MW01122267

DISCOURSE, DISCIPLINE AND THE SUBJECT

For Kay

Discourse, Discipline and the Subject

A Foucauldian analysis of the UK financial services industry

DAMIAN E. HODGSON
Manchester School of Management (UMIST)

Ashgate

Aldershot • Burlington USA • Singapore • Sydney

Published by
Ashgate Publishing Limited
Gower House
Croft Road
Aldershot
Hampshire GU11 3HR
England

Ashgate Publishing Company
131 Main Street
Burlington , VT 05401-5600 USA

Ashgate website: http://www.ashgate.com

British Library Cataloguing in Publication Data
Hodgson, Damian E.
  Discourse, discipline and the subject : a Foucauldian
  analysis of the UK financial services industry
  1.Financial services industry - Great Britain
  I. Title
  332.1'0941

Library of Congress Control Number: 00-135322

ISBN 0 7546 1495 6

Printed and bound by Athenaeum Press, Ltd.,
Gateshead, Tyne & Wear.

Contents

1 From Foucault to Financial Services

Introduction

> "The 'packaging' of the major financial institutions within the broad category 'financial services' *cannot* be seen merely as a verbal convenience. It reflects and reproduces a discursive formation which has certain effects upon the construction and development of contemporary social relations." (Knights, 1997a: 1)

> "It's not just sticking to rules, it's a question of changing their mindsets!" (Doug, Project Manager in Lifelong)

> "I am a bringer-home of income, I am! I am a Susan's husband, Jamie, Gareth and Nicolas's father, and they *need* me to earn money!" (Brian, Financial Consultant at Lifelong)

> "I don't believe there can be a society without relations of power, if you understand them as means by which individuals try to conduct, to determine the behaviour of others. The problem is... to give one's self the rules of law, the techniques of management and also the ethics, the *ethos*, the practice of self which would allow these games of power to be played with a minimum of domination." (Foucault, in Martin et al, 1988: 18)

The preceding quotations outline in the broadest sense the structure that this book will take, and reflect the diversity of currents the book attempts to integrate. The key areas on which I have drawn include current debates over the theorisation of power and power relations, traditional perspectives in the sociology of work, the contemporary restructuring of the UK financial services industry, as well as my own empirical analysis of aspects of two organisations within this industry. My immediate intention in this book is to gain some insight into the ongoing effects of the construction of a 'Financial Services' industry in the UK. My wider intentions, however,

1

are to build on an analysis of this specific context so as to contribute to the development of a critical social science which, without recourse to essentialised structural 'interests', is nonetheless grounded in some form of ethical and political commitment. By this, I refer to my own attempts through the writing of this book to develop for myself an basis from which to critique the operation of specific forms of power relations.

As a central theme, I intend to focus on the development of reflexive forms of control within the fields of Sales and Information Technology (IT) in the 'Financial Services' sector. I will contrast the emergence of diverse strategies intended to inculcate a self-disciplinary form of control with more traditional forms of bureaucratic surveillance and direct control, without obscuring the inter-dependence of these regimes. In addition, I will pay particular attention to the actual operation of the variety of mechanisms and discourses through which self-monitoring is inscribed in the individual subjects and tied to the subjects' own attempts to construct a consistent and worthwhile identity through their work. My empirical focus on the day-to-day operations also reflects my concern for the ways in which such strategies are routinely rearticulated and thus internalised and potentially reinterpreted, subverted and/or resisted. My intention here is to discuss the effects of different forms of conduct within such modes of control, and through the adoption of a specifically ethical form of analysis, to draw some conclusions regarding effective means of resisting and transforming such forms of domination within the workplace.

Themes and Intentions

The book will therefore be based around two interrelated themes. My general focus is on the changing forms of control which may be discerned in work organisations in the sector described as 'Financial Services', looking specifically at two organisations, which I will call Buzzbank and Lifelong Assurance. In doing so, I will discuss in some detail the notion of 'power' and the attempts that have been made to theorise an approach to the study of power in organisations which can encapsulate the breadth of forms of power. In particular, I will examine the concept of 'culture management' and related forms of control which depend in some way on the attempts to manipulate the subjectivity of employees. At the same time, drawing on work in Labour Process analysis, I will outline and assess the diverse forms of dissent, discretion, subversion of and resistance to these forms of control.

My broader concern in examining these processes, hence the second theme of the book, is to contribute to the development of a critical approach to the study of work organisations, which incorporates the insights of post-structuralist social theory without sacrificing political and ethical commitment to relativism. I will draw on the work of Michel Foucault in particular, building on his treatment of power and power relations to expand the perspective of traditional critical research in the field of management, labour relations and the organisation of work. I will also attempt to integrate Foucault's notion of 'the self' with other writings on identity, particularly those critical of orthodox psychology, so as to understand forms of control predicated on the subjectivity of the individual and also to develop an appreciation of ethically grounded forms of critique and resistance to such control.

My objectives in writing this book, then, exist on two levels. In a specific sense, I hope to be able to gain some insight into the ongoing effects of the recent transformation of the 'Financial Services' industry in the UK. I will attempt to trace the implications of these changes for both employees of my subject organisations, with particular emphasis on the IT and Sales divisions of the companies. In doing so, my research will examine in some detail issues such as professionalisation, the growth of Project Management as a discipline in IT, and the manipulation of masculinity as a form of control. I will also pay some attention to the implications of these changes for social relations more generally, particularly as these relate to the construction/transformation of the consumer of financial services. From a wider perspective, however, I will then reconsider the form and intent of critical social science in this light, and reflect on possible directions towards the development of an ethically grounded and theoretically sophisticated analysis of relations at work.

'Writing' Research: Power and Reflexivity in the Research Process

Before describing the empirical focus of the book in more detail, it is appropriate that I explain the reflexive mode of writing that I intend to employ in the book. My basic position rejects the notion that the aim of social research is merely to 'report' a pre-existent and external 'reality' as objectively and impersonally as possible. My discussions in the next two chapters take issue with the declared objectivity and neutrality of scientific discourse in general, and my own articulation of a social scientific discourse cannot be excepted from this critique. Drawing on the insights of phenomenology, Berger and Luckmann (1966) describe the everyday reification of 'reality', such that it is perceived as an *objective* rather than an *intersubjective* phenomenon. In particular, they stress that "man (*sic*) is capable of forgetting his own authorship of the human world, and further, that the dialectic between man, the producer, and his products is lost to consciousness" (Berger and Luckmann, 1966: 106). This reification obscures the operation of the values and assumptions which frame the individual's construction of meaning, and which lead to the inevitable partiality of these subjective representations of reality. Despite the more formal manner in which a social scientist presents his/her constructions of reality, I would contend that he/she is no more capable of attaining a transcendental and objective account of a unitary social reality. Instead, research and the presentation of research must be understood as "written" rather than "reported" (Barthes, 1986, in Game, 1991: 27), in the sense that the research process involves the *construction*, rather than a mere *reflection*, of a 'truth' about society and social relations. My own writing of this book is not a mere representation of the constructions of my 'research subjects', but my *own* construction, rearticulation and transformation of 'reality', albeit informed by a different set of discourses. As such, it is important that I stress the 'openness' of my interpretations; as Gherardi notes, "arguments never reach a closure; they are ongoing conversations which any reader is able to conclude in the way that s/he finds most congenial and my own conclusion is no better than any other" (1995: 2).

However, the insights of a Foucauldian approach point to a second operation of power through research reflecting the interrelationship of *power* and *knowledge* (which will also be examined in more detail in Chapter 2). Thus Knights describes the *process* of social scientific research itself as "irreducibly bound up in exercises of power", i.e. dependent on "the deployment of tactics, strategies, mechanisms, and technologies that transform individuals into subjects whose sense of meaning and subjective well-being become tied to those social practices sustained by such power" (1995: 235). An important point is that Knights' position here reflects the wider attempts in social science to dissolve the distinction between the action of the researcher/expert and that of the researched, such that the researcher's constructions of meaning should not be privileged as closer to 'knowledge' than those of his/her subjects (Winch, 1958). More fundamentally, this warning reflects Foucault's analysis of power working through the construction of individuals as the *objects* of the human sciences. Through the techniques employed in research, the researcher adopts a position of power over his/her 'subjects', exercising surveillance and judging/defining the subject so as to construct knowledge which reveals the 'truth' of these subjects. As Foucault notes, "the fact that societies can become the object of scientific observation, that human behaviour became, from a certain point of view, a problem to be analysed and resolved, all that is bound up, I believe, with mechanisms of power" (Foucault, 1988: 106). The operation of these 'mechanisms of power' is evident in the systematic promotion and reproduction of certain constructions of reality to sustain certain forms of power relations, and the marginalisation and suppression of other constructions. All such 'constructions' of social reality should be seen as instances of the operation of power, embodying certain values and in pursuit of certain objectives, *including* (but not limited to) my own representations presented in this book.

This identification of power and subjective interests within the research process has fundamental implications for the approach I will take to 'writing' this book. Firstly, the impossibility of value-free social research shifts the debates, such that "the question is not whether we should take sides, since inevitably we will, but rather whose side are we on?" (Becker, 1967, in Silverman, 1985: 178). The way in which research is presented is directly implicated here; the purported objectivity of the more positivist forms of social research not only *fails to appreciate* the power effects of all social research, but more importantly *obscures* the operation of power through the research process itself. Effacing the *narrator* in the text, through the use of passive constructions and the objective style typical of 'scientific' writing, "leaves the impression that the story is not told; rather, it simply exists. Because the story asserts itself, self-reflection is unnecessary and the narrative act is rendered unquestionable by being placed outside the frame of discussion" (Hatch, 1996: 363). This operation of power and the potential truth effects of social research means that, as Knights stresses, "researchers have a greater responsibility than lay persons to reflect on their motives and desires for doing what they do - research" (1995: 279). A *reflexive approach* is therefore required, whereby researchers should not only recognise their active creation of reality but should make this clear *in the writing* of their research. At the very least, this should serve to undermine the representation of research as an objective search for 'Truth'. Moreover, the inevitable operation of socially constructed and subjectively held values in this 'objective' constitution of knowledge means that it is incumbent on the researcher to reveal his/her position and make *explicit* his/her adoption of an ethical and political stance in the work. I would underline that this is not merely a methodological position but more fundamentally an *ethical* position, derived from a number of currents in feminist theory; to write otherwise represents a "denial of subjective experience ... a dismissal of the ways in which people make sense of their lives" (Townley, 1994: 154).

However, the development of this ethical-political stance is complicated by certain debates which have brought into question the researcher's right to speak for and represent a group, frequently designated as 'the oppressed' or 'the powerless'. Such debates reflect the importance of the question of *authorship* and *voice* in contemporary social research. The concern can be traced back to critical anthropology, where certain forms of ethnography which attempt to provide an 'insider account' of a group or society were attacked for their tendency to "give to one voice a pervasive authorial function and to others the role of informants" (Clifford and Marcus, 1986: 15). The power of authorship present in such work is discernible in the use of rhetorical devices to construct the subject(s) of the account as objects; thus in sociological research, critical accounts are frequently justified as "*we* sociologists (who) give *them* a voice" (Game, 1991: 30). Such debates have been rearticulated to particular effect in feminist theories, where the importance of political engagement has led to the deliberate blurring of distinctions between the *researcher* and the *researched*. However, these debates over authorship and representation have highlighted the dangers implicit in claiming to represent 'women' en masse; "the very idea of representing women, even if in the form of 'letting them speak', is to constitute women as an object" (Game, 1991: 31). The question of authorship underlines the power implicit in the role of the researcher in 'speaking for' others, and indicates the potentially dominating effects of accounts which attempt to provide totalising explanations and thus exclude and obscure other accounts.

The operation of power is also implicit in the connection many theorists have made between these constructions of reality and the identity projects of those engaged in their construction. The importance of 'identity projects' here stems from the impossibility, and more importantly, the *undesirability*, of direct representation; as Game emphasises, to seek to represent reality "is to presuppose that it is possible for a subject of knowledge, a consciousness, to have direct access to a world which is given, to know and to represent an object" (1991: 7). The construction of a coherent understanding and representation of 'reality' is therefore intimately tied up with the construction of this subject, the author who knows and can represent objective reality. My own action in writing of this book should therefore be seen as a fundamental and substantial element of my construction of my own identity as an academic, by defining the relationship between myself and the world. Clough underlines the defensive function of this process of constructing oneself as subject through writing; thus she emphasises that "the subject identity that underwrites knowledge is a formal construction, found in a text as 'a semiotic structure emerging from defensive transformations of an immanent, intrinsic, threatening pressure' (Green, 1988: 68)" (Clough, 1992: 19). This position again breaks down the distinction between researcher and researched, emphasising that just as the subjects of research attempt to secure a sense of identity through negotiating constructions of reality, so the researcher is engaged in the bolstering of his/her own identity in the creation of accounts of 'reality'. This process is clearly explained by David Knights;

> "the hidden agenda behind the production of knowledge, then, is the stability and/or elevation of the author's self or identity, for in providing some degree of certainty, orderliness and perhaps even predictability through representations of the world, one has created a space in which identity can feel safe" (Knights, 1995: 234).

Accordingly, in even the most reflexive research accounts, a range of rhetorical devices are employed in the 'writing' of research to convince the reader of the persuasiveness of the researcher's representation of a situation or phenomenon. [1] I do not mean to imply that rhetoric should (or can) be eliminated from an account, only that its very inevitability reflects the links between the author's identity and the persuasiveness of the construction of reality.

The reflexive style in which I have attempted to 'write' this book is therefore a deliberate effort to highlight that it constitutes the conscious construction of an account of reality, tied to my own identity project, by myself as 'author'. In doing so, I am attempting to effect what Hatch identifies in Dickens' *Great Expectations*, where "the regular interjection of self-referential statements ... serves the dual purpose of constructing the narrator and periodically reminding the reader that what might seem to be objective or factual statements could well be, or are indeed, colored by ... personal views of the situations and events (I) comment on" (1996: 365). At the same time, one must bear in mind that the notion of 'the author' is itself a construction, and I do not aim to deny the social construction of my own position, nor claim to embody some pre-social originating consciousness in writing this text. However, I would concur with Willmott's defence of the need to adopt the (albeit problematised) position of author, where he states that;

> "*Heuristically*, it is ethically and pragmatically defensible to identify human existence with selves who make choices... as I do when I adopt the convention of attributing authorship to my-self. But it is also necessary to recognize and deconstruct the fictional, ego-inflating quality of the autonomy ascribed to human beings whose very sense of self-identity is inescapably interdependent upon others and nature" (Willmott, 1997: 262).

---

[1] Indeed, one should be aware of the use of reflexivity itself as a rhetorical device, lending authenticity to an account.

This discussion itself is part of my attempt to achieve this, by adopting a reflexive approach to the research process, through which I myself, as researcher, will attempt to recognise the social and historical specificity of my 'writing' and my own position as 'author'.

In conclusion, then, I will reiterate that what I intend to highlight through this discussion are the dangers inherent in carrying out critical research; of presuming to attain a transcendental viewpoint from which 'Truth' may be established, or else claiming to have privileged access to the perspective and interests of an oppressed minority. In making this point, I am aware that there is a danger of undermining the very basis of any critique that I might attempt; if the researcher has no privileged access to 'Truth', nor to the interests of a subjugated and marginalised group, why should he/she (or indeed I) be listened to? To a large extent, this book may be seen as an attempt to tackle this central problem in the development of an effective critical perspective in social research.

Why Study 'The Workplace'?

This shift in perspective in the course of researching and writing the book has had direct implications for the way in which I may justify the focus of my work i.e. power relations within 'the workplace'.[2] Without pre-empting my discussion of Foucault's work in Chapters 2 and 3, it is important that I draw on a Foucauldian perspective at this point to frame the book as a whole. In line with my previous discussion of the importance of reflexivity, I will attempt to briefly explain how I as a person came to be writing *this* book, on *these* specific organisations and taking *this* particular perspective. In doing so, I am aware of the dangers of such *post-hoc* rationalisation, in creating a narrative account of the development of my 'self' as the heroic, liberal and morally-committed academic. However, these dangers seem significantly less pressing than the danger of representing my account as depersonalised, and therefore objective, 'knowledge' and thereby undermining the personalised and embodied ethical stance I am trying to develop through this book.

The work contained in this text is largely based upon my doctoral research, conducted at the University of Leeds between 1994 and 1998. My original justification for starting work towards a doctorate in this field

---

[2] I will take 'the workplace' to mean 'the site where paid work takes place' in the broadest sense, and not restricted to the physical location of the office/factory/branch - much of the work of the sales representatives in Lifelong, for example, occurs in the homes of clients or prospective clients.

reflected a mixture of fascination and repugnance with regard to widespread managerial practices in work organisations. My repugnance at these practices stemmed not only from my own personal experiences of work organisations, but from a deep discontent and anger at the degrading and soul-destroying nature of the work which continues to monopolise the waking life of many of my friends and relations; from friends resigned to a lifetime working on the line in a local factory in my hometown to others whose entire personality appeared to be annexed after starting well-paid jobs with large corporations. At the same time, my knowledge of management theories and techniques picked up during my undergraduate studies towards a degree Management led to a simultaneous fascination with the functioning and reproduction of such forms of manipulation and control. My ill-defined perception of work relations as non-egalitarian, oppressive, exploitative and somehow unacceptable was crystallised on finally encountering a critical literature in studying towards an MA in Human Resource Management; a literature that apparently had not been considered relevant in 4 years of study towards a degree in Management. Harry Braverman's reference to "a dissatisfaction centered not so much upon capitalism's inability to provide work as on the work it provides, not on the collapse of its productive processes but on the appalling effects of these processes at their most 'successful' " (1974: 14) seemed to me to sum up the moral inadequacy of the self-imposed limitations of management in both theory and practice, as well as providing a Marxist hook for my ongoing moral concern.

My initial intention in starting work towards a PhD was therefore to critique contemporary managerial practices through an empirically grounded form of academic work, founded on the traditional rationale behind Labour Process work; i.e. relying on Marx's analysis of capitalist societies, and in particular, the importance Marx attaches to control over the labour process for the reproduction of unequal social relations under capitalism. The rationale I would use for researching power relations and forms of control within work organisations, as opposed to attempting a political analysis of the role of the State, or even an Marxist analysis of the UK economy, for instance, was therefore fairly straightforward, and drew on the specific reading of Marx's theory developed within the Labour Process Debate. However, as noted above, my engagement with critical work in the broader sense, as well as discussions with my colleagues and friends while studying towards this doctorate, has repeatedly forced me to re-examine my philosophical and ethical position, and to question fundamental tenets of both Labour Process Theory (insofar as a 'core theory' exists in this area) and of a neo-Marxist perspective more generally. While I will discuss this in more detail in Chapters 2 and 3, it merits a mention here as this process has progressively led me to reappraise the importance of the workplace to an understanding of social relations more broadly. Without such Marxist foundations, was there any particular importance in the analysis of power relations at work (as opposed to power relations in the family, for instance, or power relations in government)? Clearly, research in the Marxist tradition extends beyond Labour Process work and engages with aspects of society other than industry and commerce, such as the role of the State, for example, or the education system. However, the choice of focus of such work is determined by that which can be related (often functionally) to the maintenance and reproduction of the capitalist system. Hence in the case of Foucault's key subjects of interest, the economic or political function of, say, the asylum, or the prison system, is very difficult to discern and can lead the operation of power and domination in these areas to be ignored. As my research shifted from its original foundations in Labour Process Theory, it became clear that the 'workplace' could no longer be taken as the self-evident site in which to trace the operation of power.

Nonetheless, the workplace still holds a significant position within a capitalist society, not least because of the simple proportion of an individual's life that he/she can expect to spend within a workplace. This lends support to the approaches of those commentators who highlight the vital importance of work as a source of meaning and identity to individuals in modern Western societies. Pahl, for example, sees; "work done by members of households (as) the central process around which society is structured" (1984: 14), and later argues that "work is becoming the key personal, social and political issue of the remaining years of the twentieth century" (1988: 1). The recognition of the workplace as a significant site for the construction of identity is widespread in (but not limited to) critical work; mainstream managerial psychology since the development of Human Relations has emphasised 'Social Man' and the importance of work as a source of social support and meaning (e.g. Mayo, 1946). However, it is the precise understanding of identity construction, sources of insecurity/anxiety, and the ways in which these may be manipulated and exploited in an organisational context which are of interest in this book. Hence, in the workplace, it is suggested that identity is constructed and reinforced, and insecurity can be precariously held at bay, through acting as a 'professional', displaying the requisite 'entrepreneurship', etc. I will stress, however, that I do not mean to ignore the specific nature of the capitalist system; the capitalist workplace has particular importance due to the *systematic* use of techniques of control and domination to achieve economic goals, at the expense of wider social and ethical concerns where these are not instrumental to economic performance and profitability.

My move beyond a traditional Labour Process perspective has thus broadened my interest in more general social concerns. Decoupling (although not divorcing) the operation of power from class relations, accumulation and the capitalist economic system seemed to allow critical research to identify and examine a far wider range of instances of domination and subjugation. Implicit in this is the project of enlarging the context of critical research to account for effects of such discourses on society beyond the workplace, of which a pertinent example might be the recent work on the 'discourse of enterprise' and the rise of consumerism in Western societies (e.g. du Gay and Salaman, 1992). While consumerism (and consumption generally) is not a direct focus of this book, the changes in social relations which have resulted from the restructuring of the 'Financial Services' industry in the UK is clearly a highly significant contemporary issue. I would therefore emphasise the importance of analysing recent changes in terms of their effects *beyond* the workplace, such as the pivotal position 'Financial Services' holds in the construction of what has elsewhere been termed the 'suburban subject' (Grey, 1997b). A key example of this is the continual reconstruction of individuals as 'consumers of financial services' in ways that would have been unthinkable forty years earlier. While the focus of this book is on the importance of power relations within the workplace, then, this will not be to the exclusion of related issues, which include consumption, forms of masculinity, and power relations within the home, among others.

Why 'Financial Services'?

Clearly, the nature and structure of financial institutions in the UK have always been particularly important to the performance of the UK economy as a whole. More broadly, however, the structure of certain aspects of finance, such as the mutual status of traditional building societies, or the welfare role fulfilled by the industrial branch policies of insurance companies, has had direct implications for the nature of social relations in the UK. Although change has occurred progressively over the last century in all areas of finance, it is only in the last twenty years that the most extensive restructuring of the financial markets has taken place. In common with several Western states, the last twenty years has witnessed a transformation in the assumptions underpinning individual conduct in regard to what is now termed 'personal finance'. This is evidenced by the rapidity of the change from, say, the universal provision of a state pension to the present situation where private and company pension schemes are seen as essential to anyone wishing to maintain a decent standard of living on retirement. Knights, attributing this social change to the solutions put forward in line with New Right political doctrine to deal with the demographic problems of Western economies, emphasises the subjective implications, stating that "welfare crisis talk is continually transforming consumers to seek private solutions to their security problems" (1997a: 20). While the framework of financial institutions has always been relevant to the individual's way of life, then, the gradual retreat of the State from its welfare commitments and the entrance of the private sector has given these institutions an unprecedented direct and personal relevance. To an extent, my interest in this sector reflects the contemporary focus on finance and the related restructuring of social relations through the reorganisation of financial markets and the attempted reconstitution of those subjects implicated in them.

The main thrust of the restructuring of finance in the UK has stemmed from the strategy of 'deregulation' (and, de facto, *re-regulation*) pursued by the Conservative government of the 1980s, involving the removal of the institutional and legal barriers between banking, the building societies, insurance companies, the Stock Exchange, investment brokers and other financial institutions in the UK. This restructuring has led to the emergence of what has been described as the 'Financial Services industry', wherein the interpenetration of markets has brought about an intensification of competition in all sectors. This fierce competition has also been exacerbated by the globalisation of markets as a result of the Single European Act, and can be expected to be intensified further by the introduction of a Single European Currency should the UK choose to enter. At the same time, however, the threat posed by new entrants has been offset slightly by the retreat of the UK government from the provision of a variety of forms of social security. The concurrent encouragement of private sector provision in these areas has significantly increased the turnover of the 'Financial Services industry' as a whole. The potential for (albeit smaller) slices of a substantially larger cake has been sufficient incentive for many companies to make notable efforts to break into other areas of 'Financial Services'. A pertinent example of this is the growth of what is termed 'bancassurance', as all of the main UK banks, without exception, have begun to provide insurance and other investment products since the Financial Services Act (FSA) in 1987 (see Knights and Sturdy, 1997, for a discussion), and to a lesser extent insurance companies have more recently begun to acquire demutualised building societies (Mintel, 1995b).

The notion of 'bancassurance' is a key linkage between the two organisations studied. The first, Buzzbank, although primarily a banking outfit, also provides mortgages, advice on investment and brokers the insurance products of its parent company, TN Banking. Equally, while Lifelong is primarily a life assurance company, and offers financial advice on investments of all kinds, it has recently set up a telephone banking operation, known as Lifebank. Significantly, one direct link involves the individual chosen to oversee the setting up of Lifebank, Mike Hazard - the original Chief Executive when Buzzbank was set up in the late 1980s.[3] More broadly, however, both organisations are coping with a similar recent history and general environment; deregulation, intensification of competition, attempts to diversify into adjacent sectors, and on their present courses, both can expect to come into more direct competition with each other in the near future. More pragmatically, my choice of both Buzzbank and Lifelong was partially motivated by their proximity and their generosity in allowing me a significant level of access into each organisation.

To a large extent, the choice of department within organisations in the Financial Services sector was arbitrary; my focus here, power and control in work organisations, could have been researched in any of a number of departments in Buzzbank and Lifelong. My original choice of the IT function owed something to my early interest in the ambiguity of technology and the role of technology in the operation of mechanisms of control in financial institutions. At a more pragmatic level, I had also assumed that gaining research access to the IT department of a company might be significantly easier than researching somewhere more politically sensitive, such as Human Resources, for instance.[4] In the course of my empirical work in Buzzbank, a personal contact with whom I was discussing my research mentioned a similar situation in his company, Lifelong, where an extensive IT system based on bureaucratic surveillance had been implemented. It was while conducting and interpreting the empirical research that my interest in forms of discipline broadened to cover notions of identity and self-discipline in more detail. Pragmatism and accessibility were thus key concerns in my selection of both the organisations and the specific functions within each organisation that I would research.

I do not, however, mean to represent this choice as meaningless. In the case of IT, there are a number of reasons why this function holds particular

---

[3] To maintain the anonymity of my respondents, I have used pseudonyms as far as possible in referring to individuals, companies and locations throughout the book.

[4] Indeed, this proved to be the case in Buzzbank; through my period of research in the company, the Human Resources department at Buzzbank refused all of my requests for interviews, insisting they would only respond to questions put to them in writing (and even then, the responses I received were as evasive and obscure as possible).

importance within the organisation; the role of IT in the restructuring and automating of a number of clerical and financial work processes in Buzzbank, for instance, reflects the growing status and strategic discretion accorded to the function. Equally, recent changes in Lifelong have increased the influence of the IT function, as I will discuss in Chapter 6. However, such changes could not have been assumed or hypothesised before embarking upon the empirical research itself; at the same time, the function would in no way be 'power-free' if it had not recently gained in status and influence. My focus on the Direct Sales function in 'Financial Services' can also be seen to reflect an intensification of forms of control (or 'motivation') as a consequence of the reorganisation of the industry as a whole and the move away from a paternalist ethos in many institutions. At the same time, the conduct of the salesforce in general is instrumental in reconstructing the modern client as a 'consumer of financial services' and, as noted elsewhere, reinforcing a particular *individualised* form of subjectivity. Having said this, had my research focused on other aspects of the organisations, or even of other organisations, I could well have developed an alternative justification; this would then have been a different book.

Methodology and Methods

My empirical research in Buzzbank and Lifelong took place intermittently over a period of eighteen months, with my work in Buzzbank preceding and slightly overlapping the research conducted in Lifelong. The original process of arranging access in Buzzbank took some weeks and innumerable phone calls while I attempted to convince senior management in the company that the disturbance I would cause would be minimal and that I could comprehensively anonymise any work on Buzzbank I might publish. At this time, I spent several weeks trying to arrange an interview with Mike Winter, a research contact in Buzzbank recommended to me by one of my colleagues. Without my knowledge, however, Mike Winter had recently been promoted to Chief Executive of Buzzbank; unsurprisingly, he proved to be permanently unavailable. It was only after a substantial amount of badgering that I was passed on to Alan, the director of IT at Buzzbank, whom I met in June 1996.

Although conducted over coffee in the relaxed surroundings of the Buzzbank canteen, my opening meeting with Alan was a nerve-wracking mixture of research interview and screening process, in which I tried to make some preliminary enquiries and negotiate further access while Alan assessed the disturbance I might cause, the risk I might pose and the potential benefit I might offer in terms of allowing Buzzbank access to undergraduates entering the local job market. The role I adopted in this meeting, of an uncritical and technically ignorant (therefore 'harmless') student, proved to be somewhat constraining as the research progressed; as I felt bound to conform to this role, I found it difficult to ask more cutting questions. At the same time, my harmlessness allowed me access to a number of sensitive meetings and may well have set a number of interviewees and other employees more at ease in my presence. I appeared to have passed the initial screening, as Alan agreed to allow me to conduct further interviews within the Buzzbank IT division. By negotiating further meetings with other employees in each interview, I managed to conduct 10 formal interviews with 9 different employees, ranging from heads of departments to team leaders and team members. These interviews took place on site at fairly regular intervals over the next 8 months, the last taking place in February 1997.

I followed up this work with two periods of 'non-participant observation' in April 1997, each of which lasted two days, in which I shadowed different members of two teams in the IT division. In these periods, I was able to build upon the relationships I had made in earlier interviews through daily contact with employees, and both observe and question the day-to-day practices and conduct of these employees in a less formal context than arranged interviews. In the course of this observation, I also took the opportunity whenever possible to conduct a number of ad hoc, informal interviews, to discuss a wide range of issues informally; over coffee, in spare moments, over lunch or over a quick pint after a shift. Without claiming to have gained 'unbiased' access in the positivist sense, the marginal increase in trust gained through longer acquaintance clearly affected the nature of information that my 'subjects' felt willing to discuss with me. In return, the sympathy I felt for some (although by no means all) of my contacts greatly complicated my ethical position. Nonetheless, the ambivalence and discomfort I experienced while gaining the confidence of employees in interviews was more intense during these periods of observation, as I frequently felt unable to reciprocate for fear of jeopardising my access to the company.

At the same time, I became interested in practices at Lifelong after discussing my research in Buzzbank with a friend who had recently been taken on by Lifelong as a Financial Consultant. He described parallel practices in his own branch and offered to help me negotiate research access if possible. Unfortunately, management at this branch proved very reluctant to allow any sort of access, reflecting a wariness engendered by general adverse publicity endured by Lifelong as a whole. Closer to home, the recent closure of another local branch after revelations of misconduct in the local press also exacerbated the 'siege mentality' in the Lifelong Sales division at the time. I then attempted to negotiate access through Head Office, which proved considerably less difficult - after one phone call, I was invited to Head Office for an 'chat'. After my early difficulties, I was surprised and relieved to find that my contact, Simon, a Business Manager in National Sales Operations, to be helpful to a fault. Simon helped me to arrange 5 further interviews in Lifelong Head Office, mainly in the IT and IT-related departments. These interviews took place across three further visits to Head Office, in June, August and September 1997.

Contemporaneously, I attempted once again to set up interviews with the direct salesforce in the Lifelong branch network. This time, dropping the name of a contact in Head Office proved to be a much more effective means of entry, and by the end of June 1997 I had interviewed the managers of two local branches of Lifelong. Again, I found myself acting as the keen yet naïve young researcher, a role which led many interviewees to attempt to enlist my sympathy by presenting their own account of the recent accusations of misconduct, such as the pensions mis-selling scandal (discussed in more detail in Chapter 4). In the months up to November 1997, I conducted 7 interviews with different combinations of a total of 8 staff across the two branches, from Branch Manager and Sales Manager to Financial Consultant and Sales Support Analyst. Immediately before and throughout this period, I was also engaged in an analysis of a range of documents from both organisations, mainly consisting of official company literature, such as brochures, training manuals, PR information, staff association newsletters, etc., which both informed and were informed by my interviews. In addition, a considerable amount of my time was spent collecting and analysing all media articles I could find which in some way concerned either organisation or the industry as a whole, as well as marketing information reports and press releases/reports by the industry regulators, most notably the Securities and Investments Board (SIB) and the Personal Investment Authority (PIA).

The interviews I conducted in both Buzzbank and Lifelong tended to be 'semi-structured', in that I outlined in advance a number of general themes I hoped to cover while allowing the interviewee to bring other issues into the discussion and pursuing these as seemed appropriate. The majority of the interviews were conducted on a one-to-one basis, out of earshot of his/her colleagues. However, there were a number where either time pressure or the preference of the interviewees meant that I interviewed them either in pairs or, on one occasion, as a group of 3. Most interviews tended to last about an hour, although one or two were as short as fifteen minutes, particularly when they were arranged *in situ* and conducted on the spot. While I was originally reluctant to interview more than one person at a time, this was at least partly due to a fear of losing control of the process and a misconceived belief that this would 'minimise bias' in the interviews. However, both my reading on methodology (Winch, 1958; Hatch, 1996) and my experience of the larger interviews challenged this belief in the possibility of accessing a 'natural' and 'authentic' account of the interviewees' experiences. Indeed, some of the most interesting interviews occurred as a consequence of the interaction of interviewees, often suppressing the conflict between their positions, scoring points off each other, engaging in detailed discussions and shared reflections about their work, and so on. All of these interviews were tape recorded with the prior consent of the interviewee, with the exception of 4, in which consent was not given. However, no objection was made to my taking of notes in these cases, and I also relied on note-taking to record pre- or post-interview comments or actions. All tape-recorded interviews were then transcribed in full within a week or so of the interview before being analysed, so that I could still recall and reflect on the meaning I constructed at the time.

In the periods of 'non-participant observation' at Buzzbank, I was allowed to shadow, in the first period, an IT Operations PC Support team, and in the second, an IT Applications project team. As noted, I found these periods to be significantly more demanding than the interviews, not only because of the difficulty of continually interpreting and taking part in such diverse processes but also because of my ambivalent position as both researcher and acquaintance, and my discomfort with what I felt to be instrumental role-playing. In each period, the reaction to my presence was variable; frequently staff appeared oblivious to my presence, while at other times remarks made were clearly intended for my benefit (references to 'management bullshit' by some staff, for example, appeared directed towards me as the perceived representative of this world). I do not take this 'reactivity' to invalidate the participant observation, however - as in the interviews, my intention was not to access some 'pure', authentic and natural data. Indeed, when employees explained and justified their actions to me, the process of reflection occasionally elicited significant insights from them into the taken-for-granted conduct of employees.

Structure of the Book

Before outlining the structure of this book, a cautionary note is necessary. I do not mean to imply that this structure reflects the temporal order of the research process itself. The structure of the book is by necessity a construction which traditionally mimics the ideal model for positivist research i.e. objective problem definition, literature review, construction of hypotheses, choice of methodology, hypothesis testing, interpretation of results and proof/rejection of hypotheses. This may be contrasted with the sequence of the actual research process itself, which I would suggest is intimately linked with my own identity project as an academic and a researcher, and is characterised by a recursive, discontinuous mélange of empirical work, theorising, interpretation and reflection, not only in this book but in social research more widely. As Hatch notes, "we begin writing ... at the moment we conceive of our projects. We write ourselves into our conception as narrators and thus constitute our relationship with our work" (1996: 369). Nonetheless, I have imposed an order and coherency on this book retrospectively, mainly so as to conform with certain conventions of writing and to maximise the clarity and accessibility of the book to yourself as reader. The outline given below should therefore be seen as a heuristic construction, to facilitate the reader's critical engagement with my argument, and one which owes more to the conventions of academic writing (and reading) than to any innate structure of the research process.

In the next chapter, Chapter 2, I will outline the theoretical foundations of the book, starting with my early interest in *Labour Process Theory* as a useful form of critical analysis of capitalist work relations. I will then assess a number of criticisms of the Labour Process work, focusing on the limitations of the concept of power which is central to such work, before examining the potential of *'power relations'* as developed in the early work of Michel Foucault to overcome these problems. As well as reflecting my personal shifts in perspective, I would argue that this discussion reflects the general (although not unproblematic) movement towards Foucauldian work in critical fields such as Labour Process Theory (e.g. Knights and Willmott, 1985; Sakolsky, 1992). I will, however, raise a key difficulty with Foucault's early articulation of his perspective, raised by Marxist and feminist critics, related to his avoidance of a *theory of the subject* and the implicit determinism in his work as a result. Chapter 3 will examine Foucault's engagement with this problem in his later work, specifically in his writings on sexuality which dealt with *the discursive construction of the subject*. This involves a discussion of two related subjects; firstly, the Althusserian concept of *ideology*, closely linked with Foucault's *discourse* and the notion of *'truth'*, and secondly, the parallels between Foucault's discourse and the concept of *difference* developed in linguistics and, more recently, in critical psychology. These discussions underline the importance of *identity*, and in particular, of what Foucault terms "the relation of self to self" (1988: 30) in the operation of power. I will assess this change of perspective in Foucault's work, and the extent to which it enables the incorporation of an ethical perspective, by drawing on the critical interpretations of a number of contemporary social theorists including Lois

McNay, Jana Sawicki, and Barbara Townley. Finally, I examine the problems associated with the ambiguous ethical position that Foucault adopts throughout his work, and tentatively suggest that in place of universal moral commitments, an ethical stance will be developed through this book in relation to the competing representations of situations on the part of the participants.

Chapter 4 then defines the context and focus for the empirical work in the book, concentrating on two companies, *Buzzbank* and *Lifelong Assurance*, both of which operate in the broad field now described as *'Financial Services'*. In this chapter, I will discuss the emergence of a 'Financial Services' industry, focusing on the implications of this in terms of levels of competition and the action of regulatory agencies. Chapters 5 to 7 will then detail the empirical work, which focuses on the *IT divisions of both Buzzbank and Lifelong Assurance*, as well as the *direct salesforce of Lifelong*. I have first attempted to trace the effect of what has been described as *'cultural change'* in transforming each organisation and their respective workforces, thus Chapter 5 will focus therefore on attempts at strategic cultural change on the part of management. Here, I will develop my understanding of *discourse* within each organisation, based on the importance of *difference* to the construction of *identity* and on the consequent limitations of 'culture management' in the discursive construction of the work identity of employees. In Chapter 6, I will outline the cardinal mechanism of control/body of knowledge in operation within the IT function, one which to my knowledge has not as yet been subjected to any serious critical analysis; the discipline of *Project Management* and its role in both exercising a direct form of surveillance and in articulating and enforcing a form of self-discipline based on the notion of *professionalism*. I will also highlight the role of this discourse of professionalism in undermining *resistance*, by providing a form of security for the identity projects of IT staff and legitimating the expanding influence and status of the IT function. Chapter 7 will then complement this by examining *modes of control* to which the *direct salesforce* in Lifelong was subject, focusing on the interrelated use of financial incentives and control through the *manipulation of subjectivity*, while highlighting the self-defeating nature of the predominant forms of resistance to such control. Finally, in Chapter 8 I will review the book as a whole and make explicit the links between the various aspects of the empirical work, using the schema of the construction of the individual as both *subject* and *object* drawn from Townley (1993a; 1994) to revisit the key issues raised in Chapters 1 to 3.

2 Power and Discipline

Through Marx to Foucault

The purpose of this chapter is to articulate basic aspects of the theoretical perspective I adopt through this book. To ground this ongoing discussion, however, I will concentrate here on introducing certain concepts which are central to the argument, and I will trace the debates which underpin my theoretical stance. In particular, I will examine in some detail the related concepts of *power* and *control*, specifically as they relate to the organisation of work, through an analysis of theory in this area. I will start therefore with a brief examination of the position of Karl Marx and the implications of his writings for a critical understanding of the sociology of work. Marx's writings in this area have been seen as centring on the notion of the *labour process* in capitalist economies, an approach which has been rejuvenated by its application in Harry Braverman's *Labor and Monopoly Capital* (1974). I will therefore examine Braverman's rearticulation of Marx, before looking at some of the well-rehearsed criticisms of his position which have been explored in great detail by the ensuing Labour Process Debate. These criticisms, I suggest, can be traced back to flaws in Braverman's conceptualisation of power, inherited from Marx's broadly structuralist analysis.

To examine these criticisms, I will then explore some of the wider sociological and philosophical arguments over the nature of power and its definition, which centre on the debate over the respective influence of *structure* and *agency*. At the risk of distorting the competing positions through oversimplification, the debate can be said to be held between those theorists who would explain social behaviour by reference to structural constraints operating *through* individuals and those who would explain social behaviour as an *aggregation* of individual traits, inclinations and motivations. These arguments have traditionally been conducted between proponents of relatively structuralist and relatively individualist approaches to social theory. More recently, social research has attempted to explore the possibility of unifying both sides of this argument in a 'post-dualist' (or 'anti-dualist') approach, which integrates both a structural and an agentic

20

understanding of power in society. To explore the potential of this approach, I will examine such post-dualist work and specifically the *theory of structuration* as set out by a key writer in this area, Anthony Giddens. I will then go on to assess the main criticisms of his position, which highlight the implicit voluntarism which Giddens' model is seen to retain.

It has been suggested by a number of writers that the work of Michel Foucault, without sharing in any project of unifying social science, may nonetheless offer some resolution to these difficulties. I therefore turn next to the work of Foucault, examining in detail the understanding of power and power relations revealed in his work. After setting the work of Foucault in context, particularly with regard to the discontinuous and even self-contradictory nature of his writings, I will go on to outline his distinctive approach to an understanding of power. His approach is set apart from that of many contemporary writers by two key elements; firstly, by his rejection of a unitary concept which can define power; secondly, and relatedly, by his extension of 'power' beyond repressive and negative understandings. The potential of Foucault's wider understanding of power is that it offers to highlight the habitual operation of power in situations where traditional definitions may lead to it being overlooked. To examine how this might be possible, the next section will focus on a critical assessment of three aspects of Foucault's perspective on power; its *productive* nature, its *polyvalence* and the *capillary* nature of its operation. I will then end the chapter with an examination of the implications of this conception of power in regard to the notions of *strategy* and of *resistance*. Chapter 3 will then build upon this discussion, concentrating on a critical examination of this notion of *discourse* as developed by Foucault and the relationship between discourses and the constitution of subjectivity, before drawing some tentative conclusions regarding the role of critical research and the importance of ethics.

From Marx to the Labour Process Debate

The Work of Karl Marx

In common with most researchers aiming to critically examine the sociology of work and the relations between work and society as a whole, my theoretical position in embarking upon this research was founded in the writings of Karl Marx (1951; 1976; 1978).[5] In the course of researching

---

[5] The dates of the original publications are provided in the bibliography.

and writing towards this book, my theoretical and indeed political position has shifted, not least due to my encounter with a wider literature and a significant number of 'critical' theorists in a wider sense. Nonetheless, clarifying the position adopted here requires a critical appraisal of the body of Marxist work, as little if any critical work can claim to have developed entirely independently of this canon which has dominated critical perspectives on society for over a century. In saying this, it must be noted here that a comprehensive appraisal of Marx's vast body of work is beyond the scope of this chapter. Instead, certain key points developed by Marx which underpin a critical analysis of capitalist relations of production will be brought out and considered in the light of more contemporary work.

Before tackling the key elements of a Marxist analysis, I must highlight the dangers of treating the almost innumerable articulations of contemporary Marxism as a unitary approach. However, all stem back to the modernist, post-Enlightenment conception of *reason* adopted by Marx, reflecting its elevation beyond its previous confines of God or Nature (Cooper and Burrell, 1988). Hence the defining characteristic of modernity can be taken to be its "belief in the essential capacity of humanity to perfect itself through the power of rational thought" (Cooper and Burrell, 1988: 92). Marx does accept the existence of different forms of reason specific to different historical contingencies, but nonetheless claims the right to privilege one above the others as reliable and, therefore, totalising. The logic through which Marx defends his adoption of the reason of the proletariat is succinctly summed up by Mark Poster;

> "The historical dialectic moved through the class struggle; the class that represented the negation of the present was the privileged agent of history; the perspective of this class was therefore the true perspective, the perspective the theorist could adopt to grasp the totality. The theorist was then in a position to formulate the Truth" (Poster, 1984: 10).

So it is that Marx takes it as unproblematic that one theorist can be perfectly placed to conceptualise the totality. In Marx's modernist stance, therefore, whilst there exist multiple forms of reason, access to the *correct* rationality is feasible, and, indeed, the duty of the theorist. Marx's reconstruction of history is based on a recognition of reason as historically specific, an approach which has been described as 'historical materialism'. This is based upon Marx's understanding of *production* as;

> "(the) fundamental condition of all history ... Men must be in a position to live in order to be able to 'make history'. But life involves before everything else eating and drinking, a habitation, clothing and many other things. The first historical act is thus the production of the means to satisfy

these needs, the production of material life itself" (Marx, 1978 in Poster, 1984: 47).

This leads Marx directly to focus upon the organization of production throughout history, and the role of power, as defined by class and ownership of the means of production, in shaping it.

It is important therefore to emphasize those points which are fundamental to a Marxist analysis and which set him apart from other political economists of his era and before. In particular, there are two very general aspects which must be brought out here. Firstly, there is his conception of the organization of production as historically contingent and specific, linked to a refusal to accept the inevitability of the existing system. This is one clear way in which Marx can be seen as a decisive break with traditional political economy, "accusing the political economists such as Adam Smith of taking 'the conditions of the existing system of production for the necessary conditions of production in general'" (Weiss, 1976 in Thompson, 1989: 56). The recognition of this dangerous misconception frees analysis from an uncritical acceptance of any particular social and economic system as natural and inevitable. Secondly, and relatedly, there is what might be seen as the fundamental point of his major work, the socially determined nature of production. Here, Marx illustrates his thesis by highlighting the direct link between, on the one side, the pervasive system of class relations in society and, on the other, the particular form of the organization of production characteristic of capitalism. In particular, certain tendencies within capitalist relations of production, including the division of labour, deskilling, task fragmentation and hierarchical organization, are analysed to demonstrate how they were social constructs founded on the ideology of capitalism, rather than economic necessities. The specific aims of these tendencies are rather to ensure that a surplus may be created in the labour process, a process defined by Marx as *valorisation*. This can be seen as a defining tenet of the Marxist theory of capitalism; that "capital is ... not just money exchanged for labor; it is money exchanged for labor with the purpose of appropriating that value which it creates over and above what is paid, the surplus value" (Braverman, 1974: 413). The production of such a surplus is seen to be guaranteed in early capitalism through the *formal subordination of labour*, whereby capital owns the means of production and pays labour a wage, leaving the organization of production to labour itself. This arrangement limits the ability of capital to increase productivity to indirect forms of action, such as the extension of the working day. The shift of capitalism towards centralised factory work, in contrast, enabled the *detailed* control of the organisation of work, particularly through the use of technology, and it is this detailed control of the labour process which facilitated the appropriation of surplus value through the *real subordination of labour*. Surplus value is of such central importance to capitalist organization of production that it can be said that "the social function of hierarchical work is not technical efficiency, but accumulation" (Marglin, 1976: 14). It is this surplus which ensures the levels of profitability necessary for the reproduction of the system of class relations which underpins the capitalist organization of production.

As noted, it is beyond the scope of this chapter to cover exhaustively the work of Marx in this area, particularly with regard to the specifics of Marxist economic theory. Rather, it is the general standpoint, not a coherent and intricate body of work, which is of interest here. Although certain aspects of Marxist theory will be elaborated below with regard to specific authors, I mean to draw attention to the tenets alluded to above which *underpin* Marxist analysis. Beyond this, certain aspects of Marxist and Neo-Marxist work will be considered in detail, and assessed in the light of a number of bodies of critique. In particular, a fuller application of Marxist theory with regard to the organization of production merits examination. This can be found in the seminal work by Harry Braverman, *Labor and Monopoly Capital* (1974). This work is not only an update of Marx's analysis of the labour process, it is also aimed as a corrective to the traditional neglect of this aspect of Marx's theory (Baran and Sweezy, 1966). Indeed, as is admitted in the foreword, "In terms of theory ... there is very little that is new in this book" (Braverman, 1974: xi). Rather, it is an attempt to apply Marx's analysis to modern techniques and systems of work organization.

The Contribution of Harry Braverman

Braverman draws upon extensive industrial experience and a thorough grounding in Marxism to assess modern management techniques and work organization from this viewpoint. He therefore begins with Frederick Taylor, the so-called 'father of modern management', and his techniques of 'scientific management', which Braverman understands as a system which "renders conscious and systematic the formerly unconscious tendency of capitalist production" (1974: 121). In *Labor and Monopoly Capital*, Braverman interprets the intent behind each of Taylor's principles and depicts them as steps towards 'the real subordination of labour', in Marx's terminology, whereby substantial control is gained over labour itself through taking *direct* control of the labour process (Cressey and MacInnes, 1980). Scientific management was therefore seen by Braverman as a relatively sophisticated and deliberate attempt to tackle the enduring and endemic problem of the control of labour under capitalist production. From a Marxist point of view, the reasons for the existence of this problem of control are fundamental to an understanding of how capitalism operates. This can be explained with reference to two elements of Marx's analysis. Firstly, capital cannot buy labour itself, only 'labour power'. This must be understood as a *potential*; "not an agreed amount of labor, but the power to labor over an agreed period of time" (Braverman, 1974: 54). It is this malleable potential inherent in labour power which not only gives rise to the difficulties of motivation and control, but also a potential greater than any other element in the labour process to yield surplus and hence profits. Secondly, therefore, the aim of capitalism, which, as noted, is "not efficiency, but accumulation" (Marglin, 1976: 14), means that some form of control is *required* to elicit a surplus from labour. This surplus, which may be extracted from labour above and beyond the subsistence level for the workers themselves, may be skimmed off by capital as profits. These profits are then hived off for accumulation to ensure the reproduction of the capitalist system.

From this perspective, Braverman then analyses Taylor's 'Principles of Scientific Management', which Taylor saw as the basis of a system which could take control of the work process from the workers themselves, and overcome the workforce's inclination for what Taylor described as 'natural soldiering' (inherent laziness) and 'systematic soldiering' (tactics deliberately aimed to minimise effort and maximise job security). Taylor's first principle, "gathering the knowledge of the workforce in the hands of management" he interprets as "the disassociation of the labor process from the skills of the workers" (Braverman, 1974: 113). This is effected by means of a careful observation and analysis of the labour process, to unearth the methods and shortcuts that constitute the workers' 'craft' and embody these in a corpus of 'best practice'. "Centering brainwork in the office, not the shopfloor", Taylor's second principle, is interpreted as "the separation of conception from execution" (Braverman, 1974: 114). This step, described by Hales (1980) as "pre-conceptualization", enables, and indeed requires that working methods and equally importantly the working pace of the labour process should be imposed by the capitalist (or his/her agent). This is presented by Braverman and certain other writers as a fundamental element in Taylorism's dehumanisation of the workforce. These two principles are supplemented by a third principle, "the systematic preplanning of the workforce's activities", which Braverman interprets as "the use of this monopoly over knowledge to control each step of the labor process and its mode of execution" (Braverman, 1974: 119). As Littler later notes, the control of the process cannot be effected by the planning department alone, and Taylorism was dependent for its success on the reorganisation of the position of the supervisor and the introduction of incentive payment systems. Through this analysis, Braverman demonstrates the overarching aim of this mode of production to be predicated not purely upon imperatives of *efficiency* but also of *control*. Braverman defines this process of wresting control from the workforce under Tayloristic management practices as *deskilling*, i.e. "the subordination of the autonomy of manual production workers through simultaneously decreasing the level of skill in production tasks and increasing managerial control over their execution" (Jones, 1982 in Thompson, 1989: 72). The process of deskilling is supported by the fragmentation of the tasks which make up the labour process, reducing the level of skill and discretion of the worker, and the reintegration of these with the foreman, manager or planning office as the co-ordinating agency (a technique expanded to the maximum in the Fordist assembly line). Two methods of achieving this control are therefore posited; firstly, the use of organizational and disciplinary measures, and secondly, the application of technology. Moreover, Braverman does not restrict his analysis to manufacturing, but extends it to the use of automation in offices, and further, to services and retail industries.

Labor and Monopoly Capital can legitimately be said to have had a seminal influence, both upon diverse pre-existent debates in fields from industrial relations to sociology, and also in spawning a wealth of work related specifically to the labour process. It appears therefore that Braverman has achieved his intention of providing "an invitation and a challenge to a younger generation of Marxist economists and sociologists" (Braverman, 1974: xii). Accordingly, while many works have paid tribute to the insight of Braverman's analysis, they have at the same time taken up the challenge in raising trenchant objections to key elements of the thesis. Many of these objections have been raised within a disparate school of thought collectively known as the *Labour Process Debate*, in a general and on-going critique of Braverman, with specific recommendations from a number of authors aiming to bolster the weaker parts of his thesis. Other criticisms, however, cut much deeper than many of these rectifiable objections, and question the emancipatory potential of the Marxist project as a whole.

A Critique of Braverman

At the most basic level, Braverman's conceptualization of key elements of his thesis has been widely attacked. The passivity and lack of awareness which he attributes to labour, in clear contrast with the omniscience and strategic intent on the part of capital, have been characterized as a distinct flaw in the argument. On the one hand, evidence of both collective and individual resistance on the part of labour to attempts to deskill workforces has been brought forward in contradiction with Braverman's implicit characterization of labour (Edwards and Scullion, 1982; Edwards, 1990). On the other, extensive contemporary studies have emphasized the widespread inability of management both to formulate and to accomplish clear strategic objectives (Child, 1985; Mintzberg, 1975; 1978). The idea of a strategy as "a rational consideration of alternatives and the articulation of coherent rationales for decisions" (Child, 1985: 108) has been contrasted with empirical evidence characterising "much management policy-making and execution (as) piecemeal, uncoordinated and empiricist" (Jones and Rose, 1985: 98).

Furthermore, the conclusions that Braverman draws from these assumptions have been subject to equally severe criticism. These characteristics of the relevant parties, labour and capital, have led Braverman to imply that the tendency to deskill is not only the universal aim of capital in its organization of production, but that in the existing situation it must always be successful. Both of these propositions have been directly challenged by a large number of theorists. Firstly, the recognition of the importance of *tacit skills* (Manwaring and Wood, 1985) which cannot be fully accessed and monopolised by Tayloristic work practices has led to the identification of alternative strategies available to capital, most notably those of *responsible autonomy* (Friedman, 1977). Friedman in particular argues that;

> "Braverman ... must be criticized for confusing one particular strategy for exercising managerial authority in the capitalist labour process with managerial authority itself. Taylorian Scientific Management is not the only strategy available for exercising managerial authority, and given the reality of worker resistance, often not the most appropriate" (1977: 80).

Responsible autonomy, in contrast with Taylorist *direct control*, acts by encouraging the identification of labour with the aims of an organization so as to *minimize* supervision, and hence capturing the benefits of tacit skills. A higher order of control is seen to be necessary to ensure that the increased discretion of subordinates is used positively in organizational terms in the fulfilment of their widened responsibilities. Secondly, the existence of these same tacit skills provides a basis for the resistance to, and subversion of, attempts to deskill labour in particular labour processes. Wide evidence of instances of this can be found within Labour Process Theory, both in a collective form of action, such as 'working to rule' in the car industry (Beynon, 1973; Thompson, 1983), and in individual forms of action, such as the work of Armstrong *et al* (1976; 1977) on the chemical industry.

However, despite the clear implications these criticisms pose for core elements of *Labor and Monopoly Capital*, they do not, in and of themselves, invalidate the overall thrust of Braverman's thesis. With regard to the first point, the possibility of labour resistance to management control initiatives does not contradict the existence of these initiatives, only the assumption of their success as inevitable and unproblematic. Referring to the second objection, which attacks the simplicity of Braverman's conception of managerial strategy, Salaman (1992) warns against using "too limited and focused a view of management strategy... " or seeing strategy as implying "conscious and explicit choices" (Salaman, 1992: 360). Instead, decisions which affect the labour process must be put in perspective; the foremost preoccupations of capital and management are more likely to reflect cost reductions, profit margins, and so on. So, for instance, a recognition of the place of the labour process within the "full circuit of capital" (Kelly, 1985) allows that "these preoccupations will have implications for what is expected and required from employees' work, and so will have consequences for job design" (Salaman, 1992: 360). Nonetheless, within these constraints there still remains space for managerial discretion in their choice of job design strategies. Child therefore argues for an understanding of how "managerial strategies ... establish corporate parameters for the labour process which are unlikely to be inconsequential even when there is attenuation between policy and implementation" (Child, 1985: 112).

The same applies when considering the impact of the notion of tacit skill for Braverman's thesis. Should the importance of tacit skill be accepted, then one can no longer assume that task fragmentation and deskilling are the only options open to capital in its struggle to control the labour process. The concept of tacit skills adds weight to the impact of worker resistance and the need for management to move beyond Tayloristic practices in many circumstances. However, this is not to deny the existence and intent of Taylorism, even if, in Burawoy's words, it was "a failure ... as a practical tool of increasing capitalist control" (Burawoy, 1979: 278). The core of Braverman's thesis, that the defining aspect of capital's influence on the labour process is to maintain and extend control, remains unchallenged by these critiques - indeed, most provide further evidence of this tendency. However, the understanding of the labour process has by necessity become more complex. Wider research has pointed to numerous ways in which capital may attempt to increase its control over the labour process, which may or may not be conscious strategies, which may or may not be resisted, and which may or may not prove successful. More importantly, a contradiction has been discerned throughout this struggle; it is argued that while the value added by the labour process derives from the malleability and creative potential of labour, it is this very creative potential which affords labour the possibility of resisting capitalist control. Capitalist strategies of control, therefore, have been represented as a continuing attempt to reconcile this contradiction; to harness this creative potential without sacrificing control of the labour process itself.

To further complicate matters, numerous authors have questioned the idea reflected here of an endemic antagonism between capital and labour, which implies a zero-sum conception of the relationship. Such writers have highlighted that within the present socio-economic system, "since labour can only gain access to the means of production through selling its labour power to capital it has an interest in the maintenance of that relationship and therefore the viability of the unit of capital which employs it" (Cressey and MacInnes, 1980: 15). This is not to contradict the fundamental divergence of interests which set labour and capital against each other in capitalist relations of production, nor to deny that in any interdependent relationship capital would occupy a dominant position. However, they argue that a more complete picture will take into account "how the values which guide the strategic choices of managers and workers are themselves shaped and constrained by a structure of relations that can pull capital and labour apart at the same time as it renders them more mutually dependent" (Knights and Willmott, 1988: 7). Analysis must therefore take into account "the tension underlying the dual character of the relationship wherein a productive interdependence is framed within a structure of antagonism over power, knowledge and allocative resources" (Knights and Willmott, 1988: 7). Such a 'productive interdependence' implies therefore a "potential terrain of compromise and consensus" (Littler and Salaman, 1982: 253), at least in the short term, as well as conflict.

As noted, such criticisms generally aim to rescue the essence of Braverman's thesis by correcting minor deficiencies in his formulation. Deeper criticisms, on the other hand, focus on the very foundations of Braverman's revision of the Marxist theory of the labour process. One of the most fundamental criticisms of Braverman's thesis emerges from discussions of the nature of subjectivity and its role in the control of the labour process, an issue which will be examined in detail in the next section.

The Question of Dualism

A number of criticisms of Braverman's work have been appraised in the previous section. These criticisms should not be taken to fundamentally undermine the thesis, but rather to *fortify* it, by offering constructive alternatives. This broadening of Labour Process Theory enables it to be convincingly applied to a wider range of work processes and more diverse aspects of resistance and conflict. However, there remains a crucial issue which reveals a tension inherent to the labour process field; the recurrent debate over *structure* versus *agency*.

This may be dealt with on two levels. The first approach is to argue either in favour of a structuralist or a voluntarist perspective. From a voluntarist approach, the focus is predominantly on individuals as 'agents', who "deploy a range of causal powers, sometimes on behalf of others who command greater resources, sometimes to bend or break rules, but always purposeful and reflexive" (Thompson and McHugh, 1995: 362). This forms the basis for most liberal schools of thought, which display a reliance upon the concept of society being a conglomeration of these generally rational, generally utility-maximising individuals, in the mould of the 'Rational Economic Man' beloved of neo-classical economists. To the other extreme lie structuralist models, wherein individuals are not truly free but, by acting in keeping with what they consider their nature or best interests, serve to make their decisions in accordance with structural imperatives, even if unaware that these imperatives exist. Traditional Marxist writers tend to steer clear of psychological interpretations which risk privileging individual choice and action, whereas partisans of action-based research and ethnomethodology remain dismissive of structural explanations of social tendencies.

It has been noted above that the key aims of Marx's project were to free political economy from an uncritical acceptance of the existing socio-economic system and enable an appreciation of its socially contingent nature. This may be contrasted with a continuing current of mainstream literature which Marx sought to challenge, which is founded upon an understanding of capitalism as a construct of the free actions of a multitude of sovereign agents. In this way, the existence of this particular form of capitalism may be justified as natural and inevitable. As Willmott puts it, Marx's entire thesis is *"pitted against* atomistic, individualistic and psychologistic forms of explanation" (Willmott, 1995: 5 original emphasis). His aim therefore was to illustrate how power relations and historical contingencies influence the action of individuals who nonetheless conceive of themselves as "independent, autonomous agents who float free of social relations" (Willmott, 1995: 8). Consequently, Marx stated directly that "individuals are dealt with (in *Capital Volume I*) only in so far as they are the personifications of economic categories, the bearers of particular class relations and interests" (Marx, 1976: 92). In defending this fundamentally structuralist analysis, Marx does not deny the existence of subjective understanding and action. However, the implication is that structural effects will override any subjective tendencies to the contrary. Likewise, Braverman describes his own perspective as reflecting "a self-imposed limitation to the 'objective' and the omission of the 'subjective'" (Braverman, 1974: 27). A large part of Braverman's introduction is devoted to an earnest critique of the aims and methods of bourgeois sociology as having forsaken any emancipatory objectives regarding the working class, and restricting themselves merely to the accommodation of the working class to prevailing conditions in the mode of production and domination. Like Marx, this accounts for Braverman's focus on the structural imperatives of monopoly capitalism, rather than subjective, psychological explanations of reactions and resistance to these conditions. However, this 'subjective' aspect is recognised very clearly in Paul Sweezy's foreword to *Labor and Monopoly Capital* as a complementary line of research; "Harry Braverman ... does not attempt to pursue the inquiry into what might be called the subjective aspects of the development of the working class under monopoly capitalism. That task remains to be tackled. Whoever undertakes it will find in the present work a firm and indispensable foundation upon which to build" (Sweezy in Braverman, 1974: 10). The implications of this are concisely summed up by Willmott;

> "(Labour Process Theory) challenges an inherently conservative, action-centred focus upon essentially 'free' individuals who simply choose what they do (and therefore believe that they are able to distance themselves or 'stand above' the relations in which they are embroiled). But in focusing upon structure, it excludes, or at least marginalises, the role of action in the reproduction and transformation of structural imperatives" (Willmott, 1995: 9).

It is difficult to overestimate the importance of this legacy of structuralism for subsequent work on the Labour Process. In drawing upon and extending the groundwork laid down by Braverman, many accounts magnify the structuralism of the original account in making no reference to nor justification for the disregard of subjective aspects.

This neglect of subjectivity has been highlighted as a key flaw in the approach of Braverman and subsequent structuralist work in the labour process tradition. As Burawoy notes, Braverman "makes no reference to the psychological and other processes by which subordination to capital is secured, the processes through which workers come to comply with and otherwise advance their own dehumanisation" (Burawoy, 1981, in Thompson, 1989: 153). As noted above, the focus on 'class' independently of subjectivity is a deliberate choice on Braverman's part, seen as true to the spirit of Marx and avoiding the conservatism of bourgeois psychology. However, Burawoy's focus on mechanisms which elicit the consent of the workforce to their own exploitation underlines the importance of control of the labour process *through* the subjectivity of the workforce. Burawoy therefore examines the construction of subjectivity on the shopfloor, specifically through the self-management of workers involved in workplace 'games', or 'making-out' (maximising bonuses). Burawoy's analysis does indeed suffer from a number of problems, particularly regarding his essentialist view of an immutable human nature, based on an innate creativity which the capitalist labour process stifles. Nonetheless, Burawoy's recognition of the importance of subjectivity may be seen as an indication of the future direction of Labour Process work, recognising "the unacknowledged power of this (capitalist) organisation of the labour process (which) resides in its constitution of the subjectivity of labour in ways which render it self-disciplinary" (Knights and Willmott, 1989: 552).

Even in work where the significance of subjectivity is recognised, the structuralist tendency within Labour Process Theory has frequently led to a somewhat one-sided application of the constraints of structure. This is related to a criticism made of Braverman above, specifically of his attribution of omniscience and strategic intent to capital. This error is repeated by numerous commentators within both Marxist and labour process literatures; that the organization of production under capitalist social relations is a conscious and deliberate construct of the actions of capital alone, as a unified entity. In contrast, evidence quoted above suggests an irrational, unreflective and ad hoc approach by capital to the labour process, often all but dictated by other preoccupations (Mintzberg, 1975, 78; Kelly, 1985). Discretion does play its part, and it has been suggested that the 'logic of capital' should be conceptualised as constraints upon the 'strategic choices' of management (Child, 1985). The key point here is that understandings of precisely how far structures determine managerial action and the role of discretion in translating these influences remain distressingly undertheorised in much of contemporary Labour Process Theory.

The shortcomings of both of the former positions can be appreciated from the discussion above. An excessively structuralist analysis makes no attempt to theorise how structural imperatives act upon individuals, simply conceptualising that individuals are endowed with interests as a result of their position within the structure of (capitalist) society. As Burawoy warns, "the crucial issue is that *the interests that organise the daily life of workers are not given irrevocably; they cannot be imputed; they are produced and reproduced in particular ways*" (Burawoy, 1985: 28-9). On the other hand, to err too far on the voluntarist side risks losing the cornerstone of the debate, the historically contingent nature of social, economic and productive organization. Labour Process theory is effectively caught between what has been termed the Scylla of structuralism and the Charibdes of voluntarism (Willmott, 1994). Recent work by Hugh Willmott (1995) has been particularly useful in tracing the origins of this schism in sociological analysis and explaining the powerful structuralist bent in Labour Process Theory. David Knights makes a similar point where he emphasises that the "polarization between 'action' and 'structural' theory" (1997b: 9) is not specific to Labour Process Theory, nor attributable to Braverman, but reflects the broader debate on structure/agency which divides the field of sociology and the social sciences in general. As a consequence, it is appropriate that I return to wider sociological and philosophical debates to tackle this dualism in social theory, through an discussion of what have been described as 'post-dualist' theories of power.

Post-Dualist Theories of Power

The debate between proponents of the more exclusive structuralist or voluntarist theories has continued without resolution or prospect of resolution for some time now. Arguments over the relative merits of voluntarist and structuralist perspectives are regarded by many jaded observers as the theoretical equivalent of the 'chicken and the egg' conundrum; "Perhaps, when it has been remounted and relanced many more times, we may even have trophies for the most stylish blows struck against it" (Clegg, 1994: 130). Most modern commentators are reconciled to the fact that this 'dualistic' approach is self-defeating, and that a comprehensive social theory must incorporate at one and the same time the apparently sovereign actions of individuals and also the wider forces acting upon the choices and actions of these individuals. Such 'post-dualist' approaches are aimed at breaking down the division between structuralist and voluntarist positions and developing a unifying theory which "recognises the interdependence of action and structure in both theory and practice and seeks thereby to undermine the conflict and tension between them" (Knights, 1997: 13).

The most noteworthy contributions in this field have been developed by theorists such as Stephen Lukes, Norbert Elias, Roy Bhaskar, and Anthony Giddens. The condition that their approaches try to account for is succinctly expressed by Roy Bhaskar, who asserts; "society is at once the ever present condition and continually reproduced outcome of human agency: this is the duality of structure" (Bhaskar, 1986: 123). This perspective, it is hoped, will lead to an eventual escape from the circular arguments surrounding the structure-agency debate, and is ascribed to a "growing number of organizational theorists ... in their attempt to develop explanatory logics encompassing both the enabling and empowering aspects of 'structure', as well as its constraining or limiting influence" (Reed, 1992: 187). One of the most influential approaches to squaring this circle has been made by Anthony Giddens, whose *theory of structuration* (Giddens, 1979; 1993) appears at first glance to be the perfect solution to a potentially insoluble problem. However, it is in the detail of these theories that serious and familiar problems recur.

As noted, the objective of these 'post-dualist' theories is to reconcile the structuralist and subjectivist extremes of the continuum, and resolve the apparent dilemma by reconciling the two perspectives within one theoretical framework. Difficulties arise when examining the specific manner in which this reconciliation is attempted. Lukes' (1974) work on power relations focuses on extending more traditional models of power beyond the two basic dimensions; on the one axis, formal decision making and resource utilization, and, on the other, a more subtle prior definition of agendas, which defines in advance what issues are negotiable and covers "non-decision-making" (Clegg, 1994: 76). In addition to these, Lukes was keen to include a third dimension, the notion that the needs and wants of an individual "may themselves be a product of a system which works *against their interests*, and in such cases, relates the latter to what they would want and prefer, were they able to make the choice" (Lukes, 1974: 34 emphasis added). In this way the idea of structural imperatives may be included without losing the more traditional and common-sense understanding of power entailing deliberate action to further ones own interests. Lukes is forthright about the need for an inclusive model, stating that "social life can only properly be understood as a dialectic of power and structure, a web of possibility for agents, whose nature is both active and structured, to make choices and pursue strategies within given limits ... Any standpoint or methodology which reduces this dialectic to a one-sided consideration of agents without (internal or external) structural limits, or structures without agents, or which does not address the problem of their interrelations, will be unsatisfactory" (Lukes, 1977, in Reed, 1992: 63).

Despite this being a considerable advance on previous models, Lukes has been taken to task over the difficulties in attributing a 'real' *interest* to an individual. This criticism reflects problems with notions of 'ideological hegemony'; namely, on what basis can an observer identify what they consider to be the 'true' interests of an individual and decide that what the individual considers to be his or her interests are 'false' (Clegg, 1994)? There is a need for a sound basis for asserting that the observer's assessment of 'real interests' is more trustworthy than that of the individual or group concerned, a basis which transcends individual preferences. Although not explicitly adopted by Lukes, one perspective which clearly offers this is classical Marxism. Here, a Marxist analysis of capitalist production enables the determination of the objective interests of an individual or group, and traditionally these correspond to class position. However, numerous subsequent theorists (Benton, 1981; Abercrombie *et al*, 1980; Knights and Willmott, 1982) have dismissed this notion of a unitary, all-encompassing ideology, proposing rather that distinctive groups live and work under broadly differing ideologies. It is here that differentiated, fragmented *ideologies* begin to resemble a distinctive, postmodern concept, that of *discourse*, a point which will be taken up below. It is important to note here that the traditional opposition between ideology and some objective, modernist notion of 'truth' is also eroded by the use of this concept, giving way to a more relative conception of multiple discourses.

Moreover, Giddens (1979) accuses Lukes of preserving the dualism in his 'radical' conception of power, insofar as he considers that structure and agency may coexist, but only on distinct axes. "While Lukes regards the relationship between power and structure as dialectical, Giddens wants to sever the relationship as being between two distinct concepts, a *dualism*, and instead, reconstitute it as a *duality*, in which power and structure are interpenetrated. He refers to this as the 'duality of structure'." (Clegg, 1994: 138). Rather than understanding individual agency as an alternative to structural imperatives, Giddens' structuration theory seeks to show how structure can act through agency itself. Hence Giddens asserts that "to enquire into the structuration of social practices is to seek to explain how it comes about that structure is constituted through action and reciprocally how action is constituted structurally" (Giddens, 1993: 169).

In some quarters this has been optimistically received; Reed describes Giddens' "attempt to construct a theory of structuration which will synthesise institutional analysis of structural forms with strategic analysis of social action" as "the most influential development in this domain" (Reed, 1992: 187). It is here, however, that the traditional debate rears its head again. From a review of the reactions in the literature to Giddens' work, Clegg concludes that "Giddens' 'duality of structure' promises but does not deliver because ... it is a duality which remains tightly coupled to the individualist and voluntarist side of the argument" (Clegg, 1994: 140). We are now on familiar ground; there is an acceptance that both structure and agency are relevant and that they are intricately connected, but this formulation *still* carries the original sin of dualism. Thus in the case of Giddens, his formulation has been criticised for erring on the side of voluntarism.

There are two substantial objections to the agentic predominance recognised in Giddens' structuration theory, which relate to the same central problem. One objection is that the reproduction of structure in this model is dependent on the separate "instantiations in such as practices and as memory traces" (Giddens, 1984: 18). That is to say, structure only exists in the actual moments where individuals act to reproduce it. The implication of this is that a deliberate choice taken at that moment by an individual is enough to undermine the structural constraint, which, as is suggested, is a very fragile basis for something as enduring as structure (Clegg, 1994). This fragility is exacerbated by the fact that the reproduction of structure relies upon a *knowledge* of structure (in the form of social institutions) held by individuals. Giddens goes so far as to emphasise this in a recent response to critics, stating that "even the most enduring of habits, or the most unshakeable of social norms, involves continual and detailed reflexive attention. Routinization is of elemental importance in social life; but all routines, all the time, are contingent and potentially fragile accomplishments" (1993: 7). If one turns here to abiding structures of domination in modern society, such as patriarchy and capitalism, it becomes more difficult to accept the implications of this thesis, whereby it appears that "the 'structures' and 'systems' concerned are inchoate and evanescent, appearing and disappearing at the behest of specific individuals in specific encounters" (Layder, 1985, in Clegg, 1994: 144). To convincingly include the productive nature of power acting through structure, a model must demonstrate the ability of structure to continually shape the subjectivities of individuals. Clegg argues convincingly that the arrow needs to swing the other way, such that "what agents can or cannot do depends very much on their position in relations of production and ... in other forms of social relations in the state and civil society as well as the economy" (1994: 145).

To summarise, it has been argued that there remain significant weaknesses in the theoretical basis of Labour Process work, and that these weaknesses are hampering the ability of the work to accurately conceptualise developments in the field. The main problems emphasised here are fourfold: Firstly, Labour Process Theory has inherited a structuralist bent from the avowedly 'objective' focus of its foundational authors (Marx, 1974; Braverman, 1974). Secondly, recourse to Lukes' (1974) three-dimensional 'radical' model of power founders on his continued dualistic separation of structure and agency, and on the need for a transcendent, objective designation of 'real interests'. Thirdly, Giddens

(1976; 1977; 1979) despite being more persuasive in his integration of structure and agency, discounts the dominance of structure as his 'structuration theory' is predicated upon individual agency and choice. Finally, a comprehensive and inclusive theory must incorporate the influence of discourse as a channel of power, and integrate this with the active agency of individual subjects. It can be argued that all of these difficulties may be reduced to one central flaw; the inadequate conceptualization of power and power relations. An acceptable model of power must move beyond individual intent and action, and also beyond the prestructuring of decisions and negotiations, both intentional and unintentional. A sound conceptualization of power must indeed account for phenomena which can be interpreted as the above. However, the crucial aspect of a satisfactory conception of power must be the ability to convincingly incorporate enduring structural imperatives directly constituting the subjectivities of individuals based on their position in the structure. The next section will examine the work of Michel Foucault and assess the possibility of applying the insights afforded by his writings, specifically concerning power and discourse, to these ongoing difficulties.

The Contribution of Michel Foucault

In search of a resolution to some of the dilemmas facing contemporary Labour Process Theory, a number of writers have turned to the work of Michel Foucault, with some considerable controversy. Foucault, over a period of some twenty-three years, produced a body of work so diverse as to defy easy classification. With books and articles ranging from the fields of philosophy, social theory, sociology, the history of medicine and sexuality, it is unlikely that many areas of study have entirely escaped some attention, if not by Foucault then by writers adopting his perspective. Although Foucault does not directly attempt to resolve the structure-agency dualism, his wider writings on the discursive construction of fields of knowledge (Foucault, 1972; 1975) highlight the operation of power in the discursive development of a taxonomy which distinguishes between structure and agency. In particular, his work draws attention to the role of the human sciences in the construction of the individual as a sovereign, autonomous agent. The importance of his work does not, therefore, reside in its direct relevance to the structure-agency debate *per se*; rather, it lies in the philosophical insights provided by his discussions of power, knowledge and later, the human subject. Before entering into an examination of Foucault's work, however, I will first discuss the tentative, discontinuous and at times self-contradictory nature of his oeuvre.

Almost as striking as the *breadth* of Foucault's thought is its *originality*, firmly dedicated to a radical analysis of conventional wisdom and unsurprisingly engendering enormous amounts of criticism. This applies equally to social sciences and the sociology of work, where writers from a range of theoretical positions have either dismissed his relevance or refuted his analyses (Habermas, 1987; Callinicos, 1990; Thompson and Ackroyd, 1995). This controversy is intensified by the disjointed nature of his work. It is perhaps impossible for a body of work of such breadth and diversity to remain consistent and comprehensive in its perspective and conclusions. It is common for even sympathetic commentators to openly acknowledge as much; indeed, Cousins and Hussein state "Foucault's writings are interspersed with argument and remarks that slip back into the very themes he himself has so trenchantly criticised. An immanent critique and assessment of Foucault's work by pitting one argument against another is indeed possible" (1990: 253). However, this is exacerbated by Foucault's playful approach to several issues and his often rhetorical style. "Foucault himself has described his tactic as a 'slalom' ... between the traditional philosophy and an abandonment of all seriousness" (Dreyfus and Rabinow, 1982: 205). His work as a result tends to pose questions rather than provide answers, questions which Dreyfus and Rabinow suggest we interpret as "markers on the course that modern thinkers must follow" (1982: 205).

Consequently, much of the work which builds upon Foucault displays a tendency to apply his thought piecemeal. If we take it that his intent is more to provoke than to devise universal theories, can this selective application therefore be justified? One clear example of this is Sewell and Wilkinson's *Someone to Watch Over Me* (1992a), which applies Foucault's concept of the *panopticon* (to be examined in greater detail below) to surveillance in industry without reference to his wider points on the constitution of the subject or power/knowledge discourses. This selectivity with regard to Foucauldian theory remains a particularly common approach in some areas of Labour Process work, and this is particularly the case when writers are importing his understanding of the panopticon, which is often presented as the crux of Foucault's work on discipline, rather than another situationally specific example of a disciplinary technology. Indeed, it is noted by Mark Poster that Foucault himself is "tempted by the totalizing impulse at several points in his text (*Discipline and Punish*)" (1984: 103), where Foucault risks presenting the panopticon as a universal form of normalization. This appears as a striking contradiction to his basic tenet, that "critical theory is best served by detotalizing analyses which restrict themselves to particular clusters of dominating practices"(Poster, 1984: 104). Is it justified, then, to 'pick and mix' among Foucault's writings?

Within *Discipline and Punish* (1977), the panopticon is linked in with Foucault's conceptions of discourses in the human sciences and the specific nature of power relations, issues which are neglected in Sewell and Wilkinson (1992a; 1992b), and in similar works (e.g. Zuboff, 1988). Sewell and Wilkinson invoke a commentary by Anthony Giddens (1985) to defend their interpretation of *Discipline and Punish*, where he claims that;

> "there is no need to accept the whole sweep of Foucault's arguments to acknowledge that Disciplinary Power becomes associated with a range of organizations involving new modes of regularising activities in time and space ... In this sense, prisons and asylums share some generalizable characteristics of modern organization, including the capitalistic work place" (Giddens, 1985, in Sewell and Wilkinson, 1992a: 274).

I would accept this argument to some extent, although Sewell and Wilkinson's work remains dangerously reductive in its interpretation. However, this means that it is vital that the theorist is very careful in specifying which aspects his/her perspective will adopt, and which conclusions it will draw. To an extent, Foucault vindicates this position when he stresses the hypothetical and tentative nature of much of his writings. He explains that "the notion common to all the work that I have done since *Histoire de la Folie* is that of *problematization*" (Foucault, 1988: 257 emphasis added), and states that the role of the intellectual is "to question over and over again what is postulated as self-evident, to disturb people's mental habits... " (Foucault, 1988: 265). This approach is celebrated by numerous commentators on Foucault;

> "For (Foucault) uncertainty causes no anguish ... He advances hypotheses with the delight that others reserve for the revelation of truth ... As he remarks in an interview ... the uncertainty is genuine, not a rhetorical device. He compares his last book to a Gruyère cheese, with holes in which the reader can install himself" (Sheridan, 1980: 222-3).

This view of his oeuvre is reflected by Gibson Burrell, who denies that Foucault's work can be, nor that he intended it to be, integrated into an overarching 'Grand Theory'; "In the place of widely-held views, he substituted tentative hypotheses which invite, indeed beg for, heated discussion and debate" (Burrell, 1988: 222). Further evidence can be found in several of Foucault's interviews, which echo one of Foucault's most quoted phrases, "Do not ask who I am and do not ask me to remain the same: Leave it to our bureaucrats and our police to see that our papers are in order" (Foucault, 1972: 17).

It seems therefore that it would be unwarranted, indeed dangerous, to adopt the thought of Foucault wholesale and uncritically. Taking any of Foucault's works as a Holy Book wherein all Truth can be found is clearly antithetical to any project that Foucault may be seen to have been pursuing. As Foucault once described his attitude to Nietzsche, so it would seem reasonable that writers should approach Foucault;

> "Myself, I prefer to utilise the writers I like. The only valid tribute to thought such as Nietzsche's is precisely to use it, to deform it, to make it groan and protest. And if commentators then say that I am being faithful or unfaithful to Nietzsche, that is of absolutely no interest" (Foucault, 1980: 53-4).

By the same token, the obligation is placed firmly upon the reader to explore all the avenues opened by Foucault's research and situate his or her own work on sufficiently firm theoretical foundations. Bearing this forewarning in mind, then, the following section will aspire to critically assess the impact of Foucault's writings in three main steps. I will commence with a recap of Foucault's work which is by necessity far from exhaustive but will concentrate on the areas pertinent to a study of power and the labour process in its broadest sense. I will then highlight those areas where his approach provides some insight into the problems of dualism identified above, with particular reference to the issues of strategy and resistance which are central to traditional Labour Process Theory. Finally, I will introduce Foucault's concept of power/knowledge and its relations with discourse, which will be critically assessed in more detail in Chapter 3.

Power and Genealogy

In analysing Foucault's conception of power, an immediate difficulty is encountered. In his work, Foucault questions whether there is any value in attempting to glean the 'essence' of power, of sources of power, and of ways power is used. Indeed, Foucault goes so far as to claim that "power in the substantive sense, *'le' pouvoir*, does not exist" (Foucault, 1980: 198). As has been noted, "there is in Foucault's writings no theory of power, not even a sketch of such a theory" (Cousins and Hussein, 1990 226). As a result, any comparison with existing work either directly or indirectly relevant to power is hampered by a complete shift in perspective and terminology, rendered more difficult by Foucault's idiosyncratic style and exploratory nature. Nonetheless, it is only through such an analysis that any benefits of insights on the part of Foucault will be gleaned.

The orthodox conception of power is remarkably similar in mainstream management and Marxist texts. In the first, power is almost universally associated with resource dependency, such that resource bases such as 'reward power', 'coercion power', 'legitimate power', 'expert power' and 'referent power' are defined (French and Raven, 1959). In Marxist theory, economic domination of the organization of production is the source of power, with particular reference to the ownership of the means of production. Hence in both cases, the cause and consequence of power are confused, being, in both cases, resource dependency. "How is power to be recognised independently of resource dependency? ... The cause of power is resource dependency. At the same time, its consequence, of resource dependency, is equivalent to its cause" (Clegg, 1988: 99). It is such circular reasoning which draws attention away from what Foucault sees as the main issue; the mechanisms of power. Clegg (1988), in common with Foucault, presents as the source of the problem the tendency to consider power as a thing, rather than a 'property of relations'.

Foucault's perspective may be clearly contrasted with orthodox and Marxist notions of power. The basis of Foucault's treatment of power is this very point: that power "should not be treated as a proper noun, standing for relations with definite features in common" (Clegg, 1988: 228). This in itself invalidates the introductory question to innumerable texts on the nature of power: 'What is power?'. All questions in this vein begin by essentialising power, reducing it to a unifiable entity, and hence missing the 'open texture' of what Foucault prefers to term 'power relations'. He defines power, therefore, as "relations, a more-or-less organised, co-ordinated hierarchical cluster of relations" (Foucault, 1980: 198), and never reduces the concept to a more precise definition than "an ensemble of actions exercised by and bearing on individuals, which guide conduct and structure its possible outcomes" (Cousins and Hussein, 1990: 229). Whittling away such an embracing concept as 'relations' or 'ensemble of actions' to a unitary entity inevitably means losing some essential elements and cases of power relations will then go unnoticed. Foucault therefore suggests that the appropriate approach is to "provide oneself with a grid of analysis which makes possible an analytic of relations of power"(Foucault, 1980: 199).

At least as many difficulties as benefits are thrown up by the adoption of this framework. The immediate advantage that this wider perspective provides is to move the analysis of power beyond what Foucault terms the "negative, narrow, skeletal conception of power" (Foucault, 1980: 119) which defines power only as repression, censorship and constraint. From this conception, described by Foucault as the *repressive hypothesis* (Foucault, 1979), a number of key aspects of the working of power are misinterpreted and overlooked. If this wider conception is adopted, then, phenomena such as the fields of psychoanalysis and psychotherapy may be examined as examples of power relations, in imposing norms on individuals, rather than being seen as defying repression by allowing individuals freedom of expression. Aspects of the functioning of power relations which this basic approach allows Foucault to consider will be dealt with in more detail below. However, it becomes apparent in attempting to apply this concept of 'power relations' that its very malleability makes it difficult to apply in analysis. For instance, when it comes to differentiating between the interrelated phenomena of power and resistance, there is a tendency in Foucault's work to reduce an enormous divergence of activity to the notion of 'power relations'. This, again, will be tackled in more detail when examining the *polyvalence* of power relations, below. However, it is important to note the difficulties in definition entailed in this all-inclusive understanding of power.

Foucault then continues with one of his most controversial and misinterpreted postulates; that 'power is everywhere'. By this is not meant that all interpersonal relations are merely power relations, nor that repression is everywhere, nor that there remains no space for resistance or discretion (Cousins and Hussein, 1990). What Foucault is stressing here is that much of the areas in social life habitually considered 'liberated' are in fact saturated with power relations, which are never complete and coherent and are always open to resistance. They are better conceptualised as "open-textured ... exercised from innumerable points ... tak(ing) a wide variety of forms and ... only partially co-ordinated" (Cousins and Hussein, 1990: 228). These three aspects of the Foucauldian concept of power, that it is *capillary*, *polyvalent* and *without a co-ordinating strategist*, will be added to the *productive* nature of power to provide a framework for its analysis below. The whole perspective adopted by Foucault is underpinned by the postulate that "there is nothing more to power relations beyond their exercise" (Cousins and Hussein, 1990: 229). This implies that the objectives of technologies of power are understandable by direct analysis, either of the practices themselves or of the discourses that justify their implementation. Unlike the Marxist perspective, these discourses are taken at face value, not as 'ideologies' to conceal the true objectives of technologies of power. The most direct route to an understanding of power, therefore, is through the practices and discourses accompanying particular technologies, approachable through Foucault's use of *genealogy*. Hence the first question Foucault poses in his analysis of power is not 'what is power?' but 'how is power exercised?'.

Throughout his work, Foucault's idea of the appropriate method of examining these issues, indeed his conception of the issues themselves, developed from text to text. From his early work which he characterised as *archaeology*, he later preferred the term *genealogy* to describe the approach adopted in his later work, stating that he no longer used the term 'archaeology' (Foucault, 1988: 31). Essentially, archaeology was used to describe Foucault's study of differing objects of knowledge (e.g. madness, sexuality, etc.) in terms of what led to their constitution as 'knowable' objects at a particular conjuncture of history. Archaeology focused on the conditions in which discourses arose regarding certain phenomena, regardless of the parties who were primarily involved in the discourse, hence displacing the individual subjects from the central concern. As he explains;

"Studying the history of ideas, as they evolve, is not my problem so much as trying to discern beneath them how one or another object could take shape as a possible object of knowledge. Why, for instance did madness become, at a given moment, an object of knowledge corresponding to a certain type of knowledge?" (Foucault, 1988: 31).

However, it is in *Discipline and Punish* (1977) and *The History of Sexuality Vol. I* (1979) that Foucault wholeheartedly adopts the term genealogy, to represent a switch of focus to the superficial rather than the deep and hidden. Genealogy is, in contrast to archaeology, a longitudinal analysis of the minutiae of empirical events to understand the construction of present objects, "locating traces of the present in the past" (Burrell, 1988: 225). The aim of genealogy, as summed up by Poster, is to "undermine the present order by reversing its images of the past" (Poster, 1984: 89). The way Foucault attempts this is by;

"go(ing) back in time until a difference is located ... These alien discourses/practices are then explored in such a way that their negativity in relation to the present explodes the 'rationality' of phenomena that are taken for granted. When the technology of power of the past is elaborated in detail, present day assumptions which posit the past as 'irrational' are undermined" (Poster, 1984:89-90).

Genealogy attempts to bring home the fact that "we are nothing but our history, and that therefore we will never get a total and detached picture of who we are or of our history" (Dreyfus and Rabinow, 1982: 122). Hence *Discipline and Punish* traces the development of the notion of 'disciplinary power' up to the present day through a "grey, meticulous and patently documentary" (Foucault, 1984: 76) study of concrete practices, rather than 'discourse' alone. The approach has drawn criticism from traditional historians as well as writers in other fields for the selectivity of the evidence Foucault draws upon. Despite the persuasive nature of Foucault's conclusions in *Discipline and Punish* (1977), this point reflects one of the more trenchant criticisms of Foucault's work; if Foucault is adamant that all aspects of society are suffused with power relations, on what basis can he extract his own writings from this and adopt what appears at times to constitute a transcendental standpoint with regard to power, morality and discourses?

Power/Knowledge and the Creation of Discourse

As his thought has evolved, Foucault has emphasised the fundamental interconnection between power and forms of knowledge while simultaneously attempting to avoid oversimplifying the relation. As he has emphasised;

> "as far as the general public is concerned, I am the guy who said that knowledge merged with power ... If I had said, or meant, that knowledge was power I would have said so, and having said so, I would have nothing more to say, since, having made them identical, I don't see why I would have taken the trouble to show the different relations between them" (Foucault, 1988: 264).

In his clearest definition, Foucault makes this explicit in *Discipline and Punish*; "there is no power relation without the correlative constitution of a field of knowledge, nor any knowledge which does not presuppose and constitute at the same time power relations ... In short, it is not the subject of knowledge that produces a corpus of knowledge, useful or resistant to power, but power/knowledge, the processes and struggles that traverse it, and of which it is made up, that determine the form and possible domains of knowledge" (Foucault, 1979: 28-9). Significantly, Foucault does not describe power as evolving from knowledge, nor knowledge as being constrained by power, but considers their interdependence as better described by single notion, 'power/knowledge'. The interrelationship is made even clearer elsewhere,

> "No body of knowledge can be formed without a system of communications, records, accumulations and displacement which is in itself a form of power and which is linked, in its existence and functioning, to the other forms of power. Conversely, no power can be exercised without the extraction, appropriation, distribution or retention of knowledge. On this level, there is not knowledge on the one side and society on the other, or science and the state, but only the fundamental forms of knowledge/power..." (Foucault, 1980, quoted in Sheridan, 1980: 131).

A crucial point here is that any idea of a split between knowledge and practice must be dispensed with. Knowledge exists and can be understood within the functioning of technologies of power, while power is itself an intrinsic part of any form of knowledge. This is a key issue exposed by Foucault's genealogical approach, which "forces us to reconsider the relations between knowledge and power ... Power and knowledge are two sides of the same process. Knowledge cannot be neutral, pure. All knowledge is political not because it may have political consequences or be politically useful, but because knowledge has its conditions of possibility in power relations" (Sheridan, 1980: 220). A key aspect of this is Foucault's renunciation of truth as the measure of knowledge and his emphasis of the practical power effects of knowledge. Thus Foucault uses genealogy to "deprive knowledge of its apparent objectivity. It denounces the illusion of truth. Knowledge is not so much true or false as legitimate or illegitimate for a particular set of power relations" (Sheridan, 1980: 220). It is this conception of the relativity of truth that provides the foundation for Foucault's understanding of *discourse*, which will be developed further in the next chapter.

Already, in this brief introduction to Foucault's understanding of power relations, the enormous gap in perspective between Foucault and previous theorists of power is self-evident. Rejecting the economic model of power, Foucault conceives of power as a property of *relations*, rather than residing in either voluntaristic agents or institutional forces, thus side-stepping the structure/agency debate. Critically, he stresses the productive, constitutive role of power, in contradistinction to repressive and coercive understandings, based on the fundamental interdependence of knowledge and power, which he expresses as regimes of 'power/knowledge'. As Townley explains, "the process of making something known or visible (...) also makes it potentially governable. To 'know' something is to create a new power relation" (1993b: 224). In the next section I will develop this further by examining key aspects of Foucault's conception of power relations, and critically assessing their implications for the theoretical and methodological position informing my arguments here.

Aspects of Foucauldian Power Relations

As noted in the previous section, there are four aspects of Foucault's conception of power which merit explanation. Each of these will be examined in turn; the *productive* nature of power; the *polyvalence* of power; the *capillary* nature of power; and the lack of a co-ordinating strategist behind power relations. Each of these characteristics will be shown to be interrelated and mutually reinforcing. At the same time, there are fierce objections which have been made regarding numerous aspects of Foucault's conception of the nature of power. One of the most widespread of these objections will be considered in some depth; the allegation that Foucauldian power relations leave no space for, or at the very least marginalise, resistance to power. These objections will be assessed in turn, before turning to an examination of power/knowledge and the links with discourse.

Power as Productive

Firstly, the *productive* nature of power in Foucault's understanding will be contrasted with what he terms the 'repressive hypothesis' evident in certain alternatives. The crux of this perspective is that what is implied by power is simply negative, coercive restraint. This is a tendency revealed in a large number of mainstream, liberal texts, and is conspicuous in numerous Marxist works, associating power with censorship and repression, particularly with regard to the growth of capitalism. Foucault attacks this as a negative conception of power, stating that;

> "What makes power hold good, what makes it accepted, is simply the fact that it doesn't weigh on us as a force that says no, but that it traverses and produces things, it induces pleasure, forms knowledge, produces discourse. It needs to be considered as a productive network which runs through the whole social body, much more than as a negative instance whose function is repression" (1980: 119).

Sheridan highlights this productive aspect when he explains that "power is not simply repressive; it is also productive. It is here that the role of the body becomes crucial. Power subjects bodies not to render them passive, but to render them active. The forces of the body are trained and developed with a view to making them productive" (1980: 219). This can readily be related to the links between the growth and effects of the social sciences and the needs of capitalism for docile yet productive labour. Also, in many Marxist texts which subscribe to this 'repressive hypothesis', truth is taken to be "intrinsically opposed to power and therefore plays a liberating role" (Dreyfus and Rabinow, 1982: 127), 'truth' here referring to that which can be determined through rigorous Marxist analysis. As noted, Foucault is careful to question the basis of this truth, preferring to examine the formation of the rules which decide what should be acclaimed as truth within separate discourses. The dangers of this 'repressive hypothesis', then, are threefold; firstly, that truth should be considered an absolute, untainted by power/knowledge effects and discourses; secondly, that power associated with this 'truth' should then be uncritically regarded as liberatory rather than repressive; and thirdly, that productive effects of power relations in society should be disregarded or conceptualised as somehow unrepresentative of power.

One striking feature of Foucault's early understanding of power as productive is his almost complete omission of any 'innate' creative capacities of individuals, an enduring theme in feminist critiques of Foucault's position (for example, Fraser, 1989; Sawicki, 1991; McNay, 1992; 1994). Foucault's understanding is firmly rooted in his notion of power/knowledge as intimately interdependent and of power/knowledge discourses as *constituting* the individual as a subject, *including* all capacities, desires and intentions. This can be interpreted as a legacy of Foucault's structuralist background, excluding all conceptions of agency on the part of an individual other than those bestowed upon him/her by some power/knowledge discourse. This determinism is mitigated in part by the variable and dynamic representation of such discourses, and Foucault's insistence on the inevitability of resistance as an integral part of a power relationship. However, in applying this theoretical perspective in empirical work, the reduction of all action on the part of the individual to effects of power/knowledge fields becomes difficult to maintain. In rejecting subjectivist psychology as an example of a liberal humanist discourse, Foucault abandons all recourse to notions of individuality or agency as an explanation for social action. This can also be seen reflected by Foucault's insistence that power acts materially upon the *body* of its subject, hence again bypassing psychologistic and subjectivist explanations. As noted by Cousins and Hussein, "implicit in Foucault's concern with the body, conduct and actions is the concerted attempt on his part to steer the analysis of power away from the theme of ideology" (1990: 229). While the expansion of power to cover its productive nature is welcome and indeed crucial if research is to adequately account for enduring relations of power and domination in society, the complete obliteration of any essence of an individual, in favour of the dynamics of structural imperatives, risks eliminating any possible source of deviation. In the following chapter I will examine the notion of the subject that Foucault develops in his later work, and assess the extent to which this resolves the flaws in his earlier writings.

Power as Polyvalent

A related aspect of Foucault's rejection of the constrictive definition of power offered by the repressive hypothesis is his insistence on the *polyvalence* of power relations. If power is indeed taken to be a characteristic of relationships, identifiable across the gamut of interpersonal or intergroup relationships, then it seems evident that attempts to confine definitions of power to 'coercion', 'resource dependency' or 'persuasion' must be misconceived. This reflects the comment by Sheridan, that;

> "(power) is not unitary; it has no essence. There are as many forms of power as there are types of relationship. Every group and every individual exercises power and is subjected to it. There are certain categories of person - children, prisoners, the 'insane' - whose ability to exercise power is severely limited, but few members of these groups do not find some means of exercising power, if only on each other" (Sheridan, 1980: 218-9).

This important point again contradicts attempts to reduce power to an essence which can be pinpointed across situations.

However, as noted above, this breadth of definition, accepting that both power and, necessarily, resistance are almost infinitely variable does pose serious problems as regards the reliability of research, including Foucault's own, based on this conception. In drawing upon a vast array of empirical evidence in *Discipline and Punish* (1977), Foucault appears at times to interpret events and practices as either examples of power or of resistance, often in keeping with the thrust of his thesis, but without any grounding to explain why the phenomena should be classified in this way. At times, therefore, the same phenomena may be interpreted as both power and resistance, or even as resistance which serves to justify and reinforce the power relation. It is not inconceivable that certain phenomena might act as examples of power relations in one field while equally serving as resistance in a distinct yet connected field. Such an interpretation is fully in keeping with Foucault's general theoretical perspective, particularly insofar as it allows the writer a significant freedom of interpretation, not bound by any immutable essentialisation of 'power' or 'resistance'. However, from this position the charges of relativism which are regularly levelled at examples of post-structural research remain difficult to counter.

The force with which the charge of relativism has been levelled at Foucault's position does not stem from the concerns of the critics over the taxonomic consistency of Foucault's analysis. What is far more unsettling, particularly for those involved in 'critical' social research, are the implications of Foucault's anti-essentialist stance, in undermining and questioning the taken-for-granted ethical position frequently adopted in critical social research. The distinction, or rather the act of distinguishing between power and resistance becomes fundamental if the ethical position of the theorist rests on an unreflective support of 'resistance', however the concept is defined, over the dominatory operation of 'power'. Thus the contribution of this 'polyvalence' lies in its undermining the security of such an unquestioned moral position, which is particularly useful in the critical study of the workplace which is dominated by the categories and moral judgements of Marxist approaches. However, if it is not to fall into a relativist position, then alternative criteria for moral or ethical judgement must be developed, a point which will be examined in some detail in Chapter 3.

Power as Capillary

Power relations are also described as *capillary*. By this, the point is being underlined that power relations do not emanate from a central source, whether this be the state, the sovereign or concentrations of capital itself;

"The state is rather an overall strategy and effect, a composite result made up of a multiplicity of centres and mechanisms, so many states within states with complex networks of common citizenship. Factories, housing estates, hospitals, schools, families are among the more evident, more formalised of such 'micro-powers', the relations that are made between them and their relations with the strategic aims of the state apparatus" (Sheridan, 1980: 219).

Rather, power relations are constructed from individual instances, reactions to local circumstances, which interconnect from the bottom up to form an ensemble of power relations in society. As a result, any conception of 'power' should reflect its nature as "a shifting, inherently unstable expression in networks and alliances" (Clegg, 1994: 158). This suits the aforementioned polyvalence of power technologies; each technology arises in response to local issues, reflecting conscious decision making at the local level. "The emphasis on the local nature of power relations goes hand-in-hand with the importance of placing power relations in particular domains such as the prison or the family within a wider strategy" (Cousins and Hussein, 1990: 247).

Cousins and Hussein (1990) suggest that a useful analogy to employ in this respect is the military notion of *strategies* and *tactics*. It is crucial that power is analysed primarily with respect to local *tactics*, which then interrelate to form patterns in what might be termed general *strategies*. While the implications of this postulate for the analysis of power relations are significant enough, this leads directly to the final aspect to be discussed, the level of strategic intent that one can infer from this conception of power. The question that this begs is then, does this focus on 'micro-politics' imply that politics as traditionally considered, including 'top-down' research focused on the decisions of 'power élites' should be disregarded? While power is rooted in relations and practices at the local level, should this be taken to mean that political and economic decisions on a large scale have no influence? This is an important question to bear in mind in the following section, which assesses the conception of strategy implied by the understanding of power outlined above.

Power and Strategy

The final point is possibly the most controversial departure from traditional Marxist conceptions of power; namely, *the lack of a co-ordinating strategist* behind power relations. Given the heterogeneous and bottom-up nature of technologies of power, it seems difficult to imagine how they could evolve in keeping with a deliberate strategy conceived by an individual, group or even class. Nonetheless, there are similarities, interrelationships and synergies between distinct local technologies, which have given rise to attempts to inductively derive an essentialised definition of power from these local technologies, of which a striking example is Braverman's deskilling thesis (1974). Braverman's discussion of deskilling has been taken to task for many reasons, one of which is the assumption on the part of Braverman that deskilling is the *universal* strategy deriving from the impetus of capital logic (Wood, 1982; Friedman, 1977). Foucault's understanding therefore reverses the causal relationship between such practices and a central 'power', such that "political transformations are not the result of some necessity, some immanent rationality, but responses to particular problems, combining not in a totalising, centralised manner, but by serial repercussion" (Sheridan, 1980: 219). Returning to the 'structure-agency' debate highlighted above, Foucault's work, characteristically, may be seen to suggest an original approach to the dilemma. Foucault first rejects the possibility of deducing instances of power technologies from an overarching structural determinism, such as the case of Braverman (1974) who deduces tendencies to deskill as inevitable from the logic of capital. Equally, he rejects voluntarism by insisting upon the intelligibility of dispersed technologies of power, such as disciplinary power. The solution he arrives at, therefore, is that of "intentionality without a subject, a strategy without a strategist" (Dreyfus and Rabinow, 1982: 187).

The use of terms such as 'strategic objectives' must, however, be qualified somewhat. It is important here to be clear that in using such terminology, Foucault implies no notion of intentionality or non-intentionality. Searching for a band of conspirators responsible for the evolution of 'power' reflects a fundamental misconception of Foucault's understanding of power. Foucault's basic premise is that while the objectives of power relations may be intelligible across situations, this does not imply a co-ordinating strategist, whether this be the state, capitalists, or the bourgeoisie. From Foucault's perspective, therefore, strategies are relevant "not so much to explain power relations as to render them intelligible in terms of a macro-pattern" (Cousins and Hussein, 1990: 247-8); there is no underlying intention implied by the term 'strategy'. At the local level, it is true that tactics are understandable in relation to the actions and statements of specific decision-makers. However, the grand power strategies, such as disciplinary power, are described by Foucault as "great anonymous, almost unspoken strategies" (Foucault, 1980: 95). His position is made clear in an interview, where he states;

> "If you ask me 'Does this new technology of power take its historical origin from an identifiable individual or group of individuals who decide to implement it so as to further their interests or facilitate their utilisation of the social body?" then I would say 'No'. These tactics were invented and organised from the starting points of local conditions and particular needs. They took shape in a piecemeal fashion, prior to any class strategy designed to weld them into vast, coherent ensembles" (Foucault, 1980: 159).

The key point here is the lack of co-ordination, the lack of an organised force deliberately manipulating power relations in society across time. Nonetheless;

> "There is a logic to the practices. There is a push towards a strategic objective, but no-one is pushing. The objective emerged historically, taking particular forms and encountering specific obstacles, conditions and resistances. Will and calculation were involved. The overall effect, however, escaped the actors' intentions, as well as those of anybody else" (Dreyfus and Rabinow, 1982: 187).

The local actors, therefore, are clear of what they are doing and why. The development of these local initiatives into a larger strategy is demystified succinctly by Foucault; "People know what they do; they frequently know why they do what they do; but what they don't know is what they do does" (Foucault, quoted in Dreyfus and Rabinow, 1982: 187). The idea of dominance by particular individuals and groups is accepted, but this is not simplified to general dominance and subservience. Even though positions of dominance are held by certain groups, it is noted that "all these groups were involved in power relations, however unequal and hierarchical, which they did not control in any simple sense" (Dreyfus and Rabinow, 1982: 186).

Space for Resistance

One of the most misunderstood and criticised features of Foucault's work on power relations is his conceptualisation of resistance. The key misunderstanding is to infer that if 'power is everywhere', that this should leave no space for resistance. Rather, Foucault's early position is to place resistance at the very heart of power relationships, not as an external force with an independent source acting contrary to the will of 'power'. This should not, however, be understood as denigrating the importance or potential of strategies of resistance; as Foucault elaborates;

> "there are no relations of power without resistances; the latter are all the more real and effective because they are formed right at the point where relations of power are exercised; resistance to power does not have to come from elsewhere to be real; nor is it inexorably frustrated through being the compatriot of power" (Foucault, 1980: 142).

This conception of resistance can be seen to reflect the aspects of power technologies detailed above; if we cease to consider power as monolithic and centralised, there is no reason to take resistance as dispersed, autonomous and in direct opposition.

The first issue to make clear, then, is the omnipresence of resistance in power relationships, which reflects the similarities between Foucault's understandings of both power and resistance.

> "Where there is power there is resistance, Foucault argues. Resistances to power are, he goes on, diverse in form, heterogeneous, mobile and transitory; more important, they should not be attributed to some unique locus of revolt, a spirit of resistance" (Cousins and Hussein, 1990: 242).

The resemblance between conceptions of power and of resistance are striking. It is dispersed, polyvalent, situationally contingent and stems from a number of sources. Hence Foucault rejects the application of military metaphors to power and resistance, the idea of two ranks of opposing forces from which one side will crush the other and emerge victorious. It is rather a case of a constant and endemic struggle within a power relationship, although "not a struggle to the death ... the fixing of a power relationship becomes a target - at one and the same time its fulfilment and suspension" (Foucault, 1982: 225). This also turns attention to "the existence of those who seem not to rebel...", which Gordon suggests conceals "a warren of minute individual strategies which counter and inflect the visible facts of overall domination, and whose purposes and calculations, desires, and choices resist any simple division into political and apolitical" (1980: 256-7). As far as this understanding of resistance goes, the potential can be seen to reconcile this with the long tradition of studies of worker behaviour in industrial sociology.

This is related to Foucault's insistence on localised and differential struggles. In direct conflict with the core tenets of revolutionary Marxist politics, Foucault asserts that his analysis aims to undermine not only those who exercise power but what he terms the 'vanguard party', the 'revolutionaries' who aim to 'seize' power. François Ewald is quoted in Sheridan (1980) stating;

> "there are three, not two, parties to every power struggle; not only those who exercise power and those who would exercise it in their place, but also those on whom it is exercised. Because one speaks against power, one does not necessarily speak with those who suffer it" (Sheridan, 1980: 220-1).

This then is one of the most radical points made in all of Foucault's work, which questions the legitimacy of all who consider their actions acting as or for the 'oppressed'. Instead, Foucault appears to identify with an anarchic approach to resistance, seeing the true potential for resisting power as lying with isolated, individual struggles, and not with a unified resistance based on solidarity and class-consciousness.

To further complicate matters, Foucault also highlights the role of power in actually producing resistance. Not only does he suggest that the elimination of resistance is not necessarily the aim of power, but Foucault goes on to propose that power technologies may "generate, confront, 'manage' or even promote resistances" (Knights and Vurdubakis, 1994: 179). Furthermore, the very existence of forms of resistance leads to a multiplication of the technologies of power. The example has been given of the consultancy industry, where the specific discourse of consultants define what are examples of resistance to their intervention and thus legitimate further extensions of their influence. This, in contrast to earlier comments on resistance, appears far more contentious. To subscribe to this point would be to question the use of any form of worker resistance, and traditional Labour Process Theorists seem fully justified in highlighting this proposition as antithetical to the prevailing thinking on the Labour Process. While the fact that this contradicts Labour Process thinking is not in itself reason for opposing this idea, there are significant inconsistencies in Foucault's account here. To state that resistance may lead to a multiplication of the original forces of power is not difficult to accept. However, the implication that resistance may be encouraged and nurtured in order to justify extensions of power attributes an enormous amount of strategic intent to what have previously been posited as disparate, localised power practices. This proposition would indeed undermine resistance and add fuel to the flames of those critics already suspecting Foucault of a 'neo-conservatism' (Habermas, 1987). As noted above, some restriction upon the excessive fluidity of Foucault's definitions may well reduce the risk of these interpretations. However, without an explicit foundation to Foucault's critique of power relations based on some moral or ethical principles, closer definitions may prove elusive.

Conclusion

In this chapter I have discussed some of the key elements of the theoretical approach I will take, particularly with regard to the notion of power which will be central to my empirical research on two organisations within the UK 'Financial Services' industry. I have started therefore by outlining the foundations of my early theorising, which are grounded in neo-Marxist work on the labour process, and in particular research in the Labour Process tradition in reaction to Harry Braverman's reinterpretation of Marx, *Labor and Monopoly Capital* (1974). However, my attempts to develop a coherent and cogent theoretical foundation based on such work involved the consideration of a wide range of alternative schools of thought which could also be considered as 'critical' in the broadest sense. My engagement with such work has served to highlight for me the limitations of such neo-Marxist approaches as traditional Labour Process Theory, on philosophical, epistemological and empirical grounds. In particular, the flaws and inconsistencies in the notion of *power* implicit in such work represent a fundamental problem with such approaches, and so it is through the conceptualisation of power that I have approached the critique of traditional Labour Process theory in this chapter. The structure-agency controversy is one which has permeated (and arguably has undermined) the whole of social theory, and fierce, ongoing debates demonstrate that the field of Labour Process Theory is no exception. I have underlined the implicit structuralist bent to Labour Process work, inherited from Braverman's interpretation of Marx, before considering attempts to incorporate some notion of agency, and the accusation of *dualism* levelled at theorists on both sides of this controversy. I have then examined the attempts of Lukes (1974) and Giddens (1979; 1991) to construct a post-dualist framework for the understanding of power in social science, and highlighted the main criticisms of these attempts. My discussion then turns to the radically different approach to power, or more accurately *power relations*, embodied in the work of Michel Foucault.

The second half of this chapter has been devoted to a *critical* assessment of the relevance and potential of Foucault's writings for the development of an approach to the study of power and society. For the moment, I have concentrated on his earlier writings; in the next chapter I will make greater use of his later works, with a particular focus on his writings and interviews in the years leading up to his death, where he refined his earlier work and on occasion made significant changes to his position. Nonetheless, the conceptualisation of power which can be read from his work up to around 1980 opened up a number of avenues along which research could develop without being disabled by a dualist understanding of social action. There are a number of aspects of a Foucauldian approach to power which I will highlight as being of particular relevance to this area.

The first and most fundamental implication of Foucault's perspective is that, in emphasising the *polyvalence* and *productive* nature of power relations, he suggests the expansion of our understanding of power beyond its association with *repression*, especially in critical work. What this allows is a broadened sensitivity in the researcher to the operation of power, frequently in mechanisms and situations where it has traditionally been overlooked, without recourse to problematic notions such as 'real interests', found in Lukes (1974), for instance. The second implication of Foucault's writings is his focus on power/knowledge as a concept, and his unmasking of the operation of power through the construction of truth, particularly in the human sciences. Thus a cardinal example of a 'broadened' sensitivity is evident in Foucault's analysis of the operation of power through the discipline of medicine (1975). This leads to the third point, Foucault's rejection of the Marxist distinction between ideology and truth (as accessible through the science of historical materialism), which will be examined in more detail in Chapter 3 in my discussion of the concept of *discourse*. Fourthly, it is important to underline the capillary nature of power relations in this formulation, pointing the researcher's attention towards the operation of power in multiple locales, not as determined by an overarching source of power but as articulations of a number of competing and interacting discourses. In focusing on the 'micro-politics' of power, however, it is vital that the researcher continually makes the links to highlight the relationship between the specific situation and the wider context, in terms of power/knowledge configurations and discourse. As well as rejecting the search for a conscious, originating strategist behind this operation, either as a group or a class, this position also encourages the identification of dispersed examples of resistance, and subversion through the rearticulation of power.

Nonetheless, there remains a significant *lacuna* in the theoretical position as set out in the writings of Foucault's early and middle period. Partly as a consequence of his structuralist background, he has been frequently accused of implying a fundamental determinism in his early work (despite Foucault's protestations to the contrary in interviews and lectures at the time). There seems to be some justification for this criticism, in that the operation of power through the production of the human subject in discourse appears to leave little or no space for the transformation of such discourses, save through other (existing) discourses. The problem here has been traced by a number of writers to Foucault's rejection of subjectivist approaches, such as phenomenology, and as a consequence *the neglect of the subject* in his work. In effect, Foucault's earlier work implies an understanding of the subject as 'tabula rasa', without any essence other than that inscribed by discourse. The problem with such an understanding is that it has difficulty accounting for any form of action which might be classed as resisting, or even just departing from, the dominant forms of discourse. At the same time, Foucault is fundamentally opposed to the reintroduction of the sovereign subject of humanism through the back door, with the ability to extract him/herself from power relations through an effort of will and rational reflection. In the next chapter, I will trace Foucault's engagement with this dilemma, and assess the usefulness of his conception of the *self* in overcoming this fundamental difficulty.

3 Discourse, the Subject and Ethics

Enter the Subject

Having outlined the notion of Foucauldian analysis in general, focusing on his early understanding of power, I now turn to a concept central to his later writings which will also be central to the remainder of this book; the notion of *discourse*. The aim of this chapter is to make explicit the reading of discourse which will be adopted and examined here, drawn from the work of Foucault. The apparent ubiquity of the concept of 'discourse' in contemporary social research is reflected in the numerous definitions of the term, which frequently have their roots in irreconcilable theoretical foundations. At the same time, a number of alternative terms are used in different fields of study which appear to represent broadly similar phenomena to that implied by 'discourse'. It is necessary therefore that I make clear from the outset my understanding of the concept, broadly based on a Foucauldian perspective although with a number of significant caveats. Through adopting such an approach I hope to avoid the significant problems posed for social research by certain deterministic or exclusively linguistic understandings of discourse. In particular, the precise conception of 'discourse' I will adopt will attempt to avoid certain pitfalls, including the neglect of the material in linguistic discourse analysis, and the displacement of the human subject in the more deterministic structuralist variants.

To distinguish discourse from related concepts, I will first examine the role of the *'linguistic turn'* in social theory resulting from the work on language by Wittgenstein and similar philosophers. In particular, I will focus on the widespread adoption of discursive approaches emerging from the import of insights from Saussurean structural linguistics into the fields of sociology and philosophy. I will then approach discourse by distinguishing the specifically Foucauldian notion of discourse from Althusser's closely related concept of ideology, and in particular Foucault and Althusser's contrasting positions with regard to the notion of *truth*. Clearly, this relates to Foucault's development of the relations between power and knowledge, as discussed in the previous chapter, and the role of what Foucault has described as 'truth effects'. Similarly to Althusser, Foucault's approach stresses the *material*, as well as the non-material aspects of discourse, which also reflects his productive conception of power outlined in Chapter 2. A key point is that Foucault attempts to avoid the charge of determinism by stressing the operation of multiple and often contradictory discourses in the same locality, and indeed operating on and through the same human subjects. This then leads to a discussion of a cardinal instance of the productive nature of discourse; *the discursive construction of the subject* and hence the concept of *subjectivity*.

The first point to be made on subjectivity regards the criticism levelled at orthodox notions of the unitary, individual subject from a range of theoretical viewpoints. Thus writers in fields as diverse as anthropology, feminism, social constructionism, and Critical Theory have attacked the taken-for-granted notion of the subject evident not only in mainstream social science but in everyday understandings of human behaviour. Instead, what has been emphasised is the construction of the subject as an individual with a stable, coherent identity, through a variety of social processes, from the disciplinary operation of the human sciences to the daily *'interpellation'* of subjects through interpersonal relations. The concept of discourse developed earlier is instrumental here in enabling an understanding of these processes and the mechanisms by which they act upon the individual, from family and school to the focus of the book, their operation in the workplace. Indeed, the adoption of discourse to understand identity constitution also provides an appreciation of the fragmented and disparate nature of identity, founded on the discursive construction of *difference*.

This leads into a fundamental debate on the role of the subject in this process of identity construction; should the individual be seen as directly *constituted* by such discourses, or as actively drawing on discourses, in a strategic and selective manner, in pursuit of a unitary and worthwhile identity? As the question has elsewhere been posed, "Is the subject constitutive or constituted?" (Henriques *et al*, 1984: 95). Notions of the active subject, where subjects are seen as positioning themselves within discourses, have been criticised for their reliance on the "pre-social individual", a subjectivity formed before and outside of the operation of discourse. At the same time, understandings of the subject which deny any active role to the individual in identity construction have difficulty in accounting for instances of resistance to discourse and diversions from the norm, and risk falling into a structurally determinist position. Equally importantly, particularly given that the identity of the researcher/writer/theorist is also constructed through such discourses, this position also has difficulty in conceiving of and justifying the source of any form of critique. The position adopted by Foucault in his later works (1985; 1986) reflects precisely this tension, one which he attempts to overcome by his focus on '*the self*'. In an implicit critique of some of his earlier work, Foucault turns here to a more *active* conception of the individual's contribution to the construction of his/her identity. In the final section, then, I will assess the extent to which Foucault's conception as the self as a creation provides space for not only a level of autonomy in the subject but in doing so introduces the possibility of identifying ethical (and by implication non-ethical) conduct. This allows Foucault to remain committed to a concept of emancipation while avoiding essentialism by refusing to define this as "the recovery of an authentic, 'natural' self" (Dews, 1989: 38). Finally, then, I will examine the implications for the critical theorist of Foucault's constant refusal to explicitly propose the fundamental requirements of such an ethical position.

Discourse

The concept of *discourse* has come to predominate in contemporary discussions within many fields of social research, often linked with post-structuralist and postmodern perspectives. Where it is applied, however, it is often inadequately defined, and the breadth of the term can mask a number of fundamental epistemological differences. There is indeed a danger of what has been referred to as 'discourse babble', a term used to highlight the "extravagant vagueness concerning the limits of application of the term." (Henriques *et al*, 1984: 105). This vagueness leads Henriques *et al* to ask where the limits of this concept of 'discourse' lie; "Is everything discourse? Are all practices and all subjects captured within the expansive nets of the discursive?" (Henriques *et al*, 1984: 105). Not only is the concept of discourse often ill-defined, but competing terminology such as 'culture' (Kunda, 1992), 'ideology' (Benson, 1973), 'knowledge' (Knights and Morgan, 1994), 'institutions' (DiMaggio and Powell, 1991), 'rationalities' (Parker, 1995a), 'narratives' (Law, 1994), etc. appears to cover very similar territory. In very general terms, what each of these terms signifies is *a socially and historically specific system of assumptions, values and beliefs which materially affects social conduct and social structure*.

In Foucault's earlier work (1975; 1977), his emphasis is firmly on discourses as large-scale power-knowledge regimes, such as the discourse of medicine, or of humanism, whereby individuals are constituted as *objects* through calculation and normalising judgement. Foucault's structuralist background is evident in his attempts to demonstrate the hegemony of such regimes at particular historical junctures, and the position Foucault adopts in his major early works frequently obscures the potential for the resistance to and transformation of such regimes. At the same time, however, when clarifying his theory in various other writings and interviews, Foucault is explicit in underlining the existence and subversive potential of subjugated discourses within such regimes (see, for instance, Foucault, 1980). The change of focus in Foucault's later work (1979; 1985; 1986) was accompanied by an overdue empirical focus on the operation of unofficial discourses, and here he finally makes reference to concrete examples of these subjugated discourses. For the purposes of this argument, therefore, discourse will be understood to incorporate both these hegemonic power/knowledge regimes and subjugated, localised systems of knowledge and practice.[6] Within this broad definition of discourse, however, there lie significant theoretical differences.

Textual and Material Aspects of Discourse

A clear distinction must also be drawn between the Foucauldian concept of discourse and the more textual understanding of discourse in much sociological research which promotes and practices 'discourse analysis'. While discourse has become a common focus in many areas of social research, its roots frequently lie in the related fields of linguistics and literary criticism, and in particular Saussure's development of structural linguistics (1974). Saussure's argument is founded on two basic premises. Firstly, he asserts that the relationship between signifier (word or sign) and signified (object to be referenced) is arbitrary and socio-historically contingent. Thus there is no fundamental connection between the term 'employee', for example, and the physical individual to which the term refers. Moreover, the identification of someone as an 'employee' reflects social conventions and does not reflect the essential nature of the person but rather a social orthodoxy of classification (Jacques, 1996). Secondly, and consequently, the *meaning* of a signifier is not intrinsic but depends on its differentiation from other signifiers. The term 'employee' itself only has meaning insofar as it can be classified as different from other signifiers such as 'employer', 'unemployed', 'worker', 'customer' and so on. While

---

[6] To take a contemporary example, elements of accounting discourses may be transformed in specific instances and used to subvert the disciplinary regime imposed through the power/knowledge regime of accountancy (for a discussion, see Ezzamel, 1994).

this understanding of meaning as difference will be returned to later in connection with identity, the key point for the moment concerns the insight gained into the role of language. Saussure's 'semiological' approach underpins a significant development in the field of linguistics; that language should be seen as *constitutive* rather than *representational*.

The representational view of language is the traditional perspective and is not only prevalent in common-sense understandings but underpins a number of orthodox fields of knowledge, such as mainstream psychology. From this perspective, the function of language is understood to be merely mimetic, serving to reflect as accurately as possible an external reality. However, Saussure's approach, in highlighting the arbitrariness of the link between signifier and signified, indicates the role played by language in giving shape to 'reality' through *signification*. As Henriques *et al* explain, "The argument is not that words determine but that those practices which constitute our everyday lives are produced and reproduced as an integral part of the production of signs and signifying systems" (1984: 99). This semiological conception of language built upon the focus on language in 20th century philosophy (Wittgenstein, 1953; Winch, 1958) and paved the way for what has been described as the 'linguistic turn' in social studies and in particular in the development of a social constructionist perspective in the social sciences.

While the insights offered by this work have been very useful in highlighting the relevance of relations of meaning and the constitutive power of language in society, in the work of writers as diverse as Silverman (1970) and Kristeva (1986), there are nonetheless dangers in this approach. The suspicion is neatly summed up by Parker; "Language may be the medium for all forms of enquiry into that social world, but it does not follow from that premise that language is all there is" (1995b: 557). While most research based on discourse analysis claims that it would be a mistake to see discourse as simply concerned with language, the work itself often does not reflect this, implying that the social world essentially consists simply of talk and text, with material practices a secondary effect. This is often the case in approaches based in the linguistic tradition, where theory, action and communication are conflated into one term. Stubbs (1983), for example, is more explicit on this point than many similar writers in his book on sociolinguistics *Discourse Analysis*. Although he first states that "the terms text and discourse require some comment, since their use is often ambiguous and confusing", he goes on to say "I do not propose to draw any important distinction between the two terms (...) they often simply imply slight differences in emphasis, on which I do not base any important theoretical distinction" (Stubbs, 1983: 9). This should be contrasted with more sociologically-inclined accounts, such as that of

Norman Fairclough, who makes an important distinction here; "whereas all linguistic phenomena are social, not all social phenomena are linguistic (...) discourse refers to the whole process of social interaction of which a text is just a part" (Fairclough, 1989: 23). One fundamental failure in the more textual approaches to sociolinguistics is the neglect of *interpretation* in the operation of discourse. Fairclough, by contrast, emphasises the central importance of interpretation, stating that "the particular way in which a coherent reading is generated for a text depends again upon the nature of the interpretative principles that are being drawn upon" (1992: 84). The need to focus on these "interpretative principles" forcefully underlines that discourse should *not* be understood as merely a form of *representing* abstract concepts, but as a *system of ideas itself*. Although traces of discourses may be discerned in particular texts, be they interview transcripts, official documents or physical artefacts, social research must bear in mind the dependence on a *discourse* for the interpretation of a text.

The centrality of language is an key issue here. Without discounting language and linguistic analysis, I mean to reject the implicit notion that language is the base matter for society, and the notion, epitomised by the Sapir-Whorf hypothesis, that language *determines* how people perceive the world. The reduction of social diversity to text seems to reflect a humanist belief that all life revolves around a social construct (language), which is at the same time somehow a transcendental matter which overarches and constitutes human life. This focus on language may reflect the ease by which language may be isolated as a resource for research and studied. Less cynically, this may also reflect the influence of the recent growth of linguistics, socio-linguistics and the more esoteric postmodern work, with the implication that all life is text. While such work has been useful in countering an uncritical use of language, particularly in social research, its importance should not be exaggerated. Language does indeed reflect social contingencies and acts as a medium for their reproduction and reconstitution, and as such is therefore a key focus for social research. Nonetheless, society is not *reducible* to language and linguistic analysis, and the restrictions of language as a *human* construct rather than as some transcendent, universal base matter must therefore be appreciated in social research. As a counterbalance to this linguistic conception of discourse, therefore, the next section will examine the significantly more materialist concept of ideology as developed by Louis Althusser.

Ideology and Discourse

An alternative approach to the social construction of meaning is adopted by Althusser in his discussion of the role of *ideology* in the reproduction of capitalist society. This conceptualisation of ideology is developed in Althusser's hugely influential paper *Ideology and Ideological State Apparatuses (Notes Towards An Investigation)* (1971), based in turn on part of the writings of Antonio Gramsci on hegemony. The aim of Althusser is to account for what is elsewhere termed 'false consciousness'; the apparent complicity of those exploited by the capitalist system in its reproduction. To do this, he refers in the first place to the *Repressive State Apparatus* (the army, police, judiciary, prisons, etc.), predominantly based on violence. However, Althusser goes on to propose the existence of what he terms *Ideological State Apparatuses* (ISAs) to account for the day-to-day reproduction of the social division of labour fundamental to capitalism. The ISAs mentioned by Althusser include religion, education, the family, law, the political system, the trade unions, the media and culture (including literature, the arts, sport, etc), which he describes as plural and existing in the main in the private domain. He identifies the Church as the most significant ISA in the past, now replaced to a large extent by 'the school-family couple'. The function of these institutions, along with several others, is "to ensure that people's apparently freely-chosen patterns of conduct coincide with the systematic requirements of capitalist social (i.e. class) relations" (Beechey and Donald, 1985: xiii). Thus ideology functions through the daily images and rituals which produce at a subconscious level the sense of self and forms of behaviour necessary for capitalism, while simultaneously obscuring this and convincing people that such behaviour is conscious, autonomous and self-determined. This constitution of the subject is defined by Althusser as *interpellation*, or 'hailing', whereby an individual is identified and attributed a position by both individuals and institutions, even before birth. Althusser describes the operation of ideology through this process of interpellation which constitutes the individual as a *subject* who comes to recognise him/herself as fixed with a particular identity.

Foucault's understanding of 'discourse' displays a number of distinct similarities with this notion of 'ideology' set out by Althusser, his friend and mentor for several years. The initial similarity between Althusser and Foucault's perspectives is evident in their shared concern with the *combined* disciplinary effect of socialisation in a range of modern institutions. Although Althusser is more restrictive in the examples of ISAs he provides, both emphasise the importance of expanding the scope of analyses of power relations to cover the full range of social institutions. More significantly, the phenomena that both Foucault and Althusser would consider as the functioning of ideology/power relations are remarkably similar. For example, both firmly insist on the *materiality* of ideologies/discourses i.e. their embodiment in concrete practices, rather than in abstract ideas. The materiality of ideology is a substantial part of Althusser's thesis, and he states unequivocally that "ideology exist(s) in a material ideological apparatus, prescribing material practices governed by a material ritual, which practices exist in the material actions of a subject" (Althusser, 1971, reprinted as Althusser, 1985: 79). Examples of such practices range from Althusser's main example, religion and religious worship, to those practices at funerals, school days, sports games, political meetings, etc. where subjects conform to and thus reproduce a socialised form of conduct. Foucault is at equal pains to stress that his concept of discourse, although evident through the analysis of statements, "is not reducible to language and speech. It is not the analysis of signs, or linguistic analysis - the 'mere intersection of things and words, or a slender surface of contact between a reality and a language' (Foucault, 1972: 48)" (Townley, 1994: 21). Instead, a Foucauldian understanding of discourse suggests a broader term; "Because (discourses) are knowledge constituted not just in texts but in definite institutional and organisational practices, they are *discursive practices*" (Clegg, 1994: 277). For example, Foucault includes as elements of an eighteenth-century discourse of education "the space for classes, the shape of the tables, the planning for the recreation lessons, the distribution of the dormitories" (Foucault, 1981: 28). Neither the material or the non-material should be seen to dominate here; "discourse (...) is to be understood as an amalgam of material practices and forms of knowledge linked together in a *non-contingent* relation" (McNay, 1992: 27, emphasis added). This perspective has been influential in much post-structuralist work, although it appears to have been ignored in more linguistically-based areas of social constructivism, as well as some postmodernist work. Thus John Law asserts that 'narratives', which he bases upon Foucauldian 'discourse', "generate and perform modes of talking or writing (...) But crucially they generate other materials too; for instance agents, machines, naturally occurring entities and processes and materially heterogeneous social arrangements" (Law, 1994: 259). This concept clearly has significant implications for social research, emphasising the equal importance and intrinsic interdependency of the material and non-material.

Foucault's Critique of Ideology

Nonetheless, this should not obscure the more fundamental theoretical differences between the two writers. Foucault expressed a dissatisfaction with the term 'ideology' in his 1977 interview *Truth and Power* for three main reasons (Foucault, 1980: 118), relating specifically to their understandings of truth, the subject and the role of economic theory in their respective work. Firstly, ideology implies the existence of a 'truth' to which ideology is opposed and aims to obscure. A large part of Foucault's work aims to refute the distinction, drawn in both common-sense and social scientific understandings, between ideology and science, and unmask the operation of power through the 'truth effects' of scientific discourse (Foucault, 1975; 1977). Similar to the realist position of natural science, Althusser was careful to differentiate the idea of ideology from the real, material Truth which can be arrived at through careful analysis based on Marxist political science. Thus a key principle of Althusser's approach was that ideology is a "representation of the *imaginary* relationship of individuals to their *real* conditions of existence" (i.e. capitalist exploitation) (Althusser, 1985: 75, emphasis added). He also implies that ideology may be contrasted with science, although he remains ambiguous as to his position here, making the point that "the accusation of being 'in ideology' only applies to others, never to oneself", before stating "But let us leave this point, although it is heavy with consequences..." (Althusser, 1985: 82). Foucault, in contrast, is careful to problematise such a notion of one, incontrovertible 'truth' or 'reality', and he attempts to illuminate how particular truths are formed by the conditions of distinct discourses (including, by implication, Marxist or Althusserian discourses).[7] Indeed, the multiplicity of these potential truths are emphasised when Foucault employs the terms 'discursive fields' and 'discursive practices'; "we must not imagine a world of discourse divided between accepted discourse and excluded discourse, or between the dominant discourse and the dominated one; but as a multiplicity of discursive elements that can come into play in various strategies" (Foucault, 1984: 100).

The intimate relationship between discourse, power and knowledge is stated very clearly by Foucault in *The History of Sexuality Vol. I*; "it is in discourse that power and knowledge are joined together" (Foucault, 1979: 100). This relationship can be understood by grasping "how relations of power delineate fields of knowledge and produce objects of knowledge" (Cousins and Hussein, 1990: 250). In *The Birth of the Clinic* (1975), for example, Foucault traces how madness has been constructed as an object of knowledge through the operation of such a power/knowledge nexus and field of knowledge. These 'fields of knowledge', or discourses, cannot therefore be taken as neutral, but should rather be seen as reflecting the power relations which acted as their preconditions. The implication Foucault draws from this is that analysis of these discourses will lead to an understanding of their objectives. As "the objectives served by relations of

---

[7] Although Foucault may be accused of exempting his own position from such a problematisation (Habermas, 1987, among others), as shall be seen below.

power are immanent in their exercise (...) although not necessarily transparent, they can be (...) rendered intelligible in terms of the programmes and pronouncements accompanying the exercise of power" (Cousins and Hussein, 1990: 229). Much of Foucault's later work therefore focuses on the construction of the modern sovereign individual by the subjectifying effects of power/knowledge, operating through discourse and discursive practices in contemporary societies (Foucault, 1977; 1985).

His second objection to the term ideology regards its links to this classical idea of the conscious and sovereign human subject "which power is then thought to seize on" (Foucault, 1980: 58). Much of Foucault's work is based on the notion that the focus and object of discourse is more worthy of examination than its subjects i.e. those engaged in producing the discourse. In his earlier work, this reflects his preoccupation with decentring the individual agent as the focus of enquiry. However, as noted above, this has been identified by some as leading to a determinist dead-end in Foucault's critical thought "which attempts to bypass the concept of the subject and consequently destroys any coherent notion of freedom at all" (Dews, 1989: 38). Whilst Foucault allows greater scope for individual agency in his later work (Foucault, 1985; 1986), he insists upon the primacy of the *productive* nature of power relations, and the operation of power through discourse in the *constitution of the subject*, a point to be explored in more detail below.

Foucault's position on subjectivity and agency is linked to his refusal to attribute strategies to any central subject which acts as a source, including a social force, such as 'the bourgeoisie', or 'the State'. Thus Foucault explains "One can say that the strategy of moralising the working class is that of the bourgeoisie (...) But what I don't think one can say is that it's the bourgeois class on the level of its ideology or its economic project which, as a sort of at once real and fictive subject, invented and forcibly imposed this strategy on the working class" (Foucault, 1980: 203-4). To some extent, this is a criticism which applies less to Althusser than to theorists of a more vulgar Marxism, for in many ways, Althusser also refutes the more simplistic Marxist notion of "a 'clique', a group of individuals (Priests or Despots) who are the authors of the great ideological mystification" (Althusser, 1985: 77). Nonetheless, despite the relative sophistication of Althusser's account of ideology, he insists that the operation of ideology can only be explained with regard to its functional role in the reproduction of the relations of production, and hence in capital accumulation, which leads us onto Foucault's third criticism.

This criticism directly tackles ideology's final dependence on more traditional Marxist concepts, and in particular the implication in Althusser's essay that "ideology stands in a secondary position relative to something which functions as its infrastructure" (Foucault, 1980, 91). This is to reject Marx's metaphor for society, adapted by Althusser, of an *infrastructure*, an economic base, supporting the *superstructure*, i.e. the politico-legal system and different ideologies, and in particular, the idea that "it is the base which in the last instance determines the whole edifice" (Althusser, 1985: 61). Rather, Foucault insists that power/knowledge discourses cannot be reduced to economic functionalism, and notes that the economic importance of certain instances of the functioning of power, such as "psychiatric internment, the mental normalisation of individuals and penal institutions", is difficult to perceive, to say the least. "So long as the posing of the question of power was kept subordinate to the economic instance and the system of interests which this served, there was a tendency to regard these problems as of small importance" (Foucault, 1980; 93). In breaking the link between power/knowledge discourses and economic necessity, the field is therefore widened to cover other forms of domination and subjection.

There are therefore fundamental theoretical differences between the positions of Althusser and Foucault, not least because of the Marxist foundation to Althusser's notion of ideology. Nonetheless, Foucault's concept of discourse can be seen to be not unrelated to Althusserian ideology, particularly in the mechanics of its operation. Of particular importance here is Foucault's description of the operation of technologies of power, which clearly reflects Althusser's notion of *interpellation*. This is borne out by Foucault's later focus on the subject, insofar as Althusser himself states "there is no ideology except for concrete subjects, and this destination for ideology is only made possible by the subject" (Althusser, 1985: 80). However, this insistence on the subject as constituted by discourse and by discourse alone has led to a fundamental critique of key implications of Foucault's work.

Discourse and the Subject

The material component of discourse also serves to emphasise the importance of discourse in *constituting* reality, including subjects themselves. This can be seen as reflecting Foucault's view of power as not merely repressive but as *productive*, and the constitution of active, productive individuals is a cardinal instance of this. However, a more contentious conclusion which might be inferred from Foucault's position is that material practices reproduce perfectly the objectives of the unitary discourse they embody. Were this to be the case, then this would signify a truly deterministic dystopia, where there is no hope of resisting dominating discourses. Thus a neo-Marxist critique sees a real danger of pessimism in the Foucauldian perspective; "Given that post-structuralists believe that language constitutes reality, perhaps it is the case that the language of the prison, of docile and obedient workers (Sakolsky, 1992: 239; O'Neill, 1986: 55), of colonisation and conquest, becomes the Foucauldian's own conceptual cage" (Thompson and Ackroyd, 1995: 624). Admittedly, several of the articles which have adopted Foucault's power/knowledge as a concept appear to have at least sidelined, if not rejected, all possibility of resistance in some form (e.g. Sewell and Wilkinson, 1992a; 1992b). Indeed, there is some justification for theorists who see this implication in Foucault's work, particularly in *Discipline and Punish* (1977), where the focus is on the growth of a specific form of power, disciplinary power, and the discourses which accompany and embody it. One key failing of the work is that "Despite his assertions to the contrary, Foucault in fact produces a vision of power as a unidirectional, dominatory force which individuals are unable to resist" (McNay, 1992: 40). This is accounted for by at least one theorist (Dews, 1987) with reference to Foucault's focus in *Discipline and Punish* on the *official* representations of disciplinary technologies, such as architects' plans, political treatises and legal documents, to the neglect of subjugated discourses or subcultures. Foucault's tendency to overestimate the effectiveness of discourse and to therefore neglect resistance, contrary to his own tenets, goes some way towards explaining the myopia in some research which uses his work as a base.

In his interviews and later work, however, Foucault is far more explicit on the subversive potential of discourses, and ties this in more clearly with his more empirical work. Rather than portraying a deterministic process whereby dominant discourses imply perfectly-effective material practices with no hope of resistance, Foucault is keen to emphasise the instability and complexity of the process; "discourse can be both an instrument and an effect of power, but also a hindrance, a stumbling block, a point of resistance and a starting point for an opposing strategy" (Foucault, 1979: 101). This interplay and indeterminacy of discourses, in both their material and non-material aspects, is repeatedly stressed by Foucault to avoid the charge of determinism and fatalism in his analyses. Thus Foucault notes, "there can exist different and even contradictory discourses within the same strategy; they can, on the contrary, circulate without changing their form from one strategy to another, opposing strategy" (Foucault, 1979: 102). As an example, he highlights the subversion of psychological discourses regarding the deviancy of homosexuality so as to support arguments for the legitimacy and naturalness of homosexuality, often by the use of the selfsame language (Foucault, 1979). Nonetheless, without outlining any theory of the subject through whom these discourses operate, Foucault is left by default with a conception of the subject as 'empty vessel', and it is indeed very difficult to see how (or even why) such a transformation of discourse should take place. Foucault implicitly recognises this point in his change of tack for the second and third volumes of *The History of Sexuality* (1985; 1986), and his introduction of 'the self' into his work. To clarify this change, however, I must contextualise this shift in Foucault's position by reference to movements in critical/social psychology and the sustained critique on the notion of the unitary, atomistic individual as base unit for understanding.

The Deconstruction of the Sovereign Subject

The process by which discourse can be understood to materially affect the formation of an individual's identity is clearly a complex issue. There are a number of schools which critique the orthodox, humanist definition of a unitary, atomistic individual, and each implies the possibility, indeed necessity, of presenting an alternative notion of the individual to that proposed by the traditional social sciences of mainstream psychology, classical economics and socio-biological approaches. The lines of critique are clearly summed up by Sampson (1989), and can be summarised with reference to the words of Geertz; "The Western conception of the person as a bounded, unique, more or less integrated motivational and cognitive universe (...) organised as a distinctive whole and set contrastively against other such wholes and against a social and natural background is, however incorrigible it may seem to us, a rather peculiar idea within the context of the world's cultures" (Geertz, 1979: 229 in Sampson, 1989: 1). The first critique therefore focuses on cross-cultural, anthropological analyses which highlight differing, less individuating alternative conceptions of the person (e.g. Geertz, 1973). Similarly, feminist re-conceptualisations of psychological accounts have offered processual, relational notions of the person which contrast with traditional, patriarchal models (e.g. Lykes, 1985). Thirdly, social constructionism has emphasised that contemporary ideas of traits, selves, and identity are socially and historically constructed, not universal (e.g. Harré, 1984; Gergen, 1985). A fourth critique relies on the interpenetration and inter-dependence of the individual and society, objecting to the self-contained, bounded conception of the independent individual agent (e.g. Giddens, 1979; Willmott, 1990). Finally, Critical Theory has tied the concept of the individual in mainstream psychology to capitalist ideology and emphasises the role it plays in constructing productive subjects and reproducing structural inequalities (e.g. Habermas, 1971a). While the issues raised by each of these schools are palpably different, the effect of all of these is to undermine the common-sense notion of the stable, self-contained individual, and emphasise the specificity and hence transformability of contemporary ideas of the subject.

The implication of this, then, is that serious attention must be paid to the process by which subjectivity is constituted, and it is suggested that one of the key aspects of discourse is the way in which it constitutes the individual subject. This process is persuasively described by Shotter (1989), who highlights the continuous transformation of the identity of an individual through the operation of discourses via communication. Essentially, the focus here is on the way in which discourses are "constitutive of our actual relations to one another, and, to the extent that we constitute ourselves in our relations to others, constitutive of ourselves" (Shotter, 1989: 136). Shotter describes the project of accounting for our actions as something *learnt*, rather than as an innate capacity of humanity, in order for us to "sustain our status as responsible members of our society" (Shotter, 1989: 141). Furthermore, he draws upon the interdependence of the subject and society, related to the structure-agency debate tackled in the previous chapter, to suggest that this learning and reproduction of discourses which account for action is part of the ongoing constitution of subjective identities. In this way it is suggested that human communication, which must rely on some shared discourse in order to be intelligible, "must be seen as ontologically formative, as a process by which people can (...) help to make each other persons of this or that kind" (Shotter, 1989: 145). This position clearly reflects the idea of interpellation put forward by Althusser, in this day-to-day process of 'hailing' which fixes the individual with an identity.

Overall, then, the approach I adopt will attempt to cover both of these related aspects of the operation of power/knowledge and discourse; the *objectification of the individual*, through 'techniques of domination', and the *subjectification of the individual* through 'techniques of the self' (McNay, 1994: 134; Townley, 1998: 200). Thus Foucault's work on discipline (1979) demonstrates how this occurs through the operation of mechanisms within social institutions throughout the lives of individuals in modern Western society. However, as he was later to concede, this somewhat monolithic concept of power must be supplemented by a theorisation of the subject and how individuals are routinely constituted as subjects. The implication of this is to emphasise the importance of studying the operation of discourses within organisations, the construction and reinforcement of the identities of its members, and thus its effects upon their action and on the reproduction of the organisation.

Identity and Difference

The conception of identity to be adopted and explored within this book owes much to the work by Saussure indicated above, and in particular to his notion of meaning as constructed through *difference*. To briefly recap, the structuralist position in linguistics views meaning as not intrinsic but as constituted by the difference between signs and other signs in the linguistic chain, such that meaning is derived from the *relations* with other signifiers. The transposition of this insight into social science more generally has focused on the process of identification i.e. the "construction (of identity) on the back of a recognition of some common origin or shared characteristic with another person or group" (Hall, 1996: 2). Thus the construction of identity relies on what Hall describes as "the binding and marking of symbolic boundaries, the production of 'frontier effects'" (Hall, 1996: 3).

Difference and differentiation play a similar role for identity as for meaning; as Clegg explains, "identities are not absolute but are always relational; one can only ever be seen to be something in relation to some other thing. Identity is always defined in terms of difference, rather than as something intrinsic to a particular person or category of experience" (1989: 151). The construction of an individual's identity thus relies upon the construction of a relation with something other to the subject, to which it can be opposed. Hall emphasises that positive identity depends on the construction of negative relations of difference by drawing on Derrida's notion of 'the Other' (1981); "it is only through the relation to the Other, the relation to what it is not, to precisely what it lacks, to what has been called its *constitutive outside* that the 'positive' meaning of any term - and thus its 'identity' - can be constructed" (Hall, 1996: 4-5). Such work has been developed to particular effect in feminist writings, in which the masculinist ideal of the autonomous and sovereign individual is critically undermined by work which demonstrates the reliance of the self on 'external' objects for its definition (e.g. Weedon, 1991). An important aspect of this concept of 'the Other' in the analysis of identity construction is that it is frequently used to imply the simultaneous privileging of one side of the dualism (of the masculine over the feminine, for example) and the establishment of a hierarchical relationship with regard to other perceived identities (Butler, 1993). This 'marginalisation' of the Other will be returned to below; specifically, in its use in the work of Willmott (1986), Townley (1994) and Parker (1995), among others, on the role of the subject. For the moment, what I mean to emphasise are that these structures of difference are not chosen at random or at will by the independent and sovereign subject. Instead, they can be seen as constructed collectively as *discourse* and thus transferred (and potentially transformed) through social practices similar to Althusser's interpellation, as described by Shotter above.

In keeping with the critique of the unitary, sovereign subject outlined above, however, it is essential to counter any implication that the identity of the subject is fixed either by one dominant discourse or even that it is definitively fixed by a range of discourses. Rather, I will underline Deetz's assertion that "the subject is subject to a range of discourses, some of which conflict. Meaning is not a singularity claimed by an individual text or even an intersection of texts. It is pluralistic and deferred in the sense that there can be no final determination" (Deetz, 1992: 34). Thus Parker (1997) examines the organisation and operation of difference within three work organisations, proposing that the organisation, or rather the process of organising itself, produces identity through classifying similarity and difference between the subjects. Importantly, however, Parker underlines the multiple and contested bases for differentiation within and between organisations, departments, areas and teams. While he suggests that bases of division may include gender, location, profession, department, and so on, he adds "it is vital to note that the pattern of fractures recognised and reproduced by one member will be different from that of another member" (Parker, 1997: 120). Moreover, the differences recognised and represented will also be different for the same member at different times and in different contexts, which Parker interprets as reflecting the insights of 'role theory' of post-war sociology (e.g. Becker and Geer, 1960, and to a lesser extent, Goffman, 1959).

This form of analysis is crucially important, in that it demonstrates in a practical way the multiple and dynamic nature of identity, or rather of *identity construction* as a process. A key question which remains, however, regards the role of the subject in this process, which will be examined in the next section. Essentially, the question focuses on the degree to which individuals can be seen to construct their own identity by *drawing on* discourses. If this marks a return to a naïve humanism, should such discursively-constructed difference instead be thought of as *acting upon* an individual in directly constituting their identity?

The Active Subject?

The first perspective which one may adopt here is to see discourses as *directly* constituting subjects, without action or indeed recognition of the process on the part of the individual. I have already outlined the significant arguments against sociological and psychological approaches which rely on a notion of the unitary, atomistic and sovereign subject as the foundational unit of analysis (see Shotter, 1989, etc). Instead, what should be emphasised is "the temporal and logical pre-existence of the social process to the self-conscious individual" (Mead, 1934: 47). Ian Parker, therefore, emphasises the *involuntary* aspect of identity construction, suggesting therefore that "selves should not be seen as parts selected at will, but as set in a variety of power-infused discourses. We do not rationally 'choose' to display our-selves as willing participants, for example, in the rituals of close personal relationships or to experience our-selves as discerning readers in the presence of an academic text" (Parker, 1989: 67). While the recognition of the construction of the individual as a sovereign subject is welcome, taking the active and deliberate element out of this process raises the danger of implying another form of determinism and a return to structuralism. Such an approach would again struggle to account for both resistance to the more transparent discourses, such as attempts at culture management, and for the breadth of difference between subjectivities discursively constituted in similar positions. Moreover, this would again close off any recourse that critical sociology might have to autonomy, ethics and indeed responsibility, a crucial point returned to below.

The question then is, how far can discourses be seen as resources to be *drawn upon* deliberately by an active agent? The introduction of the notion of a subject actively, although not necessarily rationally or even consciously, positioning him/herself in often contradictory discourses does allow for the inclusion of some potential for emancipation and some level of autonomy. The term 'investment' is adopted by Hollway (1984) to describe this action on the part of the individual on the grounds that other definitions carry unfortunate connotations; as she explains, terms such as 'drive' or 'motivation', for instance, imply instinct and biological determinism, whereas 'choice' is strongly redolent of models of rational decision-making.[8] However, this alternative idea of the individual 'investing' in discourses to achieve certain objectives poses a problem of equal weight. The first is, where do such objectives arise from? If these are not constituted through discourses, are they therefore essential desires intrinsic to the subject prior to the operation of discourse? Effectively, this argument risks resurrecting the idea of the 'homunculus', the 'core of insight within the brain' which once again implies the existence of the pre-social individual. The return to subjectivism is clear in the presumption that the individual has a self which pre-exists discourse, and which stands back, untouched by the effects of discourses and, more or less rationally, *chooses*

---

[8] Surprisingly, Hollway does not question the financial instrumentalism implicit in the notion of 'investment' (nor does she make any particular note of this implication, if this inference is deliberate).

to invest in particular discourses, in the pursuit of pre-given desires. Such an approach once again risks letting in through the back door the humanist ideal of the rational, unitary subject. A formulation is therefore required which can allow for the conscious or subconscious participation of an individual in the constitution of their identity, but without essentialising a natural, pre-discursive individual.

Foucault and the Construction of the Self

Foucault, even in his last works, can be seen as treading a thin line in this regard. While he remains committed to a social theory which does not rely upon a universal subject, there is a clear change in his perspective vis-à-vis the individual, reflecting a shift from a focus on 'docile bodies' to a concern with 'techniques of the self'. This represents a highly significant and timely development in Foucault's thought from his position in his middle period, especially the position set out in *Discipline and Punish* (1979). As Habermas notes, Foucault acknowledges the restrictions of his earlier perspective, stating "one has to take into account not only the techniques of domination but also the techniques of the self" (Foucault, in Habermas, 1987: 273). Foucault's later work therefore displays a particular concern with what he describes as "the relation between forms of reflexivity - a relation of self to self - and hence between forms of reflexivity and discourses of truth, forms of rationality and effects of knowledge" (Foucault, 1988: 30). He now recasts the constitution of the self through discourse in terms of "those *intentional and voluntary actions* by which men not only set themselves rules of conduct but also seek to transform themselves, to change themselves" (Foucault, 1985: 10, emphasis added). This recognition of subjectivity in some form is a significant advance on the determinism implicit in his notion of disciplinary power in earlier writings. The recognition of an *active* role on the part of an individual is also necessary if Foucault is to clarify and develop the emancipatory alternative to disciplinary technologies and subjectification which is merely implicit in his earlier work.

A number of commentators from both humanist and structuralist schools have, for different reasons, celebrated what has been interpreted as Foucault's final admission that the subjective and reflexivity cannot be written out of critical social research. Elsewhere, however, this change has been interpreted not so much as a renunciation but as an *elaboration* of his earlier work. McNay, for example, insists that "although Foucault still believes that power constitutes individual subjects, he no longer locates it exclusively in external and impersonal mechanisms and institutions. Rather, a more specific and diffuse idea emerges of individuals actively constructing their day-to-day existences in a relatively autonomous fashion" (1992: 82). Although *The History of Sexuality* and associated writings do serve as a corrective to the more deterministic and monolithic implications of his earlier work, the analysis used can be most productively understood as *complementary* to the work on discipline and power/knowledge regimes (Townley, 1994). Thus Foucault continues in the quote used by Habermas; "...one has to take into account the interaction between those two types of techniques, the point where the technologies of domination of individuals over one another have recourse to processes by which the individual acts upon himself" (Foucault, in Habermas, 1987: 273). Hall describes this development as supporting an analysis of subjectification, "the production of self as an object in the world, the practices of self-constitution, recognition and reflection, the relation to the rule, *alongside* the scrupulous attention to normative regulation and the constraints of the rules without which no 'subjectification' is produced" (Hall, 1996: 13, emphasis added), a process which Townley identifies as central to the construction of 'management' as a practice (Townley, 1995). What this leads us to is an analysis which distinguishes broadly between two forms of power effects; "the discursive constitution of the self, and the social construction of its interests" (Willmott, 1994: 100), and thus avoids recourse to the prediscursive individual.

A useful reading of Foucault's position here can be found in the work of David Knights and Hugh Willmott. In a seminal article questioning the basis of labour process theory, Knights and Willmott turn their attention to what they term "the significance of *identity-securing strategies* in the reproduction of power relations" (Knights and Willmott, 1985: 22). Attempting to reintroduce subjectivity into labour process work without compromising critical intent, they highlight the operation of what Willmott later described as processes whereby "individuals are routinely constituted to develop and demonstrate a sense of themselves as sovereign agents" (Willmott, 1994: 89). It is suggested that through socialisation and subjectification, the modern individual *learns* to act as a unitary and sovereign subject. This leads Knights and Willmott to emphasise the importance of the modern individual's *anxiety* over the construction of a stable identity for him/herself. In an attempt to resolve this existential anxiety, they suggest that individuals are placed in "a competitive struggle over the symbolic and material resources that are seen to sustain an unproblematic sense of self" (Knights and Willmott, 1985: 26). This reading does allow an active role to the subject in drawing on certain discursive resources in the creation of difference in the struggle for a coherent identity. So while discourses may constitute the subjectivity of an individual without the individual's awareness or complicity, discourses are also drawn on, often in conscious and strategic ways, either to bolster one's sense of identity or to achieve more material goals. The most radical point put forward here, and reasserted in much of each writer's subsequent work, is that such a struggle is self-defeating, in that it undermines the creative potential of interdependence and reinforces the very insecurity it aims to relieve (see Knights, 1990; Willmott, 1990; Willmott 1994).

Nonetheless, there is a crucial omission in Foucault's revised conception of how discourse operates on the subject, regarding his relatively undifferentiated notion of discourses. Here, it has been argued that "Foucault does not distinguish sufficiently enough between practices that are merely 'suggested' to the individual and practices that are more or less *imposed*" (McNay, 1989: 74). Hollway reinforces this point when she states "Of course some discourses are more hegemonic and thus carry all the weight of social approval. But successful positioning in these discourses is not automatic, else there would be no variations" (1984: 238). At the same time, while the importance of recognising the deliberate and active ways in which individuals draw on discourses has been emphasised above, the amount of leeway available in the construction of one's own identity must not be exaggerated. McNay raises the subject of discourses around gender, and suggests that Foucault's position in his later work ignores the "involuntary and biological dimensions to sexuality" (McNay, 1989: 80). Without in any way advocating a reintroduction of biological determinism here, this criticism usefully reflects the cautionary comment elsewhere, that "in an attempt to escape the reactionary implications of biological determinism, sociologists and some psychologists have fallen into the trap of denying biology altogether" (Henriques *et al*, 1984: 21). Furthermore, in an interesting reversal, McNay (1989) notes that Foucault now risks *underestimating* the embedded nature of cultural constraints which operate outside of consciousness and rationality. The importance of differentiating discourses on this basis, and examining each on its own merits, is an issue that will be returned to with reference to the empirical work in the following chapters.

In an organisational context, this diversity of discourse is evident in their operation on (and through) the identity of employees, from relatively transparent cultural initiatives to more enduring and embedded discourses regarding individuality, masculinity and duty in capitalist organisations. Through the structuring of the understandings of employees, discourses may define for the individual what is inevitable and fixed, and by implication what is contestable and negotiable, about the organisation. Discourses within managerial thinking therefore serve to reproduce a pattern of behaviour by managers in general when faced by similar circumstances; "they discipline themselves in order to shape what they feel to be appropriate, acceptable and valued identities, which in turn allow them to maintain their participation in social actions" (Thomas, 1995: 10). These discourses include not only the more fashionable movements such as Business Process Re-engineering, Total Quality Management and the like, but also fundamental assumptions about the role, duties and concerns of a manager with reference to masculinity, understandings of hierarchy and discretion, appearance and conduct, etc. Similarly, discourses among the employees in general will frame their day-to-day behaviour and their reactions to managerial interventions such as the implementation of new technology, the introduction of new working practices, etc. The variety of these discourses and their constant interaction give rise in part to the fluidity of social and organisational life. Nonetheless, the identification of discourses by a researcher in a given situation should *not* be taken as final, and far less as universal (Parker, 1995a; Law, 1994). The discourses identified should reflect the subjective, often tacit, representations of the organisation constructed and used by those who not only inhabit but in both senses of the word *constitute* it. An understanding of these discourses and how they are invested in, resisted and/or transformed is therefore essential in critical social analysis.

The Moral Foundations of Foucault's Critique

This understanding of discourse and subjectivity in Foucault's later work has led to a fundamental debate over the ethical or moral justification for any critical intent Foucault may assert. As noted, a key element of Foucault's work has been to displace the sovereign human subject from its position as the source of meaning and autonomy in humanist discourses. The very fact that Foucault's understanding of power is *productive*, and that power/knowledge regimes *discursively constitute* subjects, contradicts any assumption that forms of resistance adopted by subjects must automatically provide the possibility of 'freedom' (Knights and Vurdubakis, 1994). The question then becomes 'Can resistance be justified?'. Foucault argues that it can, but problematises the idea of a universal 'legitimacy' of resistance underpinned by 'human rights'. In his earlier work, Foucault justifies his genealogical approach by emphasising its role in articulating the subjugated discourses of the oppressed; thus he says: "One does not have to be in solidarity with them. One does not have to maintain that these confused voices sound better than the others and express the ultimate truth. For there to be a sense in listening to them and in searching for what they have to say it is sufficient that they exist and that they have against them so much which is set up to silence them" (Foucault, in Knights and Vurdubakis, 1994: 190). In promoting this pluralist egalitarianism, however, Foucault has no grounds on which to assess the claims of subjugated discourses, as he lacks what Fraser describes as "an alternative, posthumanist, ethical paradigm capable of identifying objectionable features of a fully realised autonomous society" (1989: 50).

What I intend to do in this section is to examine the implications of the link forged by Foucault between *power* and *truth*, particularly where he has been accused of promoting a postmodern relativism which undermines critique and reinforces conservatism. At the same time, I will examine the implicit normative position which has also been identified in his work, leading to contrary accusations of 'cryptonormativism' (Habermas, 1987). In the judgement of some commentators, this normative ambiguity is finally dealt with as Foucault admits some theory of the subject linked to ethics in his later work. Nonetheless, certain complications remain in Foucault's attempts to address ethics without imposing norms. I will approach these complications, firstly through a discussion of Foucault's refusal to posit a normative code, which derives from his distinction between morality and ethics, and secondly through an assessment of his understanding of normativity as inevitably normalising in the disciplinary sense.

Relativism or Cryptonormativism?

The fundamental difficulty Habermas identifies in his reading of Foucault lies in the latter's rejection of truth as an ultimate basis for critique, stemming from his insistence on the intimate relationship between power and knowledge, and the production of 'truth effects' through discourse. From Habermas's perspective as a critical modernist, this limits Foucault to an essentially relativist position, where he has undermined any founding principles, or 'meta-narratives of rationality and justice' (McNay, 1992: 119), which might justify his critique. As noted by Lyon, Foucault "carefully eschews the metaphysical, but in doing so indulges in moral outrage without either acknowledging it or elaborating on its basis" (Lyon, 1994: 167). Instead, then, Foucault's justification relies, as noted above, on the potential of alternative truths, or 'subjugated knowledges', to destabilise 'absolute truth' - it does not depend on such subjugated knowledges being 'closer' to an absolute truth, a more accurate representation of the world.

Such a formulation of resistance has been roundly attacked, not only from the modernist perspective, but from a range of other epistemological positions. These include feminist work in particular which has forcefully criticised Foucault's complete renunciation of any universal normative commitment in favour of what is perceived as a celebration of postmodern difference. Taking issue with the relativity of discourse, Felski suggests "it would be hard to imagine a feminist theory which did not espouse as a bottom line a belief in women's subordination and their right to equality and autonomy" (Felski, 1989 in McNay, 1992: 122). Nancy Fraser's criticism of Foucault sums up this dissatisfaction, asking; "Why is struggle preferable to submission? Why ought domination to be resisted? Only with the introduction of normative notions of some kind could Foucault begin to answer this question. Only with the introduction of normative notions could he begin to tell us what is wrong with the modern power/knowledge regime and why we ought to oppose it" (Fraser, 1989: 29). In avoiding meta-narratives and 'truth', Foucault has been accused of adopting a relativist position which can only rest upon a postmodern amorality and nihilism.

At the same time, as a number of authors have stressed, this superficial relativism is contradicted by the normative values implicit in the work of his middle period, and in particular, in *Discipline and Punish*. In some quarters, this 'cryptonormativism', in Habermas's terms, has been used as a defence of Foucault against accusations of conservatism; thus McNay states that "at an unarticulated level, Foucault clearly makes value judgements about what constitutes progressive political behaviour and what constitutes an abuse of power or domination of truth, yet he fails to make these assumptions explicit" (1992: 141). While these normative values are indeed unarticulated, a number of aspects can be identified as objectionable to Foucault, including, as Habermas notes, "the asymmetric relationship between power-holders and those subject to power, as well as the reifying effect of technologies of power, which violate the moral and bodily integrity of subjects capable of speech and action" (Habermas, 1987: 284). Other writers have interpreted this as indicating some confusion in Foucault's analysis, reflecting his failure to understand his own construction, as author, within regimes of power/knowledge. Fraser thus associates this cryptonormativism with Foucault's lack of reflexivity, as "he fails to appreciate the degree to which the normative is embedded and infused throughout the whole of language at every level and the degree to which, despite himself, his own critique has to make use of modes of description, interpretation and judgement formed within the modern Western normative tradition" (Fraser, 1989: 30-1).

The criticisms of Fraser (1989) and Habermas (1987), however, only cover the earlier writings of Foucault, specifically in his work in the late 1970s, and McNay sets out a defence of Foucault by asserting that the attention paid to 'the self' in Foucault's last works directly tackle a number of these criticisms. I will turn now to these works to assess the way in which Foucault's later work attempts to develop a critical perspective based on his understanding of ethics in the reflexive concern with the self.

The Self as Ethical Creation

In *The History of Sexuality Vol. II: The Use of Pleasure* (1985) and *Vol. III: The Care of the Self* (1986), ethics becomes an explicit issue in Foucault's work thanks to his renewed focus on a 'critical ontology of the self'. In particular, his emphasis on *reflexivity*, as "the relation of self to self", enables space for some form of autonomy in the creation of self which requires a form of ethical conduct from the individual *within* discourse. Nonetheless, Foucault still refuses to specify a moral or ethical normative basis for his critical position, for two main reasons, The first relates to his understanding of the role of the intellectual, and in particular his lifelong refusal to impose "alien forms of morality on groups who are able to struggle for themselves" (McNay, 1994: 158). He clarifies this in response to an interviewer who, referring to Foucault's turn from politics to ethics, asserts that people will expect an answer to the question "what must one do?". Foucault's reply is revealing; he states clearly "The role of an intellectual is not to tell others what they have to do. By what right would he do so? (...) The work of an intellectual is not to shape others' political will; it is to question over and over again what is postulated as self-evident" (Foucault, 1988: 265). Nonetheless, his dilemma here in evident in his inability to avoid an *implicit* normative position, which persists in his later work, if only at the basic level of promoting the values of reflection and of autonomy in subjects. I will return to the role of the normative in critical work in my discussion below.

This position is also related to the second reason for Foucault's reticence on ethical norms, which derives from his understanding of *morality* and his distinction between *morality* and *ethics* (Foucault, 1985; 1986). In *The Use of Pleasure*, Foucault defines morality as an externally-imposed system of rules regarding conduct, as distinct from *ethics* which refers to the 'real behaviour' of individuals in relation to these systems; "the manner in which they comply more or less fully with a standard of conduct, the manner in which they obey or resist an interdiction or prescription" (1985: 25). His analysis relies on his perception of this distinction between the rule of ethics in ancient Greek culture and its transformation into a moral code in Roman civilisation, from which Christian codes of morality evolved. In classical Greek thought, Foucault discerns a toleration of self-determination and a dynamic relationship whereby the individual (presumed to be male) has a level of freedom in his (*sic*) ethical conduct and how he (*sic*) relates this to moral and social codes. He interprets the erosion of this autonomy of conduct within Roman culture to be linked to the emergence of a universal notion of the subject as a 'truth' against which conduct would be judged in terms of compliance, leading to the normalising tendency of moral codes.

The criticism of the essentialist concept of the human subject here relates directly to a fundamental objection Foucault maintains against humanist discourse. It has been asserted that in his later work, Foucault retreated from a relatively postmodern i.e. anti-essentialist, anti-humanist position to one in line with the aims of Enlightenment thought, with a belief in the possibility of emancipation through the application of a universal rationality. From this reading, Foucault's later position might even be termed 'critical modernist', insofar as it can be seen as relying upon humanity's capacity for rational thought to achieve some form of emancipation. However, McNay (1989) refutes such an inference by highlighting the distinction Foucault makes between humanism and the Enlightenment in his early article on Kant, *What Is Enlightenment?* (1984). She argues persuasively that here Foucault clearly differentiates between these based on the essentialism he identifies as inherent in humanism, where emancipation requires a discovery of the 'authentic' self. Foucault's critique of modern psychoanalytic discourses aimed at uncovering such an 'inner nature' or 'true self' is a key part of his identification of disciplinary mechanisms in the modern world. Equally, Foucault stands opposed to forms of universal reason implied by the Enlightenment, identifying these as linked inextricably to rationalisation and domination. Rather, Foucault's notion of agency and autonomy rely on an understanding of *the self as a creation*, rather than a rediscovery. Hence Foucault's reliance on critical self-awareness and experimentation as a source of autonomy can be seen to reflect the Enlightenment project, while at the same time rejecting its static conception of a universal rationality and essential human nature. As McNay makes clear, it is *"the principle of a critique and a permanent creation of ourselves in our autonomy* that Foucault attempts to salvage, whilst rejecting the humanist theme of a fixed human nature which lends itself to modern practices of the normalisation and the homogenisation of individuality" (McNay, 1989: 90).

As a final but key point, then, I would suggest that this conception of the subject in Foucault's last work does indeed indicate a potential way out of the determinism and nihilism implicit in his earlier studies of discipline. As I have noted, there is considerable potential in Foucault's insistence on the contingency of resistance; as summed up by Jana Sawicki, "the question whether some forms of resistance are more effective than others is a matter of social and historical investigation and not of a priori theoretical pronouncement" (1991: 26). However, the refusal to posit even the most basic of criteria against which behaviour might be judged makes it all but impossible to distinguish between conduct which is emancipatory and ethical, and that which is merely a function of disciplinary and/or subjectifying mechanisms. Certainly, the political activism of Foucault himself outside of his writings, and his commitment to a range of causes, reveals his willingness to act upon value judgements of an ethical nature, albeit without the underpinning of an explicit agenda or framework of values. Fraser (1989) makes a significant point when she accuses Foucault of confusing *normativity* in his own work with *normalisation* as the imposition of 'regimes of truth', such that the articulation of an ethical framework is seen to imply domination. McNay attacks this refusal to judge as "border(ing) on a libertarianism which does not distinguish between acts that are predatory and oppressive in relation to others and actions that are genuinely progressive" (1989: 147).

Foucault is not alone in struggling with this dilemma, however; from different theoretical positions, the work of Richard Rorty (1989) and Zygmunt Bauman (1993; 1996), among others, have also approached this problem. What may be imported from this work, however, is the recognition of *contingency* in the determination of ethical conduct. Thus Rorty cites Isaiah Berlin (quoting, in turn, Schumpeter); "To realise the relative validity of one's convictions and yet stand for them unflinchingly is what distinguishes a civilised man (*sic*) from a barbarian" (Rorty, 1989: 46). While the source might not be immediately compatible with a Foucault's perspective, the notion of tentative and contingent ethical commitments does offer a solution to the dilemma of norms and normalisation indicated above. This is not to seek a transcendental legitimation for resistance or critique; the criteria may indeed be situationally specific, and more fundamentally, *should* remain contingent and open to criticism and transformation. My position here reflects that put forward in his own defence by Parker, who argues "I do not claim access to a transcendental Truth to speak for others, only to state my own truth because I wish to condemn (...) I put these views forward with the willingness to have them changed by the arguments of others" (Parker, 1996: 576). The practical requirement of such a position is therefore clear, and is one which I will attempt to adhere to below; it is the responsibility of the writer to make as clear as possible (or to 'out', in Willmott's (1997) term) his/her ethical commitments in constructing an account of a situation or process such that they can be assessed, debated and potentially changed.

Conclusion

As this chapter should make clear, the concept of discourse will be central to my analytical approach, particularly with regard to the empirical work presented and discussed in the next chapters. Consequently, I have taken care to distinguish the conception I will adopt from two alternative understandings of discourse. The first is the purely linguistic understanding; this does not exclude the analysis of discourse through language, only that language should be seen as a component of discourse alongside material articulations. Secondly, I have distinguished discourse from Althusserian ideology in terms of its epistemological and theoretical underpinnings, while at the same time recognising the significant continuities, including the identification of power relations throughout society and the materiality of the operation of ideology/discourse. More generally, I have examined Foucault's adoption of a relativist, post-humanist (even anti-humanist) position, insofar as he refuses to oppose discourse to a fundamental, and obscured, Truth, and he is intent on decentring the human subject from its central position in social research. Throughout his work, Foucault emphasises the historical construction of the subject though discourse. However, the need for a theory of the subject is recognised and accepted in Foucault's later writings in order to overcome the difficulties regarding the source of subversion due to the implicit determinism of his early work. I have therefore related this transformation in Foucault's thought to concurrent concerns in the field of critical psychology over the sovereign subject, which have led to widespread efforts to conceptualise identity as a process or project, frequently depending on the discursive construction of *difference*.

To develop the notion of subjectivity, it is necessary here to depart from the slightly artificial construction of the book as a logical progression from literature review through empirical work to conclusions. The concept of *difference* and its importance in the construction of meaning and identity is not one which emerged directly from my review of literature and theory in this area. Instead, I was struck by the constant use of difference on a day-to-day basis by those employees I interviewed to construct accounts of the processes within their organisations, and to situate themselves in relation to these processes. What this interpretation did not offer was a substantial insight into the role of the subjects here; were these differences *active* constructions of meaning/identity or mere articulations of discourses *imposed* upon them? This dilemma reflects the dilemma in Foucault's own position after his *The History of Sexuality: Introduction* (1979): If identity is a involuntary and imposed construction, how can one account for departures from imposed discourses (as this can only derive from other forms of discourse)? On the other hand, if discourse is drawn upon actively, even strategically, by the subject, in pursuit of certain objectives, where do these objectives arise from? The assumption of such pre-discursive 'needs' implies a return to an essentialist concept of a universal subject, which risks imposing this concept in a totalising fashion by imputing uniform needs on all subjects.

What is useful here is a complementary reading of Foucault's analysis of discipline and the construction of the self as an object through power/knowledge regimes *alongside* his work on subjectification and the self's action on the self. Where objectives are imputed to subjects, such as the perceived need for a coherent and cohesive identity (leading to anxiety and insecurity when (or *as*) this cannot be achieved), this should not be seen as reflecting an essentialist understanding of the subject; following Knights, I would also emphasise that "it is the *particular historical conditions* wherein subjects become individualised (...) that generate their anxiety and insecurity" (1990: 328).

Finally, I do not intend to establish a definitive moral position here to underpin the critical analysis throughout the book. In a sense, I have now adopted a focus for ethical debate in engaging with the empirical material, based around the operation of power relations on and through the constructed identities of those working in each of the chosen organisations. In interpreting and analysing the material, I will attempt to make as clear as possible the ethical positions I take and have taken in directing the research into these areas. Moreover, as noted above, such ethical positions should be seen as contingent; they will directly depend on the situation and its construction by those involved, and by clarifying my interpretation as far as possible, I hope to facilitate the critical engagement of others on the issues which I have taken to be important and in need of such engagement.

4 The Discursive Construction of the Financial Services Industry

Analysing Financial Services

In this chapter I will examine the context of the subject organisations, Buzzbank and Lifelong Assurance, specifically focusing on the legislative and social changes associated with the emergence of the 'Financial Services' industry. This transformation has been brought about largely as a result of the Financial Services Act (1986) and related legislation, which set in motion what was represented as the 'deregulation' of all aspects of finance, including banking, life assurance, building societies, stockbrokers and other institutions. The first section, therefore, will examine the main aspects of this 'deregulation', paying particular attention to the New Right political philosophy which provided a rationale for what was effectively the 're-regulation' of financial markets in the early 1980s. The ground was prepared for full 'deregulation' by the Single European Act, ratified by the member states of the EC in 1987 for implementation by December 1992. The intention of this act was the encouragement of the globalisation of competition within a single European market, to be achieved through measures such as such as the abolition of exchange controls on capital flows, and the elimination of non-tariff barriers to trade. This process of harmonisation, with the long-term objective of monetary union, depended on the implementation of common frameworks for regulation within the EC, and in keeping with the political inclinations of the main EC members, this implied widespread deregulation in European financial markets. Despite conflicts between Europe and the Conservative government of the time, this push towards deregulation corresponded to the latter's own objectives vis-à-vis the UK financial markets. A significant part of this New Right philosophy entailed the establishment of a system of regulation for these newly-deregulated financial services, to be overseen by the

Securities and Investments Board (SIB) through a network of Self-Regulatory Organisations (SROs). The role of regulation will be critically assessed before entering into an examination of the specific contexts of each organisation; the banking industry and the life assurance industry. Here, I will discuss the effects of deregulation in terms of competition and the action of the regulators as background to fundamental changes in the nature of banking and life assurance in the UK, as well as the relations between the two sectors. This provides the context for a detailed discussion of the two organisations, which will be referred to here as Buzzbank and Lifelong Assurance. In this chapter, I will detail the major changes in the recent history of each organisation, before looking at the key departments for the purposes of this argument; the IT function in each organisation and the distribution network of Lifelong Assurance. The chapter concludes by summarising the key points of the discussion and tracing the framework for the book as a whole.

The Construction of 'Financial Services'

The focus in the book is on two organisations, Buzzbank and Lifelong Assurance, which until recently would have been seen to function in related but entirely distinct industries; *banking* and *insurance*. Before discussing the recent changes to the structure of financial markets in the UK, however, I will set this in context by defining in very broad terms the nature and role of the major types of financial institution in the UK prior to 1986. The principal financial institutions before this date could be classified as either *banking* financial intermediaries (BFI's) or *non-banking* financial intermediaries (NBFI's). Those classified as BFI's could previously be divided into the *retail* (or *'High-Street'*) *banks*, with extensive branch networks which provide current accounts and money transmission services for personal and business customers, and the *wholesale* (or *commercial*) *banks*, specialising in the provision of finance directly to major corporate customers. However, in recent years the distinction between the High Street banks and the wholesale banks has blurred somewhat, as the High Street banks have acquired controlling interests in major merchant banks and similar institutions to form 'banking groups' offering a range of services under one roof (Beecham, 1994). Those institutions traditionally classified as NBFI's, on the other hand, included the building societies, insurance companies, investment trusts, pension funds, etc. These institutions could broadly be divided into the profit-making, *joint-stock* institutions, owned by shareholders, and the non-profit-making *mutual* institutions, owned by their members. Of particular significance here are the insurance companies, who provide policy holders with both *general insurance*, as cover against specific risks such as fire or theft, and *long term insurance*, which includes life assurance, pensions and permanent health insurance and leans more towards *investment* than *insurance*. The size of the premiums received by the insurance companies means that they also act as custodians of large funds within the UK economy, and thus tend to dominate the purchase of ordinary shares in the Stock Exchange.

As noted, prior to 1986 legislation existed which defined and thus limited the operation of banks, building societies, insurance companies, and other financial institutions to given markets, such that each industry was generally seen as fundamentally distinct, involving "its own distinct set of customers, marketing/distribution systems, management skills and regulatory practices" (Knights, 1997a: 2). This is not to say each industry did not have relations with the others; banks, for example, were a traditional source of advice on insurance and other matters. Nonetheless, barriers did exist, such as those which maintained the cartel enjoyed by the 'big four' high-street banks, which since the Second World War had been seen as essential to stave off fears of bank failure and thus maintain financial confidence and stability in the UK economy. In the late 1970s, the banks took advantage of their oligopoly in their own sector to make inroads into the building societies' domination of the mortgage market, to compensate in part for poor returns on personal banking and on their loans to developing countries. Motivated by this and other evidence of the imbalance in the 'free market', some legislative moves had been made by the government prior to 1986 to encourage competition in the area of banking. Nonetheless, a wider and more substantial restructuring of financial markets was perceived as necessary by the Conservative government of the time.

Such a restructuring was in keeping with certain aspects of New Right political doctrine in the 1980s, particularly regarding the primacy of free markets and 'healthy competition'. The favoured form of restructuring centred on the 'deregulation' and breaking down of legal barriers between the stock exchange, banking, investment, life assurance, the building societies and other sectors so as to enable interpenetration and thus enhance competition. It is essential to recognise the connections here with key elements of New Right/Thatcherite discourse. Firstly, and most fundamentally, there can be discerned a reliance on neo-classical economics to support what are termed *laissez-faire* policies, on the assumption that the unrestricted operation of market mechanisms leads to optimal resource allocation in pursuit of profits. Related beliefs include the need to cut back on state intervention via the transfer of welfare, pension provision, etc. to the markets and the economic importance of service industries (particularly financial services) as opposed to manufacturing/primary industries. Underlying much of this discourse are basic assumptions of individualism and self-interest, founded on neo-classical conceptions of individuals as economically-rational agents. The intention here is to give a flavour of broadly-related New Right discourses in the late 1980s and early 1990s, without imputing any *specific* intellectual coherence to these positions; indeed, the contradictions within this liberal, New Right position have been raised by a number of commentators, drawing on a range of positions ranging from neo-Marxist to postmodern debates. A key criticism regards the use of the term 'deregulation' to describe the relaxation of legislative constraints in favour of the economic regulation of free markets. As Grey notes, "once it is understood that economic law is not 'naturally given' but rather determined by our collective construction of it, then it becomes clear that the unregulated market is ordered by the application of this historically specific construction" (1997: 57b).

The impetus towards 'deregulation' stems more broadly from certain New Right concepts of individualism, and is legitimated politically by recourse to the 'rights of the consumer' which it is represented as defending. As such, the move towards deregulation in the late 1980s can be linked with a wider inscription of New Right discourse on individuals, in their reconstruction as 'consumers of financial services' through participation in these changes. Crucially, the political implementation of such discourses has the potential to reproduce them in the subjectivities of those involved, although this cannot be seen to occur in a deterministic fashion. The promotion of personal pension plans, for example, linked with the freezing of the state provision of pensions can be seen in the first instance to forge a material dependence of individuals on the life assurance industry, and by implication the Stock Exchange and 'Financial Services' more widely. More fundamentally, however, the "selling of life insurance and associated investment contracts 'plays on' but also stimulates anxieties and uncertainties concerning the accomplishment of successful masculine identities" (Knights and Morgan, 1994: 143), a point I will return to in Chapter 7. This provides a key example of the deep social changes which financial deregulation/re-regulation potentially engenders. Even if a future change of government or of policy should lead to substantial reinvestment in state pension provision, it seems likely that the connection between control and personal pension provision in the masculine identity would prove more enduring. As has been pointed out, resistance in the form of campaigns for consumer rights have the effect of reaffirming subjective status as consumers, and refusal to partake in (and thus reproduce) such practices, through investment in a personal pension, for instance, can lead to serious material consequences (Grey, 1997b: 64-5). Nonetheless, these discursive, social changes should not be assumed to occur without resistance, particularly at a subjective level.

Importantly, the attitudes of the main financial institutions regarding deregulation should not be seen to have been uniformly positive either. The possibility of deregulation in this area, in terms of the freedom of institutions to enter other financial sectors, elicited contradictory reactions in different sectors of the market. In the first place, there was a certain amount of resistance on the part of established institutions based on the fear of losing the relatively secure position they held in the status quo. On the other hand, there was considerable support for moves which would provide the same companies with potential areas for growth outside of what were often stagnant and over-populated industries. The fear of new entrants encouraged by deregulation was generally offset, therefore, in the case of most financial institutions; by the recognition on the part of banks of the opportunities in insurance markets, the awareness on the part of insurance companies of the opportunities offered by the potential privatisation of welfare in the UK, and so on. This deregulation came about in 1986 with the introduction of a range of legislation centred on the Financial Services Act (FSA).

The Financial Services Act of 1986 brought about the deregulation (and, *essentially*, the re-regulation) of not only the banking and life assurance industries but of the UK financial markets as a whole. A large part of this legislation, linked to the parallel Building Societies Act (BSA) and Social Security Act (SSA), both in 1986, entailed the relaxation of restrictions on the activities in which different types of financial institution could engage. Related actions included the 'Big Bang', which abolished the 'closed shop' of the Stock Exchange and thereby attempted to encourage the wider participation of small investors in dealing with stocks and shares (although, as noted by Knights (1997a), a main beneficiary of this has been the large, institutional investors who enjoyed reduced commissions for large volume transactions). The key effect of the deregulation, however, was indeed to break down the restrictions on competition between the three main types of financial institutions (banks, insurance companies, and building societies) by enabling these institutions to operate in other sectors. Indeed, the FSA reflected and reinforced the gradual reconstruction of all of these sectors into one industry, to be known as 'Financial Services'. As Knights notes, "the packaging of the major financial institutions with the broad category 'financial services' cannot be seen merely as a verbal convenience" (1997a: 1), as it implies and effects the discursive construction of a particular form of social relations. Through participation in the practices of 'Financial Services' institutions, individuals may thus be constituted as 'consumers of financial services', or 'financial services professionals', reinforcing certain contemporary discourses founded on notions of 'customer service', 'the sovereign consumer', 'professionalism', and so on.

An essential part of the deregulation was the provision in the Act for the installation of a system of watchdogs to monitor behaviour in these sectors. The specific provisions were drawn from the recommendations of Gower's *Review of Investor Protection* (CMND 9125), which was itself incorporated into the Financial Services Bill (CMND 9432) which preceded the Act. This review came down in favour of the institution of Self Regulatory Organizations (SROs), regulators specific to each area which were set up, funded and partially staffed by practitioners. These were to be overseen by a main regulatory body, the Securities and Investments Board (SIB), set up by the government in 1984 to monitor the operation of a number of professional organizations and self-regulatory bodies. The SIB was also established and funded by practitioners, although it was subject to the approval of the Department of Trade and Industry (DTI), and reported annually to the Chancellor of the Exchequer. In banking, the main source of regulation was still the Bank of England, except where banks engaged in other areas such as investment advice, where the appropriate body was responsible. In the case of life assurance, the main bodies were originally the Life Assurance and Unit Trust Regulatory Organization (LAUTRO) and the Financial Intermediaries, Managers and Brokers Regulatory Association (FIMBRA). The other two SROs were the Investment Management Regulatory Organisation (IMRO), looking after fund management, and the Securities and Futures Authority (SFA), regulating the organised City investment markets. LAUTRO and FIMBRA were wound down from 1994 onwards as a unified regulatory body, the PIA (Personal Investment Authority), took over their responsibilities. Self-regulation is also the fundamental form of control for associated professionals such as accountants and lawyers, operating through the relevant professional body.

The operation of the regulatory bodies can be interpreted in a number of ways. A conventional understanding would take the existence of regulators to be a entirely natural means to ensure fair-play within free markets. The perceived need for regulation relies on New Right concepts of human nature as primarily motivated by self-interest, even where this may involve infringing on the rights of others by cheating, etc. On one level, this contradicts liberal assumptions regarding the operation of markets, particularly regarding the effectiveness of market discipline in controlling the conduct of firms. This does reflect the point made above, that such free market theories, by "maintaining a rigid separation between institutional law (what governments do) and economic law" (Grey, 1997b: 57), obscure the construction of free markets through the action of the state (in providing legal structures for wage labour, contract law, etc.). Moreover, without resorting to a Marxist 'ruling ideology' argument, the existence and symbolic action of regulators in a very real sense legitimates the privatisation of the financial industry and the operation of free markets. In doing so, they provide a model of how the 'Financial Services' industry *should* operate, and reinforce the truth claims of New Right and liberal philosophy which underpin deregulation.

This process can be seen to have continued despite the departure of the Conservative government responsible for deregulation. Almost immediately on the arrival to the Labour administration in May 1997, Gordon Brown as chancellor announced that the responsibility for the supervision of banks would be taken from the Bank of England and allocated to SIB, which would then become a 'super-regulator' covering virtually the whole of British finance. While simplifying the regulation procedure and promising tougher action on those infringing the regulations, in sanctioning the 'truth' of deregulation and competition, this radical move all but completed the reconstruction of the UK finance industries as a single market for 'Financial Services'.

Restructuring in Banking

The construction of a 'Financial Services' industry has meant radical change in both the banking and life assurance sectors in the course of the last 12 years, particularly involving the commercial interpenetration of each sector. In the following section I intend to examine the structural changes which have occurred in each industry, as a consequence of the FSA and associated developments, so as to place the subsequent examination of the subject organisations in context.

Despite the protected oligopoly enjoyed by the big four banks in the UK, significant levels of competition in the late 1970s were reflected by the decision, quickly taken up by all the main banks, to provide personal banking accounts free of normal charges. In search of profitable areas to compensate for this and the poor rate of return on many loans to developing countries, many of the banks, as noted above, moved into traditional building society markets and in the early 1980s began to offer mortgages at very competitive rates, thanks to their access to wholesale funds. It has been suggested that the perceived 'market imbalance' of the protected banks undercutting other sectors was instrumental in arguments supporting a relaxation of restrictions on the building societies and contributed to the New Right discourse for deregulation.

This relaxation of constraints in the BSA (1986) allowed the building societies to compete with the banks directly through the provision of unsecured loans and current accounts. The demutualisation which occurred in many building societies, most notably with the TSB, Woolwich, Abbey National and the Halifax, further broke down the traditional distinction between these forms of institution. This was soon followed by increased competition on other sections of the banks operations from other institutions, notably the life assurers and credit provision agencies offering unsecured personal loans. At the same time, the banks have gained a significant foothold in the mortgage provision market, accounting for more than 50% of the new loans by 1993 (Mintel: 1995a). The advance of the banks into the direct provision of life assurance, which had started prior to the FSA, was accelerated by the legislation, replacing the traditional approach within banking whereby the bank manager might recommend outside insurance brokers at his/her own discretion as part of their 'professional' service to clients. These advances have been mainly achieved by either the establishment of insurance arms, in the case of Barclays, Lloyds and the TSB, or by the acquisition of life insurance institutions, such as Lloyds' acquisition of Abbey Life in 1990.

The emergence of 'bancassurance', as this is known, has given rise to significant problems which have served to highlight what has been referred to as 'cultural change' in the banking sector. In particular, widespread attempts to instil a 'sales-oriented culture' within banks have led to conflicts over a variety of issues, as the "mildly aggressive sales and marketing orientation sits uncomfortably with the 'gentlemanly' (sic) professional image associated with traditional banking" (Knights, 1997a: 13). Knights and Morgan (1991) case-study illustrates the potential for considerable conflict where the paternalist ethos of traditional banking comes into contact with the 'hard-sell' of life insurance salesforces. While the banks have a significant advantage over the life assurers in their substantial networks of branches and the frequent contact with their customers, they are nonetheless criticised by life assurers and other competitors for their sub-optimal exploitation of this advantage. The banks and building societies have tended to favour a less aggressive, indirect approach to selling, relying on socially skilled, mature female receptionists in the branches to sound out and pass on prospective consumers of investment products, etc. (Kerfoot, 1993). Nonetheless, 'cultural change', frequently associated with an intensification of pressure to pursue sales in a more systematic or aggressive way, can be linked to the developments in banking after deregulation.

Concurrent developments, however, have had an enormous impact on the status of the banks' branch networks, which have fallen by almost a fifth from 15 346 in 1980 to 11 351 in 1995 (Mintel, 1996b). This movement is widely presented as driven by two particular aspects of the unstoppable progress of information technology and communications. The first of these is the development of nationwide networks of ATMs (Automated Teller Machines), more commonly known in the UK as 'cashpoints'. The increasing acceptance of ATMs for a wide range of everyday banking transactions, particularly as regards current accounts, has motivated a greater investment in research and development to enable cashpoints to facilitate more complex transactions than simply cash withdrawals, covering cash transfers, statements, etc. In tandem with this, the banks have attempted to increase the use of ATMs for these transactions by installing them in branch foyers accessible outside of working hours rather than the less comfortable and secure external machines.

A second development undermining the use of branch networks has been the rapid growth of telephone banking in the UK, originally led by the Bank of Scotland, with the subsequent establishment of Buzzbank as the UK's first 'stand-alone' telephone banking outfit. Although slightly slower to follow, most UK high-street banks and to a lesser extent building societies have since acted on the success of Buzzbank and established their own telephone banking operations to back up the branch networks. Although the widespread development of current account banking via domestic PCs and the emergence of the 'virtual bank' has been touted more recently with the emergence of more secure Internet and e-mail connections, very few have been actually brought into operation, with Barclays and the Bank of Scotland being notable exceptions. A partial consequence of this has been the representation of branch networks as prohibitively costly, an argument which has gained the strength of an essential truth in the industry, leading to enormous job losses in banking over the last ten years. A report by the British Banking Association suggests a loss of 110 000 jobs in banking since its peak of 450 000 in 1990 (Mintel, 1996c). While there has been some resistance to the progressive closure and centralisation of branches by customers, this may have had less effect than otherwise as discontent is perceived as limited to the lower-income sectors of the banks' clients from whom minimal profit margins are gained.

The figures representing the reduced employment in banking branch networks are offset by the increasing numbers employed in call centres across the UK, where employees in a centralised site deal with telephone calls from customers nationwide, administered through automated call distribution systems. These call centres are generally situated in northern England and Scotland and outside of major conurbations to reduce overheads and take advantage of lower regional wage rates. It has been estimated that 250 000 workers were employed in call centres in 1997, about 1.2 per cent of the UK labour force, and the same report predicts an increase in the number of call centres from 4 - 5 000 now to around 10 000 by the year 2000 (FT 24/6/97). Telephone clerks within these call centres rely upon access to client details through networked PCs linked to a central database known as a Customer Information System, or CIS. The development of these CISs draws on significant developments in the storage and rapid-access capabilities of IT, which is often portrayed as the driving force behind such change. Quite apart from the technological determinism of this explanation, the use of CISs comes partly in response to compliance regulations enforced by the PIA, requiring that financial institutions which provide investment advice 'know their client', which involves keeping detailed records on their customers financial situation. In contrast to the much-publicised potential IT affords for enabling 'tele-working', many of the advantages perceived in the development of call centres stem from the control facilitated by the centralisation of labour on a single site. Again the IT function is instrumental in the development of Management Information Systems (MISs) which routinely report on the behaviour and performance of targeted aspects of the organisations. The introduction of shift patterns to enable 24-hour cover and the establishment of Taylorist management practices based on direct observation and the imposition of 'call-answering' quotas are cited as key benefits of call centres (Fernie, 1998). According to a report by Incomes Data Services, "The seven-day continuous nature of the operations is more akin to manufacturing than a more traditional day-work arrangement ... Productivity targets or piecework quotas are also borrowed from a more manufacturing background" (quoted in FT, 24/6/97). The widespread reliance on CISs is not restricted to call centres, but extends to branch networks and, to a lesser extent, to field agents (particularly in financial services more generally). As a consequence, this dependence has significant implications for the control of relations with the *consumer*, as well as modes of organisational control.

The first key implication of the use of CISs is in facilitating the growth of what has been termed 'Relationship Banking'. This involves the development of a central resource of detailed data-files on customers for sophisticated targeting of marketing, as well as providing such details to front-line employees "so that they can sound and act as if they know their clients individually" (Mintel, 1996c: 12). Knights and Sturdy (1997) draw on the work of Rose (1990) to illustrate how the techniques of 'relationship marketing' segment the market in an attempt to constitute the consumer by suggesting attractive and 'secure' identities through advertising, tied to the consumption of the individual. At the same time, a second implication of this development is that the technical requirements of constructing a CIS tend to require significant levels of specialist knowledge, which is perceived by financial institutions to reside outside of their workforce, in IT consultancies. This fuels the increasing reliance on 'professional help', in banking and elsewhere, to develop CISs and to restructure the operations of the institution to fit in with the CIS installed. This growing influence of IT consultancies will be developed in much further detail below (see Chapters 5 and 6); for the moment it will suffice to highlight the support this provides for the wider application of BPR, Project Management and other disciplines associated with IT and IT consultancies. More generally, I would also emphasise that the central role adopted by the IT function in the restructuring of workplace operations contributes to the establishment of a specifically *technical* form of rationality in financial institutions.

Restructuring in Life Assurance

As in banking, the FSA instigated a fundamental reorganisation of the UK life assurance industry, as well as leading indirectly to a number of related changes in the environment within which life assurers operated. As noted above, the general attitude within the industry could be characterised as welcoming the opportunities to take over areas of state security provision, tempered by some concern at the potential entrants into the life assurance industry. However, the most important aspect of the reorganization for life assurance was undoubtedly the effect of the Social Security Act (SSA) in 1986 to encourage the public to consider opting out of the State Earnings Related Pensions Scheme (SERPS), and to transfer their DSS contributions into personal pension schemes. The rapid growth in this area was largely stimulated by the government campaign, with the offer of cash rebates for those 'opting out' of SERPS, and the fear that the government would not fund an adequate state pension in the future, following the de-indexation of the state pension. In addition, the rush to 'opt out' of company pensions was given fresh impetus by the emergence of Maxwell pensions scandal, where the businessman Robert Maxwell was found to have raided his company pension funds in an attempt to prop up his failing business empire. Both of these occurrences were exploited by the salesforces of life assurance policies with the effect of significantly boosting demand in the pensions market as a whole, which rose from £1 370 million in 1986 to £5 540 million in 1993 (Mintel, 1995a).

The combination of all of these circumstances led initially to a drastic increase in the numbers of life assurance salespeople, where the FSA also insisted on a principle of 'polarisation'. This was to ensure there was a clearly perceived difference between the Independent Financial Advisers (IFAs), those who sold the products of all life companies, and the Tied Agents/Company Agents, those who sold the products of only one life agency. The expansion of the personal pension market as a result of the SSA meant that a large number of staff were recruited in this area in a relatively short period of time. However, the brief boom enjoyed by life assurance companies, including Lifelong, was soon hit by increased levels of competition encouraged by the FSA, competition which was particularly attracted to the expanding market for personal pensions (Knights and Morgan, 1994). This coincided with a recession in the UK economy in the early 1990s, which hit investments and related business particularly hard; indeed, the boom in personal pensions is the main reason why most life assurers business managed to increase in this period, albeit marginally (Mintel, 1995a). As a consequence, the early 1990s saw large scale redundancies throughout the financial services industry, a phenomena hitherto unknown due to the constant expansion and oligopolistic suppression of competition in the industry. It was reported that two-thirds of financial services companies cut their staff in this period, (CBI/Coopers and Lybrand, in Knights and McCabe, 1995). The salesforces in the life industry took much of the brunt of this; according to LAUTRO, the number of people registered to sell life policies fell from a peak of 190 000 in 1990 to just over 70 000 in 1995 (Mintel, 1995b). Following this, many institutions took advantage of the redundancies to reorganise their distribution network, balancing their reliance on Tied Agents/Company Agents and IFAs.

In the course of the SIB's regulation, two incidents in particular proved to be of considerable importance for the operation of life assurance companies in the 1990s. The most shattering of these emerged from an investigation by the SIB into the selling of personal pensions in 1994. Concern was raised on publication of a study commissioned by the SIB in December 1993 which indicated cause for concern in 90% of cases where people had switched from company pension schemes to personal pensions. On October 25 1994, the results of the ensuing investigation were finally released. The SIB stated that more than 1.5 million people who were persuaded to invest in a personal pension instead of the company pension to which they were entitled may have been wrongly advised. The SIB ordered the relevant life insurers to compensate in full those who had lost out financially, and given that they might number around 350 000 individuals on initial estimates, this was likely to cost the industry as a whole over £2 billion. The effect of this on the industry was enormous, and the clearest immediate effect was to severely undermine the public's confidence in life insurance and the pensions industry, and to greatly exacerbate the slump in the pensions market. This finding did not appear to be an isolated incident; between May 1992 and October 1994, nearly £3 million in fines were levied against life insurers for assorted breaches of regulations, often regarding the conduct of the salesforces (Economist 29/10/94).

The second incident was the introduction of a regime of disclosure from January 1995, whereby life assurance and other investment companies were required to provide the consumer with a transparent statement of the true cost of a policy over its lifetime, including the charges and commission made by the salesperson. This was widely expected to increase pressure on life insurance companies to reduce costs, and to simplify their policies (Economist 29/10/94). The life assurers later claimed that disclosure had not directly discouraged sales, but that it had increased the time each sale took, thereby hitting profit margins (Mintel, 1995b). However, other research by the PIA concluded that disclosure had resulted in a fall in charges and some loss of business among the direct salesforces, who had both higher commission levels and higher general costs than IFAs.

Public confidence in life insurance salespeople was already very low in the early 1990s, therefore, and the market was struggling with the competition of PEPs, unit trusts and other alternative investment products. The steady trickle of revelations regarding the mis-selling of private pensions reinforced the poor reputation of the life assurers, and pension premiums fell from a peak in 1993 by around 15% per year in 1994 and 1995 across the industry (Economist 5/10/96). This distrust, coinciding with continuing lack of consumer confidence as the recession receded, led to a switch from regular premium investments to single premium (i.e. lump sum) investments. As this market was monopolised by the IFAs, this put further pressure on the direct salesforces of the life assurers.

Although the large life assurance institutions suffered a great deal from both economic conditions and the repercussions of the misbehaviour of the salesforces, the effects of this on the market as a whole were not entirely negative. In the first place, the enormous publicity engendered by the pensions mis-selling significantly raised the profile of the life assurance industry as a whole. The status of the regulators could also be said to have improved, mainly through their constant depiction in the media threatening the major companies with fines for dragging their feet (obscuring the failure of regulation which had led to the scandal in the first place). Moreover, in a wider sense publicity has increased public awareness of what is represented as 'crisis talk' regarding the state pension provision (Knights, 1997a). In essence, this 'crisis talk' highlights the increasing number of elderly dependants within the Western economies and the "inability" of the state to provide sufficient support in terms of pensions, and highlights the inevitability of some form of privatisation of welfare. Knights notes that "crisis talk is as much a function of New Right political ideology as it is of demographic analysis since the data, by definition, has been available for years without arousing these concerns" (1997a: 12). Nonetheless, this argument appears to have been relatively persuasive with New Labour, who even prior to the election in 1997 had displayed their willingness to entertain an increasing role for the life assurers in the provision of welfare (Mintel, 1995b).

As sales fell for the troubled life assurers, then, they were also put under increasing pressure by the growing ingress of other financial institutions into the personal investments market, attracted by public interest and the promise of a greater role in public welfare provision. On one side, a number of 'direct' insurers, such as Direct Line and Virgin Direct, entered the arena through telephone sales, without the expense of sales networks. At the same time, a bigger threat came from high-street banks and building societies moving into the market; as noted above, many became 'bancassurers' either by taking over existing life insurers or by setting up their own life insurance products. The significant growth in merger and acquisition activity was presented in many quarters as the direct and inevitable effect of the deregulation brought about by the Financial Services Act (Economist 5/10/96). Indeed, this growth in bancassurance was explained by the Financial Times as "the logic of the financial services revolution, point(ing) firmly in the direction of combining the traditional functions of banking and life assurance" (FT 25/10/95).

In the meantime, pressure was kept up by the SIB on the life assurers to compensate those who has lost out through the mis-selling of personal pensions, and this pressure was redoubled after the change of government in May 1997. The pensions companies were widely perceived as dragging their feet in the review of cases by issuing overly elaborate enquiry forms and other tactics (SIB Press Release, 13/5/97). Helen Liddell, economic secretary to the treasury, delivered a speech to the heads of the insurance companies at the same time accusing them of "reprehensible behaviour", referring to the PIA's assertion that more policy-holders had died than had received compensation since the review began. She also required written proposals from each company within a month detailing how they intended to speed up the process. The behaviour of the insurance companies was also cited by the new chancellor Gordon Brown in explaining the reason for instituting a 'super watchdog' a week later. In addition to the ongoing cost of reviewing possible cases of mis-selling, then, the major institutions also face substantial bills for compensation. Nonetheless, increasing profits in most areas despite increased competition and the probability of further involvement in the provision of state welfare may be seen to have relieved some of the pressure on the major life assurers by the late 1990s.

This section has presented a brief overview of the recent history of the banking and life assurance sectors and their relationship with the construction of a unitary 'Financial Services' industry in the course of the last 12 years. While concentrating on large-scale change, I have tried to keep in perspective a number of fundamental processes which have taken place at a social and subjective level, in the discursive reconstruction of both employees and consumers in line with prevalent discourses which can be associated with New Right philosophy. The following section will attempt to build on this in a detailed manner with analyses of each of the subject organisations and their recent development in the course of these changes in the industry and UK society as a whole.

Organisation 1: Buzzbank

The concept of personal banking by telephone was pioneered in the 1980s by the Bank of Scotland from 1985 onwards, building on a scheme originating in the Nottingham Building Society in 1982. Nonetheless, Buzzbank has taken on the status of pioneer in the field, and many of the developments in the financial services market in the last few years have been attributed to its success. The burgeoning interest and investment in banking services via telephone and personal computer over the last few years has been accredited by many in the business to Buzzbank's performance, and it is claimed that Buzzbank's success "has compelled the high street institutions to offer telephone banking simply to defend their market positions" (Datamonitor Consultants, in FT 23/9/96). All of the 'Big Four' UK banks have launched telephone banking services in addition to the branch network and it has been estimated that 30% of all current accounts could be telephone-based by the year 2000 (Datamonitor Consultants, in FT 3/4/96), although whether this is meant as a forecast or marketing target is unclear.

Although not the first UK bank to implement telephone banking, when Buzzbank was established in 1989 it became the only 'stand-alone' UK telephone banking organisation, operating without the support of a dedicated branch network. Buzzbank exists as a subsidiary of TN Banking, one of the larger high-street banks in the UK, and Buzzbank has relied on TN Banking since its inception for a number of technical and procedural necessities. The origins of the idea for a stand-alone telephone banking operation allied to TN Banking go back to a meeting legendary among Buzzbank staff, of a number of TN Banking managers in a Chinese restaurant in 1987, and an apocryphal plan drawn up on a tablecloth. The importance of this image of the company's roots as radical yet informal is evident in the frequent retelling of this story and repeated references to it by Buzzbank managers. The project which emerged from this meeting, 'Project Raincloud', came to fruition in October 1989 when Buzzbank was opened. Within six years, Buzzbank had grown to a company with 500 000 customers by April 1995, and gaining around 10 000 extra customers every month. This increased drastically in September 1996 as Buzzbank moved into credit provision with the addition of the Creditable group, another subsidiary of TN Banking. Thus by February 1997, the total number of customers exceeded 1 million, including 350 000 within the new arm, which was renamed Buzzbank Business To Business (BTB). By January 1996, the number of employees at Buzzbank had risen from 250 at start-up to 2 300 people across two sites in Northern England. By February 1997, the number had increased to over 3 000 (plus around 500 in BTB), and the company was planning to open a third, larger site to be situated in Scotland. The existing sites are around four miles apart, and are linked electronically and through telecommunications to enable either to continue business should an emergency force one site to close. Buzzbank defines its telephone banking system as "a full person-to-person banking service available over the telephone 24 hours a day, seven days a week, 365 days a year" (Buzzbank Information Sheet (BBIS) 1). Since 1989, Buzzbank has developed its services to cover cheque accounts, credit cards, savings accounts, mortgages, loans, share dealing, and travel services, as well as car, home and personal insurance. The customers themselves are mainly aged between 25 and 44, roughly evenly split between men and women, and the majority fall in the ABC1 socio-economic classification (FT 3/4/96).

While Buzzbank was touted as the first UK 'stand-alone' telephone banking service, it did originally adopt the existing TNB banking system, including TN Banking arrangements for current accounts, savings accounts, etc, before adding on its own products later. Similarly, the original IT processing system was inherited from TN Banking, although a number of systems specific to Buzzbank have since been added to this base. Furthermore, as a 'stand-alone' outfit, Buzzbank depends upon TN Banking's branch and cash machine networks for withdrawals, the paying-in of cheques, etc. The reliance on TN Banking's financial and technological systems has also resulted in the recruitment by Buzzbank of a significant number of TN Banking employees at different levels of the organisation, a process which has continued since its inception. As Buzzbank's business has expanded, the relationship between Buzzbank and

TN Banking has grown more complex in a number of significant respects which merit discussion below.

In terms of internal organisation, Buzzbank appears in many ways to conform to a divisional model, led by a Management Team made up of 6 divisional heads and the Chief Executive. This Management Team is "effectively what would be the Board of Directors if Buzzbank were a Plc.", according to one head of division. The divisions themselves include *Information Technology* (IT), *Finance and Operations*, *People and Organisational Development* (P & OD), *Customer Services*, and *Commerce*. There are also a number of Heads of Departments who report directly to the Management Team; the connected departments of Credit Services and Analysis and Development, and also Mortgage Services, Lending Services, Savings and Investment, and Insurance. Within this structure, however, Buzzbank management are keen to stress the flexibility throughout the organisation, reinforced by initiatives such as 'hot-desking' and the like. The innovative cultural aspects of Buzzbank have been extensively covered in the media, and the company's 'creed' encompasses a number of contemporary managerial ideals. These ideals, including Single Status, Openness, Responsiveness, Commitment, Respect, Contribution, and a recent addition, 'Kaizen' (Continuous Improvement), are randomly displayed on idle computer monitors throughout the buildings on a company-wide screen-saver.

While all of these departments are based on the ground floor, there is also the basement, containing the Print Services department and the stores, and a mezzanine floor, reserved for Management Information Systems staff who monitor and collate information on the performance of each division. Interestingly, this area is kept well apart from the rest of Buzzbank, such that there is no direct evidence of monitoring on the ground floor apart from the overt surveillance system in the telephone centre, Customer Services. Architecturally, then, the open-plan layout of the Buzzbank centres appears to fit well with the image of the progressive company, promoting workplace democracy and single status throughout the shopfloor. The Chief Executive, Mike Winter, has been quoted in the media as "asking fundamental questions about why we need offices" and declaring that "the challenge for UK industry is to tear down the boardrooms" (FT 19/8/94). Both sites, A (the original site rented by the company) and S (a larger site, owned and in the process of expansion), consist therefore of vast, air-conditioned warehouse-like buildings, where departments are generally grouped in specific areas. Filing cabinets and moveable screens serve to separate sections of the floor, acting as partial soundproofing as well as demarcating departmental territories. While PR documents claim that the company practices "what has been dubbed hot-desking" (BBIS 5), this was carefully described by one director as "a sort of semi-hot-desking" (Alan: 1). Each department still has its own geographical situation, and each employee appears to have their own workspace, decorated with personal items and signs. However, there are no dedicated offices in terms of enclosed and private spaces, only rooms which may be reserved for private meetings. This was represented as being linked to the culture of 'openness', where most of the activities of the employees goes on 'in the open', and much of the communication appears to occur by desks, in aisles, etc. The main aim of this was said to be to encourage approachability and communication between staff, linked in to the single status ideal. Another effect of this was to heighten the visibility of employees, such that the actions of anyone in a department, including who they communicated with, could be visible to other employees and management present at almost any time.

In terms of the composition of the workforce, Buzzbank has been careful to recruit a 'green' workforce, where only 5% of employees have prior experience of banking (FT 19/8/94). In selection, the traits focused upon in applicants are primarily 'behavioural' as opposed to experiential (i.e. based on banking knowledge). In appraisal also, pay is mainly related to behavioural skills, such as "communicating, decision making, judgement, influencing, using information and handling stress" (FT 19/8/94). A team reportedly monitors 5-10% of all calls to Buzzbank, and the above factors, along with harder measures such as call duration and time logged into the workstation, go to determining the employee's bonus level, as well as being passed back to the individual in feedback sessions (FT 19/8/94). Hence it is claimed that "(Buzzbank) is not simply interested in telephone answering rates, even though call rates are logged... Calls are monitored to assess tone of voice and response so that the human touch does not go missing" (FT 15/5/96). In prominent locations in both sites, electronic notice-boards visible to all staff display the previous day (or night)'s service level, and whether the performance standard was achieved, along with various other messages.

In material terms, Buzzbank management stress the provisions made for its employees, 69% of whom are female and a quarter of whom are part-time. These include crèche facilities, which "have enabled many more women to return to work after having children, either on a part-time or full-time basis" (BBIS 2). The sites also contain subsidised restaurants and there has been a significant investment in on-site security, both in the design of the sites and in their day-to-day operation: "safety is an important issue ... with a predominantly female workforce (and) women coming to work at night" (BBIS 2). Due to the 24-hour availability of Buzzbank, the majority of employees, over two-thirds, work on a shift basis (FT 19/8/94).

While this is flexible and up to the individual employee to some extent, the staffing tends to be focused on the peaks and troughs of customer demand. The single status ideal has eliminated all significant perks short of the company car, and, according to interviews, the Chief Executive Mike Winter remains unhappy about the existence of company cars (FT 19/8/94). In keeping with this ideal, terms such as 'junior' and 'senior' are discouraged as "non-PC" (Politically Correct) (TA1: 236), in favour of a language that promotes 'team-members', although an appreciation of hierarchical differences are still clear in employees' representations of the company structure.

Buzzbank: IT Division

The IT Division is divided into five "areas of specific expertise" (BBIS: IT Overview); *IT Applications, IT Operations, Strategic Systems, Emerging Technology* and *Business Analysis*. While IT Applications and IT Operations were grouped together, Strategic Systems was based on the floor above, Emerging Technology in the basement and Business Analysis nearby on the same floor.

All but Business Analysis are directly involved with the development, operation and maintenance of the IT systems of Buzzbank. Business Analysis is officially concerned with "providing consultancy to IT projects, as well as other areas of the organisation" and is "closely involved with the Emerging Technology department" (BBIS: IT Overview), according to company documentation. However, the actual links between BA and the rest of the IT division appeared weak, however, as one head in IT noted that "no IT projects (had) come from Business Analysis as yet" (LW1: 185), and the head of BA joked that "if we were removed from it the rest of the department wouldn't actually notice" (TA1: 165). The two main departments in the IT division appear to be Applications Development, which manages IT projects, developing software and hardware for the three computer platforms, and IT Operations, which is responsible for the installation and the day-to-day running of the computer systems. Strategic Systems looks after the infrastructure of the computer system and acts as an intermediary with outside organisations, particularly TN Banking "as Buzzbank uses TNB systems, and therefore ... depend(s) on continued support from TNB" (LW: 20). Finally, Emerging Technology acts as the Research and Development department, looking at "leading edge developments such as voice recognition technology" (BBIS: IT Overview). As Strategic Systems is mainly a liaison department with TN Banking, and Emerging Technology limited to technical R & D, my research focuses on the 3 largest and most influential areas within the organisation; Business Analysis, IT Applications and IT Operations.

Business Analysis Business Analysis is a relatively new department, introduced originally to act as "the interface between systems developers and the business" (TA1:23), but evolving later into a more traditional Business Process Re-engineering (BPR) role. This 're-engineering' of Buzzbank's work systems has occurred since then according to a typical 'moving feast' arrangement, with a handful of projects in different divisions going on at any one time. Based on a number of factors including size of potential return, specific work systems or departments are chosen, analysed through Process Mapping and restructured, with the intention of minimising "non-productive delays" (TA2: 208). The department is also involved in a 'benchmarking' exercise, which essentially involves the comparison of processes with companies which are not direct rivals. In both these activities, but particularly in the BPR projects, there is a clear accent on formalisation, reflected elsewhere in the IT Division. Throughout a project in the BA department, there is an emphasis on the establishment of a detailed project plan, the clear recording of all data, and the production of a report and action plan for every project; "a number of stages we always go through, which the business doesn't require but again we think we should do, in order to be professional and do it properly" (TA1: 133). Furthermore, the BA team is seen by its head as the "centre of excellence for project work" (TA2: 310) and as such plays a key role in the training of management from elsewhere in Buzzbank in the formal techniques of Project Management.

IT Applications The Applications Team is split into three areas, focusing on three IT platforms. Firstly, there is the SEQUOIA mainframe which supports the 24-hour Telephone Support System (TSS). This TSS is the basic Customer Information System of Buzzbank, which "holds customer personal information and demographics, performs the customer identification procedures and records details of every contact with the customer" (BBIS: IT Overview) It also provides access to numerous TN Banking systems processing direct debits, cheques, Visa, etc. Secondly, there is an IBM mainframe, based on the TNB systems, which supports the employees' PCs and associated Office Automation applications, running on Windows. Finally, there are the DEC/VMS platforms, which support the Management Information (MI), the Customer Work Bench (CWB) and also the Account Enquiry System (AES). The MI provides customer data for the use of departments, while the CWB is predictive software which can manipulate data for sales projections, informing marketing initiatives. The

AES holds data on customer account transactions, and performs behavioural analyses on these data to inform more complex calculations of the CWB. In addition to the staff dedicated to each platform, there is a group of what are termed "business analysts" (LW1: 96), who discuss possible projects to decide which platform a project should be built on.

Both the Sequoia and the IBM groups include one support/maintenance team and three involved with longer projects, lasting from 2-3 months. These smaller projects are planned and prioritised by a Small Projects Forum which meets monthly, while the larger projects are "usually championed by a director" (LW1: 41) and take up a dedicated team for 2-3 years. The DECs have a small number of staff dedicated to maintaining their operation, and according to the head of IT Applications Development, appear to have proved rather troublesome in their recent installation. Finally, the 'business analysts' are described by the department head as part of the aforementioned efforts to create professional 'project managers', experienced in the disciplines of managing substantial projects.

Again, there can be seen a concerted attempt to formalise the operations of the Applications department, tracing back to the appointment of a new head two years ago. In the first instance, this took the form of a restructuring of the teams, such that they were no longer assessed by someone other than their team leader, and to form "enduring teams" (LW1: 83) rather than reforming teams for particular projects. Beyond this, a system was instituted known as the Systems Development Life Cycle (SDLC), to formalise the process of developing new technology and the resource planning for different projects. The SDLC, then, requires of each project "business feasibility studies, design, implementation, training and post-implementation reviews and support", and is integrated with other formalisation initiatives in IT Operations.

IT Operations The IT Operations department consists of four main 'teams', working on Telecommunications, Print Services, PC Services (focusing on day-to-day Office Automation projects) and Operations (the technical team working on installation and technical support/maintenance). As noted, these teams are intended to maintain the running of the Buzzbank IT system as a whole, and consequently, the Operations department has teams working in shifts to cover 24 hours, as well as an IT Help Desk. The department head describes the role of the department as "the hamsters on the wheel, we have to keep the bloody wheel turning" (JR2: 341). Although the majority of the teams are there to provide support, there are a number of project-based teams, mainly concentrating on a large number of relatively small projects.

In many ways the recent developments in IT Operations appear to mirror those in Applications Development, insofar as a new head of department was introduced from TN Banking at roughly the same time to pursue a similar remit; "to get some structure in place, to get some planning in place in terms of the way they do business" (JR2: 20). Again, one of the first changes made was to restructure teams and shifts, to balance out the skills of the teams on duty at a particular time, to make the teams more permanent and to synchronise the shift patterns with their counterparts in TN Banking. In the longer run, a mission statement was produced, and comprehensively broken down into the objectives for each member of the department. In a bureaucratic manner, then, the roles and duties of the department were formally defined and set out for each individual employee in the department, linked in to a "training needs analysis" carried out by an external consultancy. In a similar vein, the Operations team were integrated into the SDLC structure used by the Applications Development department. However, there is evidence of some resistance to these attempts at formalisation, as well as to other areas of change within Buzzbank, which will be developed in more detail in the next chapters.

Organisation 2: Lifelong UK

Lifelong UK is presently the one of the largest life insurance companies in the UK with a significant proportion of the total market, as well as having a major presence in personal investments and now incorporating a fledgling banking division. It is a subsidiary of Lifelong Corporation, a holding company established in 1978 to allow Lifelong Assurance to diversify beyond its traditional market of insurance. Within the UK, the Lifelong Corporation also covers *Lifelong Portfolio Managers*, one of the leading UK institutional investors, and *Lifelong Services Limited*, which provides certain functions to the other divisions, including *Group Personnel*, *Legal Services*, *Group Financial Services*, *Administrative Services* and *Central Actuarial Services*. The corporation also has a significant stake in the world market, with half its profits and sales in 1996 coming from overseas operations, including the subsidiary in the US, James Federal Life, and smaller operations in Asia, Australia, New Zealand and Italy. Nonetheless, the bedrock of the profits for the Lifelong Corporation are still provided by Lifelong UK, which made £344 million of the Lifelong Corporation's £733 million global operating profit in 1996.

The Lifelong Assurance Company itself was formed in 1848, and at first grew rather slowly, focusing on 'ordinary insurance', selling life and endowment policies to the middle classes. It was in 1854 that it moved into what was to become its most well-known business, the field of 'industrial' life assurance. Industrial assurance involved the provision of "very small policies, often only large enough to cover the cost of a funeral, to working-class clients, and arranging for agents to call and collect the tiny premium payments every week", as they were paid weekly (Jordan, 1996: 71). In this area too, Lifelong's market share remained relatively small, until the company began a series of amalgamations from 1860 to 1870, leading to a rapid expansion in the industrial policy business. Indeed, at the peak of its industrial life business in the 1940s, Lifelong Assurance was reportedly calling at a third of all homes in the UK (Lifelong Assurance Company, 1948). In 1919, Lifelong Assurance moved outside life insurance for the first time into general insurance, and in the 1920s began to expand overseas. Following the Second World War, Lifelong Assurance took advantage of a boom in pensions to such an extent that pensions now form a core part of the company's business. The last thirty years of Lifelong have been characterised by acquisitions, the main events being the purchases of RPM Reinsurance in 1968, of an estate agency in 1985 (sold in 1991) and of the US firm James Federal Life in 1986. However, the life insurance industry was inevitably affected to an enormous degree by the far-reaching changes in the financial services legislation described above. The following section will detail the main aspects to these changes, and attempt to trace some of the reactions of Lifelong Assurance.

Recent History of Lifelong Assurance

Lifelong Assurance itself suffered financially in the early 1990s, relying on the performance of its subsidiaries and overseas concerns to make up for the poor performance of its key business, the UK life assurance industry. In line with other life assurers, Lifelong Assurance made sweeping redundancies, particularly in its salesforce, in the early 1990s, in a move ominously referred to by sales-persons now as 'Scenario Three'. This refers to the strategy adopted by Lifelong Assurance, taking the opportunity of substantial redundancies to implement a number of related initiatives, including Total Quality Management programmes. Significantly, a number of employees unable to adapt to the new *sales-oriented* culture were also made redundant at this time. The life assurance industry was reported to have "underperformed the market by 15%" since the introduction of the disclosure regime in 1993 (FT 21/1/94). Despite improvements in some parts of the industry, the sales figures for Lifelong Assurance were seen as consistently disappointing for the next two years, particularly in the area of life assurance. The poor sales figures in this area were only compensated for by subsidiaries such as RPM Reinsurance (FT

23/3/94) and James Federal Life (FT 15/9/94; 19/4/95), in US life assurance. In general, this seemed to reflect the performance of the industry as a whole, which was blamed by senior management on the aftermath of the personal pensions selling scandal and the compulsory disclosure regime, along with the recession and job insecurity of the time. It was only by the summer of 1996 that the sales of Lifelong Assurance began to pick up, a revival which coincided with a number of other significant developments at Lifelong.

The early 1990s were also characterized by a number of clashes between Lifelong senior management, under the leadership of the Chief Executive Jim Gordon, and various regulatory bodies over a range of issues. This turbulent relationship was not helped by the aggressive stance adopted by Gordon over such matters as his own pay increases, the provision of three-year rolling contracts for directors, the personal pensions mis-selling scandal, his share dealings and the introduction of a new regulatory body. The first controversy to hit Lifelong involved the award of a 43% pay increase to Gordon in 1991 after his first year as Chief Executive, a year in which Lifelong's profits fell sharply. His response to shareholders at the time, as it would prove to be in many situations, was unconciliatory and rebarbative. Later, the use of rolling three-year contracts for top executives at Lifelong was criticized as expensive, indulgent and inefficient, as well as damaging to industrial relations, in a campaign by leading pension fund managers. It was argued that such contracts allowed badly-performing executives to receive large pay-offs if forced to resign. Nonetheless, under Gordon, Lifelong resisted calls to discontinue this practice for several years, until finally capitulating after a change in chairman in early 1995. The main source of discord, however, continued to be the attempts to resolve the scandal over the mis-selling of personal pensions. On one hand, Lifelong consistently denied that their salesforce had in any way behaved improperly in the selling of personal pensions. To back this up, Lifelong launched an advertising campaign in 1993 to reassure customers of this, and stated in 1994 that they would not make any provision against possible claims for compensation, so certain were they of their case. On the other hand, however, Lifelong was one of the major pension providers in the UK at the time, and independent reports suggested that up to 9/10 of occasions where customers were advised to opt-out of company schemes did not comply with regulations (FT 26/3/94). This uncertainty was exacerbated in Lifelong's case by a leaked memo from LAUTRO in July of that year, referring to an unofficial investigation which stated that there appeared to be 'significant cause for concern' in the practices of Lifelong salespeople (FT 19/7/94).

This stormy relationship between Lifelong and their regulators, the SIB, was not improved by the investigation of Gordon's share dealings following a meeting with the Chancellor of the Exchequer in October 1994. This meeting was requested by Gordon in order to complain about the intrusive behaviour of the regulatory body, the SIB which he claimed was affecting the industry's business. In the course of discussions, Gordon learnt that a framework would shortly be set-up to reimburse the victims of pensions mis-selling, information which might have been presumed to adversely affect the Lifelong share price. The chairman of Lifelong, Sir Patrick McConville, later authorised the sale of a significant number of Gordon's share options, just before the release of the SIB report mentioned. The ensuing investigation into the behaviour of Gordon and McConville went to two appeals, before the final findings cleared both men, although it was very critical of their behaviour. Another indication of the hostile relations between Lifelong and the regulators was the Lifelong board's refusal to accept regulation from the Personal Investment Authority, a self regulating organization set up by the SIB to act as watchdog in the pensions and life assurance industry. Instead, in a move which baffled many commentators, they chose to exercise their right to demand direct regulation from the SIB instead of self-regulation, on the grounds that this would give them "greater opportunity to influence the regulatory environment" (FT 25/3/94). This led to the increased isolation of Lifelong as the other firms in the life assurance industry chose to ignore Lifelong's lead and subscribe to the PIA, and the situation was only altered by the sudden change of stance at the time of the appointment of a new Chief Executive in March 1995.

The tenure of Gordon as Chief Executive came to a suitably dramatic conclusion with his abrupt resignation in January 1995, in the midst of revelations concerning the investigation into his share dealings. In the official statement, the board explained that Gordon felt the "current relationship between the UK retail financial services regulators and both himself and the company (had) become unacceptable to him", as well as mentioning the Stock Exchange investigation into Gordon. While the board publicly regretted the resignation of Gordon, there then appeared to be a concerted effort to move away from the confrontational position adopted by Lifelong in previous years. This was seen to be confirmed by the choice of Peter McCourt as the new Chief Executive, whose background in marketing was described, prior to his appointment, as making him "well-placed to help LL meet the challenge for the life insurance sector generally in attracting back customers who have lost confidence" (FT 17/3/95). Along with the appointment of a new Chief Executive, the arrival of Sir James White as chairman was taken to imply a softening in Lifelong's stance on several disputes. White himself was one of the architects of the Financial Services Act and, being considered a reliable establishment figure, as well as a former member of the SIB (FT 1/11/94), this was taken to indicate a possible stepping-down from Lifelong's outright refusal to be regulated by the PIA. Indeed, the appointment of Peter McCourt coincided with a number of announcements which could be interpreted as climb-downs; provision was to be made for reimbursing the victims of pensions mis-selling, a relatively ungenerous pay package was announced for McCourt and three-year rolling contracts were to be converted to one-year contracts for senior executives, while its executive share scheme was to be ended. All of these announcements were interpreted in the media as indications of a "less abrasive stance at LL" (FT 22/3/95), and McCourt himself described his first priority being to "settle things down" (FT 22/3/95).

While one of McCourt's original declared priorities was the overseas operations of Lifelong, within months he had publicly shifted the focus of his interest to the UK business, with two objectives announced within months of his arrival. The first was the acquisition of other life insurance companies, as part of what was described as the "widely-expected shake-out of the British industry" (FT 14/9/95). Referring to the slump in life insurance, McCourt stated "There is bound to be some rationalization, and we are interested in taking a part. The attractions are in running funds under management without duplicating back offices and sales forces" (FT 14 /9/95). The implications of such a move would be expected to be a number of redundancies in salesforces, back-office and investment staff, and consequently it was predicted that mutual life insurers, without shareholders to force the issue, would be more likely to resist take-over attempts. A second objective, announced in October 1995, was to set up a bank and enter the personal savings and mortgages markets within the year. This was the first significant attempt by a life insurance company to enter the 'bancassurance' market; all previous initiatives combining life assurance and banking had been made by banks expanding to sell life and investment policies. The move was explained by McCourt as "part defensive, part offensive... As banks become bancassurers, we must become assurer-banks" (Economist 5/11/96). The intention was to invest £70 million in setting-up telephone and postal banking services, and to effect this the appointment was made of Michael Hazard, the original Chief Executive of TN Banking's telephone banking subsidiary, Buzzbank. The decision to enter the mortgages market was received with some surprise, however, given the level of competition in that sector. Overall, this move appeared to be welcomed by market analysts and the media, and was seen by many as confirming Lifelong's intention to focus predominantly on the UK market.

As a consequence of these announcements, there was increased speculation that Lifelong might attempt to acquire a building society, instead of, or possibly as well as, a mutual life assurer. This speculation increased on the announcement in March 1996 that Lifelong was belatedly to track down its 'orphan estate'. Lifelong's 'orphan estate', the "amount of money in a 'with-profits' life fund beyond what is needed to meet the reasonable expectations of policyholders" (FT 16/3/96), was estimated to be anything between £1 billion and £5.5 billion. McCourt suggested at the time that the money so retrieved could then be used to fund the acquisition of a mutual life assurer, to capture a fresh customer base and a set of independent financial advisers to complement Lifelong's Direct Sales division. The funds available to Lifelong were then further boosted by the sale of Lifelong's Dutch subsidiary, Nivel, and more significantly, the sale of RPM Reinsurance, in August 1996, for £1.75 billion. The size of what was described as Lifelong's 'war chest' appeared to increase the pressure on Lifelong to begin acquisitions, and the company was repeatedly linked with the forthcoming flotations of the Woolwich and the Alliance and Leicester building societies, as well as Scottish Widows and Friends Provident, the mutual life assurers. However, the breakthrough finally came in March 1997 with the acquisition of Independent Life, the mutual life assurer, for £2.15 billion. The access this provided to a network of Independent Financial Advisers may well have been a key concern for Lifelong in negotiating this deal.

In the meantime, the opening of Lifelong Banking in October 1996 signified the accomplishment of another of the projects announced by McCourt a year earlier. One key aim of this subsidiary was described by the Executive Manager of Lifelong UK, John Weston, as using the deposit accounts to "capture a significant proportion of the money we currently pay out" (FT 26/9/96) in maturing policies. However, he also expressed a continued interest in acquiring a building society to give access to a branch network, although initially a deal was struck to allow Lifelong customers to deposit or withdraw funds through TNB banks. The positive trend in Lifelong's fortunes was also reflected in two other areas over the same period. Firstly, the PIA announced in October 1995 that at the end of an 18-month investigation, they had decided not to take disciplinary action against Lifelong over its selling of personal pensions, at the same time as the SIB set stricter rules on the future conduct of all companies selling personal pensions. Secondly, there was a sharp increase of profits in the first period of 1996, and sales rose to their highest level in two years in April 1996, although this appeared to be roughly in line with the market as a whole. Overall, then, after a period of instability, poor market performance and radical change, Lifelong appeared in a much more comfortable position by 1997, although many of the internal changes appeared to still be very much in progress.

Lifelong UK: IT Division

Throughout these upheavals, the IT division of Lifelong has continued remarkably unaffected by structural changes in the industry. The basic formation of the IT function is based around three areas; *Development Services, Technical Services* and *Delivery Services.* Development Services focuses on the construction of new systems and upgrades, in terms of both software and hardware. Technical Services concentrates on development and maintenance of the technical infrastructure of the Lifelong systems. Delivery Services covers the operational and support side of IT, with responsibility for arranging and carrying out the testing and installation of new systems as well as providing support for these systems once they are in operation. In addition, *National Sales Operations* (NSO) is a related although non-technical department which is formally part of Lifelong's Financial Services. NSO acts as a Business Analysis department, deriving IT requirements from strategic decisions at senior management level which are then passed on in the form of a Business Project Management Plan (PMP) to Development Services. Development Services then operationalise this as an IT PMP, which then forms the basis for their projects. The role of NSO will be examined in more detail in Chapters 5 and 6; for the moment, the key point to emphasise is that NSO is perceived within IT to wield considerable power, and IT is seen in many ways to be a service function, subservient to the wishes of senior management as articulated by NSO. As Technical Services is concerned with the technical functioning of hardware and basic systems only, the discussion below will focus on the remaining departments within IT; Development Services and Delivery Services.

Development Services Development Services is one of the larger parts of Lifelong's IT division, with over one hundred employees based in Lifelong Head Office in London. Development Services staff are mainly IT analysts, IT developers or project leaders, and are based in a number of project teams of varying sizes, depending on the size of the project, with most teams incorporating around five members. A certain amount of staff rotation occurs between the teams, although each employee tends to specialise in certain areas of IT, such as PCs, networking, mainframes, etc. While a number of the teams are involved in fairly short-term projects, a substantial minority of the department are more-or-less permanently engaged working on upgrades to the key systems used within Lifelong. The largest of these rolling project teams consists of 16 people (2 analysts and 14 developers) under one project manager, and is dedicated to the development of BASIS, the Lifelong Management Information System (MIS) which monitors the activity of the direct salesforce. As my original interest lay in the implications of IT systems for the organisation as a whole, I selected BASIS after some initial discussion with Lifelong management as a focus for research which would allow me access to both IT staff and those other employees directly influenced by their behaviour. At the same time, looking at BASIS would also allow me to pursue other themes in the Lifelong not directly connected to the IT application itself.

Essentially, the BASIS system covers a number of objectives in Lifelong, providing a form of monitoring of the direct salesforce for revenue forecasting, staff appraisal and regulatory compliance purposes. The system itself is installed on the information systems in all branches, which are not networked but exist as stand-alone servers. BASIS then produces forms for the sales staff to complete with details of the amount of business they have written, etc. These details are then passed on to administrative staff in each sales team for manual input into the system, and for weekly uploading to the main database (held at the Lifelong offices in Oxford). Employees in Oxford check a proportion of this information to make sure it complies with the requirements of the regulators, then much of this transferred to microfiche and sent to a private company in Sri Lanka, who carry out the manual keying-in of information onto databases. This is then returned to the Lifelong head office in manipulable form, collated and produced in aggregate form for the use of senior management and in report form for the use of the branches. The branch reports are intended to be used as a framework for one-to-one meetings between the salesperson and their sales manager each month, for appraisal and ideally motivational purposes.

As this brief overview should make clear, BASIS can be seen to be central to the control of the direct salesforce in Lifelong, and the team involved in the perpetual upgrades to BASIS therefore occupied a privileged position in the IT hierarchy. To examine the application of IT in the control of the workforce in general, I chose to focus on BASIS in Lifelong, concentrating on both the direct salesforce in the branches and the section of Development Services dedicated to BASIS at head office. However, it soon became clear that Delivery Services were also implicated in the operation and support of BASIS to a significant degree, as well as providing a complementary perspective on the changes occurring within Lifelong.

Delivery Services Delivery Services is by far the largest and most wide-ranging department within IT, with over 200 employees in five areas; Systems Delivery, Service Planning, Desktop Implementation, New Service Implementation, and Customer Services. Systems Delivery is a technical area, with 45 staff dedicated to the maintenance of hardware and the mainframe systems. Service Planning had recently been renamed from Capacity and Planning, and had the basic responsibility to ensure there would be is sufficient storage space for incoming information and any planned IT expansion. Desktop Implementation is fairly self-explanatory, with 32 employees responsible for all aspects of the Microsoft Windows desktop, from customising aspects to carrying out upgrades and providing specialist support where required. Apart from technical aspects, however, none of these department had a significant role to play in the development and support of BASIS. The two areas with the greatest involvement in BASIS are New Service Implementation, or more specifically the subsection known as Release Management, and Customer Services.

New Service Implementation (NSI) is divided into two sub-sections of roughly equivalent size, one involved in the technical/hardware issues of putting new servers in place, the other, Release Management, with the responsibility for co-ordinating the release of substantial IT projects. This involves communicating details of the change to concerned parties, which often includes the IT help-desks and other support functions, Service Planning to ensure the system has the capacity to support the new application, Systems Delivery to ensure they have the resources free to install any necessary hardware, and so on. While the 12 employees in this sub-section are all IT-literate to some degree, the crux of the job is more administrative, frequently involving negotiations over scheduling arrangements and prioritising the implementation of different projects. All upgrades and installations which may be done from head office and downloaded to the branches (i.e. those not requiring specific hardware installation) are managed by a specific utility called TIVOLI, although such downloads must be carried out in at specific times (usually outside of office hours and over weekends). The members of NSI not belonging to Release Management tend to travel quite considerably, doing manual installations of hardware in the branches themselves.

Customer Services is a substantial sub-section of Delivery Services which comprises around 70 employees operating from both the London and the Oxford offices. Its main responsibility is the provision of IT support to their 'internal customers' i.e. the whole of Lifelong UK. Similar to Buzzbank, this is split into three 'lines' of support in each main office, although the facilities in the Oxford office are comparatively limited. The first-line support consists of the two Service Desks (i.e. telephone helpdesks), one of which is situated in the London office and one in Oxford. The Response Centres, again in London and Oxford, make up the second line of support, and deal with more complex queries passed on by the Service Desks. The third-line support, Service Management, is rather more complicated; in both London and Oxford, Service Management employees take on the most difficult problems. However, the role of the Service Management staff is not to solve the problems but to bring together related IT specialists from different areas and 'manage' the problem-solving process. The interaction between these three departments is supported and monitored through an IT application called InfoMan, in which the severity of problems must be logged, along with the actions undertaken by the relevant sections.

Without going into all areas of IT in Lifelong, I have tried to give a brief overview of those sections involved in the development of IT systems for the monitoring of Lifelong Assurance direct salesforce. Shortly after I commenced my fieldwork, it became widely known within Lifelong that the IT section was to be entirely restructured. This was not generally referred to with any surprise, as a number of interviewees both within IT and (more often) outside IT were explicit about the archaic standard of the IT throughout the company and the reputation for incompetence and insularity that the IT function as a whole possessed. Increasingly, instances of this lack of competent IT systems came to more general notice; for example, it was revealed (with astonishment) in Marketing Week (25/10/96) that Lifelong did not have a central CIS on its 6 million policy holders. During the period of my research, an IT consultancy was employed to review the IT division and develop a new structure for the function. As a consequence, there was a significant amount of job insecurity, particularly in certain areas of IT, and in this atmosphere, a number of interviewees suddenly became 'too busy' to take part in further interviews.

I will now briefly contextualise the related focus of my empirical work; the Life Assurance division of Lifelong and the direct salesforce in particular.

Lifelong UK: The Life Insurance Division

Unsurprisingly, there had been a significant number of major changes within Lifelong's UK life insurance division in the time immediately preceding my research. Lifelong Assurance found itself relatively unprepared for the boom in the pensions market in the late 1980s, and in sales, the growth placed pressure on the company to recruit large numbers of new staff in a short period of time and to train them very quickly. The first major reorganization took place under Gordon, as a result of which the number of staff in the field was reduced considerably and, according to several sources, the morale of the staff suffered considerable damage. The main effect of this reorganization was described as changing the nature of the salesmen (invariably referred to as masculine); "to transform the much-loved 'man from LL' who calls at peoples' homes to collect premiums and soft-sell new policies into a more aggressive salesman" (Economist 19/3/94). This does not seem to have occurred without some resistance, and reports of "old hands who did not want to be pushier (who) have been ousted from their old jobs or induced to leave the firm" were repeatedly referred to in assessments of Gordon's reign in the media. Nonetheless, this reorganization and cost-cutting was described as having "pleased the City" (FT 24/1/95), and was seen to have prepared Lifelong Assurance well for the disclosure regime introduced in 1995.

This reorganization of the salesforce was to be extended in 1994 by the cancellation of one of the most traditional aspects of the UK life insurance business; the industrial branch policies. As noted, the tradition of the 'man from LL' carrying out door-to-door collections of relatively minor amounts harked back to the 1850s, although it now accounted for less than 2% of Lifelong's business and proved very expensive in comparison with the more modern methods of payment such as direct debit. While existing industrial branch policy holders would still receive their monthly visits, Lifelong announced in October 1994 they would no longer be issuing such policies. Lifelong also claimed that there would be no redundancies among its sales and collection force as a result of the change. Despite this, the image of the 'man from LL' was to be resurrected in 1996 in advertising, possibly in part to combat the loss of faith in Lifelong and in Financial Advisers in general. As explained by Peter McCourt in the annual report, "The Man from LL is a very powerful brand image... The new Man from LL is designed to build on our traditional values of security, reliability and individual service, and to add to the more modern attributes of efficiency, flexibility and investment excellence" (Annual Report 1996: 8).

A further restructuring after the redundancies of the early 1990s occurred in 1995 under McCourt, merging the two Lifelong salesforces to form a single subsidiary, Lifelong UK. The two salesforces were the home service (the direct sales staff), and Lifelong Financial Services, made up of the Independent Financial Advisers. This merger was only to occur at the level of administrative and customer service functions, however; the salesforces were to remain separate. The aim of this, according to Weston, the new Executive Manager of Lifelong UK, was to reduce rivalry between the two salesforces, and to reduce costs through duplication, although he stated that he did not expect any redundancies. Weston is reported to have earned his promotion to heading Lifelong UK by a tough programme of cost-cutting in the home service, reducing costs by £100 million in the three years preceding the merger.

A final point worth mentioning here regards the strategic direction of Lifelong's acquisitions and projected acquisitions in the mid 1990s. As noted, one of the major benefits of the take-over of Independent Life was seen by Lifelong to be the adoption of a force of IFAs. This must be seen in the light of the public disillusionment with direct salespeople after the personal pensions mis-selling scandal of the early 1990s and, indeed, the subsequent conduct of the major life insurance companies in delaying the reimbursal of the victims. While there is little evidence to suggest that IFAs were any less implicated in the pensions mis-selling scandal than direct salesforces, it is the direct salesforces which appear to have borne the brunt of public distrust. Reflecting this, one industry report forecasts that IFAs may take £70 million in business from direct sales forces by 2001 (Financial Adviser, 16/1/97). This swing can be seen, not only in public sympathy but equally in the focus and investment of the major companies, away from the tied, company financial salespeople and towards Independent Financial Advisers. This reflects a number of prevalent beliefs in the industry, including a perceived need for a "multi-channel distribution strategy" and the increased costs of training and monitoring a direct salesforce (Mintel, 1996b).

Conclusion

The fundamental changes in the structure and nature of financial markets in the UK have had wide-ranging implications for both employees and consumers. While deregulation is portrayed as having increased levels of competition and having (finally) ensured effective regulation within a single 'Financial Services' market, the transformation which has occurred runs much deeper than this. The political philosophy of the New Right which underpins the process of deregulation has to a large extent implicated individuals in its project through both their material dependence on the private sector and their subjective reconstruction as 'consumers of financial services'. In banking and, to a lesser degree, life assurance, 'cultural change' has been attempted in many organisations to elicit an aggressively sales-oriented approach from workforces, often at odds with the ingrained paternalistic, 'professional' ethos of the established institutions. Although this change may be seen as instrumental in causing the very damaging pensions mis-selling scandal in life assurance, it does not appear that the scandal has harmed the long-term expansion of the personal pensions market, thanks to continuing state efforts to encourage the private provision of welfare. Hence in both industries, whilst organisations develop operations in adjacent financial sectors, they are also engaged with an attempt to maintain and increase their own market share despite growing competition from other financial institutions.

To this end, information technology has been used in both sectors in an strategic attempt to secure some competitive advantage in circumstances of increased competition. The most visible indication of this has been the enormous job losses due to the automation of numerous back-office operations and the centralisation of many branches, replaced by telephone-based services. The switch from huge mainframes to networks of PCs has reflected the flexibility deemed to be necessary in these deregulated industries, and work systems have been fundamentally restructured around these networks, taking advantage of the surveillance potential of IT. Partly to comply with the requirements of the regulators, a great deal of effort has gone into the creation of both Management Information Systems, to monitor and record the conduct of employees, as well as instantly-accessible Customer Information Systems, leading to the emergence of what is termed 'relationship banking', utilising comprehensive data for more precise marketing and a careful management of customers, linked to the sudden growth in call centres in financial services.

These trends can be seen to support moves towards a more influential role for the IT function in financial institutions of all kinds. In both centralised call-centres and geographically-dispersed sales-forces, at the same time as cultural initiatives have attempted to change the work identity of 'financial services professionals', IT has been applied to control and inscribe a mode of discipline upon employees. The discretion of this rejuvenated IT function, however, is controlled by the disciplinary operation of Business Process Re-Engineering and, in particular, Project Management techniques. At the same time, the expertise and professionalism accredited to IT Project Managers and IT consultancies is to a large extent legitimated by their adherence to the discipline itself in terms of technical knowledge and conduct. Chapters 5 and 6 will examine this process in more detail, with reference to the empirical material in both organisations, and evaluate forms of dissent, deviation or resistance to such changes.

In a similar way, the direct salesforces of life assurance companies are finding themselves in a position of considerable significance in the restructured 'Financial Services' industry of the mid-1990s. The Financial Services Act (and the Social Security Act in particular), boosting the personal pensions market, instigated a rapid increase in the numbers of direct life assurance salespeople employed not only by assurance institutions but by banks and a range of new competitors. The effect of this was to dilute the levels of profits achievable in the rapidly expanding personal pensions market, a blow which coincided with the recession of the early 1990s. Consequently, the number of life assurance salespeople fell as swiftly as it had risen, with companies choosing to sub-contract the risks, to some degree, by balancing their reliance on direct selling with the use of IFAs. The reputation of life assurance selling as a whole was then hit, first by the pensions mis-selling scandal in 1993 and then by the requirements for the disclosure of commissions in 1995 (with particular effect on the direct salesforces, it would appear). However, the negative headlines which recurred throughout the mid-Nineties, particularly as compensation was delayed and fines were publicly imposed, did have the effect of publicising the 'need' for the private position of pensions in the light of the supposed 'crisis' in the UK welfare system. Partly as a consequence, increasing profits and the promise of further opportunities in the provision of welfare under New Labour may account for the increasing number of competitors willing to enter the life assurance industry, including the emergence of direct providers and the growing interest of banks and building societies in 'bancassurance'.

Even by the standards of this turbulent decade for life assurers, the recent history of Lifelong has been particularly dramatic, with a generally poor economic performance exacerbated by the difficult relationship between a controversial CEO and the industry regulators before his resignation in 1995. The 'consolidation' which took place under a new CEO involved a focus on the UK market, and reinforced the aggressive sales ethos that Lifelong attempted to establish in the boom of the late 1980s. I will return to particular aspects of this context again in Chapter 7; for the moment, I would like to highlight two particularly significant influences on the sales staff that I interviewed. The first is that, although this 'change in culture' towards aggressive selling may well have contributed to the company's relatively poor record in terms of pension mis-selling, the need for aggressive selling was nonetheless reinforced by senior management in an attempt to recover in the aftermath of the scandal. Secondly, I would underline that alongside the pressure to sell aggressively, it was clear from unprompted references by Lifelong sales staff that the pensions mis-selling scandal was frequently in their thoughts. It is in the light of this context that the changing modes of control among the Lifelong salesforce will be interpreted in Chapter 7. I will then conclude in Chapter 8 with a general discussion of the parallels and discontinuities between discourses, forms of control and forms of resistance in the IT and sales staff in Buzzbank and Lifelong Assurance.

5 Identity and the Discourse of Culture Management

Using Discourse

In this chapter I will attempt to develop the notion of discourse through engaging with the empirical research conducted within both Buzzbank and Lifelong Assurance. In the course of the research, I have paid particular attention to discourses in various forms, from the physical and structural to textual and verbal examples of discourses, which I understand here as *a socially and historically specific system of assumptions, values and beliefs which materially affects social action and social structure*. The intention below is to critically examine some of the more complex and contentious aspects of *discourse* in the light of empirical work. This involves in the first place an examination of the number and scope of such discourses, distinguishing 'official' discourses, frequently aligned with an 'organisational ideology' (Kunda, 1992), from more unofficial or marginal(ised) discourses. This distinction is drawn, not as a taxonomic definition, but as an heuristic aid, of considerable relevance to the next section where I will discuss the relevance of 'culture management' initiatives, and what will be analysed here as the *discourse* of 'culture management'. Although there are indeed grounds for scepticism regarding much of the more managerialist writing on culture management, I suggest, following Willmott (1993) that the concept cannot be dismissed; instead, organisational 'culture' can be seen as dependent upon the constitution of oppositions through discourse (Parker, 1995). These 'oppositions' may be sanctioned and promoted by management or reproduced independently of managerial intentions; indeed, they may be in direct conflict with managerial objectives. Their importance, however, stems from their instrumental role in the construction of (relatively) stable workplace identities, in line with the relational concept of identity as outlined in Chapter 3.

To illustrate this understanding of culture, I will trace a number of these oppositions in Buzzbank and Lifelong, specifically those which I could discern in the interviews and observation as central to the subjects' constructions of organisational realities. In particular, oppositions are constructed externally - between Buzzbank and TN Banking - as well as internally to Buzzbank - between permanent and contract staff, between 'fire-fighters' and project workers, and so on. In Lifelong, such discursive oppositions are equally important, constructed between the IT function and 'the Business', between IT and the Business Analysts, and from a different perspective, between Head Office and the Branches (despite the fact that the notion of 'culture' does not appear to be used explicitly in Lifelong). It is important to emphasise here, however, that I gradually became aware of the importance of these oppositions to the employees' constructions of organisational reality and identity as I looked for a way to interpret the empirical material; I did not enter the organisations with the specific intention of seeking out such oppositions to bear out this theory. Nonetheless, the notion of oppositions provides a useful way to understand the relationship between identity and discourse, and the place of 'culture management' initiatives in attempts to manipulate the identity of employees. I therefore go on to explore the operation and interaction of such discourses, primarily through the example of *formalisation initiatives in Buzzbank*, emphasising their dynamic and heterogeneous nature. Moreover, I mean to underline the use of 'culture management' as an instrumental form of manipulation through which discourses are rearticulated by managers so that employees may be reconstituted to conform with the latest definition of corporate goals.

At the same time, I do not mean to exaggerate the dominance of formal discourses and culture management initiatives; as noted in Chapter 2, where there is power there is also resistance. I therefore conclude the chapter with an examination of instances of *resistance and subversion*, which question the level of conscious/unconscious adoption of such discourses. My intention is that through such an analysis, not only should a clearer picture evolve of the dynamics at work within the subject organisations, but that a more sophisticated appreciation should evolve of the operation of discourses in work organisations more generally.

Discourse in Buzzbank and Lifelong

The first point to be examined is the extent to which discourses identified through empirical work should be taken to be comprehensive, stable, and universal. There is an abundance of discourses which could be identified through an analysis of the accounts, behaviour and communication among the employees. Issues such as workplace democracy, professionalism, the role of IT staff, and the relationship with the 'parent company', for instance, are a relatively small number of examples of the types of discourse within which employees positioned themselves. The identification and analysis of discourses on my part in such a context should not therefore be taken as final and exclusive - the discourses examined below are those which emerged during my empirical work and appeared to me to hold some importance for employees in their attempts to make sense of their social environment. It is probable and indeed inevitable that there exist numerous other discourses which escaped my notice in conducting the research; as noted in Chapter 1, my research is a subjective rearticulation, *not* an objective reflection, of specific discourses. Furthermore, given the dynamic nature of discourses, were the research conducted at a different time the discourses identified would also have differed. Thus it is important to emphasise here the time-bound and context-bound nature of the specific discourses articulated, and the *inevitable* limitations of my own role and perspective in interpreting, rearticulating and thus transforming these discourses through this book.

Consequently, the relationship between discourses and wider social tendencies is, as noted in previous chapters, rather complicated. The discourses identified within Buzzbank and Lifelong should not be assumed to be universal and generalisable, although many may have resonance outside this specific workplace, and all are likely to interact with other systems of discourses in the home, in the family, and in wider social relations of all forms. By the same token, these discourses are located within societal discourses of such widespread significance that they are often seen as structural forces in modern Western societies, such as those related to capitalism, patriarchy and the like. With regard to this link between power/knowledge discourses and local instances of discourse, Foucault explains that while there is no discontinuity between the two levels, this does not imply that they are homogeneous. Instead, "one must conceive of the double conditioning of a strategy by the specificity of possible tactics, and of tactics by the strategic envelope that makes them work" (Foucault, 1979: 100). Hence it would be exceptional to find that systems of discourse generally prevalent in society, regarding gender relations for instance, were not present in practices, forms of communication and artefacts in Buzzbank and in Lifelong Assurance. An apposite example in this case might be the presence in each organisation of generic disciplinary mechanisms predicated on systems of surveillance, temporal and spatial control of the working day, etc. However, as in any context, these will interact with numerous historically and situationally specific discourses in a relatively fluid fashion, and cannot therefore be 'read off' from such large-scale discursive tendencies.

Furthermore, a distinction will be made between those discourses which have been appropriated and promoted by management, often in quite a conscious, strategic way, as opposed to the 'unofficial' discourses, subjugated and marginalised by officially-sanctioned discourses, drawn on by the employees (and in some instances, the management) in the organisation. The immediate difficulty is finding an adequate term to reflect the former concept, one which does not attribute to it unwarranted coherency nor a monopoly over employees' interpretations of organisational reality. Kunda uses the term 'organisational ideology' to reflect these discourses, comprehensively defining them as "publicly articulated and logically integrated 'reality claims' concerning the company's social nature and the nature of its members, formulated and disseminated by those who claim to speak for 'the company perspective'" (Kunda, 1992: 52). For the sake of brevity, I will also employ the term 'organisational ideology', although used in Kunda's sense rather than a Marxist/Althusserian sense. In adopting this term, it is important to reiterate that this does not imply a coherent, strategic entity; corporate ideology is a relatively fluid, internally contradictory construct, interpreted and articulated in conflicting ways by different managers/departments/divisions at different times to serve different purposes. What the term does offer is a general distinction between strategically-promoted discourse and attempts at ordering organisational reality which occur without the explicit sanction of senior management. Although these forms of discourse are necessarily linked in a complex and dynamic way, an appreciation of strategic attempts at promoting discourses on the part of management and the interaction between these and less formal, often antagonistic, systems of beliefs offers a way out of simplistic conceptualisations of the workplace in terms of control and resistance. Concerted attempts by management to promote and enforce a framework of beliefs and understandings lead the discussion into the field of culture, or more specifically, the discourse of culture management itself.

Culture and the Discourse of Culture Management

The concept of organisational culture is one that has risen to prominence not only in managerial literatures but most strikingly as an everyday, taken-for granted concept drawn on by members at all levels of modern organisations. The unproblematised notion that organisations possess and can be identified as possessing a unitary, definable culture, and that this is amenable to modification and engineering by management is well on the way to assuming a taken-for-granted status in modern discourses. The academic and managerialist writing on culture has focused very much on the identification and potential for manipulation of organisational culture to achieve productivity gains, at the same time as displaying a concern for employees welfare (for example, Pettigrew, 1979; Peters and Waterman, 1982; Deal and Kennedy, 1988, among others). The roots of this specifically managerialist concern with culture lie in a number of fields, including the discourse of human relations and the humanisation of work arising from the integration of psychology into work organisations (see Rose, 1990: 102-118 for an account of this). It is important therefore to put notions of organisational culture in context by tracing the origins and implications of this discourse of culture management.

The theme of organisational culture emerged during the 1980s as a key component of various contemporary managerial discourses, including Total Quality Management (Crosby, 1984), Excellence (Peters and Waterman, 1982), Theory Z (Ouchi, 1981) and more recently, Human Resource Management (Beer and Spector, 1985; Fombrun, Tichy and Devanna, 1984). As is the case for much of the hybrid field of management, the term itself was originally borrowed from another discipline, in this case anthropology. However, as is highlighted in a seminal paper by Linda Smircich (1983), the underlying assumptions and theoretical underpinnings of the concept of culture were, in the main, not included in the managerialist import of the notion of culture; consequently, many of the ongoing debates over 'culture' in anthropological literature have been disregarded in the mainstream management literature.

The key point made by Smircich (1983), picked up with varying degrees of critical awareness by subsequent writers, regarded the distinction between the use of *'culture' as an organisational variable*, similar to 'technology', for instance, or *'culture' as a 'root metaphor'*, "promoting a view of organizations as expressive forms, manifestations of human consciousness" (Smircich, 1983: 347). Here, she draws on the framework proposed by Burrell and Morgan (1979) which differentiates between culture as something an organisation *has*, and culture as something an organisation *is*. In both the comparative management and the corporate culture literature, Smircich identifies a mechanistic, functionalist philosophy which underlies the conceptualisation of culture. In these fields, culture is conceived of as a clear-cut variable of the social world with a distinct potential in "the search for predictable means for organisational control and improved means for organisation management" (Smircich, 1983; 347). She contrasts this with the cognitive, symbolic and structural branches of anthropology, which understand culture as systems of shared knowledge, or shared meaning, or, in the case of structural anthropology, emerging from the inbuilt constraints of the human mind. Leaving aside the debates between these different fields of anthropology, it is interesting to note that these perspectives share the same foci of attention as managerialist work on culture, described by Smircich as "language, symbols, myths, stories, and rituals" (Smircich, 1983; 353). Nonetheless, the uncritical extraction of the concept of 'culture' clearly obscures and ignores a number of related anthropological debates. One consequence of this which Smircich identifies is the ability of managerialist work on culture to pass over the *constructed* nature of social life, and hence to avoid "questioning taken-for-granted assumptions, raising issues of context and meaning, and bringing to the surface underlying values" (Smircich, 1983; 355).

Ten years of literature on culture management later, Willmott (1993) reprises and develops many of these arguments, significantly indicating possible directions for attempts to contextualise the use of 'culture' both socially and economically. He also makes the highly salient point that despite the enormous number of citations of Smircich's article, its critical points had been disregarded in many interpretations of her work. In particular, he highlights the many 'cultural purists' (Willmott 1993: 520) who take up Smircich's implied criticism of the theoretical superficiality of work on corporate culture, while ignoring Smircich's more fundamental conclusion regarding the need for an appraisal of culture to "question the ends it serves" (Smircich, 1983: 355). In part, this is an aim of Willmott's article; to highlight the specific social context in which the *discourse* of culture and culture management evolved. He rejects outright the implication that the rise of corporate culture management can be attributed to the foresight and inspiration of management gurus and the receptiveness of a number of top executives. Instead, Willmott highlights the insecurity of Anglo-American businesses in the face of global threats, as well as the growing moral vacuum in modern Western societies, which serve as preconditions for the emergence of a 'new' management theory, one which promises employees "meaning as well as money" (Peters and Waterman, 1982: 323). He focuses therefore on the existential insecurity of individuals in Western societies, reinforced by economic insecurity, which encourages a reliance on strong institutions, and in the case of work organisations, on a corporate ethos which can bolster individual identity. At the same time, Willmott is careful to situate culture management within the history of struggles over managerial control of the labour process, emphasising that such an approach "repeats and embellishes prescriptions advocated by earlier advocates of post-Taylorist management theory" (Willmott, 1993: 523). He therefore draws on insights from the labour process debate to highlight what are seen as the organisational benefits of a strong corporate culture; the extension of employee control *beyond* direct control by requiring employees to *internalise* corporate values and thus ensuring that self-direction and autonomy will only occur within the constraints of such values.

In the culture management literature, therefore, a key assertion is that the creation of a 'strong' organisational culture is a pre-requisite for a 'committed' and/or flexible workforce, which is in turn necessary for a productive organisation as a whole. One of the most influential writings in this field is Peters and Waterman's *In Search of Excellence* (1982), despite severe criticism from even mainstream managerialist writings (see Guest, 1992 for an overview). Entirely in keeping with Smircich's (1983) description of mechanistic culture management, Peters and Waterman posit a "positive relationship ... between strong cultures and the performance of individual organisations" (Beaumont, 1992). Without oversimplifying the diversity of managerialist literature which has since flourished in this area, there appears to be a general assumption that a key role of management is to define corporate values and inculcate these values and beliefs into the employees themselves at a deep level. The values themselves are often embodied in 'mission statements' or expressions of 'core values', many of which represent either bland ideals (e.g. 'to be the best at...') or generic terms (e.g. 'responsiveness', 'to be proactive', etc.). There are also those, however, which appear relatively specific to particular sectors, such as 'customer care' in service industries, or 'continuous improvement' in manufacturing (although these boundaries are often, and increasingly, blurred). Those corporate values which are prescribed can also be linked to other contemporary discourses in Western society, such as 'customer care' cultures and the rise of consumerism (Ogbonna and Wilkinson, 1990; Du Gay and Salaman, 1992). Indeed, the recent explosion of 'culture talk' in managerial literature can be ascribed to its relationships with other contemporary discourses; drawing, for instance, on the anti-bureaucratic ethos of what Du Gay terms the 'discourse of enterprise' (Du Gay, 1994), which serves to present culture management as an emancipatory force (Willmott, 1993; 527). The burgeoning managerialist literature on culture can also be interpreted as interacting with the spread of 'commitment' in managerial jargon in the 1980s and into the 1990s. Whether or not such 'commitment' can be achieved through such culture management initiatives, it seems clear that the notion has taken hold in managerial discourses that areas of the employee beyond his/her overt behaviour are not only open to manipulation but indeed central to an organisation's ability to cope with competitive threats.

The revolutionary insight of culture management, therefore, is seen in many quarters to be that it is the 'hearts and minds' of employees that must be captured; management initiatives must now "define (the employees') purposes by managing what they *think and feel*, and not just how they behave" (Willmott, 1993: 516, emphasis added). This is brought out in Schein (1985), who differentiates between three levels of culture; overt behaviour and physical manifestations, underlying values of what 'ought to be', and beneath this, taken-for-granted, often tacit, basic assumptions (Ogbonna, 1992; 76). It is claimed that what is novel about culture management approaches is that for the first time, the *subjectivity* of employees is directly and explicitly targeted as a means to achieve corporate ends. As this is defined by Kunda, the organisation fashions and imposes a role for the employee which "includes not only behavioural rules but *articulated guidelines for experience*" (Kunda, 1992: 11, emphasis added). It has been claimed that the novelty of this approach has been overstated (Thompson and McHugh, 1995), as arguably traditional Human Relations and Organisational Psychology approaches had this as a more-or-less tacit aim. Nonetheless, the fact remains that much of the recent management literature explicitly distinguishes between changing behaviour through coercion and/or remuneration, and "changing deep values which, by implication, is changing culture" (Ogbonna, 1992; 76), and wholeheartedly recommends the latter.

Hand in hand with this understanding of organisational culture is the assumption that the 'hearts and minds' of the employees *are* directly accessible through management interventions, and that a strong, unitary culture can therefore be *deliberately* constructed in line with the management's values. The point is raised by numerous critics that the evidence on the effectiveness of such management interventions tends to be anecdotal and often simple propagandising, such that "much of the time even corporate slogans are taken as virtually incontrovertible evidence of culture and effects" (Thompson and McHugh, 1995; 209). The debate over the effectiveness of culture management is far from resolved, with numerous writers from a variety of fields disputing the claims for the concept on both theoretical and practical grounds (see, for instance, Fitzgerald, 1989; Ogbonna and Wilkinson, 1990; Rowlinson *et al*, 1991; Anthony, 1994; Sturdy, 1998, among others). This school of criticism is in the main founded on two key points. Firstly, it is claimed that what is defined by the management as a unitary (therefore 'strong') culture in fact obscures, and in doing so vainly seeks to homogenise, the vast variety of perspectives and networks of beliefs that make up an organisation. Secondly, it is claimed that the hype surrounding culture management hides the practical inability of transparent managerial programmes to effectively manipulate the deeply-held values of employees, and instead interprets instrumental, behavioural consent as a deep change in employees' values and beliefs.

At the same time, however, Willmott warns against the tendency to dismiss culture management as a 'pipe-dream', claiming that it is "too well established and too influential to allow its gurus and corporate devotees to monopolise assessments of its theoretical and practical worth" (Willmott, 1993: 517). There are, indeed, analyses of culture management, such as Kunda's *Engineering Culture* (1992), which are neither theoretically naïve nor empirically impoverished. The next section will engage with both of the above criticisms in the light of the research into the very different implications of 'culture' in Buzzbank and Lifelong Assurance. By focusing on interviews and observation, I hope to avoid interpreting corporate propaganda as evidence of subjective transformation as I assess the extent of change effected through 'culture management'. At the same time, I will use the notion of *discourse* to examine the way culture was articulated in each organisation, before looking at the inconsistencies and conflicts within such models of a 'unitary' culture. I will then discuss the level of 'internalisation' or indeed dissent and resistance to 'culture management' initiatives.

'Culture' in Buzzbank

In Buzzbank, an understanding of culture as unitary, manipulable, deep-seated, and positive was apparent in many interviews with staff at all levels. The majority of interviewees had no hesitation in describing Buzzbank's culture, generally in ways which were almost identical; as open, non-hierarchical, unitary, innovative, etc. The common-sense belief in the existence of a unitary culture, encouraged externally by managerialist literatures and internally by both official and unofficial communications, serve to reinforce this acceptance of a definable 'Buzzbank' culture. Thus management of all levels at Buzzbank appeared to use the term 'culture' very frequently and fluently in interviews, often introducing the term into the discussion themselves to clarify points. The instrumental and mechanistic understanding of culture within Buzzbank became apparent in references made to the acquisition of the Creditable Group, a credit management organisation which provides unsecured loans via retailers. This was transferred from TN Banking to Buzzbank, and this was raised by one manager, Lee, as an example of a cultural problem;

> "We've just acquired a big outfit ... which very much has its TN Banking hat on, and it will be a fairly large challenge to instil Buzzbank values and

culture into them ... I think if they're part of the Buzzbank group they should be encouraged to *buy into* the same philosophies and approach as the rest of the company" (Lee 2: 219, emphasis added).

Culture is seen therefore as relatively manipulable; it can be identified, defined, reproduced, transferred and possibly even imposed, depending on the intentions of management; indeed, Lee's use of the phrase 'buy into' arguably reflects an financially instrumental understanding of culture.

What was interesting here, however, was that when pressed for any examples of literature on Buzzbank culture, in terms of official documentation, all responded that Buzzbank did not produce anything actually *on* their culture. Indeed, none of my contacts could provide, nor had any recollection of, a written definition of Buzzbank's actual culture. At the same time, the official documentation I gathered referred directly to "a banking service with its own systems, *culture* and operating philosophy" (BBIS 1: 1). However, there was no folder, document, or section in any brochure on 'culture' specifically, the nearest equivalent appearing to be the section on "People", defining what "the Buzzbank employee" was "like" (BBIS 4). This section opens with a quote from the CEO which states that "broadly speaking, this company's only long-term assets are its people and the culture in which they operate" (BBIS 4: 1). Throughout, repeated references were made to key employee attributes such as "responsibility towards their customer" (BBIS 4: 2), "efficiency, consistency and a friendly response" (BBIS 4: 1), "leadership and guidance, not interference and instruction" (BBIS 4: 2), etc. What should not be ignored, however, is the extent to which the distinctive 'culture' of Buzzbank is used in communication with the media, PR and direct advertising. In interviews, for instance, the CEO is keen to emphasise the importance of culture, defined as "a set of shared values" (People Management, 10/8/1995). However, in the same interview the CEO refuses to reveal Buzzbank's five 'shared values', claiming that this would compromise the company's 'competitive edge'.

This contradictory position on corporate culture and its management in Buzzbank might be explained by the CEO's public assertion that he;

"deliberately avoids writing down (core values) and circulating the values to all staff for fear it could be counter-productive to formalise them this way" (People Management, 10/8/1995).

This response is backed up by the IT Director Alan's description of the IT division at Buzzbank as "relying on a sort of creeping culture". He explained this approach with a careful smile, referring to the fact that IT staff had a "tendency to be... ahh... a tendency towards cynicism about these things", with a clear implication that he shared this mature scepticism regarding 'culture' initiatives. Within IT, he went on, the company was aware that "people showed commitment in different ways" (Alan: 3), a position reflected in the accounts of a number of employees in the IT division. The deliberately amorphous nature of culture in Buzzbank might be seen as undermining the relevance of the concept. Another reading, however, might point to an intensification of the sense of insecurity engendered in staff attempting to measure up to such indefinite or tacit Buzzbank standards, promoting a *perpetual* process of self-monitoring. The ways in which the discourse of 'culture' is invoked and articulated in an *everyday* sense must therefore be examined in order to assess its specific relevance and implications in Buzzbank.

In interviews and general conversation, then, the concept of culture was commonly used at Buzzbank, at least in interactions with myself as an 'outsider'. The typical description of culture by the permanent, male managers interviewed was that of "a very open culture" (Lee 2: 141), typically followed up by some personal explanation, such as;

> "as a team we're directly in communication with the users ... we have quite a good relationship with a raft of individuals out there" (Lee 1: 200).

Most could describe some aspects of the culture; for instance, the head of IT when asked could reel off "equal status, openness, responsiveness..." (Alan: 3) before trailing off. At lower levels, there were similar examples, such as a middle manager in IT backing up accounts of his actions with reference to Buzzbank culture, explaining "one of its core values is communication" (Lee 1: 222). This general impression of Buzzbank can be contrasted with an alternative view of the 'culture' which was expressed to me in casual conversation with, significantly, a female contractor, Debbie. Here, she directly contradicted the emphasis on openness and communication, giving this as a reason why she would not be staying long despite offers of a lengthy contract;

> "the lack of communication between the departments and teams here means they can't solve anyone's problems, and that's what they're here to do" (Debbie: OBS1: 3).

It seems likely that this view was related in part to her status as contractor, therefore outsider to Buzzbank, and in part to her status as female in a predominantly masculine department (and profession). Although this is only one perspective, the statement points clearly to alternative interpretations of the company's purportedly unitary culture, one not expressed directly to me by permanent, male employees in the IT division. The diversity of interpretations not only undermines the notion of culture as unitary and unifying, but points to the importance of '*difference*' to the construction of a 'culture', which I will develop below. First, however, I will examine the very different understanding of culture within Lifelong.

A Lifelong 'Culture'?

The most striking contrast to emerge between the interviews and document analysis conducted at Lifelong and those at Buzzbank was the *absence* of the notion of 'culture' in the accounts of the Lifelong employees. While the term 'culture' was readily and frequently utilised in Buzzbank to convey aspects of working there, not a single employee so much as mentioned the word 'culture' in my discussions at Lifelong. This may reflect to some extent a lack of focus among Lifelong senior management on culture management initiatives, in clear contrast to both formal and informal efforts in this area at Buzzbank. This should not however be seen as excluding the concept of *discourse* from an understanding of developments within Lifelong, as 'culture management' is merely one articulation of discursive techniques of control. Nor does this mean that management do not attempt to manipulate meaning and sense-making within and around the organisation to further what are defined as organisational goals.

It does, nonetheless, imply a slightly different situation where discourses evolve without explicit and openly recognised attempts to manage them through the construction of a unitary corporate 'culture'. While the apparent absence of cultural initiatives is a strategic managerial decision (or lack of decision), it does not imply that generic work identities are not constructed, albeit in a more limited form than in Buzzbank. The size of Lifelong as a company, its geographical dispersion and the diversity of the departments and roles within the company all play a part in the establishment and differentiation of these identities. As a consequence, even general conceptions of Lifelong Assurance as an organisation proved very difficult to discern in the interviews, and there was only one unprompted reference to what Lifelong was perceived to be 'like', one manager's very brief description of Lifelong as "having always been a very open company - we certainly try hard!" (Simon: 563).

Instead of a immediate notion of a Lifelong 'culture', then, each division appeared to have its own set of oppositions, which may or may not correspond with those constructed and drawn upon elsewhere in the organisation. Similar to the discourses perceptible within Buzzbank, the discourses represented in the accounts of Lifelong staff also appear linked to their constructions of a valuable and valued identity within the work organisation. As in Buzzbank, although certain discourses appeared to have greater prominence in employees' understandings and representations, those examined below should in no way be taken to be a final and comprehensive analysis of conflicting discourses constitutive of employees' identities. Numerous oppositions can be envisaged other than those analysed below, such as those implied in general discussions with staff, including the antagonism between particular Lifelong sites (London and Swindon, in particular) and between sections of departments themselves. However, through research conducted in a number of areas of Lifelong, certain discursive oppositions were discerned to have particular importance in employees' accounts, and these are examined below. Such discourses include relations between the salespersons in the field and Lifelong head office, and between the IT department and 'the Business', both of which play significant parts in the construction of the identities of employees and in framing their attempts to make sense of organisational processes.

Culture, Difference and Oppositions

This constructed opposition seemed to point towards a theoretical connection with *relational concepts of identity*, derived in the main from the influence of linguistics and post-structuralism in the social sciences. From this perspective, as noted in Chapter 3, identity should be understood as relational, constructed through setting up oppositions between *the subject* and that which he/she is not i.e. '*the Other*'. As noted, it is through the construction of *difference* that meaning is formed, and that identity, the attribution of certain characteristics to one's self, depends on systems of difference which can be considered as discourses. While such discourses are not deterministically imposed on individuals, nor fundamentally connected as an omnipresent 'dominant ideology', neither is the individual free to select and conform to given discourses at will; a plurality of discourses operate on and through an individual at any time, all of which are resistible and transformable in their articulation. However, the objectification of the individual by a range of disciplines in modern society exacerbates insecurity and anxiety, and lays him/her open to discourses which offer relative security and stability through the construction of such oppositions which maintain the subject's privileged position.

What I mean to highlight in the next section is the *strategic* use of such oppositions on the part of senior management in order to build a sense of a unitary culture within organisations. Thus Garsten refers to a process whereby "directives from headquarters or top management set the framework within which the construction of meaning can take place, and provide *reference points* for organising" (1994: vi). The clearest example occurred within Buzzbank, where the construction of an identity for their 'parent' company, TN Banking, was but one external 'reference point', setting up an opposition to reinforce understandings of a (superior) organisational culture specific to Buzzbank. Indeed, it has been suggested that "the 'culture' of an organisation is constituted by, and through, these oppositions" (Parker, 1995: 542). At the same time, identity is also constructed in a less strategic sense through the operation of alternative discourses, which interact constructively and frequently operate to resist or transform others. What I will highlight below, then, is the construction and maintenance of a variety of oppositions in each organisation, which point to a fragmented and contested range of 'cultures' corresponding to the diversity of discourses in each site.

Oppositions in Buzzbank

Buzzbank and TN Banking

A key element in the identities and perspectives of Buzzbank staff was the opposition constructed between TN Banking and Buzzbank. Despite close links on a strategic and day-to-day basis, significant rivalry and animosity existed between employees of the two organisations. The relationship is further complicated by the contrasting cultures attributed to each company by staff, made explicit by one manager in Buzzbank who explained that "the cultures are very different - comparing cultures is chalk and cheese, really" (Lee 2: 139). The attention paid to these issues in one form or another at Buzzbank testifies to the structuring of discourses in terms of culture; for instance, the issue of building a unitary culture was highlighted as the key concern when the second site was opened, with the slogan 'One Mission: Two Sites' widely promoted (Lee 2: 214).

What was particularly interesting was that Buzzbank staff appeared *unable* to define the culture of Buzzbank without setting this against their perception of the culture at TN Banking. Thus the culture of Buzzbank was described by interviewees as "youthful, positive to change, willing to experiment - a real sense we can go a lot further" (Jack 1: 28), and "a bit of a chick" (Lee 2: 172). This is invariably contrasted with a depiction of TN Banking as "bureaucratic" (Ian 1: 118), "straight-laced, three-piece-suit, you know, 'nod and a wink'-type outfit" (Lee 2: 140), and "a bit of a dinosaur" (Lee 2: 172), often in the same breath. Interestingly, this has a very clear parallel with the situation reported in a study of Apple

Computing (Garsten, 1994). Here it is claimed that Apple strategically used the image of IBM as monolithic and corporate to serve as an orientation point to position Apple, in the perceptions of both staff and customers, as a democratic, entrepreneurial culture.[9] The tension between Buzzbank and TN Banking is all the more striking as, unlike the fierce competition between Apple and IBM, these companies were supposed to be complementary operations within the same group. In the construction of a relatively cohesive identity for Buzzbank, a forceful opposition had developed between the two interdependent organisations.

The perceived differences between TN Banking and Buzzbank were raised by the interviewee in almost every interview, often without any reference to TN Banking by myself, and discord is evident in many areas in Buzzbank where the relationship with TN Banking is more direct. What should be emphasised here is that such differences are not represented in neutral terms by Buzzbank staff; there is a very strong impression of the superiority of Buzzbank's approach over TN Banking's. The negative portrayal of TN Banking values is made explicit in many statements by Buzzbank staff at all levels; thus in response to a general question about the open-plan office, Lee replied;

> "I mean, on the whole, it's a very good environment - it's better than TN Banking!" (Lee 2: 160)

Another IT manager, Martin, was more specific on the perceived shortcomings of TN Banking (and by implication the superiority of Buzzbank's approach).

> "The problem with TN Banking is ... there are a lot of people who've been there a long time, and as such there's a lot of deadwood, really. You know 'That's the way we've always done it, that's the way we'll continue to do it', that sort of thing, and you know, that might not be the best way to do it, that might be why you're in the problems you're in now" (Martin: 206).

This criticism was not restricted to the middle management at Buzzbank, however. Jack, a head of department who had recently moved from TN Banking was equally disparaging;

---

[9] As is powerfully represented in the famous '1984' advert, in which a huge screen of Big Brother, depicting the domination of IBM (at the time), is shattered by a hammer hurled by a young woman running through the ranks of grey-clad 'citizens'; Apple's 'spirit of independence'.

"I've learnt more about banking in ten-twelve months here than in twelve years in TN Banking - it's a different world" (Jack 1: 26).

This hostility does not appear to be one-sided; several of the heads of departments attest to a belief among parts of TN Banking that Buzzbank needs to be reined in. Another head of department who had also been transferred from TN Banking explained with obvious satisfaction;

"we were here to bring Buzzbank back in line and if anything we've gone the other way ... we're seen by colleagues in TN Banking as having betrayed them" (Angus 1: 170).

The continued dependence by Buzzbank on the IT systems of TN Banking appears to be a particularly sensitive area, and one which caused some resentment among Buzzbank employees. Certain situations brought this dependence into sharp focus, such as changes made by TN Banking and imposed on Buzzbank. One major source of change, for instance, was what Lee resentfully described in unusually autocratic terms as a "group dictat" from TN Banking, "saying 'Get yourselves off the existing platform'" (Lee 1: 2), which caused a number of large-scale changes in the department. To return to the Apple-IBM relationship, it is noted by Garsten that while recent strategic alliances between the two companies have complicated Apple's representation of IBM as their nemesis, this has not put an end to Apple management's continuing use of this opposition to "stag(e) a unique corporate culture" (Garsten, 1994: 12). Tensions became evident in my own empirical work when I was dissuaded from researching an IT project at Buzzbank which had been delayed for some considerable time while waiting for TN Banking support. After initial consent by senior management in Buzzbank, I was later informed indirectly that it was likely to unearth difficult political situations, and I would not be able to pursue this interest, which seemed to attest to the somewhat volatile state of inter-company relations. Overall, then, the relationship between employees in TN Banking and Buzzbank may be seen as characterised by rivalry, a somewhat strained interdependency and perceptions of a (slightly) veiled antipathy.

What I aim to emphasise here, however, is not merely the tension between TN Banking and Buzzbank but rather the construction of contrasting organisational identities by employees of Buzzbank at least, and quite possibly on the part of TN Banking employees also. It should be stressed at this point that these discursive oppositions need not be interpreted as *either* promoted by management *or* emerging independently of/in spite of attempts at culture management. At all times, the *interaction* between 'organisational ideology' and 'embedded' discourses must be emphasised, and the distinction should be seen to be, in many senses, of heuristic value only. No clear and sharp distinction is possible in referring to the dynamic operation of a multiple discourses in any setting. At the same time, this should not be taken to imply that discourses cannot be differentiated with regard to certain criteria, including the level to which they become *embedded* in subjects, or the level of conscious, strategic intent behind their propagation as a 'culture'. The discourses which may be identified with Buzzbank's organisational ideology tend to be articulated around the discourse of corporate culture and culture management. Nonetheless, the actions of senior and middle management throughout my research appeared instrumental to the reproduction and propagation of the opposition with TN Banking, regardless of the strategic intent behind their actions.

Insofar as it can be seen as a mainstay of the identities of Buzzbank employees, then, the importance of Buzzbank/TN Banking tension is very clear. However, this should not obscure the numerous other oppositions which are crucial in constituting the identities of members of any number of subgroups within Buzzbank. Even within the IT department, there are numerous examples of such oppositions, evident in both the research interviews and the day-to-day interactions observed. The discursive oppositions examined below are not apparently congruent with the strategic aims of Buzzbank, and not directly traceable to the efforts of the senior management engaged explicitly or implicitly with the construction of an organisational ideology. Nonetheless, each opposition examined below appears *embedded* in the subjectivities of IT staff to a greater or lesser extent and thus framing their understandings, not only of Buzzbank but of the world more widely.

Permanent Staff and Contractors

One clear example of such oppositions was the differentiation of permanent staff at Buzzbank from contractors and temporary staff. Within the IT department, there were a relatively small number of contractors employed in purportedly specialist roles on short-term (3 to 6 month) contracts, either working alongside permanent staff or in a specialist project team. There appeared to be considerable resentment and insecurity among the permanent staff, mainly directed against management for "trying to buy-in experience instead of taking on staff and training them up" (Dan: OBS1: 8). This tension between the groups was considerably heightened by the widespread knowledge that the contractors were paid significantly more than permanent staff; one contractor admitted when no permanent colleagues were within earshot to being embarrassed to be sitting around doing nothing when she was paid almost twice as much as her permanent supervisor (Debbie: OBS1: 3). This tension was frequently evident in the banter between contractors and permanent staff. For example, in a typical distraction from their duties, Debbie, a contractor, and her permanent supervisor, Dan, spent a few minutes showing off the short-cuts on the keyboards that they knew, each claiming that theirs were faster. When Debbie accepted that one of her supervisor's short-cuts was more useful, Dan clearly appreciated the opportunity to make a number of jibes about Debbie being "paid a fortune when you know nothing!". Debbie's good-humoured agreement reflected both her discomfort at the imbalance in pay, and equally the usefulness of humour in giving the impression of redressing the imbalance and relieving the tension.

The same tension is perceptible in the telling of certain stories by permanent staff. At one point, Dan related to me a story, in the presence of Debbie, regarding a firm of contractors who offered to fit PC servers in vertical cases for what his incredulous tone implied was the exorbitant cost of £60 000. He said that the permanent staff fitted the cases themselves instead, "it was glorified Meccano really", and it cost nowhere near £60 000. Debbie objected in the defence of the contractors that it must have cost thereabouts, and Dan replied scornfully "What, *three* of us working for a *year*? You must be joking!". This story can be read as a defence of Dan's identity, based on the capacities and value of permanent staff ('us') compared to the contractors, particularly in the light of the threat they pose to his promotion prospects. The fact that Dan and Debbie had earlier discussed the difference between Dan's £20 000 salary and Debbie's £30 000 plus adds spice to this exchange; Dan's resentment of the difference, carefully concealed in the earlier discussion, now showed through.

In contrast, the sense of a worthwhile workplace identity is reinforced by Dan's efforts to differentiate himself as PC Support officer from other, implied inferior, groups among Buzzbank, such as the low-grade temporary staff (who lack the status of the contractors) and particularly the Banking Representatives, or BRs. Dan's view of these was unequivocal;

Debbie: "So what are the BR's like?"
Dan: "Lowlifes. It's not a job I'd do myself"
Debbie: "Why's that?"
Dan: "They probably enjoy the first few weeks - they do all the training and they get them all pumped up about the job. Then they start the proper job and most of them don't last more than a few months... the pressure of the job, they have to take days off just through the stress, answering the phones and taking the shit non-stop..." (Dan: OBS1: 2)

This opinion of BRs appeared relatively widespread, although the officially-sanctioned view was considerable more appreciative. In casual discussions with another member of staff in the Commerce department, he at first declared his admiration for the BRs, who he described as the "heart and soul" of Buzzbank. Later, however, when the conversation became more informal, he stated he "couldn't imagine how anyone could do that job, taking the shit, getting paid bugger all..." (OBS1: 3). Hence there appeared to be a clear hierarchy, at least in terms of each employee's conception of his/her own identity, an identity constructed in opposition to what are perceived to be other groups within the organisation.

Fire-fighting and Project Work

Another dualistic construct involves the differentiation of those engaged in project work from those on permanent call, the 'fire-fighters'. Indeed, on arriving for my first spell of observation within the organisation, this was the first distinction used to distinguish for me the different functions of IT Operations. The heroic and quite dramatic language used by Dan to describe the role of PC Support seemed quite significant; PC Support was described as a "firewall" which allowed other members of PC Services to work undisturbed on projects. (Dan: OBS1: 1). The members of the PC Support team appeared to resent the recent expansion of PC Support's responsibilities in this area. It was claimed by team members that the helpdesk lacked the knowledge to fulfil their role as the "first line of defence", and that the technical support team lacked the practical knowledge to fulfil their role as "second line of defence", so the PC Support had been forced to change from a "third line of defence" to handling the vast majority of PC problems. This change in responsibility appeared to raise significant issues regarding status,

This situation appears to have caused a significant amount of ambiguity, even tension, in the PC Support staff. On the one hand, many of the IT Operations staff professed that they preferred the operational, fire-fighting side of IT to the more project-based work of IT Applications. Such assertions tend to employ generally similar heroic imagery; for example, the Head of IT Operations claimed;

"Personally, I prefer working in this environment, I'm far more of a coal-face man, keeping the ship running... Yeah, I love it!" (Jack 2: 350).

The use of masculine metaphors, particularly those derived from traditionally masculine manual occupations such as coal-mining and seafaring, is commonplace in interviews with IT staff in both organisations.

In many cases, the context of such references to "grinding the wheel", "forging a path" (Lee 2: 74) and similar heroic activities imply their importance as attempts by male PC Support staff to validate work perceived to be secondary and inferior within the organisation.

This denigration of IT support appears linked to the valuation of autonomy and ownership in IT, and the rarity of this in the support function. For instance, while strolling back after successfully resolving a PC problem, Dan explained that what he enjoyed about the job was;

"the feeling of satisfaction from solving a problem, you know, understanding it and resolving the difficulty..."

However, he immediately followed this up by complaining;

"...anyway, most of the time the job is taken away from you - someone from another department walks in and takes it after you've spent hours and you're like - 'Great!' (sarcastically)" (Dan: OBS1: 5).

These statements by PC Support staff explaining the positive aspects of their position can be seen to be closely linked with attempts to inflate the worth of their role and by implication to bolster their work identity. The constant re-emphasis of this does seem to indicate a level of insecurity and tension. This tension can also be discerned in a number of references made to the other side of the department; the project-based workers. Dan, for example, joked during my shadowing of him;

"Lucky you're not shadowing the IT (Development) Team - watching them sleep, more like! No, I don't mean that...!" (Dan: OBS1: 1).

This mild resentment was not restricted to the lower levels of the hierarchy; elsewhere, the Head of IT Operations stated rather bitterly while chatting at the end of an interview;

"Oh yeah, we're the hamsters on the wheel, we have to keep the bloody wheel turning... It's fine for these guys (IT Applications), they can down tools and it doesn't have too much impact, but if I say to my guys 'Okay, we won't answer the phones for half an hour', it all grinds to a halt" (Jack 2: 341).

The implication in many defences of employees' support roles, which becomes more explicit in references to the project teams, is that many perceive a hierarchy of work roles related to the length of undertaking and level of autonomy, such that fire-fighting is accorded a lower status than project work. Hence Angus, the head of IT Applications describes himself as;

> "luckier than most in that we don't have operational responsibilities in here at all, it's all project work" (Angus 2: 282).

Similarly, Ian of the IT Development team within IT Applications described his recent promotion and the changes in the IT Development team's responsibilities in terms of "moving on to look at more sort-of long-term goals" (Ian 1: 31). This also appeared to be related to the extension of the Strategic Plan leading to the increased bureaucratisation of several functions of IT Operations and the growing formalisation of project work, a point which will be developed in the next chapter. For the time being, it will suffice to propose this project work/fire-fighting opposition as another resource drawn upon to reaffirm identity, of particular relevance to the fire-fighters given the symbolic subservience of their position.

Oppositions in Lifelong

IT and 'the Business'

In the Lifelong IT section, based in the London branch, the main distinction drawn upon in the employees' accounts of processes and changes affecting them was between IT as a department and what they termed 'the Business'. The Business appears to be constructed by IT staff as the senior and middle management of non-IT related departments at Lifelong Head Office, although in discussions the references are often unspecific, sometimes appearing to mean the entire organisation outside of the IT department. However, in their descriptions of what their job entails, the IT staff interviewed refer to the Business as a unitary entity. Thus Rick, the head of Service Management tended to describe staff as being in "Delivery Services, Development Services, Technical Services (the other sections of IT) or the Business" (Rick: 480), and referred to the need to inform "affected-stroke-interested parties in Delivery / Technical / Development Services *and* the Business" (Rick: 41). In terms of the relationship between IT staff and other organisational members, IT managers repeatedly invoked the Business as a unitary article, almost as a subject. Thus managers stated that "(the Helpdesk staff) might go back to the Business and say..." (Patrick: 539), or "(Helpdesk staff) also ask the Business, who report (the problem), what the current impact is" (Rick: 326). There is, however, evidence that IT staff were to some extent aware of the complexity encapsulated in the term 'the Business', one describing a report which "will go out to the Business, which is pretty wide, obviously" (Rick: 239). Nonetheless, in terms of behaviour, it seems that IT staff felt that 'the Business' can be treated as a cohesive unit, even to the extent that they almost ascribed a personality to 'the Business' in some accounts of organisational processes, such as when one manager complained;

"at the end of the day, the Business is shouting 'We want our system back! We need this to work! Blahblahblah...!'" (Rick: 573).

The opposition between IT and the Business is also implicit in the role of National Sales Operations (NSO), whose Business Analysts effectively act as intermediaries between the rest of Lifelong and the IT department. The role of the Business Analysts was described by Patrick, the Head of the IT Response Centre, as;

"a key one... (they) act as *a buffer between the Business and technology in general*, who make sure that the Business define their requirements, that they know what's coming along, that they're trained now to be sure they'll be able to deliver..." (Patrick: 51, emphasis added).

Managers in NSO, occupying this transitional role in the gap between IT and the organisation as a whole, also applied the 'Business'/IT opposition in their accounts of developments in Lifelong, and seemed to position themselves on the Business side; thus describing a new application, Simon explained that;

"our project managers on the Business side were new to the area, and on the IT side this was a complete new concept... er... complex... er... of getting information from elsewhere" (Simon: 66).

The role of NSO and of the project managers proved to be of central importance, particularly in power struggles between IT and other parts of Lifelong, a point that will be developed more fully in Chapter 6.

Linked to this perception of the IT/Business opposition is a general feeling that in this relationship, 'the Business' occupied the dominant position and IT staff of all departments held a secondary and reactive 'service' role. This became most evident in explanations of the agencies which operate between 'the Business' and IT; in particular, National Sales Operations and Release Management. Thus Patrick, attempting to defend Release Management's influence on implementation decisions, stated rather unconvincingly;

"Release Management? ... I think they obviously get told from the Business side that they want this system, so it's a sort of *fait accompli* in that respect, but then the way it's released, there's lots and lots of things that they can help with..." (Patrick: 434).

This perceived dominance of 'the Business' over IT extended beyond the intermediary departments; Patrick went on to illustrate his own department's reactive position, saying;

"the Release Management area should be the key one to make sure that Delivery Services can handle what the Business wants it to handle... it's almost like it's vetted and knocked into shape before it hits us" (Patrick: 438).

Hence in the Delivery Services area, IT was seen as subservient to the demands of the Business as a whole and furthermore, as relying on 'buffer' agencies like NSO and Release Management to protect it to some extent from the demands of 'the Business'. This was backed up by Sue, a manager in one of these buffer agencies, Release Management, who explained reluctantly, after some thought;

"I think the biggest difficulty (in my job) is er the Business ... like basically they want everything like yesterday, it's quite difficult sometimes 'cos they think we're just being awkward when we say 'No we can't cover this' and it's getting them to accept the sort of constraints that we've actually got" (Sue: 328).

The IT-Business opposition can thus be seen as a key construction in the attempts of IT staff to make sense of organisational processes. Although *severe* resentment was not apparent in the interviews conducted by myself, most interviewees within IT would attribute a certain number of problematic characteristics to 'the Business' as an entity. Without overstating the stereotype, the general conception among IT staff was of a wider organisation, 'the Business', which operated as a more or less coherent entity, and stood in a dominant position with regard to their own functions. 'The Business' was thus seen as self-centred and impatient, an impatience exacerbated by its ignorance in most technical matters, and consequently unable/unwilling to appreciate the 'facts' as supplied by IT staff. Nonetheless, a certain amount of tact was apparent in IT employees' references to IT-Business relations. This seems to reflect the general appreciation that the Business was very clearly in the dominant position and IT's function in Lifelong therefore conformed to the traditional passive support role. This was reinforced by the relationship between the IT function and their main contact as regards IT development, NSO. However, for the Business Analysts in NSO, this was not the key opposition within the Lifelong. Although from the perspective of the IT department, difference is constructed around the IT/Business opposition, the Business Analysts in NSO structure their understandings on the tensions between Head Office and the Branches, an opposition to be examined below.

Head Office and the Branches

In discussions with branch staff, the opposition between IT and NSO or 'the Business' was not seen as central - indeed, many outside Head Office did not even perceive a distinction here. Instead, the key issue raised concerned the tension between the central management (generally based in London and Reading) and the regional management and sales-forces, i.e. the tied agents, sales managers and branch managers. Although this will be dealt with in some detail in Chapter 7, this opposition merits some discussion here to emphasise the diverse ways in which these oppositions are constructed within one organisation. In this case, some of the antagonism may be ascribed to the geographical distance and lack of direct contact between the salesforce and Lifelong Head Office. Instead, much of the relationship between the centre and the salesforce is structured around the surveillance and reward system embodied in BASIS, an IT-based Management Information System, as well as through the wider systems of direct managerial accountability and appraisal. The way Lifelong senior management were perceived at the branches was consequently rather contradictory; the appreciation of the considerable financial benefits the company offered was tempered by a recognition of the basic commercial exchange fundamental to the relationship, in that the salesmen earn the company X amount of money and receive a proportion of X back in salary and particularly in bonuses.

Beyond this, there was considerable (although variable) resentment at the constraints imposed via BASIS, and most of all, the pressure of the paperwork; thus one salesman, describing recent changes, explained;

> "it's really just a more streamlined sales organisation... - but the paperwork is absolutely bloody awful! (laughs)" (Brian 1: 105).

Indeed, the level of conformity to BASIS as a Management Information system was variable, as is evident in the accounts of both branch managers and sales staff, much seeming to depend on the attitude of the Branch Manager him/herself. Thus Ken, a Branch Manager, claimed that for at least one element of BASIS,

"...we're still getting the guys to note them and fill in the sheets, but loads of other branches just don't bother any more..." (Ken: 131).

His explanation for this change sums up the impression given in several other interviews;

"a hell of a lot of the guys just aren't interested, basically - they just want to get on with the job and they see it as a pain in the arse going through all this information..." (Ken: 176).[10]

From the perspective of the sales force, then, no distinction was drawn between the different functions of Head Office; indeed, Denise, a Financial Consultant, declared unhappily, to general assent, that;

"We've got no idea what goes on down there - I mean, we've really got no idea at all what they do" (Denise: 429).

This lack of understanding is one element of a general feeling of resentment at Head Office's ignorance of the realities of work 'out in the field'; thus Head Office staff were portrayed, with varying amounts of animosity, as petty bureaucrats, fixated on minor details and with little appreciation of how to aid their sales-force's efforts. This may be accounted for in a number of ways, not least the structuring of the salesforce-Head Office relationship around BASIS, and Head Office's role as enforcer of the demands of the statutory regulators. When asked directly, however, this resentment tended to be accounted for by branch employees as the constraints of bureaucracy clashing with the natural autonomy of the sales*man* (*sic*). Thus Ken explained;

"the guys don't like being monitored (...) I mean, they're in sales to be salesmen, they don't want to be in some clerical job (...) They want to be in charge of their own destiny, their future!" (Ken: 261).

The construction of the salesperson will be examined in Chapter 7 in the light of a more protracted discussion of masculinity and surveillance. For the moment, it will suffice to highlight this as a further opposition, constructed *within* Lifelong, which contributes towards the salesforce's conception of its own identity. At the same time, this is merely one aspect;

---

[10] While one reading of this subversion might be to see it as simple (and laudable) resistance to control in the workplace, the implications of this in terms of avoidance of industry regulations, customer exploitation, etc, present a much more complex picture of such behaviour.

there also appeared to be some *outside* agencies which were discursively constituted and utilised to serve as orientation points in salespersons identity construction. These may be seen as much closer to attempts to construct an organisational ideology identified in Buzzbank; for example, a significant amount of effort had been expended by the company to discard the staid image of Industrial Branches, and, internally, training, recruitment and redundancies had all been deployed to reconstitute the old IB premium collectors as a focused and incentive-driven salesforce. The antiquated, unmotivated 'Man from LL' was brought up in a number of interviews, usually to contrast with the perceived sophistication of the present practices, training procedures, information systems, etc. It is interesting to note that this is slightly different from other discursive oppositions in that in many ways this is a cross-temporal discursive construction. Moreover, it also provides an insight into references to what were seen by Lifelong sales-staff as 'unreconstructed' areas of contemporary financial services, such as the banks, which were criticised for unsystematic and suboptimal exploitation of their customer base, or "cherry-picking" (Jonathan 1: 533).

The Lifelong salesforce, therefore, can be understood as constructing and continually reaffirming an identity based on discursive oppositions which may be emergent, strategically encouraged by Lifelong senior management or founded in enduring masculinist discourses in sales (which will be discussed in more detail in Chapter 7). The sales-force provides a key example of how such oppositions, constructed discursively, become *embedded* in the subjectivity of the employees themselves. Equally, the complexity of these discourses and their interpretation/internalisation thwart simple predictions regarding their implications. The next section will examine ways in which such oppositions are reproduced and implications for the notion of 'culture'.

Discourse, Difference and Culture

The first observation to be drawn from the oppositions outlined above is to reinforce the pluralist view of the organisation, reflecting "the great likelihood that there are multiple organisation subcultures, or even countercultures, competing to define the nature of situations within organisational boundaries" (Smircich, 1983: 346). However, such oppositions should not be understood as merely demarcating classificatory subsets for the academic dissection of the organisation as a whole; such that an individual's identity can be categorised as that of a 'male, white, permanent, PC support officer', for example, or a 'female, white, contracted, network supervisor'. Those oppositions central to the discursive construction of identities in the workplace are *actively* drawn upon by employees to combat insecurity by bolstering a sense of a worthwhile and valued identity. Moreover, as will be seen below, these oppositions are the constant focus of re-negotiation and re-interpretation in the day-to-day interactions of the employees.

The complexities of such a dynamic and heterogeneous concept of discourses can be directly contrasted with the notion of a unitary, manipulable culture proposed by much managerialist literature. The danger, specifically, is that the use of 'culture' as a concept means that "what tends to be overlooked is the dynamic and precarious process in which culture is constructed and deconstructed" (Knights and Willmott, 1987: 42). To emphasise this, the approach taken draws on the permeable distinction outlined above between discourses identified with the organisational ideology and unofficial, emergent discourses. In the first case, discourses are explicitly and implicitly reinforced by official communication to the staff and symbolic behaviour, through presentations, internal memos/circulars, etc. Furthermore, discourses promoted via the advertising and PR of the organisations also necessarily have implications for employees, not least because employees are also consumers in the wider sense. This is particularly true in Buzzbank, where it is compulsory for Buzzbank employees to bank with Buzzbank. Having said this, the discrepancy between external image and what is perceived as internal 'reality' by staff can give rise to cynicism on the part of employees; for instance, one Section Manager, Martin, explained;

> "It's not a case of 'We've always got to be the latest with technology.' *Customer facing* we do, but behind the scenes, if a five- or ten-year-old application will do (...) then what's the point of fixing it if it's not broken?" (Martin: 86),

in clear contrast to the technocratic image presented in Buzzbank's PR literature,

> "ensuring that customers benefit from the most up-to-date systems" (BBIS 6: 1).

Moreover, such discourses were deliberately yet informally encouraged through the everyday actions and informal communication of management; examples of this might be the symbolic reward of certain behaviour among employees, or the forms of humour in everyday conversation between managers and employees. The explicit nature of the discourse of culture in Buzzbank should not obscure the discursive construction of an organisational ideology in Lifelong. Furthermore, the more or less deliberate construction of such a system of meaning should be seen as neither 'natural' nor engineered, but as serving certain managerial interests while frustrating others, and not amenable to direct or simple manipulation.

Thus at the same time, these discourses interact with those discourses which are *embedded* in the subjectivities of Buzzbank employees. These latter oppositions (e.g. contractors versus permanent staff, project workers versus fire-fighters, sales-force versus Head Office) do not appear to have been constructed in any strategic or deliberate way by management (although this is obviously difficult to gauge). However, they may well be reinforced by managerial behaviour, not only in terms of intentionally symbolic action and explicit directives but also in terms of the unpredictability of employee interpretations of management behaviour. These discourses can be seen as a relatively autonomous set of beliefs held by the staff of Buzzbank and Lifelong more generally; examples of these might also include notions of autonomy or creativity thought to be appropriate to IT professionals, or assumptions regarding the relative competence of contract workers. The constitutive function of discourse is of relevance here, in that many such discourses become integral to and indeed contribute towards the constitution of the identity of many of the employees themselves. Thus processes through which this might occur include storytelling, symbolic behaviour, humour, signs, the decoration and design of personal space, as well as more subliminal instances of discourses; discourses embodied in language, space, interactions, etc.

In short, then, what I have attempted to convey in this section is the effect of participation in and observation of communication and behaviour of all kinds, which serves to instil and reinforce within the individual employee the discourses appropriate to his/her position. Identity is fundamental to the rearticulation and reproduction of such discourses in terms of conduct and communication. Hence 'culture' is mobilised within Buzzbank so as to reinforce a unitary, and mutually supportive notion of an appropriate and worthwhile identity. It is important to recognise that part of the project of invoking 'culture' is to reify such understandings, by obscuring the "dynamic and precarious process by which culture is constructed" (Knights and Willmott, 1987: 42). Nonetheless, even within Buzzbank the organisation culture initiatives have had variable effects. What I would emphasise is that the construction of oppositions is a central element of this process, which employees partake in so as to differentiate their own identities from socially-constructed notions of other groups. This establishment of difference is not a neutral process, however; the discursive constitution of identity depends on the construction of a *hierarchy* in such oppositions, which privileges one side of the opposition at the expense of the other. Through this process of hierarchical opposition, a form of *distance* is constructed which is instrumental in the neglect of ethical issues with regard to those constructed as 'other'. Thus Dan can, somewhat uncharacteristically, dismiss the Banking Representatives as 'lowlifes', which allows him to avoid reflecting on the degradation of their work and the lack of monetary compensation in comparison to his own position. Clearly, not all oppositions serve this purpose; nonetheless, most of them enable employees where convenient to disregard ethical issues and avoid difficult feelings of empathy in their everyday dealings with their counterparts, particularly where this would compromise the instrumental use of others to achieve goals or further secure one's own identity.

Through an analysis of the interaction and transformation of such discourses over time, the next section will attempt to represent the operation of this 'dynamic and precarious' process. I will focus on a specific example within Buzzbank where senior management have attempted to impose a particular discursive understanding of changes within the organisation, in an attempt to increase the bureaucratisation of work systems in the company.

The Operation and Transformation of Discourse

Formalisation and Innovation in Buzzbank

Possibly the most significant change occurring in Buzzbank at the time appeared to be the concerted attempt to formalise and build a bureaucratic structure around the current work systems. Over the previous two years, a number of significant appointments had been made, particularly in the IT division, in an attempt to institute aspects of the more structured approach to banking and finance perceived to exist in TN Banking. This section will focus therefore on the 'cultural change' attempted in tandem with such formalisation measures, in the light of the *discursive understanding* outlined above. While there is a strategic rationale behind this initiative, of particular interest are the tactics used to integrate bureaucracy and formalisation into what management perceive as the traditional culture of Buzzbank; ironically, the precise opposite of most cultural change programmes which tend to equate tradition with bureaucracy and formality.

The first step in this process involved the installation of two senior managers, Jack and Angus, from TN Banking, as heads of IT Operations and IT Applications respectively. Both made it very clear that their remit in moving to Buzzbank from TN Banking was to "bring a level of discipline" (Angus 1: 130) and to "bring an idea of professional structuring" (Jack 2: 10). This can be seen as part of a company-wide strategy, involving the formal structuring of a number of processes in different departments and the introduction of formal project management techniques, even to the extent of prescribing a dress code for Buzzbank employees. Examples of measures taken within IT to achieve this structuring include aspects of what is known as the 'Strategic Plan', such as the development of a set of objectives for IT Operations, derived from a mission statement, and the introduction of a formal checklist to be completed as each project proceeds. The precise measures taken and their effects will be covered in more detail in the next chapter. What is relevant to this discussion, however, is the 'cultural change' which the new managers considered necessary to implement in Buzzbank, and the approach adopted to handling resistance to formalisation.

Both arrivals from TN Banking were equally forthright about the fact that in fulfilling their remit, some opposition appears to have been provoked, where the view had been taken that "you don't need all this discipline and bureaucracy" (Angus 1: 131). Interestingly, the head of Applications Development pinpointed Mike Winter, the Chief Executive of Buzzbank, as one of the key people unwilling to accept the imposition of a more bureaucratic form of discipline. This reinforced the general impression that the main reason behind the introduction of formalised procedures was to increase accountability and secure the now considerable income of this offshoot of TN Banking. Furthermore, this tended to imply that the source of this initiative lay outside Buzzbank itself, being imposed by TN Banking senior management. At no point was this admitted by employees, but it seems difficult to envisage how else this might come about in Buzzbank with a CEO (at least initially) opposed to such change.

The essential problem as seen from the point of view of those introducing this formalisation was the culture of autonomy and innovation which was apparent in the accounts of several Buzzbank employees. One manager, for instance, again contrasting Buzzbank with TN Banking, explained;

> "there, you'd be one of many grinding the wheel, whereas here you can forge a path, and people will listen to you" (Lee 2: 174).

As well as this sense of autonomy, significant value appeared to be placed on creativity, at least within the IT division; as we discussed career aspirations over a lunchtime pint, when I explained I enjoyed teaching, Ian asked incredulously;

> "Would you be happy doing that - I mean, not *creating* anything, or anything?" (Ian: OBS2: 7).

Such discourses appear in many ways perfect examples of discourses embedded in Buzzbank IT staff, insofar as they seem to be relatively autonomous with regard to management and central to the identity of employees. It seems highly likely, however, that much of the origins of such embedded discourses may lie in earlier discourses strategically promulgated by management which proved relatively successful in installing themselves in the subjectivities of employees. Here, encouraging, reinforcing and rewarding innovation and creative responses to challenges, within the parameters of the company's interests, may well have formed part of managerial strategy at an earlier point in time. This point is made to highlight once again the permeable distinction between different forms of discourse, as noted above. Beyond a certain point, such a 'culture' may clash with the changed strategic aims of senior management, and a new 'managerial discourse' is then invoked to alter the company's 'culture'.

This formalisation and increased accountability was justified mainly with reference to the particular size of the firm now, and the stage it had reached in its 'life-cycle'. Indeed, the rationale given for such a change referred directly to;

> "the growth, and the maturity of the organisation ... it's certainly the growth of the company, we never anticipated that it was going to grow that quickly last year, and it's a lot to do with the *maturity* of the company"(Jack 2: 247).

Elsewhere, the logic behind this as perceived by senior management was made more explicit;

> "as the business continues to grow, it becomes more demanding in what it wants to do, and we have to show we're being equally responsible as to how we meet that requirement, and that has to be within a structure" (Jack 2: 239).

So in many ways, the articulations of Buzzbank senior management appeared to draw on academic/managerial discourses which associate the *size* of the organisation with a *need for formalisation* (stemming from the Aston studies, in particular Pugh and Hickson, 1976, and Blau, 1970). The deterministic way in which this link is forged by Buzzbank management goes some way towards explaining their insistence on the initiatives' fundamental importance for the survival of the organisation.

The Insight of Metaphor

A useful perspective on this derives from the use of metaphor in senior management's attempts to explain to me (and in doing so, to persuade me of) the inevitability of such change. Metaphor has been used throughout this analysis as an indicator of discursive positions adopted by staff. Elsewhere, metaphor has been highlighted as not only representative of constructions of reality but to some extent constitutive of these constructions (Morgan, 1986: Tsoukas, 1991). This is not to revert to a merely linguistic/textual notion of discourse, as such metaphors may be seen as one *possible* articulation of the discourse. Equally, a discourse may be embodied in the conduct of an individual, the building of a prison or the construction of an IT system. However, the use of a metaphor, as an attempt to constitute reality by persuading others of the plausibility of one's own system of meaning, does serve as a particularly accessible means to analyse a discourse.

In line with this understanding of metaphor, the importance of such formalisation measures can be seen as reinforced by the repeated use of the metaphor of a parental relationship to define the relationship between TN Banking and Buzzbank; for instance, "Buzzbank is really a child of TN Banking" (Lee 2: 50). The organisation was therefore portrayed by upper management in IT and as approaching its "next stage of evolution" (Jack 1: 251). The origins of such a metaphor appear to lie in biological sciences and general models of development derived from such sciences. More specifically, however, such a metaphor comes from the introduction of such discourses into human sciences, particularly organisational studies, in the guise of Life Cycle models of organisations, positing fixed trajectories for the development of organisations (see Chapter 6 for further discussion). In drawing implicitly on such discourses which have become part of the common-sense 'truth' of organisations, the strategy of formalisation strengthens considerably the chances of its acceptance and internalisation by Buzzbank employees. The immediate benefit of such a metaphor for those members of senior management charged with introducing a level of formalisation is that it carries a very strong sense of inevitability. As such, it casts opposition to such changes as irrational and futile, standing in the way of natural 'evolution'.

Furthermore, the imposition of a level of discipline is then legitimised with recourse to the parental relationship, wherein Buzzbank is categorised as resembling "most adolescents" (Jack 1: 223). Thus;

"like most adolescents, they don't like to be told what to do, but there has to be some kind of structure around things" (Jack 2: 225).

What should be emphasised is that the effect of such a metaphor depends on how it is deployed. Garsten, for example, cites a very different deployment of the same metaphor in Apple, where she is told "Apple is still an adolescent, still looking for its shape and form" (1994: 18), with no hint that this necessitates the imposition of some form of discipline. In Buzzbank, by contrast, resistance to these initiatives were therefore described as "growing pains" (Angus 1: 139), "inevitable reactions in this ... small-village atmosphere" (Angus 1: 131). Resistance could then be categorised as unavoidable in the short term yet ultimately just a phase the organisation is going through, without any real validity and fundamentally dysfunctional for the organisation as a whole.

The Formalisation Strategy: Inverting the Discourse

It is here that the relevance of 'discourse' as a concept becomes clearer. One of the main initiatives in the formalisation strategy within Buzzbank was clearly the process of redefining and rearticulating existing discourses. The key aim of this process appeared to be to transform existing 'embedded' discourses hostile to the initiatives into discourses which were essentially compatible with senior management intentions. In this case, the previous position within Buzzbank was described by one of the new heads of department, Angus, as;

"if you did something wrong, you just said 'Oh dear, we got that wrong, let's try something different' and we haven't got the luxury of that" (Angus 1: 136).

The subtly pejorative definition of Buzzbank (prior to their arrival) as "rapidly expanding, gung-ho" (Angus 1: 158) highlights its perceived weaknesses. It is important to note the rhetorical use of these terms for characteristics which could equally be described in positive terms as growing, evolving, adaptable, proactive, flexible, etc. Represented in these terms, however, such attributes become the source of problems; for example,

"Two or three years ago, we'd start a project and never have a bloody clue when it would finish" (Angus 1:146).

As a consequence of this construction of the problem, the formalisation initiative could then be presented as dealing with this precise problem;

"If we capture how we do things right, at least it makes things repeatable, and we can record the improvement required when things don't go right, which doesn't happen in a rapidly-expanding, gung-ho environment" (Angus 1: 156).

The importance of language as raised above is very clear here in its use in a constitutive rather than a representative sense, in creating the situation, the problem and therefore the solution. Without attempting to reduce such discourses to language, what is of central importance here is how 'organisational reality' is articulated, which entails considerable sensitivity to the language used in the organisation. Such a concern over the way the situation is articulated was evident in a number of interviews with senior management, although this concern was not internally consistent. Drawing on notions of language as signification rather than representation sheds some light on this tendency; as language is constitutive of social reality, relations of meaning assume a focal position in social and organisational changes.

The central importance accorded to language is evident in the emphasis placed on the definition of the changes occurring in the IT department. Most significantly, a high degree of sensitivity was shown by management in specifying the precise terminology to be used. Hence the first definition of the changes offered to me by Jack, the other new Head of Department was;

"trying to get some structure in place, get some planning in place" (Jack 2: 19).

When later in the interview I referred back to this in different terms, my terminology was instantly corrected, politely but very firmly ;

Q: "So... this idea of formalisation...",
Jack: "Getting a structure."
Q: "Right, yeah, getting a structure..." (Jack 2:81).

This aversion to the term formalisation continued throughout the interview, Jack being careful to correct himself whenever he employed the term;

"a very formalised - well, not formalised but *formal* customer-supplier relationship" (Jack 2: 294).

In another interview, a middle manager, Martin, was equally careful to specify the precise meaning when I brought up senior management's intentions to put "structures in place". In this case however, he was unwilling even to endorse his immediate superior's characterisation of the changes;

"I mean, when you say, 'structures in place', I don't think that necessarily means hierarchical management structures as such, I think it's more procedures, yeah? ... I think it's more like a sort of structuring of work, rather than a structuring of people" (Martin: 235).

In these examples, I received a clear sense that the managers were desperately attempting to avoid giving the impression that the new initiatives involved formalisation and increased bureaucracy. One reason for this aversion may well be the widespread denigration of such terms in contemporary popular managerial discourse of the Peters and Waterman variety. In the case of Buzzbank, however, I would suggest that management were *particularly* sensitive to accusations of introducing bureaucracy due to their understanding of the existing 'culture' of Buzzbank as flexible, informal, innovative, etc.

The new senior management, introduced from TN Banking to push through the formalisation and accountability initiatives, described two potential problems resulting from this antipathy to formality and structure. The first was the potential for a backlash against formalisation efforts within the department, particularly given the association of such changes with TN Banking. To a large extent, this is a problem of senior management's own making, as the opposition with TN Banking had previously been, if not constructed, then at least fostered and exploited by management in pursuit of a positive and unitary culture. The second problem was the perceived danger that in introducing formal procedures and accountability, they risked losing the benefits to the organisation of informality and autonomy; to quote one senior manager, the challenge was;

"trying to get that formal structure together, not to become bureaucratic, not to become slow to respond, but to be anticipating..." (Jack 2: 185).

Senior management's response to this was inventive, and, I would argue, relatively strategic and purposeful. Through a *rearticulation* of embedded discourses, the discourse being introduced by senior management was cast as not only *consistent* with such discourses but, moreover, as crucial to their continuation and further development. This position can be traced through the analysis of a statement by Jack in which he comprehensively enunciated the ways in which discourses were to be rearticulated. This should not be taken to presuppose the efficacy of this approach, rather to emphasis the dynamic and purposeful manner in which such discourses may be drawn on and reconstructed.

Firstly, then, he outlined the danger of resistance (while subtly implying the perception of bureaucracy to be mistaken);

"*If we're not careful, people will see bureaucracy* - 'Why do I have to tell so many people I want to make this change? Why do I have to get you to sign this form?'" (Jack 2: 221).

He then went on to attempt to synthesise the new managerial discourse with his rearticulation of embedded discourses, such that creativity/innovation and restriction/control may be seen as congruent values. Significantly, this was supported by appeal to the 'bottom-line', the *sine qua non* of service industry - *the customer*;

"The idea is that we want to try and facilitate *more change*, but we want *to do it in a controlled way* - so it doesn't affect customer service..." (Jack 2: 222).

As the next step, resistance to such changes was then redefined as natural, irrational and transient, and unconnected to the conflict between values implicit in the last statement;

"... but the nature of the business is that it's a pretty young business, and *like most adolescents*, they don't like to be told what to do" (Jack 2: 224).

The changes, in this light, were then referred to as difficult but inevitable, such that the real issue was one of (re)presentation rather than a fundamental clash of discourses;

"... but *there has to be some kind of structure* around things, and we have to be very careful about how we sell that to different parts of the business, and indeed within IT itself" (Jack 2: 226).

Finally, the way in which both discourses can be integrated was articulated, and articulated in such a way as to present the discourses as complementary, indeed mutually dependent;

"we're not actually slowing down the ability of certain areas to change, *so that we're actually enabling change to take place*, fast but *in a more controlled manner*" (Jack 2: 228).

The way this rearticulation and integration of discourses occurs links in conspicuously with the notion of the intertextuality of discourses (Kristeva, 1986; Bahktin, 1986); specifically, "the property texts have of being full of snatches of other texts, which may be explicitly demarcated or merged in, and which the text may assimilate, contradict, ironically echo and so forth" (Fairclough, 1992: 84). This is also described as the "creative interaction of narratives" (Law, 1994), although, for reasons outlined below, I disagree with the more *structural* force that Law's formulation attributes to narratives, which almost entirely omits the role of subjects in their articulation and transformation. The account above illustrates the reflective and relatively conscious way in which subjects rearticulate and deploy discourses to achieve given ends (although this is not to endorse simple voluntarism by ignoring the role of discourse and discipline in constructing the ends themselves). What I mean to underline here is the productive process whereby discourses are transformed to align with differing, even contradictory projects. In this case, the focus is on the assimilation of a prior and embedded discourse so as to lend weight and minimise resistance to material changes to procedures and controls occurring within the organisation.[11]

It is worth noting that the attempts made to overcome resistance and transform the embedded discourse were frequently described by senior management as;

> "*education* (...) a continual management of expectations, and communication, basically" (Jack 2: 264-75).

On the one hand, this may be interpreted as simply a rhetorical device to couch the changes being attempted in unthreatening and positive language. At the same time, however, it reveals the extent to which the focus of this change was the *subjectivity* of individuals (disregarding for a moment the question of the effectiveness of such manipulation). I read this action as constituting an instrumental and relatively self-aware attempt on the part of senior managers to manipulate key discourses within the organisation so as to reconstitute employees in ways conducive to the attainment of corporate goals. Jack's extended explanation and justification of his work on the formalisation initiative indicates the conscious and instrumental way in which it has been and was being implemented by management. This self-awareness should not be over-stated, however; implicit in such forms of conduct are the identity projects of the management themselves, dependent on their ability to effect such transformations in their subordinates at the command of strategy dictated from above.

Having said that, the effectiveness of this strategy of 'culture management' was, however, questionable, given the attitudes towards the ongoing changes evident in the responses and behaviour of the employees at all levels. In the next section I will examine the forms of resistance which could be discerned within Buzzbank and Lifelong, linked with

---

[11] In this sense, what I, as a researcher, can be seen to be engaged in is the rearticulation of these discourses, incorporating a number of sociological and academic discourses.

attempts to subvert discourses and the use of humour in an attempt to distance the individual from the power effects of discourse. What I have attempted to illustrate in this section are the ways in which what are seen as 'hard' issues, involving organisational structure and power, are intimately related to the 'softer' issues of the discursive constitution of organisational reality through the construction of oppositions and the strategic deployment of discourses around these oppositions. More fundamentally, I have interpreted how 'culture management' initiatives reflect strategic and instrumental attempts at to manipulate these discourses, focusing on employees themselves, in line with corporate objectives. I now mean to highlight the potential for subversion in the face of managerial attempts to subjugate and reconstitute employees, while securing and bolstering their own identity projects.

Forms of Resistance

The above discussion should in no way be taken to imply that such discourses will readily be internalised by employees. To substantiate this position, I will analyse varied instances of resistance and subversion below. The possibility of resistance and/or subversion reinforces a key point of the previous discussion; that the operation of discourse is necessarily dynamic, and the complexity of the interaction between discourses frustrates attempts to unilaterally impose a framework of meanings onto an organisation. Here I will focus again on Buzzbank, where the most conspicuous forms of resistance ranged from the use of humour by employees to distance themselves from discourses of formalisation, to more passionate expressions of discontent and even revolt.

Thus in Buzzbank, there were conflicting signs apparent in employee behaviour and communication as to the extent to which the prevalent discourse had been successfully altered by the initiatives of senior management. Among senior management, the impression given was that despite initial resistance, the 'message had got through' that formalisation did not threaten autonomy and flexibility but actually enabled it. For instance, Angus explained;

"having come through very rapid growth in a small number of years, probably within that there's an appetite for change ... this discipline has given confidence to that tolerance of change" (Angus 1: 140).

The impression was given by senior management that such an understanding had successfully been spread through lower management and other employees. Thus Angus also claimed;

"There was a perception that by doing this (reorganisation) we were becoming less efficient - that's now been dispelled" (Angus 1: 84).

The impression given was of a change in culture which was inevitable, which gave rise to some understandable but irrational resistance, and which had now been effectively completed, for the good of the organisation as a whole.

Elsewhere, however, the impression given was very different. Some of the statements of the middle- to lower- management, mainly in direct responses to questions but occasionally in general conversation, appeared to support this, describing the Strategic Plan as "a good thing" (Ian: OBS2: 3). However, in the time spent by myself in the organisation, the tone and target of much of the humour, as well as much stronger reactions, appeared to question the extent to which this discourse had permeated among the general employees, particularly within the IT department.

The Use of Humour

Although research on the use of humour in organisations in particular is as yet fairly limited, work by writers like David Collinson (1988) and Tony Watson (1994) has traced a number of themes, particularly regarding how humour may be interpreted in organisations. The multiplicity of contexts, motives and forms of humour means that achieving some sort of definition; however, it is defined fairly succinctly in a general sense by Hatch and Ehrlich (1993), drawing on a wide range of sources, as a type or means of communication which recognises incongruities in meaning or in relationships accompanied or intended to be accompanied by laughter or at least a smile. Humour is further defined by differentiating *standardised* humour (i.e. the formal 'canned' joke) from *spontaneous* humour, emphasising that standardised humour carries its context with it, while spontaneous humour is firmly rooted in context. Thus we can distinguish narrated jokes, satirical cartoons, humorous anecdotes etc from spontaneous puns, non sequiturs, and incongruous statements which emerge from a specific situation. Watson (1994) draws on a theme common to both conservative and radical social research when he suggests that, apart from serving to 'pass the time' and distract individuals from the tedium of work, humour also fulfils an important role in that it "allows us to confront and come to terms with threats and dangers of the world around us", and enables us to "recognise the absurdity of our human condition" (1994: 188). From this perspective, recurrent topics or themes in humour can serve to indicate those things which not only *matter* to a group or individual, but which *cause anxiety and insecurity* and point to attempts to manage this anxiety.

While this connection may be seen as fairly broadly accepted in social research, there remains, however, substantial ambiguity regarding the social *effects* of humour. Considerable disagreement continues over how humour in organisations may be interpreted, from the conservative view of humour as a organisationally productive *"safety valve"* (Mulkay, 1988) to the radical view of humour as a *subversive force* (Douglas, 1975). Effectively, what is at issue is whether humour should be seen as a form of *resistance*, as a subversive force within organisations, or as a mode of *accommodation* to power relations, preventing tensions building up to more substantial and effective forms of behaviour. Thus those who interpret humour as subversive emphasise the link with anxieties and insecurities, and point to use of humour to raise disagreement or protest without the speaker taking direct responsibility for the statement as it's 'only joking'. On the other hand, the use of humour as a sociological defence mechanism to avoid more direct action is highlighted historically, with reference to the position of the 'Court Jester' whose freedom from sanction proves the ruler's tolerance and power. Humour in this sense is frequently portrayed as an individualistic and ineffective alternative to collective forms of resistance, and as such tolerated and even encouraged by those in positions of dominance. A more contemporary example is given by Kunda (1992), who identifies the use of humour in Tech as a form of 'distancing', in Goffman's sense, to relieve anxiety while conforming to imposed organisational norms. At the same time, he notes that cynical forms of humour in Tech frequently had the effect of enrolling the individual in the 'culture' of the company, through the redefinition of dissent and cynicism as confirming the 'culture' of tolerance and openness.

Examples of each merely serve to reinforce the multiple forms of humour, as noted above; humour may well act to subvert imposed systems of meaning and undermine structures, *as well as* managing tensions as a substitute for more tangible and direct forms of resistance. I would suggest that the variety of forms and instances of humour preclude such an either/or classification; however, a common thread seems to be, as proposed by Hatch and Ehrlich, that humour "contributes to the maintenance of paradoxical states of understanding by permitting recognition of fundamental contradictions without a loss of social balance" (1993: 524). The onus is on the researcher to interpret humour in its own context, and to assess the potential for subversion or resistance that each instance or form of humour implies.

Humour, then, was commonplace in the everyday banter both within teams and between teams in the IT division at Buzzbank, and the increasing levels of bureaucratisation was one of the main foci of humour, particularly at the lower levels of the hierarchy. One of the key examples was the negative reaction to what was seen as the managerial jargon employed in company literature circulated regarding the Strategic Plan. Typical comments upon receiving these documents were;

> "I don't understand any of this - it's not in English, it's in Management!" (Matt: OBS1: 5).
> "God, I wish *I* went to Management School - I'd do great here!" (Matt: OBS1: 5).

Significantly, these comments, although by no means subtle, were made when no member of senior management was within earshot. [12] A similar response was provoked by a circular which gave details of the dress code to be introduced on the site, with employees reading out excerpts in pompous, mock-upper class accents;

> "Collared shirts are essential, although the top button may be undone on hot summer days",
> "This one's for you, Ian - 'Jackets are preferred, although a smart sports coat is acceptable'!" (Martin: OBS2: 4).

Although this may be considered 'just humour', the content of the humour, and the fact that such statements were not only tolerated but encouraged by lower management and employees in more informal situations, can be taken to provide some insight into the concerns and embedded discourses within the organisation. While in themselves, the effect of such comments are indeed minimal, such statements did appear to represent the emergence of a level of solidarity among general staff, and the articulation of an informally-reproduced resistance to the formalisation initiatives which sanctioned non-compliance in the most basic sense. Links were possibly identifiable between such humour and resistant behaviour, as will be seen below.

Articulated Dissent

Without discounting the importance of such humour, then, on other occasions the response was significantly more passionate. Again, comments were provoked by the circulation of literature on the Strategic Plan, and again, excerpts of the document were read out by members of

---

[12] Although my presence may well have been instrumental in encouraging this outburst of anti-managerialist humour.

staff, adding sarcastic comments to the end to the effect that the document didn't reflect their experience of life in Buzzbank. However, on this occasion, this was followed up by a heated outburst by one member, Dan, throwing the document down and exclaiming to everyone within earshot;

> "It's all *bollocks*, it really is, it's nothing but rhetoric, just bollocks - bollocks, rhetoric and jargon!" (Dan: OBS1: 8-9).

The same employee explained his anger to me later, indicating the behavioural standards which the Strategic Plan stated IT staff were to conform to;

> "If the staff are conscientious, they do all of this stuff *anyway*! If they *aren't*, then they don't give a shit and they're certainly not going to sit around and read the damn thing!" (Dan: OBS1: 8-9).

A direct reference to those employees he would categorise as 'unconscientious' emerged when I later asked Dan if I could have a copy of the document. Throwing over the copy from Ian's desk, he retorted;

> "Well, you can have Ian's - he wouldn't look at it unless you wrapped it in pitta bread and put some red cabbage on top, or wrote 'Woodpecker' on it!" (Dan: OBS1: 9).

Here then was a more conscious and more articulate example of the resistance engendered by the attempted changes in the lower management and other staff. While this statement clearly implies that he, Dan, is one of the 'conscientious' staff, and as such 'does all this stuff anyway', it does indicate the likely response the formalisation initiative is likely to meet in some quarters (without actually implicating the speaker himself in such behaviour).

The effectiveness of such forms of articulated resistance may well be seen as debatable, especially given that these statements were not said in the presence of any of the senior management responsible. Indeed, when I attempted to pursue the issue of resistance to the Strategic Plan with Dan, I aroused some suspicion on the part of the employees, who joked;

> "See, you should have kept your mouth shut - we've got a spy in our midst" (Dan: OBS1: 9).

Although I tried to laugh this off at the time, I recognised a clear warning delivered through this statement, and approached the issue of active resistance more obliquely in later conversations. Despite such wariness about openly articulated dissent, these statements do appear to indicate the existence of other interpretations of the changes made by the new senior management. Furthermore, the articulation and dissemination of such interpretations of ongoing changes in the company may at the very least be seen as ways of resisting the ideal objective of these initiatives i.e. effecting real change by altering the basic systems of beliefs and the assumptions held by the Buzzbank employees. While the employees did appear to comply with the formal requirements of the new system, in terms of filling in the necessary forms, reporting in at given times, completing the necessary work-logs, and so on, their statements appear in general to contradict assertions by the senior management that the perceptions of the employees have effectively been changed. In effect, despite the relative sophistication of senior managements rearticulation of key discourses, compliance on the part of Buzzbank employees in many cases bore all the hallmarks of instrumental behaviour, accompanied by insubordinate statements and humour ranging from the cynical to the confrontational.

Overall, then, a number of heterogeneous means to resist and subvert discursive dominance can be seen in Buzzbank. The forms that such resistance takes range from the use of humour to undermine discourses propagated by senior management, to the more direct articulation of more or less sophisticated, conflicting forms of discourse. It is, however, difficult to assess the extent to which such forms of resistance are effective. At the very least, the use of humour can be seen as a form of distancing which resists attempts to internalise forms of discourse in employees, and articulates what in its more organised forms might be referred to as a 'counter-culture'. This humour is often connected with the articulation of dissent, anger and alternative understandings of developments in the organisation, which on the surface appears a more 'deeply-held' and constructive form of resistance. This impression is somewhat undermined, however, by the fact that such expressions of dissent, like the humour indicated above, frequently occur hand-in-hand with an instrumental obedience to disciplinary demands. I will examine the connections between humour and resistance in more detail in the next chapter.

Conclusion

In this chapter, I have examined in some detail the operation of power through the analysis of discourses, as outlined in Chapters 2 and 3, in the light of the empirical research in the subject organisations, Buzzbank and Lifelong Assurance. As noted above, those discourses which I have identified and analysed in this chapter are those which seemed to me to hold particular significance in the constructions of the employees interviewed and observed. In a broad sense, I have distinguished between those discourses strategically promoted by senior management in the organisations, linked to an 'organisational ideology', and those which are less formal and are frequently marginalised in organisations. In doing so, I do not mean to imply that these are mutually exclusive - indeed, a key property of discourses is their interdependence and constant dynamic interactions. Nor do I mean to make any simplistic moral judgements based on this distinction. However, there is at the very least a heuristic importance in differentiating very generally between 'unofficial' forms of discourse and those promoted by management to achieve organisational objectives, if only to trace the interactions between these more clearly.

Examining the structuring of the sense-making processes of individuals has necessarily involved engaging with a significant body of literature on 'culture management', in both managerialist and, to a lesser extent, critical perspectives. The position I have taken here perceives culture management as a relatively strategic and organised attempt to monopolise the construction of meaning in the workplace through the imposition of an 'organisational ideology' (in Kunda's sense) upon its members. As such, the evolution of culture management should be understood in the context of changing control mechanisms in the workplace, as culture potentially offers a powerful and economical form of 'control at a distance', as well as drawing on aspects of earlier, paternalist control mechanisms. Such attempts vary enormously in their sophistication and in the depth of change which they attempt in organisational members. Thus my research in Buzzbank indicated a widespread understanding of 'culture' as definable and transferable among employees, as well as an apparent recognition of a specific 'Buzzbank culture'. In my interviews in Lifelong, however, the term was not used at all. Nonetheless, in both organisations employees appeared to have an understanding of an identity specific to the company (in the case of Buzzbank) but, more tangibly, specific to their department or division. More importantly, this identity was conveyed to me through attempts to delineate the difference between an 'us' and a 'them', through the construction of an opposition which was portrayed as vital.

This use of *difference* seemed to reflect relational conceptions of meaning, developed in the field of structural linguistics, and the import of this notion into conceptions of identity, as discussed in Chapter 3. Such models emphasise the construction of identity through such discursive oppositions, and this is borne out in both Buzzbank and Lifelong, between permanent staff and contractors, for instance, or between IT and 'the Business'. These oppositions were not fixed, however, and different oppositions were used by the same individuals to define themselves in different contexts. Moreover, these discursive oppositions were often rooted in assumptions which were *central to the subjectivity* of the individual and upon which the individual relied to maintain a sense of a valued (work) identity in the face of anxiety and insecurity. In practice, the construction of oppositions enabled staff to maintain a symbolic distance between themselves and those construed as their counterparts. In certain cases, it became evident that this distance made it significantly easier for an individual to disregard and even contribute to practices which exploited and dominated other individuals. Both therefore use the other in the instrumental pursuit of personal objectives while at the same time shoring up a precarious sense of superiority without facing up to moral consequences of their action (or inaction).

Returning to the discussion of culture management, the strategic representation of TN Banking as bureaucratic and monolithic by Buzzbank management is a clear example of how such discourses are appropriated and exploited, through the construction of an opposition to act as a 'reference point' for the development of a 'unitary' culture. My discomfort at such practices centred on their thinly-veiled manipulative intent, to reconstitute employees to facilitate their objectification and discipline in line with corporate objectives. However, the complexity and constant dynamic interaction of discourses cast doubt on the ability of senior management to unilaterally impose a system of meaning in even the most 'favourable' situation. Such initiatives must contend with an enormously complex network of discursive oppositions which emerge unsystematically, are held collectively and communicated through everyday interaction. Furthermore, the centrality of these discursively constructed oppositions to the notion of identity held by a group of employees clearly undermines attempts at direct manipulation.

Focusing on changes in Buzzbank, I have attempted to trace the conflicts, transformations and forms of deployment of a relatively limited number of nonetheless key discourses, both emergent and strategically sponsored by senior management. Through an analysis of the formalisation of work processes within IT in Buzzbank, I have highlighted the productive interaction of managerial and embedded discourses, as management deliberately and strategically rearticulate and transform prior discourses to enrol otherwise resistant employees. At the same time, I have also emphasised the potential for subversion in the constant rearticulation of such discourses and the practical impact of this on organisational change. In my empirical work, humour was frequently used to undermine or transform elements of discourses associated with organisational ideology, and at other times I witnessed open articulations of dissent. However, in both cases such behaviour could instead be interpreted as a substitute for more directly subversive conduct.

In the following chapter I intend to build on this initial analysis by examining the power effects of *discipline* and *professionalisation*, in addition to discursive mechanisms examined above, in each organisation, mobilised around the theme of *Project Management*. Again, I will examine the potential for subversion and resistance to what proves to be the deeply ambiguous imposition of discipline.

6 Project Management and Professionalism in the IT Function

Disciplining the Professional

This chapter has attempted to trace the connections between a number of concepts, focusing on *discourse, discipline* and *professionalisation*, through an examination of the phenomenon of *Project Management*. This notion appeared to hold significant importance in the accounts and experiences of IT staff in both Lifelong and Buzzbank, and is related to many of the discursive shifts, such as formalisation, identified in the previous chapter. The chapter will start with an overview of the development of Project Management, tracing its theoretical origins and examining elements of the generic model, as well as associated tools and techniques. At the same time I will outline the specific form of Project Management which has been developed to fit the field of Information Technology, before examining its particular incarnation in Buzzbank and Lifelong. The expansion of Project Management in both organisations is driven in part by its use in promoting the notion of the *professionalism* of IT staff. Such professionalism affords improved security and status to certain IT staff, which at the same time implies associated insecurities and loss of status outside the circles of Project Management. A brief examination of some contemporary debates over professionalisation suggests a number of characteristics that Project Management shares with other fields which have attempted to engage in a discourse of professionalism.

A key part of the construction of a profession is the development of a coherent ontology and the constitution and enforcement of a specific language. Drawing on my empirical work, I will argue that the IT function's growing influence in each organisation relies heavily upon the promotion of Project Management as *an objective body of knowledge and expertise*. In this way, attempts are continually made to constitute Project Management as a *discipline*, both in a general sense and specifically through its articulation within the subject organisations. This discipline is therefore defined in the *abstract* i.e. as a neutral, transferable skill, and is understood to be promoted through training in such procedures, with an implicit effect on the subjectivity of the individual. In keeping with the modern professions, the scientificity of the discipline is fundamental to the attempts of IT staff to legitimise the expansion of their influence and control within each organisation. Through such disciplinary technologies, a specific mode of rationality is instilled in the subjectivities of IT staff, which enables such staff to adopt the position of IT *professionals*. At the same time, conforming to professional standards in both knowledge and conduct enables a form of control to be exercised over technical and managerial staff, sanctioned by senior management. Nonetheless, there is the possibility of resistance to the imposition of Project Management as a discipline, through the use of discretion and, more widely, the use of humour in each organisation. To illustrate the operation of Project Management as a discipline, I have ended by examining examples from each organisation, emphasising the contingent and often strategic transformation of discourses of professionalism, and the implications of this for power relations, work systems and structures in both Lifelong and Buzzbank.

The Emergence of Project Management

Project Management first came to popular attention in the management literature in the late 1960s and early 1970s, although it has its origins in a number of distinct fields. Seminal texts on Project Management emphasise its reliance upon Systems Theory, an approach imported from the natural and physical sciences (Cleland and King, 1968; Lock, 1968). Drawing upon Systems Theory, management writers attempted to develop an holistic approach to the emergent 'science' of management. The aim was to devise models whereby organisations could be viewed as collections of interrelated processes adapting to the environment, similar to the representations of biological or mechanical systems in the natural sciences. The emergence of this perspective may be seen in part to be a reaction to the static nature of the models of early Organisation Theory, and to the enduring perception of bureaucracy as the ideal organisational form. However, there are a number of deeper effects of the import of Systems Theory into management thought which can be discerned. One key consequence was the introduction of the functionalist assumptions of

Systems Theory in the natural sciences, or more accurately, the reinforcement of existing functionalist tendencies in management theory. By adapting Systems Theory management theorists could then presuppose that "as in such biological analogies ... system parts (or sub-systems) are interconnected and *each are functional to the viability of the organization*" (Thompson and McHugh, 1995: 367, emphasis added). The dangers of this were highlighted as early as 1975, Bertalanffy recording his "fear" that "system theory is indeed the ultimate step towards the mechanisation and devaluation of man and towards technocratic society" (Bertalanffy, 1975, quoted in Giddens, 1979: 270). Nonetheless, many systems theorists in management have since embraced and indeed continue to aspire to the technical rationality of its source in the natural sciences, again reinforcing positivist tendencies in the field.

The technicist foundation of Project Management is evident not only in its theoretical precursors but also in the sectors where the original Project Management techniques were developed. A history of the application of Project Management is traced by Morris (1994), highlighting its use in a number of substantial projects back to the Manhattan Project, developing the first atomic bomb. While the US oil and chemicals industry played a large part, the majority of the groundwork was done in US defence and aeronautics in the 1950s, including widespread use in the Apollo space programs (Harrison, 1981). From this concentration on technical projects, Project Management techniques have proliferated in the last forty years, not only within technology and engineering but expanding into areas as diverse as education, health and social services. This process appears to have accelerated in the UK in recent years in tandem with the import of managerialist models and techniques into public services (e.g. the restructuring of the NHS around internal markets, etc). Throughout these developments, the arguments behind the promotion of Project Management techniques have remained remarkably similar, referring to the increasing uncertainty and complexity of the modern world (for example, Cleland and King, 1968; Kerzner, 1995). The response to this encapsulated in Project Management, as will be outlined below, is a resurrection of the modernist emphasis on comprehensive planning, linked to a reassertion of the importance of strict managerial control.

Many writers on Project Management present their field as gradually converging on a universal model of the Project Management process, complete with standardised ontology and a standard terminology used by all professional project managers. Morris, for instance, claims that "it was only in the mid-to-late 1980s that sufficient inter-industry exchange of project management expertise and practice had occurred for a multi-industry, universal model of best project management practice to emerge in any kind of robust form" (1994: 307). Within IT, in particular, this mission has been caricatured by some authors as "the search for the holy paradigm" (Hackathorn and Karimi, 1988, in Fitzgerald, 1996: 9). Despite efforts in this direction, and the development of a vague consensus over what Project Management should be, it appears that the development and enforcement of a unitary model has had limited success. For instance, it was recently estimated that there may be up to 1000 different IT Project Management models in publication (Fitzgerald, 1996: 10), many focusing on specific sectors of industry and/or phases of the process.

It is common for Project Management authors to account for the ongoing problems with unification by pointing to Project Management's relative immaturity as a discipline, and calling for further rigorous research to achieve this perfect model. Indeed, Morris claims that "one of the greatest challenges still facing the discipline is to develop genuine generic practices and terminology" (1994: vii), and describes his book as an attempt to rise to this challenge. Tentative attempts by national professional organisations to develop an incontrovertible 'Body of Knowledge' is another approach. Even if such a universally-accepted model were feasible, however, a number of significant obstacles remain. Not least of these is the financial well-being of innumerable academics and consultancies, which relies upon some form of product differentiation in order to market their own models, applications and services. As such marketing constitutes a major source of Project Management's recent expansion, it seems unlikely that this harmonious union of models will materialise, at least in the near future. As a consequence, any attempt to analyse the field as a whole is open to the criticism that it is unrepresentative of the true nature of Project Management. In the discussion to follow, therefore, a number of key texts will be drawn on, those most frequently referenced and recommended in the literature, which cannot be *fully* representative of the field but which should provide a substantial overview of the main themes and perspectives of Project Management.

A key theme of many original texts on Project Management is the need for project-based organisations, rather than monolithic bureaucracies, to cope with the uncertainty and change of contemporary (i.e. 1970s) society. This is made clear in one of the first Project Management texts, *Systems Analysis and Project Management* (1975), later to be described as a "classic of the genre" (Morris, 1994: 76). Here, Cleland and King depict the typical modern organisation as hamstrung by the formality and hierarchy of what they imply is the universal adherence to the bureaucratic model. Reflecting a popular theme in such writings, they assert that "the realities of modern industrial competition cause serious doubt for (its) universality" (1975: 227). Thus in the 1970s the *matrix* organisation design came into vogue, based on a formation experimented with by NASA in the 1960s (Morris, 1994). This matrix organisation is described as comprising two divisions; an administrative area, carrying out routine functions, and a number of horizontal 'project teams', composed of staff from different functions and formed for fixed time-periods to handle non-routine work. A grid structure was proposed which integrated the traditional functional structure of organisations with project team-based lines of authority (see fig. 6.1). This matrix form of organisation, described as 'ad hoc', was celebrated by its proponents as capable of coping with increasing complexity, uncertainty and interdependence (Davis and Lawrence, 1977). In popular literature, the widespread adoption of matrix organisations was presented as all but inevitable, Alvin Toffler stating in *Future Shock* (1970) that "the rise of ad hoc organization is a direct effect of the speed-up of change in society as a whole" (quoted in Morris, 1994: 135).

Figure 6.1: A Matrix Structure

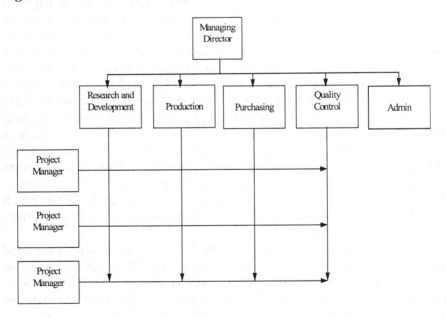

The significance of this model in the popularising of Project Management should be emphasised here. Cleland and King, for example, promote the *matrix* organisation as "the natural framework for incorporating projects into a traditional functional organisation" (Cleland and King, 1975: 202), while Harrison claims with greater determinism that the matrix "*had* to be evolved ... in order to bind all the diverse elements (of large projects) in one organisation" (Harrison, 1981: 17). Indeed, Morris claims that "Project Management was established as a popular discipline in the late 1960s and 1970s (...) crucially through the widespread adoption in business, government and the military of the *matrix* form of organisation" (1994: 216). Despite this convenient interdependence, the generic model of Project Management and the set of techniques grouped under it appear to have outlived the popularity of the matrix organisation. Nonetheless, aspects of the matrix formation may still be discerned in contemporary management vogues for team-based and project-based working. The next section will outline the predominant frameworks of Project Management, based around the Project Life Cycle, before briefly exploring the development of a body of relevant managerial practices.

The Project Management Model

Building on these foundations, a general model for the process of project work has been developed, defined as the *Project Life Cycle*, or PLC. The PLC is essentially a standardised model of the stages of a project, said to represent the "natural and pervasive order of thought and action" (Cleland and King, 1975: 186). Other writers are more authoritative; Morris, for instance, states "to achieve the desired project objective one must go through a specific process. There is no exception to this rule. The process is known as the Project Life Cycle" (quoted in Cleland and King, 1988: 19). While there are numerous broadly similar versions of the PLC of varying levels of complexity and detail, for the purposes of illustration a model will be adapted from Morris (1994). This model, in common with the models in most other Project Management texts, includes five basic phases, here defined as; *Conceptual, Definition, Production, Operational* and *Divestment.*

The *Systems Development Life Cycle* (SDLC) is explicitly based on the PLC model, and reproduces these phases in a slightly modified form for use in specifically IT-based projects; for example, the model enforced in the US by the IEEE (Institute of Electrical and Electronics Engineers) bears a striking similarity to the PLC above. However, here the stages are renamed *Requirements, Design, Implementation, Test* and *Installation/Checkout* (IEEE, 1987).

The content of each stage will be examined in more detail in the next section. On a more general level, however, it is asserted that what is needed to guide a project through these stages is not only an understanding of what each stage involves but, more fundamentally, the development of a set of management skills which "characterise a new breed of manager" (Cleland

and King, 1975: 6). It is these skills, together with the associated techniques and tools deemed necessary for each stage, which make up Project Management's 'body of knowledge'. Indeed, between 1983 and 1986 the Project Management Institute (PMI) in the USA developed what it termed 'the Body of Knowledge', to serve as a basis for certification and standardised degree programmes. The UK-based Association for Project Management (APM) produced their own version in the early 1990s, which has also been adopted by the European Project Managers' association, the IPMA, although other countries such as Australia and Germany are now developing their own. Although the 'Bodies of Knowledge' differ, both the PMI and the APM require knowledge of techniques (such as *Project Life Cycle, Budgeting, Scheduling,* etc) and management skills (such as *Control and Co-ordination, Leadership,* etc.). Before examining the tools and techniques in more detail, it is important here to understand the conception of management skills implicit in the discipline of Project Management .

Despite the proclaimed novelty of the Project Management approach, most textbooks (e.g. Cleland and King, 1975; Day, 1994; Kerzner, 1995) return to 1916 and Fayol's 5 *Elements of Management* when attempting to define the responsibilities of the project manager; *Planning, Organising, Commanding, Co-ordinating* and *Controlling.* Despite trenchant critiques of these principles from a number of writers (for instance Mintzberg, 1973; Hales, 1986), they are evident in slightly adapted forms in the vast majority of Project Management guides. Thus Morris states unequivocally that Project Management is the same as "any other kind of management, except that one moves through a predetermined life cycle. Everything else, at this level, is covered by general management practices - planning, organising, controlling and so on" (1994: 307). Cleland and King (1975) define similar skills as necessary, although later texts (such as Cleland and King, 1988) tend to add more fashionable concerns, such as 'leadership', 'entrepreneurship', etc. Very little deviation from Fayol is evident in IT-based Project Management; for example, the standards of the IEEE state; "Software project management is the process of planning, organizing, staffing, monitoring, controlling and leading a software project" (IEEE, 1987).

However, what sets these checklists apart is the emphasis on "an ability to conceptualise and to operate using a systems approach" (Cleland and King, 1975). Implicit in this requirement is the need for competence in the role and application of the wide variety of Project Management models and techniques. These techniques, examined in the next section, have been developed over the last forty years and pertain to the progressive stages of the PLC/SDLC. It is not the purpose of this chapter to go into these techniques in great detail. Rather, the section will attempt to give an overall impression of the character of these techniques before examining how they have been interpreted, adapted and employed in the subject organisations.

Techniques of Project Management

A number of tools and techniques have been developed to facilitate what is known as the *Conceptual* phase, generally aimed at structuring an analysis of the existing/potential system so that the Project Manager may develop what is known as a *Work Breakdown Structure* (WBS). The WBS is the central model throughout a project which acts a framework for timescale and manpower planning, budgeting and the subsequent monitoring and evaluation of the project. The first stage therefore involves either the design of a new system or the remodelling of an existing system. Techniques applied within the *Requirements* phase of IT projects to derive the WBS include the composition of *Data Flow Diagrams* (DFDs), constituted of system processes, and *Entity Relationship Diagrams* (ERDs),[13] constituted of events within the system. Both techniques, as part of what is known as the *Systems Analysis Oriented* (SAO) approach, provide a representation of the flow of work within an organisation, along with guidelines for identifying flaws in the system. The methods used here also form a key part of *Business Process Re-engineering* (BPR), a similar vogue in managerial circles which also emphasises the potential for IT to remodel traditional work processes (although BPR appears at present to be proving less enduring than Project Management). More recently, these techniques (DFDs and ERDs) have been combined in an approach known as *Object Oriented Analysis* (OOA), where 'objects' represent both events and processes. A variety of related methods such as Cost-Benefit Analysis and Cash Flow Forecasting may then be applied as decision-making aids, to structure the choice of solution to be implemented.

Once this decision has been made, the next step is to plan the project, defined here as the *Definitional* phase (or *Design* phase in the SDLC). Again, a number of techniques have been developed to operationalise the WBS so that it may be used for purposes of control and evaluation. One traditional method which is still widely used today is through the construction of a *Gantt Chart*, a bar chart with timescale across the top and the activities represented down the side. Slightly more sophisticated methods which could display the interrelationships between project elements emerged from the application of network diagrams. One such technique widely used for project planning is known as *Critical Path*

---

[13] Also known as *Entity Life Histories* (ELHs) achieved via *Entity Event Modelling* (EEM).

Method (CPM), which displays activities as dependent on prior activities and enables the calculation of project duration and slack time. A variation of CPM known as *Program Evaluation and Review Technique* (PERT) accentuates the quantitative basis of these techniques by attempting to integrate uncertainty and risk, specifically by including three estimates of the time for each task. Both the CPM and PERT approaches facilitate the quantification of intangible aspects such as duration and risk, while the *Gantt Chart* provides a basis for manpower and resource planning.

The *Production* stage, defined as the *Implementation* phase in IT, merely involves the administrative and technical aspects of initiating the project in line with the plan. Once the project itself has been implemented, then, the next step is defined as the *Operational* phase, wherein the project manager's duty is to control the development of the project. Here the techniques involved are essentially the same as the previous phase, as the key aim of such systematic, quantitative planning techniques is to ensure *visibility* and *accountability* in the control and evaluation stages of a project. Thus techniques such as PERT and costed versions of the WBS are referred to throughout the project as flexible representations of the project plan against which the actual progress of the project and the performance of staff may be judged. More recently, a range of IT applications have been developed to assist in the monitoring of the progress of projects, such as Microsoft Project through automatically requesting and logging status reports from team members and alerting the project manager if these are late or incomplete. Thus the comprehensive planning process is fundamental to the tight control of the project in operation, based on quantitative specifications which enable performance to be readily and continually assessed against given standards.

The tools and techniques described above are in no way intended to be an exhaustive account of Project Management techniques. The intention, rather, is to give a flavour of the technical, often quantitative nature of these techniques, representative of a particular form of rationality in management circles. These techniques are embodied not only in the numerous textbooks on how to manage projects and collections of documentation required by the procedures, but increasingly in the form of PC software, of which the most widely used, Microsoft Project, claims to have 2 million licensed users world-wide. This is not to endorse the assertion that there exists a standard Project Management ontology, nor a uniform and internationally-recognised body of techniques. The process is evocatively described by Tagg (1983), who states "Despite the fact that they are 95% agreed in their aims and their broad areas of getting there, they nevertheless manage to stay separate. Each sect jealously guards its own style and magic ingredients" (quoted in Fitzgerald, 1996: 10). Indeed, it might be supposed that each application of Project Management within individual organisations, even individual departments, constitutes a distinct interpretation and articulation of a non-uniform, abstract corpus. Despite this variety, central elements of Project Management are evident in each, such that there seems to exist a *broadly* standard basic model.

The development and dissemination of this standardised Project Management model and generally similar techniques also appears to have been accelerated by its recent popularity. The Project Management Institute, for example, reported an increase in membership from 8,817 in 1992 to 24,458 at the end of 1996 (PMI Annual Report, 1996). The last few years has also witnessed a proliferation of management consultancies offering Project Management services and a rapid expansion of University, College and privately-run training courses. In Project Management in general there has also been a multiplication of computer-based support packages in the last decade, similar to the rapid increase in the number of CASE (Computer Aided Software Engineering) tools within IT. This has been described by Fitzgerald as a process of "systematising knowledge", closely related to the "fundamental principles of Taylor's scientific management which sought to find the 'one best way' to perform work" (1996: 7).

A number of wider influences can be pinpointed which have encouraged this growth in Project Management in the field of IT, ranging from the forceful marketing of Project Management consultancies to the support and legitimation of academia, the media and governmental agencies. Without denying the importance of the efforts of the numerous IT consultancies supporting such packages, care must be taken to recognise the interdependencies with public and professional institutions. Thus, for example, reviews of academic literature on IT have revealed a widespread assumption that the problem with project work is the 'irrationality' of practitioners, and that formalised (therefore 'rational') methodologies provide the solution (Fitzgerald, 1996: 9). A further influence worthy of note is the continuation of governmental support and government-developed Project Management systems, in the tradition of the original work in the US military and space programs. In the UK, for example, the *Structured Systems Analysis and Design Method* (SSADM) was adopted in 1980 by the Central Computer and Telecommunications Agency (CCTA), the governmental department responsible for IT in the civil service. More recently it has been integrated with PRINCE, a standard set of Project Management procedures for governmental projects. Since 1984, SSADM has also been promoted in the private sector as the government-approved set of techniques for IT projects in order to improve UK competitiveness. As a consequence, it is now considered by many to be the standard methodology for IT projects in the UK today. What should be emphasised about the growth of SSADM in particular is that it challenges the widespread view that the proliferation of institutions supporting Project Management is a simple reaction to levels of demand in the industry. The expansion of Project Management approaches has been sponsored by a significant number of institutions both private and public, with critical implications for the organisation and control of work in a variety of industries and areas.

Project Management in Operation

To examine the processes by which such practices and structures reproduce themselves, the rest of this chapter will draw on empirical work in Lifelong and Buzzbank. In line with what appears to be a growing trend in IT, both organisations rely on projects as the principal means for structuring and controlling the development of the IT function. The importance of Project Management is magnified by the growing importance of IT in these organisations, and in banking and finance in general. Furthermore, in both companies (although most explicitly in Buzzbank), the notion of Project Management in IT development is being used as a model on which to restructure work in a number of other areas unrelated to IT, thus reproducing a number of technicist assumptions and norms in the organisations more widely.

In both organisations, managers, especially senior managers, appeared convinced of the importance of Project Management structures and techniques. Several interviewees attested to the crucial importance of Project Management not only for IT but for the future performance of the organisation as a whole. For example, the Head of IT Applications at Buzzbank defined the first step in formulating a departmental strategy as deciding "What do we need to excel at?" and naming Project Management as the first "critical success factor" (Jack 2: 134). His colleague, Head of IT Development, indicated what he perceived to be a significant lack in his department;

> "we need people to go and manage IT projects - we don't have *any* of these at the moment" (Angus 1: 104).

In Lifelong, the feeling was similar, although senior management were less explicit regarding their 'need' for Project Management, partly due to the ongoing political disputes between existing staff and the incumbents, versed in Project Management. Nonetheless, the very recruitment of such staff, trained and/or experienced in Project Management, and their sponsorship by senior staff reflects the premium put on Project Management expertise in Lifelong.

As to what this entailed, interpretations varied. In Lifelong, in response to my general question about IT projects, the project manager immediately wrote two lists without any hesitation, the first defining 10 *Steps* ("Feasibility Study, Outline Options, Business Analysis... (up to) Implementation") the second listing *Standards* ("Risk, Cost, Productivity, Schedule, Plans, Resources and Quality") which he described as "the balls I have to juggle" (Doug 1: 5). In Buzzbank the conception of what was implied by 'Project Management' appeared to be less clearly defined, with more variation in how it was interpreted and applied between departments. Senior managers tended to emphasise the formal procedures and techniques, characteristics which many characterise as aspects of 'professionalism';

> "Running pilots, managing third parties, all the basic things Project Management is all about..." (Angus 1: 104).

For middle management and other members of project teams, however, their descriptions of the effects of Project Management focused on the restrictions and bureaucratic demands;

> "Have you done this? Have you done this? Have you done this? Have you got it signed off? Have you thought about your project beforehand...?" (Ian 1: 189).

As noted in my discussion of Project Management techniques above, the key effect of the application of Project Management models and techniques is understood to be *enhanced control* over the conduct of employees, based on the objectification of those subjects involved in project work. In particular, the quantification and detailed planning involved in Project Management serve to enhance both the visibility and the calculability of those employees involved in projects. As tasks are broken down and allocated to staff in an almost Tayloristic fashion, both bureaucratic and technological means of monitoring are used to augment the individualising effects of the discipline. Not only does each team-member have his/her own task and individualised deadlines for completion, but the required quality can also be specified in a quantitative form. It is unsurprising, therefore, that descriptions of Project Management by a number of IT staff in Buzzbank centre on humorous references to bureaucratic control; "I can get you the documentation, if you really want - if I can carry it! (Ian 2: 211).

Nonetheless, all employees appeared to recognise project work as more prestigious than other IT duties insofar as it embodies a 'professional' approach to IT. The responses of the interviewees in both organisations pointed towards a clear association between Project Management and the valuation of professionalism. This was most clearly stated by the head of Business Analysis' explanation of their reputation for Project Management;

"...we always do written terms of reference, we always write a report, we always define our recommendations, so there are a number of stages we always go through, which the business doesn't require but again we think we should do, in order to be *professional* and do it properly" (Tony 1: 122-134).

Similarly in Lifelong, the link was made in describing the actions of the project team;

"We always carry out a thorough review, which is the proper way to do things... not used in some projects round here..." (Doug 1: 1).

Both responses indicate the importance of an attitude of *professionalism*, in addition to a knowledge of the *techniques* of Project Management and denote the centrality of the subjective aspect of the discipline, a crucial point that will be developed below. The following section will therefore commence by attempting to clarify the link between Project Management and modern discourses of professionalism.

The Construction of IT as a Profession

The discussion below will aim to unite two strands of theory relevant to a reading of the development of Project Management; Project Management as a discipline and the construction of the IT professional. As noted in earlier chapters, the discursive constitution of a discipline involves its inscription onto a variety of artefacts. The importance of training and development to Project Management serves to emphasise that these inscriptions include the construction of the *subjectivity* of the individual, in this case through the development of the 'IT professional'. To illustrate this, the following section will first briefly cover the debates in related areas, most notably on critical work on professionalisation. Parallels will then be drawn between recent issues in the debate over professionalism and the work of Foucault, as outlined in earlier chapters. This leads into an analysis of how Project Management is constructed and enforced as a discipline in both Buzzbank and Lifelong. The effects of the monitoring and disciplinary elements of Project Management will then be traced though an analysis of organisational changes in each company. The first step, however, is to examine traditional debates on the role of the professions and processes of professionalisation.

Debates on Professionalism and Professionalisation

The professions have existed as a concern of social theorists since the work of Marx and Durkheim, each taking contrasting positions as to the usefulness and ethical worth of professional organisations (Marx, 1951: Durkheim, 1992). Much of the early sociological literature on the professions, however, can be categorised as adopting either the *trait* or the *functionalist* approaches (or containing aspects of both). The *trait* approach to the professions concentrates on compiling an exhaustive list of features which constitute the core elements of a profession (e.g. Merton *et al*, 1957). As Becker (1970) indicates, the vast majority of these attempts produce checklists possessing broadly similar core elements, and Becker therefore takes up one of the earliest lists of traits, produced by Abraham Flexner in 1915. Flexner defined professions as essentially *intellectual, learned* (as opposed to routine), *practical* (as opposed to academic), possessing a *technique which may be taught*, strongly *organised* internally, and broadly motivated by *altruism*. This final point leads to Flexner's more general and more fundamental criterion, that "what matters most is *professional spirit*" (Flexner, 1915, in Becker, 1970: 88). Assessing numerous models constructed since then, Becker concludes "one is hard put to understand why anyone should want to alter Flexner's original statement, for the similarities between it and those that followed are more striking than the differences" (Becker, 1970: 88). Building on these core elements, some theorists adopted a more dynamic, *process* approach, looking instead at *professionalisation* and attempting to identify what an occupation had to do in order to become a profession (e.g. Wilensky, 1964).

However, the trait approach has attracted criticism for a number of reasons, not least for its atheoretical, inductive method and its willingness to accept the definitions of professionals themselves, thus understanding professions as they generally aim to be perceived (Johnson, 1972). The *functionalist* perspective offered a related approach which was more theoretically grounded, focusing on the specific expertise or knowledge that the professions possess and the importance of this for the functioning of society as a whole (e.g. Barber, 1963). Parsons (1968) builds on this by explaining the emergence of the professions with reference to their foundation in Weberian *rationality*, "locating their development within the rationalising tendencies of the wider society" (Witz, 1992: 40). Such an approach directs the analysis of professionalism towards aspects of this knowledge, such as the control and restriction of recruitment and education and accreditation in the field, backed up in the final instance by the state. The social and economic rewards monopolised by the professions, from this perspective, are explained with reference to their functional usefulness. The functionalist position is therefore summed up by Rueschemeyer as "positing that professions are service- or community-oriented occupations applying a systematic body of knowledge to problems which are highly relevant to central values of society" (in Johnson, 1972: 34).

There is, however, an intrinsic dilemma overlooked by the trait and functionalist approaches, which can be distinguished in Flexner's distinction between the "core elements" of professionalism and the importance of a "professional spirit". From a symbolic interactionist perspective, Becker (1970) identifies the dilemma as stemming from a confusion between elements of an objective 'ideal-type' of professionalism, and the everyday, morally-desirable concept of professionalism. His solution is to adopt the everyday concept, and ask "what are commonly agreed to be the features of a work group that can legitimately be called professional?" (Becker, 1970: 92). Pursuing this question opens up the field to cover not only professional knowledge/expertise but equally importantly what may be termed *professional behaviour*. Becker therefore emphasises that "to be accepted one must have learned to play the part" (Becker *et al*, 1961: 4). Reflecting the processual construction of professionalism, he goes on to stress that "there is *continuing* pressure for (the professional) to give the kind of service that, in the layman's eyes, is satisfactory" (Becker, 1970: 101, emphasis added). This is not to displace the importance of expertise and credentialism, but to underline the role of both knowledge *and* conduct in the ongoing construction of a profession, including the 'established' professions such as medicine and law.

The Emergence of a Critical Perspective

The focus of the professionalism debate shifted substantially in the 1970s with the emergence of a critical perspective from writers such as Freidson (1970) and Johnson (1972). Drawing on neo-Marxist and Neo-Weberian perspectives, this work fiercely criticised the tendency in the existing approaches to ignore issues of power and domination in accounts of professionalism, taking the functional usefulness of professions for granted. Instead, this critical stream highlighted the centrality of issues of power and domination to the study of the professions, emphasising what Witz terms "the conceptual indissolubility of the concepts of 'power' and 'profession'"

(1992: 40). Thus Johnson's critique defines "the institutionalised form of the *control* of occupations" (Johnson, 1972: 38, emphasis added) as the cardinal purpose of professionalisation. Larson later builds upon Johnson's neo-Marxist critique, adding a somewhat economistic dimension and defining professionalisation as "the process by which producers of special services sought to constitute and control a market for their expertise" (Larson, 1977: xvi). Larson therefore accounts for the power of the professions as derived from monopoly, "the attempt to relate one order of scarce resources - special knowledge and skills - into another - social and economic rewards" (Larson, 1977: xvii). In addition, Larson critiques the notion of 'service' seen as central to the professions by drawing attention to the efforts of professionals to control clients.

The importance of this approach is its emphasis on the symbiotic relationship between the professions and a matrix of capitalist institutions, including the state, the labour market, bureaucratic organisation and the education system. It has been noted that Larson's analysis seems to reflect aspects of Weber's, arguing that in the eighteenth and nineteenth centuries, "the rise of professionalism has been a phase of *capitalist rationalisation*" (Witz, 1992: 55). Since this period, according to Larson, a second phase of professionalisation has occurred, leading to the emergence of what she defines as the 'modern professions'. These she distinguishes from 'traditional' professions supported by aristocratic and elite sponsorship, such as early medicine, law, architecture, etc. The 'modern professions' are instead supported by the use of tactics of *occupational closure* around the professionally-defined body of knowledge. While, broadly speaking, neo-Marxist work focused on the relationship between the professions, the class structure and the state, a significant amount of neo-Weberian work pursued this notion of control via occupational closure. Thus Parkin (1979) defines *exclusionary* and *demarcationary* strategies as two modes of occupational closure whereby groups attempt to professionalise. Exclusionary strategies involve the internal regulation of the supply of professional labour in order to create a monopoly of skills and knowledge. Demarcationary strategies, on the other hand, involve the external control of barriers between the sphere of influence of the profession and that of other occupational groups. A significant amount of work has been carried out by a number of writers (e.g. Freidson, 1977; Abbott, 1988; Murphy, 1988) analysing the operation of such strategies of "occupational imperialism" (Larkin, 1983).

Knowledge and Professional Conduct

However, many neo-Marxist analyses appear to view professions as functioning essentially to ensure the reproduction of capitalist culture and class relations (Abercrombie and Urry, 1983). Ironically, this can be seen to reproduce the functionalism of much earlier work, by uncritically acknowledging the social and economic value of the knowledge monopolised by the established professions. Crucially, this omits the *social construction of professional knowledge*, and therefore disregards the processes by which such knowledge is articulated and legitimated (Abbott, 1988). Therefore analysing in great detail the processes of exclusion often entails ignoring the first step and, as Fournier notes, taking the constitution of "the field or discipline within which a profession operates as 'given', 'in the order of things'" (1991: 3). One partial exception to this tendency is Larson who focuses on the relations between 'knowledge' and 'power' to balance her analysis of the construction of "professional markets" with an analysis of how professions gain autonomy through the production of an "ideology of professionalism" (Freidson, 1970). Larson's analysis of this ideology identifies a number of elements, including individualism, expertise, service, and anti-bureaucracy, which are transferred through socialisation and education in the discipline. In a somewhat circular argument, Larson explains that "once reached, this structural position (of professionalism) allows a group of experts to define and construct particular areas of social reality, under the guise of universal validity conferred upon them by their expertise" (Larson, 1977: xiii). Nonetheless, Larson's generally sophisticated analysis returns to a rather functionalist neo-Marxist conclusion, defining the essential function of the ideology of professionalism as "reproduc(ing) the relations of production and the class structure by disguising their real nature and even their existence" (Larson, 1977: 239).

So while exclusionary strategies are of interest, of at least equal importance are the processes by which a discipline attempts to establish a monopoly over *truth* to establish its legitimacy as a profession. In this area, the parallels with Foucault's work on truth and power/knowledge suggest that Foucauldian work may offer a useful perspective on professionalism and professionalisation. In addition, Foucault's work on discipline and the self reprises a number of concerns of symbolic interactionists such as Becker (1970), specifically regarding the importance of *professional conduct* in the construction and control of subjectivity. From this perspective, professionalism is reinforced and gains legitimacy in the eyes of those external to it (e.g. directors, non-professional staff, the media, etc.) not only through claims to competence but also, as Fournier emphasises, in constituting the conduct expected of a professional. "Although competence embodies the government of truth, it is not indexed merely in terms of the extent to which the practitioner has mastered truth (i.e. the knowledge of the practitioner) but in terms of appropriate conduct" (Fournier, 1997: 7).

Furthermore, such a Foucauldian approach emphasises that while the legitimacy of professions relies upon the establishment and maintenance of appropriate norms of knowledge and conduct, such norms also act as a form of *discipline* over otherwise autonomous professional labour (Fournier, 1997). Implicit in this is the disciplinary constitution of subjectivity whereby careful socialisation and the inculcation of self-discipline allows senior management to dispense with a reliance on direct forms of control in the case of professional employees. Thus induction into professions, in terms of *both* knowledge *and* conduct, serves to construct a specifically governable subjectivity rooted in self-disciplinary mechanisms (Grey, 1998). Professional discipline therefore "does not only constitute the subjectivity of the 'other' or object of professional practice (e.g. patient with illness, legal subject with right...) but also the subject positions along which professional conduct is to be articulated" (Fournier, 1997: 5).

This insight is not restricted to Foucauldian work; Becker, for one, examined the different modes of induction and socialisation of engineering, physiology and philosophy students in *The Development of Identification with an Occupation* (Becker and Carper, 1970). However, the adoption of a Foucauldian perspective makes it explicit that moving beyond a neo-Marxist focus on the exploitation of professionalism by the powerful entails an obligation upon critical theorists to "consider the ways in which social order is reproduced through the co-production of *both the notionally powerful and the powerless*" (Grey, 1998: 31, emphasis added). The situation is summarised succinctly by Fournier, who states that "Professionals are both the instrument and the subject of government, the governor and the governed" (Fournier, 1997: 5). It is this *double-edged* nature of professionalisation which will be developed below in the context of Project Management; that *the increase in security, material rewards and social influence afforded by professionalisation is intrinsically linked to the subjection of such professionals to a significant level of discipline and domination.*

The Construction of Project Management as a Profession

The actions taken within the field of Project Management give the impression that practitioners have *explicitly* modelled a strategy based on other, more 'legitimate' professions, targeting key elements and taking specific steps to emulate them. In the discussion above, professionalism and professionalisation has been seen to involve a number of broad strategies, including the *formal internal organisation of an occupation*, the *development of a body of knowledge*, the *promotion of accredited training*

184 Discourse, Discipline and the Subject

programs and attempts to expand *credentialism within job markets*. In each of these areas, despite clear efforts, the progress of Project Management has been very uneven. The efforts made to form institutional supports through professional associations have resulted in the emergence of professional bodies in many developed countries, as well as a European association, although the international links between such bodies are as yet limited. This is borne out by the continued discrepancies between the recognised bodies of knowledge, ethical principles, etc. of the two main associations, the PMI in the US and IPMA in Europe. Moreover, accreditation by the PMI, for instance, is still practically based, involving the submission of a CV detailing the individuals level of experience in projects, to be assessed by existing members. While systematic and 'academically-grounded' training in Project Management has expanded, the provision of this has not extended far beyond consultancies and private organisations, and still lacks the support of dedicated university courses in both the US and Europe. A significant exception to this is pertinent here; in the case of IT, Project Management has become an accepted part of most Computing/Information Systems courses in Higher Education. This has not extended to licensure backed up at a governmental level; although, as noted, most governments in Western countries support and encourage Project Management models, especially in the field of IT, this does not as yet entail restrictions on practitioners in the form of mandatory qualifications.

Despite the relatively limited progress towards the professionalisation of Project Management, the relevant professional organisations continue in their efforts in all of the above areas. The PMI Annual Report (1996), for instance, details a number of aspects of its long-term strategy, which include bringing the Project Management Journal into line with standard academic journals, the release of an updated *Guide to the Project Management Body of Knowledge*, a tightening of requirements for accreditation to improve its perceived legitimacy among businesses and development of a salaried infrastructure for the accreditation process. However, such macro-level initiatives cannot be assumed to be universally effective, and can only be interpreted as a *context* for the actual constitution and operation of Project Management in individual organisations and departments. As noted, each application of Project Management constitutes a distinct interpretation and articulation of what has been seen to be a disparate, abstract body of practices. It is within this context that the interpretation and articulation of Project Management in the subject organisations will now be examined.

It will be argued here that an essential part of the professionalisation of the IT function involves *the constitution and operation of Project*

Management as a discipline. As a discipline, Project Management can be understood to exist in an abstract and purportedly objective body of rules, with a specific language and ontology. While the formation of this discipline is intimately related to particular aspects of technicist management theory, the dedicated vocabulary and terminology serve to represent the world in keeping with the ontology constructed by Project Management. This should be understood in terms of Foucault's 'productive' notion of power/knowledge configurations (Foucault, 1980), as discussed in Chapter 2. Thus Project Management, in drawing heavily on technical rationality to represent the world in certain ways, produces certain forms of knowledge and enables a particular material ordering of the world. Furthermore, this discipline should not be seen to exist merely in this abstract, ideal form; in line with the notion of discourse defined above, discipline should be seen as inscribed in texts, practices, technology and in the subjectivities of those individuals instructed in the discipline and/or subjected to the practices. In this way, Project Management forms part of a disciplinary mechanism within organisations, with a number of power effects which can be perceived within both Lifelong and Buzzbank.

In the case of Project Management, much of this project of professionalisation relies upon the significant efforts made from a variety of quarters to construct Project Management as a recognisable and coherent *discipline*. The legitimacy of Project Management therefore rests upon its claims to monopolise expertise which in some way articulates the 'truth' of organisational reality, as determined by recourse to technical rationality. I would draw a comparison here between Project Management and attempts made by mainstream management theory to constitute itself as a profession. Project Management resembles management more widely in that it draws to a large extent on its (perceived) basis in technical rationality and positivist science to support its claims to professionalism. As noted above, a significant advantage of this tactic is the image of a neutral and objective professionalism that scientism bestows, regardless of its actual relation to scientific practice. Thus, similarly to mainstream management, Project Management can be said to rely on "the twin features of an appeal to science and the claim of neutrality ... providing a strong basis for professionalisation" (Grey, 1998b: 14). Grey, however, goes on to examine the curious failure of management to achieve professional status, despite these conditions. Highlighting the social control effected by management education, he argues that the case of management should not be viewed as an example of a 'failed professionalization' but rather as a 'successful responsibilization' of managers; the creation of 'docile subjects', in Foucault's terminology. Equally, within Project Management, attempts to professionalise have already served to enforce a mode of discipline over managers and staff, and this discipline is continually reinforced despite, and as a partial result of, Project Management's lack of professional status in society as a whole.

In the following section I will develop this analysis by outlining how each of these aspects of the construction and operation of a discipline may be read from the subject organisations.

Discipline and the 'Body of Knowledge'

The first point to be made, therefore, is to refer back to the efforts made over the last forty years to build what is explicitly termed the 'Body of Knowledge' of Project Management, based on the PLC framework. Indeed, despite the variety of models and techniques, a number of attempts have been made by academics and professional organisations to regulate these and disseminate a unified model and set of rules. In the field of IT in the UK, SSADM is the most pertinent example, thanks in part to widespread usage and government sponsorship. In the subject organisations, a number of staff refer directly to a similar perception of a unitary, model applicable across a wide range of situations; one middle manager in Buzzbank, for instance, emphasised the homogeneity of the projects that he was involved in, defining the process as;

> "'What do we need from it? How are we going to do it? What are we going to use to do it?', produce it, pilot it to a sub-group of users, and get the feedback. I suppose in that way the process you go through is much the same, because it's potentially providing a solution to a problem that's needed." (Ian 1: 221)

This perception is reproduced in both organisations, reflecting a general assumption that a general model does exist with rules that can apply to all project-based work. It was immediately striking that Project Management's representation of the process was generally accepted as natural and therefore universal. What also became apparent is that a significant number of employees of all levels seemed to compare their own flawed procedures with some ideal model of Project Management. More importantly, without mentioning any other organisations by name, they generally implied that this ideal model was being implemented perfectly somewhere outside their own organisation. Thus one head of department, explaining recent changes in Buzzbank, self-consciously put the changes in perspective by stating;

> "We became a lot more formal in a lot of our projects - they're still not as formal as a lot of those *outside*, but for Buzzbank they are!" (Tony 1: 122-134)

Whether or not this 'ultimate' Project Management is actually being implemented, I mean to suggest here two possible implications of this perception of an perfect model elsewhere. Firstly, the ideal model can be seen to correspond to the notion of the 'correct' solution, entirely in keeping with the positivist doctrines of technical rationality. Secondly, it reinforces the belief that greater formalisation can overcome the difficulties of complexity and rapid change; as Townley notes with regard to technicism in HRM discourses, "this discourse is maintained, even intensified, when faced with evidence to the contrary" (1994: 140). Similarly, rather than question the effectiveness of Project Management, failures in one's own Project Management system are then interpreted as down to one's imperfect implementation of this potential panacea. In both Buzzbank and Lifelong, managers were keen to play down their expertise in the area of Project Management, usually with humorous self-deprecation and veiled references to the relative competence of their competitors in this area. I do not mean to imply by this that both companies represented the pinnacle of Project Management expertise without knowing it. However, the insecurities prevalent in each organisation highlight an important element in the power effects of such a discourse; by constructing the discipline of Project Management as 'skills' and 'experience', the potential for improvement can be represented as limitless. The head of department quoted above, for instance, used Buzzbank's relatively informal system to justify his ongoing promotion of the Strategic Plan, aimed to increase the formality of Buzzbank's Project Management procedures. Thus the "search for the holy paradigm" (Fitzgerald, 1996) mentioned above is reflected not only in the efforts of Project Management researchers to find this ideal model but in the tacit understandings of practitioners also.

Discipline, Terminology and Ontology

A second and critically important aspect of the discursive construction of Project Management is the strict enforcement of a specific *terminology*, in addition to IT staff's customary employment of a particular technical jargon. This may be interpreted in two complementary ways. Firstly, the ability to understand and employ the required terminology is a particularly conspicuous aspect of the *professional conduct* expected of initiates, as well as implying a level of knowledge/expertise. Thus to be recognised as a 'professional' project manager, the individual needs to demonstrate cognisance of the body of knowledge, as well as an ability to articulate this knowledge through the requisite terminology. Secondly, the enforcement of this terminology acts *to reinforce the ontology* of Project Management upon those subject to the discipline. Successful enforcement of the

188 *Discourse, Discipline and the Subject*

terminology effectively controls the discursive resources available to staff in their subjective attempts to make sense of and articulate social reality as it relates to Project Management. Opinions and positions expressed which do not utilise the same ontology can thereby be marginalised as 'lacking expertise' and unprofessional. This is of particular importance given Project Management's promotion of the positivism and technical rationality upon which its models, ontology and claims to legitimation are founded.

With regard to the first point, I have proposed that the correct deployment of appropriate terminology, including a significant amount of jargon, acronyms, abbreviations, etc, can be interpreted as an example of both professional conduct and evidence of professional expertise. One particularly striking example of this occurred as I sat in on the weekly breakfast meeting of the PC Services team at Buzzbank, held at 8am around a table in the canteen. The four team members of varying ranks were discussing the issue of security on the PC Banking project, and a brainstorming session developed to solve a particular difficulty. My initial impression, was of informality and collegial openness, as the team members lounged around eating scrambled eggs, gossiping and joking. However, as the debate progressed there appeared to be an element of tension and competition developing. Each participant was suggesting a more complex solution than the previous had and then immediately backing down, apparently making very little effort to defend their idea. As the suggestions increased in complexity and seeming unfeasibility, as it became apparent that an aim of each participant was to display a greater knowledge of both IT and Project Management. The session began to resemble a game of poker, with each participant raising the stakes, using more and more acronyms and abbreviations from both technical jargon and Project Management terminology. Eventually the youngest and most junior member of the team was forced to ask the meaning of a particular abbreviation, which the team leader then explained to him in a condescending manner. A weak joke was then made by another on the number of abbreviations being thrown around, which relieved the tension that had built up on all sides and allowed the discussion to resume at a more relaxed tempo.

A number of issues related to professionalism, terminology and discipline were apparent in this meeting. The strenuous efforts made by all members to display conduct appropriate to professional IT project staff emphasises the relationship between professionalism and the sense of identity and self-esteem of the staff. While it is feasible that my presence may have exacerbated this competitive display, this does not undermine, and indeed might be seen to confirm, the relevance of professional *conduct*, based on technical and Project Management expertise, to the identity projects of IT staff. In particular, this can be interpreted as indicative of a particularly competitive and masculinist environment. Most importantly, however, the specific use of language in the everyday operation of power in the organisation should be underlined. Failure to keep up with the stakes results in social sanctions which simultaneously affirms the other members' position in the tacit hierarchy of 'expertise' while emphasising their dependence on demonstrations of this expertise for security. This example is raised as the most explicit out of a number of instances in each organisation where the operation of power relations through terminology and jargon became evident. This was particularly the case in Lifelong, where anxiety over the forthcoming restructuring made competency in Project Management an issue of some concern to many staff.

This is directly related to the second issue, the connections between the disciplinary enforcement of a specific terminology and the internalisation of a defined ontology. The importance of enforcing terminology was particularly apparent in interviews with the Lifelong project manager, Doug. Doug declared very early in the interview that he had been brought in originally as a consultant to enforce project management structures within the IT division. Throughout our interviews, he was fiercely specific to the point of dogmatism on the terminology to be used not only by his subordinates and colleagues in the division but also by myself in our interviews. In the first interview, after I had posed several tentative and rather general questions, he interrupted impatiently "There's some information you want and you aren't telling me what it is...". I replied with more general references to IT development and Project Management techniques, at which point, his patience exhausted, he interrupted again "Now *there* you're being ambiguous without realising it!". Taking out a sheet of paper, he drew his model of Project Management and the criteria and techniques he employed at each stage. He emphasised with some force that these were the terms that I was to employ from then on (Doug 1: 5). Rather taken aback now, I looked over the outline and mumbled agreement, after which he seemed to relax and became even helpful, as long as the interview kept to matters within the confines of Project Management. As a consequence, the substance of the first interview was restricted to rather objective matters, relating to Project Management criteria, procedures and usual practice. Although later interviews covered less 'objective' areas, in this first encounter the power effects of the imposition of a terminology were clearly evident.

Terminology was also perceived as very important in Doug's attempts to train Lifelong staff in the Project Management approach. Explaining the reason for his employment, he began by stating bluntly that all the staff in the department, with the exception of one manager, were insular, with no experience of the world outside Lifelong and ignorant of even the basics of Project Management. Providing an example, he was evidently appalled that many could not even distinguish between 'problems' and 'requirements' (when pressed, he explained that the former means "what's wrong with the old system", and the latter "what must be added/improved for the next version"). He stated with evident disgust, even anger;

> "Some of them'll say 'We've found a problem in Version 1 so we've worked it out and now we've got a requirement', and that's absolute CRAP!" (Doug 1: 2)

His role, as he perceived it, was not unlike that of the TN Banking staff imported into Buzzbank; to instil the discipline of Project Management into unruly, informal processes and more importantly, into unruly, informal employees. The solution, as Doug went on to outline, went beyond mere conformity to rules; " - It's a question of *changing their mindsets*" (Doug 1: 2, emphasis added).

Without reducing this solution to simply the enforcement of a terminology, this statement does provide a significant insight into what precisely is implied by the *discipline* of Project Management. Implicit in this is a surprisingly profound understanding of the foundational importance of language in identity construction. Moreover, it is clearly understood by Doug at least how language may (and, in his view, must) be employed to instil this discipline in his employees at a 'deep level'.

Elsewhere in Lifelong, this concern over *definitions and terminology* appeared widespread. Management in other sections of IT, including those not directly involved in project work, appeared similarly firm in their use of language, although rather less aggressive in most cases. This often became evident when staff took great pains to define everyday terms, or to correct my use of certain terms. For example, the rather hyperactive Head of Service Management, in an elaborate description of normal procedures, seemed at first reluctant to define a 'project', although I had not asked for any definition ;

> "what happens currently is you've got a development *project* -I won't go into that..."

This reluctance was clearly transient, as he immediately 'relented' and gave a rapid rundown of phenomena which qualified as 'projects';

> "i.e. a new system, change to existing system, hardware upgrade, software upgrade, etc, they would all be seen as a *project*" (Rick: 446).

This concern to clearly demarcate the boundaries of expressions, particularly in communication with others, appeared widespread in the IT and IT-related departments of both organisations. The immediate effect of this is to reinforce the representation of the world within each organisation in Project Management terms; in this case, as fitting in with the SDLC framework. This is reinforced by the power effects of language and terminology, as noted above, and especially by the association of a given terminology and jargon with professional expertise. The effect of the interaction of these two aspects of professional language is to monopolise the representation of processes in line with the Project Management model, by attempting to sanction certain articulations of organisational processes, while delegitimising as 'unprofessional' those which do not subscribe to the Project Management ontology. The next step, examined in the following section, acts to obscure the political nature of this process by emphasising the objectivity of the professional discipline.

Discipline, Abstraction and Objectivity

It is important to note that, in the Project Management literature, the discipline of Project Management is generally promoted as centring on an *abstract skill*. This skill is therefore seen as transferable to individual managers through training and experience and then applicable in a range of diverse situations. The extraction and distillation of this knowledge is directly related by many authors to the principles of Scientific Management, "changing all subject-dependent knowledge into knowledge in an objective form" (Fitzgerald, 1996: 7). The dissemination of this knowledge amongst managers then becomes a key objective of organisations; for example, one senior manager in Buzzbank stated that their aim, not just within IT but elsewhere, was to;

> "establish 2-3 project managers who don't have teams. They can then find things that need to be done, and solutions that may be found outside the organisation, in private consultancies" (Angus 1: 104).

This perceived need for general project managers had significant consequences for one specific department, Business Analysis (BA). BA had existed within the IT division for several years, and under its present head, its role had shifted from that of a business-IT interface to acting as a dedicated Business Process Re-engineering department. As such, BA's links with the rest of IT became minimal, as it transformed itself into a predominantly non-technical "kind of internal consultancy" (Tony 1: 35). One link with IT which remained, however, was the importance of Project Management, the head describing BA more than once as "the Centre of

Excellence" in terms of Project Management (Tony 1: 214; Tony 2: 307). BA therefore came to serve as a training centre for the production of 'flying' project managers. The Head of BA explained;

> "a lot of people internally come to BA for experience of project work, because you get quite a lot of people in the line out there who have experience of managing people, and may have a management background in banking, but they haven't done much in the way of project work, and there's such a lot of change going on that people need to be skilled in lots of areas" (Tony 1: 138).

Candidates with an 'aptitude' for Project Management were therefore selected internally and initiated in Project Management techniques and processes. The (present) informality of this role was stressed, the manager stating;

> "it's not as if they have a formal development plan with a stint in the BA Team, although that may come" (Tony 1: 202).

The ancillary of this responsibility for Project Management development was the 'missionary' role of the Business Analysis department. An analogy can be drawn here with the insistence in the rhetoric of Human Resource Management that "if HRM is to be taken seriously, personnel managers must give it away" (Guest, 1987: 51). A similar responsibility is adopted by the BA department, the head explaining that;

> "a lot of people come to us either on secondment, or on a permanent basis for one or two years or whatever for that experience and then go back out into the business" (Tony 1: 138).

His explanation of the rationale behind this is even more explicit;

> "what we want are people who want to learn as much as possible about project work, and then to take that back out into the line" (Tony 1: 202).

It should be noted here that by 'people', Tony refers here to managers in a general sense, rather than specifically IT managers. What is significant here is the notion that Project Management is understood throughout Buzzbank as a form of expertise which exists independently of the situation, as a valuable, even critical 'add-on' to employees' experience of banking, insurance, mortgages, investment and the numerous other specialisms within Buzzbank. Like 'management skills', it is seen as essentially abstract and therefore able to be transferred and applied in almost any organisational context. Furthermore, this reinforces the understanding of the discipline of Project Management as embodied in practices and therefore relying on the construction of a work *identity* formed around the discipline.

In Lifelong, this transferability of Project Management was put to me very forcefully by one project manager, who seemed to interpret my inquiry about his background to be a questioning of his financial services credentials. After stating that his background was in managing projects in manufacturing, he paused, then added aggressively;

"... and there's NO difference between that sort of environment and this one!"

I was more rather unnerved by his vehement retort to what I believed to be a neutral, 'opener' of a question. Unfortunately, my rather meek "No?" did nothing to smooth the waters as he retorted even more forcefully;

"NO! None at all!" (Doug 1: 1).

This provides a very clear example of the relationship between Project Management and the subjective construction of a valued identity. After some consideration after the event, I read it that, at least in part, the vehemence reflects the fact that Doug's reputation and very identity as a consultant in Project Management depended directly upon the belief in the transferability of Project Management as a discipline.

What should be underlined here is that this understanding of a transferable Project Management discipline reinforces its objectivity, which is reflected by the frequent use of mechanical metaphors (Morgan, 1986). The model and related techniques are thus portrayed as a neutral 'toolkit' with the power to restructure not only IT systems but all work systems so as to afford greater efficiency. The description of Project Management as a 'toolbox' (Doug 2: 5) is a key example of this, which underlines the neutrality of the discipline and indicates the prevalence of discourses founded on technical rationality (Morgan, 1986). The same theme can be discerned in different metaphors; for example, the same manager describes the information made visible by Project Management techniques as "a bit like the speedometer on a car", with IT as the metaphorical driver and the Business as navigator (Doug 2: 5). A key effect of this representation is to underline the objective nature of Project Management in everyday communication, as a 'mere' technical function without an agenda of its own, divorced from political values and far removed from moral or ethical concerns.

This image of objectivity was emphasised in a number of ways throughout the interviews, often in an apparently defensive way. Thus the project manager at Lifelong, after completing his lists defining Project Management, stated;

"Now I can do both of these but I prefer this (*the right hand column*)...".

After a brief pause, as if embarrassed at bringing subjective preferences into the matter, he hurriedly added "...but that's that!" (Doug 1: 5) before moving swiftly on to another, less 'personal' matter. In Buzzbank, in conversation with a middle manager I referred to a previous conversation (with his head of department) where he spoke of "getting structures in place" (Jack 1: 19). He carefully challenged this phrase, stating;

"when you say 'structures in place' I don't think that necessarily means hierarchical management structures as such, I think it's more procedures, yeah? I think it's more a case of 'This is a Product Life Plan, and you have to fill in all the bits to make sure you're doing it right'... I think it's more like a sort of *structuring of work*, rather than a *structuring of people*." (Martin 1: 236)

At one level, this can be taken as a slight difference in interpretation, possibly indicating a sensitivity to the charge of increasing bureaucracy, in line with the discussion of discourse in Buzzbank (see Chapter 5). It also, however, reflects the assertion that Project Management models are *used* by people to structure their work, contradicting what might be taken to be the (vaguely) threatening implication in my phrase that they *act upon* people. The following section will dispute this assertion, examining the ways in which the discipline of Project Management does indeed act upon and through individuals in a very profound way. However, these examples, along with numerous less defensive and less reflexive references to the neutrality and progressive value of Project Management, serve to underline the importance that the discipline should be perceived as unthreatening by both its practitioners and those outside the discipline affected by the processes and techniques themselves. Indeed, this purported neutrality and technocratic objectivity is a crucial element of the power effects of the discourse of Project Management.

It can be seen from this discussion that a number of elements converge to constitute Project Management as a *professional* discipline, beyond the everyday sense of a branch of learning. Efforts to produce a unified model and set of procedures, along with a specific terminology, help to constitute the field as a discipline. However, equally fundamental is the specific construction of Project Management as an objective and transferable body of knowledge, serving only to improve the efficiency and effectiveness of organisational projects. The concern for training and development within both Buzzbank and Lifelong reflects the importance of inscribing this discipline of Project Management onto the subjectivities of 'professional' employees. Furthermore, in establishing Project Management in each organisation, the emphasis is firmly upon ways in which the discipline can be instilled into the staff not only within IT but elsewhere in the company. 'Changing the mindsets' of the employees relies on a number of aspects of professionalisation, whereby the IT function gains the status but equally is subject to the control of professional autonomy.

What it is important to stress here is that the operation of discipline in constituting work identities appropriate to IT professionals should not be taken to imply that responsible autonomy is the exclusive means of control over them in these organisations. As Fournier points out, "Some of these new softwares of control", (such as professional discipline, in this case), "rely on a complex interweaving of bureaucratic logic with the logic (or rule) of responsible autonomy" (Fournier, 1997: 11). Thus the self-discipline and "responsibilization" (Grey, 1997a; 1998) imposed by the construction of Project Management as a discipline does not exclude more direct methods of control. In Buzzbank, for instance, the growing use of IT applications structured around Project Management control techniques clearly served to intensify the levels of surveillance of these 'IT professionals'. Ironically, many of the IT staff were employed to develop, tailor and 'road-test' such applications which will then be used to monitor *their own* conduct and performance in project-based work.

Overall, then, the control effects of Project Management should be seen to extend beyond the surveillance and control of the project team by the project manager. The wider disciplinary effects of Project Management have been examined in detail above, particularly with regard to the links with a discourse of professionalism. In addition, the direct control of work is an equally fundamental objective of Project Management, through the monitoring of conduct enabled by Project Management's quantification and individualisation of work. This dual nature of Project Management, operating through both professional discipline and direct control, produces a complex and interesting nexus of power relations in the organisations examined. I will now examine the *limits* to the effectiveness of such a project in both Buzzbank and Lifelong, through the operation of what may be interpreted as forms of resistance and discretion in each company. I will then go on to complete the analysis by examining instances of the dynamic operation of Project Management in Lifelong and Buzzbank and its potential transformation through resistant and subversive conduct of subjects within each organisation.

Resistance and Discretion

It is important here to qualify the impression which might have been given in the ongoing discussion, regarding the *effectiveness* of the discipline of Project Management and professionalism. While analysing the interview responses in isolation, particularly the responses of management, I became aware of the danger of 'believing the hype' i.e. accepting management's portrayal of a watertight system of direct control via technological surveillance supplemented by careful socialisation. The only variation from this line was the admission by a number of interviewees that the bureaucratic control of Project Management is not followed to the letter in all cases, and that steps are omitted, documentation is overlooked and reports are missed out in the everyday practices of project managers and team members. This does seem to reflect ongoing debates in the academic literature on Project Management in IT as to whether or not the SDLC must be followed entirely faithfully (Fitzgerald, 1996). Thus one project manager in Buzzbank admitted;

> "a lot of it is overkill, we still probably cover probably the same method (as project managers elsewhere), except we don't spend days thinking 'do we really need this?'" (Ian 1: 203).

In Lifelong, a more considered response came from the project manager there, who emphasised;

> "The project life cycle involves certain tasks but you've got to tailor your cloth and cut corners where necessary - either justify your reason for missing out tasks or do the work!" (Doug 2: 4).

Far from implying that the disciplinary effect of Project Management is less stringent than represented, however, this explanation points to the 'complex interweaving' of control mechanisms noted above. Discretion in the application of Project Management is clearly possible, but the key point is that, as put by one manager;

> "you justify why you've dropped the steps you have - if you differ from the standard it's *because...* - so obviously you only get the confidence to do that through experience, and security comes from that" (Doug 2: 5).

The idea behind this is clear - only those who have 'internalised' the discipline are able to deviate from the structure.

At one level, this can be read as a simple reflection of the orthodoxy of any training programme; much like driving a car, it aims at the internalisation of a set of practices, and once this internalisation is complete the driver may then omit steps according to his/her experience and discretion. My aim here is not to challenge this model for learning sets of skills, although it might be contested that even in the transfer of skills, this internalisation represents the productive operation of disciplinary practices on the subject. In this case, moreover, it is not a question of the 'mere' transfer of skills. Rather, as reflected in the reference to the 'mindset' above, internalising the logic of technical rationality embedded in Project Management entails a far more substantial reconstruction of the subjectivity of the 'professional'. The construction of the professional attempts to reset the framework by which the individual interprets and makes sense of the world, in keeping with the logic of the discipline itself. Through this combination of supplementary and interdependent techniques, the disciplining of employees is attempted to ensure their productive and compliant conduct.

Doug's final comment, "and security comes from that", hints at the means by which such disciplines may achieve such a fundamental change; namely, that such discourses provide a level of security against the complexity and unpredictability of the outside world. This seemed to lend some weight to research which has pointed to the importance of SSADM as a 'social defence' i.e. a set of rituals which "allow practitioners to deny their feelings of impotence in the face of daunting technical and political challenges" (Wastell, 1996: 25). Thus the certainty of the structures and the social approbation reaffirm the identities of those engaged in 'professional' project work, while simultaneously causing anxiety over the employees' ability to achieve this level of behaviour. Evidently, this is a cumulative process, reinforced by months of prior technical training, scientific education, etc. and either daily discipline in the Project Management framework or secondment to a particular department can be seen as a continuation of this process on receptive individuals. Consequently, I would argue that this process should be read as far more than the acquisition of a tacit skill; the intention, if not always the effect, of instituting Project Management structures is the manipulation and construction of a particular form of subjectivity among employees.

The Ambiguity of Humour

This said, there were still instances which might be interpreted as resistance to this pervasive disciplinary restructuring of work identity, and these were generally identified during the periods of observation in the organisations. Via humour, the values and norms of professionalism and Project Management were mocked in the day-to-day practices of employees and some managers. As noted in Chapter 5, humour frequently indicates issues which cause insecurity and anxiety in an individual, and can be interpreted as an attempt to manage this anxiety in a social context. Certain instances of humour I noted in each organisation seemed to fit in with this categorisation, particularly where recurrent themes pointed to areas which cause significant conflict in the employees' maintenance of a positive and coherent identity and perspective. In many cases, they appear to point to a form of 'distancing', to use Goffman's (1959) terminology, on the part of the individual. While this may be accurately interpreted as a relatively effective form of resistance to the disciplinary effects of Project Management, this is to overlook the damaging side-effects of such 'distancing'. Furthermore, the effectiveness of this conduct is not a foregone conclusion; humour appears to be a way of dealing with contradiction but often as a substitute for action. At the very least, however, the examples below point to some recognition of a problematic state of affairs on the part of the individual, hence the potential for substantive action.

In Buzzbank, then, the focus for most of the humour seemed to centre on two general themes; *frustrations at levels of bureaucracy* and *insecurities over the 'professional' identity staff were expected to display.* For example, Ian, a team manager, in describing SSADM stated;

> "'Right, you're at the feasibility stage: Have you done this, have you done this, have you done this? Have you got it signed off? Have you thought about your project beforehand, what functions it can and can't do and how you go about it? Have you got it signed off? You've tested it? You can have an implementation review - is everything okay?' If not, back round the cycle again!"

After emphasising the pedantic nature of the procedure in this way, he added;

> "It's a formal method, to make sure you've not missed anything out, like (slaps forehead) 'D'oh! I've forgot to test it!'" (laughs) (Ian 1: 189)

This might be read as reflecting the contradiction between the competency that IT professionals are nominally credited with and the rigour of the bureaucratic controls that Project Management subjects them to. Nonetheless, constant references to professionalism in everyday banter implied that the IT staff were struggling with their understanding of what was demanded of them in their new role.

One of the most direct instances of humour in this respect occurred while carrying out my introductions at the start of my observation. As I described the focus of my research somewhat vaguely as "Professionals working in teams", one manager replied with a laugh;

> "After you've spent a while with us you might have to change that to '*People* working in teams'!". (Ian : OBS2: 1)

The theme continued in banter between staff of all levels in the IT department; later, for instance, a middle manager in Buzzbank, Lee, complained good-naturedly to the team as a whole that a frequently-used manual was kept locked in a cupboard in the basement, a good five minutes walk away. A junior team member asked "Well what do you expect from consummate professionals such as ourselves?" to which the manager replied, over his shoulder "What amazes me is how you managed to say that and keep a straight face!" (Lee: OBS2: 2).

It seemed that many members were encountering some difficulty in matching their expected identity as professionals with their everyday experience in the face of the complexity and unpredictability of interactions with humans and technology. If this may be understood as distancing, then it may be taken as evidence that the attempted reconstitution of IT staff within the discipline of professionalism was not achieving the success implied by some senior managers. Evidence of more direct resistance seemed scarce, although it is important to highlight one instance where humorous resistance to the demands of professionalism was actually converted into conduct. During a brief exchange, two IT support staff considered compiling a library of discs with frequently-used files to cover all eventualities and both agreed this to be a good idea. As the colleague walked off, however, he turned and said "Actually, no I won't - that would be FAR too proactive!". The employee I was shadowing laughed, saying "Too right - far too proactive!" (Dan: OBS1: 1).

At least in the duration of my observation, the 'library' was never initiated. I should stress, however, that this was an isolated occurrence throughout my observation period, and most of the numerous incidents involving humour seemed to be merely a verbal articulation of internal strains.

On the other hand, the *attraction* of attempting to conform to the model of professionalism became evident in instances when the opposite of this 'professional' subject cropped up in humorous exchanges. It occurred to me during the fieldwork that the notion of the 'professional' might be set against another discursive construction, the 'cowboy', which was frequently used in banter as a term of mild abuse. For example, on one occasion the team were generally complaining about the time taken by the contracting firm (referred to, significantly, as the "*professional* help") and the amount they were being paid. The full-time staff clearly felt threatened by the company's frequent recourse to outside consultancies to cover work that they might have expected to do, and the possibility that their claim to embody 'professionalism' might be better founded than their own. Thus their defence against this manifested itself in exchanges where members would engage in a reaffirmatory bout of undermining the abilities of the contractors to one another. Thus on this occasion, one team-member referred to the contractors as "That lot over there at the OK Corrall..." (Ian : OBS2: 2). Amid much laughter and renditions of spaghetti western theme tunes, reference was made to "The Lee Van Cleef of coding" and similar cowboy jokes. The recurrent references to the 'cowboy' implied that despite deep difficulties adopting and internalising the model of the 'professional', employees perceived in it an existential and material security to be contrasted with the position of the 'cowboy'. Insofar as the IT departments were successful in promoting and displaying a 'professional' image, however, there were considerable advantages in terms of their position and influence in each company, as will be examined in the next section.

Project Management and Power Relations in Lifelong and Buzzbank

My intention in this final section is to flesh out my discussion of professionalism and Project Management with reference to power struggles in Lifelong and Buzzbank which were presented to me as significant by staff in interviews. I have dealt with each separately to avoid disrupting the train of the arguments in this chapter with extended accounts of complex political and structural changes in each company. Nonetheless, each of these accounts is important to the development of my arguments in the book as a whole; through the detailed analysis of empirical material I have attempted to illustrate the inter-related nature of the issues dealt with in this chapter and their connections with the themes of the book as a whole. I will therefore deal first with the restructuring of the IT section in Lifelong during the period of my research there, before tracing the development of similar issues in a less momentous way in Buzzbank.

Power Struggles in Lifelong: The Emergence of 'Lifetech'

At the level of organisational influence and discretion, the advantages of this promotion of professionalism were considerable, at least for the project-based areas of the IT departments. In both organisations, the pre-existent system generally required parts of 'the Business' gaining some level of senior sponsorship to requisition the services of the IT function to develop or improve existing applications/hardware. In both, fairly experienced managers with a minimum of IT knowledge came to play an intermediary role in this process, acting as translator-cum-negotiator in the development process. The position of these intermediaries varied between organisations, however; in Buzzbank, these were highly-paid members of Business Analysis, often ex-consultants, performing a basic intermediary role. In Lifelong, by contrast, the influence of the intermediaries, the Business Managers in the National Sales Operations department, appeared to match their status, as they were engaged in high-level negotiations over which projects were chosen, funded and prioritised. The IT function in Lifelong seemed therefore to perform far more of a service role in attempting to measure up to the specifications set down by the Business Managers, with little or no direct influence on the choice of jobs allotted to them. The Business Managers appeared fairly satisfied with the hierarchical relationship between the two departments, and in particular with their dominant position in this relationship, one explaining;

> "you can actually *change* (senior management's) ideas about what they want to do, and we're delivering far more sensible things... there are people (in National Sales Operations) running major projects now who know exactly what we should be giving them, and they know who to talk to, to find how what to change..." (Simon: 546).

Reflecting this secure position, my interview with this manager, Simon, ended with his confident projections of his next refinement of the Customer Information System BASIS, centrepiece of the IT network, which was to be called BASIS 3.

At this point, my first visit to Lifelong, this situation was still precariously in place, although the perspective from IT Development Services implied a significantly different reading of both the problems in this area and the remedy required. The temporary recruitment of Doug, a consultant project manager on the IT side of the BASIS 3 project, appeared to be bringing some of these tensions to the surface. What Doug impressed upon me throughout the interview was what he should be seen to have brought to Lifelong; namely, knowledge of the techniques and procedures fundamental to 'professional' project management. He repeatedly stressed his unhappiness with the techniques and approaches presently employed in the department as a whole. Thus explaining the prescribed steps in a project, he stated that using this was "the proper way to do things", adding "not like in some projects round here" (Doug 1: 1). He appeared very irritated at the shortcomings of the Lifelong IT Developments Services

202 Discourse, Discipline and the Subject

staff of whom he was in charge, and constantly returned to the need to employ key principles of project management.

In a later visit, Doug seemed suddenly keen to bring up the "serious shortcomings to the present system" (Doug 2: 2). To illustrate the problem, he sketched the development process, significantly drawing a brick wall between 'the Business' and IT in his diagram and complaining that requirements written by the 'non-professional' Business Managers were simply "tossed over the wall" (Doug 2: 2). He indicated that the intermediary role of the Business Managers was a key part of the problem, as they were "brought up in the LL way - they can't see outside the way it's always been done" (Doug 2: 2). Expanding on this, he referred to "bad feelings on both sides" (Doug 2: 2) of this opposition (although this was not raised in my limited interviews with Business Analysts). In direct contrast with the position of the NSO manager, he expressed general and ongoing dissatisfaction with the situation. He also stated that since his arrival, he had demanded a "different relationship" with the Business, claiming after the interview that without control over the business analysis aspect of Project Management he would not have stayed in the company.

It seems quite likely that Doug's more forthcoming manner with regard to what might be considered rather delicate matters may well have resulted from the support and even vindication he read from a major recent announcement in Lifelong. After months of rumours, it was made official that Andersen Consulting had been brought in to restructure the entire IT department, which was to be renamed 'Lifetech'. On a company-wide level, a restructuring of Lifelong into four main parts was announced shortly after the introduction of Andersen Consulting. The new divisions were to cover the Independent Financial Advisers, the direct salesforce, telephone sales and banking, and corporate pensions. Within IT, Doug explained that to deal with the "bad feelings on both sides" (i.e. 'the Business' and IT), they were to "bury the hatchet" (Doug 2: 2) by making future projects "jointly managed" by the Business Managers and the IT project teams. After further elaboration, it appeared that rather than 'joint' control, discretion over the process and overall responsibility would instead lie to a large extent with the IT Project Team. One direct effect of this was to signify a substantial shift in the balance between 'the Business' and IT, represented by Simon and his counterpart Doug. Significantly, it appeared that 'BASIS 3' was no longer on the agenda, and Doug was now in control of the project to develop a radical replacement, 'PARTY'. The change in name can be seen to symbolise the shift in power, meant to signify a break with the traditional (now largely discredited) system and a radical redesign of the Management Information system. This shift in power is justified by Doug with reference to the discipline of Project Management, as *his* staff are trained, "professional" Systems Analysts with knowledge of industry-wide "best practice". He implied that the development of PARTY to replace BASIS 2 was a key example, indeed a pilot, of the arrangements envisaged in the new order to be instituted by the Andersen consultants. In order to "bury the hatchet", it appears that the power struggle would be resolved, but resolved in favour of IT. What was central here was the strategic deployment of the notion of the Project Manager as expert/professional in this struggle, and the weight that IT Project Management *as a discipline*, in both the everyday and Foucauldian senses, afforded the IT Development staff in their efforts.

This shift in the power relations within Lifelong seemed clearly linked to issues of professionalism and the introduction of Project Management into the procedures in the company. Although the shift in the control of IT projects from National Sales Operations to IT is the clearest example of this shift, a number of other changes seemed to back up the expansion of IT's level of influence. Other examples included the incorporation of the 'Business'-based helpdesks into the IT department, or the adoption of a field research role by the previously Head Office-bound IT staff. The arguments put forward by IT focused on the importance of having staff who were "professionally-trained" (in Project Management) carrying out these important tasks (rather than what were by implication the 'inspired amateurs' of National Sales Operations). Clearly, the poor perception of BASIS 2 and other existing IT systems was instrumental in motivating senior management to buy in outside help in the form of Doug and Andersen Consulting. However, the action being taken by both sets of outside agencies brought into Lifelong was then dictated by the tenets of professional Project Management. The system was now to be based around SSADM, utilising Microsoft Project Manager and other CASE tools. Within the department, Project Management discipline was to be enforced, and the general levels of anxiety and job insecurity while Andersen devised the forthcoming restructuring appeared to ensure the wholehearted embrace of the new discipline. Overall then, the simultaneous effects at Lifelong appeared to be an enormous expansion in the size and influence of the IT function, tied to a fervent espousal of Project Management and the new professionalism, with all the disciplinary constraints that this implied. Interestingly, the new 'joint management' arrangement appeared less a breaking-down of the hierarchy than an *inversion* of the hierarchy, to the apparent 'benefit' of a group whose professional aspirations allowed a tighter form of domination to be exercised over them.

Power Struggles in Buzzbank: Incorporation and the 'Dirty Mail' Issue

As noted, a similar situation could be traced in Buzzbank, although far more incrementally and without affording IT anything like the hegemony discernible at Lifelong. The process was superficially the same here; as noted above, the Business Analysis department had traditionally adopted a role as intermediary between IT and the rest of Buzzbank.

> "(We) were focused at the time at being an interface between systems-developers and the business, so they were what is in some areas a conventional Business Analysis team, where if you like the discussions between people in the business who wanted systems developing and the systems developers hadn't been working effectively, so there was a kind of intermediary, so if someone in the business wanted a system developing they'd talk to Business Analysis" (Tony 1: 22-26).

At the same time, senior management and Business Analysis staff alike were encouraging direct contact between the IT staff in IT Applications and departments of Buzzbank more widely to negotiate the development of new IT systems. This also appeared to be in the interests of the IT Applications department. From the Business Analysis side, their enthusiasm for this shift was explained by the Head;

> "Certainly that wasn't an appropriate role for the team if they were to fulfil their role of reviewing how the business operates, so we then pulled away completely from any systems development projects, which coincided with what the development people were trying to achieve at the time, which was to get closer to the business, so the timing was very good, so that now if someone in the business wants a system developing they go and speak to a systems developer, rather than having an intermediary, and that works very well" (Tony 1: 22-32).

The accounts in Buzzbank tended to emphasise the consensuality and co-operation that this direct contact produced, as well as the mutual transfer of expertise, such that the 'techies' come to understand the business and the 'technophobes' come to understand IT, in the terminology of the Director of IT. However, closer analysis indicated that this might well be an oversimplification of the new relationship. The centrality of Project Management to this was underlined by the Head of IT Applications;

> "I think I'm painfully aware... er, *perceptively* aware that the worst thing we can do is throw IT solutions at bad business processes. New IT proposals are really joint business-IT projects which require quite stringent work on business processes" (Angus 1: 189).

Interestingly, despite emphasising the egalitarian nature of business-IT relationships here, the reference to business processes indicates the potential for IT to dominate. In Buzzbank, Project Management is widely perceived as indispensable for the effective redesign of the IT systems which structure much of the financial and clerical work processes. As in Lifelong, the IT staff retain a firm monopoly over Project Management 'expertise', in spite of Business Analysis's development of a number of non-technical project managers. Indeed, rather than challenging IT's dominance, the *incorporation* of non-IT-based managers project management might only be expected to reproduce and reinforce the same technical rationality characteristic of IT staff in the organisation more widely.[14]

My own observation of business-IT interactions tended to suggest that they were characterised far more by political negotiations than by consensual collaboration, and the centrality of Project Management and the appeal to IT professionalism seemed to give the IT function the whip hand in these dealings. I witnessed a clear illustration of this in a meeting of the PC team about the provision of an external e-mail facility for a new department, PC Banking. As PC Banking were in charge of dealing with personal banking via the Internet, it had been agreed by senior management that they needed to be able to receive and reply to e-mails. This in itself was a significant privilege, as e-mail links for the rest of the Buzzbank network were internal i.e. could only be used to reach other members of Buzzbank. As the PC team discussed how the e-mail facility should be set up, the issue of security was raised. There was some debate over the issue of who should have access to the mail found to be 'dirty' (i.e. not conforming to standard formats for data), which was automatically re-routed to a separate mailbox. It was agreed that in keeping with present security arrangements, access to this mailbox and the responsibility for vetting 'dirty mail' should be restricted to the PC team themselves. Despite meaning an increase in their future workload, this would enable them to maintain the centralisation of control over the network by the IT department. This was then justified as one member referred to a situation where someone in the PC Banking department might attempt to import their own software or files by sending it to themselves as an attachment.

An hour later, a meeting took place between members of the project team and a representative of PC Banking to discuss the implications of what they intend to do. Interestingly, the details of the debate, the options discussed and the decision taken in the previous meeting were

---

authoritatively presented to the representative as a *fait accompli*, a technical necessity. Despite some misgivings, the PC Banking representative was thus precluded from discussing alternative systems, and accepted the technical inevitability of the project team having responsibility for this. Through a combination of their monopoly over technical knowledge and the professional control of IT over the systems analysis aspect of the project, the IT team routinely manipulated the interaction so as to maintain control over key aspects of the system. A parallel can be drawn with the IT department in Lifelong using their ability to define the status of IT problems to maintain control over wider aspects of operations in the organisation, as mentioned above. As a consequence, the discretion available to the department in their handling of incoming mail was restricted, and more importantly, the social choice taken was deliberately obscured beneath the legitimatory effects of professional expertise.

The main impression gained from the two organisations examined was that of a general expansion of the IT function into areas formerly monopolised by commercial functions. Thus during my empirical research, the work systems in customer banking, insurance sales, insurance policy processing, financial services sales and numerous other areas, including IT application development itself, were in the process of reorganisation and restructuring in both Lifelong and Buzzbank, based on the principles of Project Management and with a significant level of IT involvement. Not only basic work processes however, but wider aspects of the business operations such as employee appraisal systems, inter-departmental communication systems, incentive payment systems for financial advisors, etc. were also being restructured, again with the IT function paying a central role. Thus in each organisation a gradual annexation of operations by the IT function was apparent, not in a simplistically political sense but in the sense that this process enabled more and more aspects of the organisation to be governed by the logic of technical rationality. In doing so, this raises the status of IT employees, reaffirming their sense of a productive work identity and affording them a pivotal role with some discretion over the form and the values inherent in the restructured business processes. As in Lifelong, this discretion was significantly constrained, not only by the pressure of having to conform to norms of professional conduct but also by disciplinary construction of identity that Project Management achieves.

Conclusion

This chapter has developed the connections between a number of concepts central to the constructions of staff in each organisation, focusing on the themes of *discourse, discipline* and *professionalisation*, through an examination of the phenomenon of *Project Management*. In particular, I have looked at the rapid expansion of Project Management in the fields of IT and, to a growing extent, in 'Management' more broadly. In doing so, I have tried to avoid both functionalist arguments which see this expansion as a deterministic effect of the growing use of IT in business, and individualist arguments which attribute this to the strategic, political behaviour of a professional group. Although both these arguments reflect aspects of the process, the first do not account for the subservience of the IT function for the last 15-20 years, nor the ongoing failure of IT to deliver the much-heralded productivity benefits. At the same time, individualist arguments neglect the significant levels of internalised discipline and direct control to which these newly-professionalised IT staff are now subject. What emerges instead is a complex picture in which the construction of Project Management as a discipline by a wide variety of agencies interacts with contemporary attempts on the part of IT staff and management more widely to professionalise the IT function.

In outlining the development of Project Management over the last 50 years, I have made a very broad distinction between Project Management as practised in the fields of construction, engineering and so on, and the quite specific formulation of Project Management in the field of IT, with a distinctive basic model and dedicated techniques for each stage of the model. More fundamentally, however, Project Management in all fields tends to epitomise and reproduce a particularly technicist and instrumental form of rationality. In particular, a key effect of Project Management is to enhance the calculability and visibility of those engaged in project work, enabling a direct form of control (frequently assisted by the use of technology such as IT applications to monitor performance). In this chapter I have attempted to illustrate the direct control that Project Management attempts by drawing on examples of its use in each organisation.

At the same time, Project Management shares certain elements of *professionalism*, particularly in terms of the *control effects* of professional discipline. Radical analyses of professionalism and professionalisation have brought out the links between professionalism and a form of self-disciplinary control based on the construction of a *professional identity* and the maintenance of forms of *conduct appropriate to a professional*. Such analyses of professionalism can be seen to as similar to the Foucauldian notion of the discursive construction of the self, and in particular

Foucault's emphasis, inherited from Althusser, on the materiality of discourse and the interrelated nature of practice and subjectivity. Through a discussion of developments in both organisations, I have emphasised the double-edged nature of professionalism, subjecting IT employees to an intensive form of self-discipline while at the same time providing (relative) subjective security linked to increased material and symbolic rewards. More problematically, this security is typically attained through the objectification and instrumental manipulation of other subjects in line with technical rational goals. In addition, the increase in the strategic influence of IT is manifest in the authority IT exercises over the restructuring of a vast array of work processes in both Lifelong and Buzzbank.

Attempts to construct Project Management as a profession appear dependent upon its development as a *discipline*, both in the abstract sense and as it is articulated and reproduced within the subject organisations. A key element of this is the development of a Project Management 'body of knowledge', both universally and as construction of IT employees in Buzzbank and Lifelong, against which their own practices must be evaluated (and, typically, are found wanting). This disparity between the ideal and the actual means that failures in the application of Project Management are frequently interpreted as merely failures in *implementation*, which not only leaves the basic discipline itself unquestioned but also implies that the required remedy must be to enforce Project Management more strictly in future. The dissemination and enforcement of a terminology specific to Project Management serves two purposes. Firstly, it structures the discursive resources of project workers such that their representations of 'reality' must conform to the basic Project Management model. Secondly, in doing so it privileges the constructions of those who have mastered the terminology and marginalises the interpretations of those 'non-professionals' outside the discipline, whose constructions do not conform to the Project Management model. Although these may clearly be understood as power effects, the presentation of Project Management as an objective and transferable technical discipline, as a 'toolkit', is fiercely defended in both organisations and acts to obscure this operation of power.

Overall, then, Project Management appears to intensify the control to which the IT staff are subject, in terms of both the levels of visibility and calculability it affords and at the same time the inculcation of a form of self-discipline through professionalisation. The interpenetration of these forms of control was made clear in my examination of instances of resistance in Lifelong and Buzzbank. In the face of tighter specification of tasks and increased surveillance, employees attempted to maintain discretion over their conduct by stressing the inefficiency of the bureaucratic overkill of Project Management models. However, their use of discretion was undermined by the ongoing professionalisation of the selfsame employees, and in particular, by the construction of these subjects as 'Project Management professionals', such that discretion is only employed in line with the technical rationale of the discipline. Where the professionalisation of the IT staff was resisted, this was usually through the staff's use of humour to 'distance' themselves from discourses of professionalism. Such distancing may be interpreted as undermining the operation of the discipline at a *subjective* level. However, it was not clear that this necessarily indicated a resistant form of *conduct*; indeed, humour may often have acted as a *substitute* for deviant or resistant behaviour. The wider use of humour appeared to reflect insecurities regarding the IT staff's professional status, which brings into question the effectiveness of this distancing.

The next chapter will pursue similar themes through an examination of the forms of control exercised over the direct salesforce of Lifelong Assurance.

7 Subjectivity, Masculinity and the Control of the Salesforce

Introduction

This chapter focuses on the changing mechanisms of control in operation in the life assurance sales division of Lifelong Assurance. The effect of the deregulation through the Financial Services Act (1986) was to encourage a number of financial institutions to branch into adjacent sectors of the market, leading to a rapid increase in the number of providers of life assurance, including the development of several direct, telephone-based operations The background of public scandals and increased regulation has led to more intense pressure on the *direct* salesforce of the life assurance companies, accompanied by in many cases by a significant reduction of the size of the salesforce. To examine the changes in progress at Lifelong, I begin with an analysis of the traditional identity of the sales*man*, and the links between this subjective construction and a number of related discourses with the intention of encouraging a self-disciplinary form of control in the individual. As has been noted elsewhere, the selling of life assurance is characterised by a particular 'masculine mystique' more usually associated with manual labour occupations (Willis, 1977: Collinson, Knights and Collinson, 1990). The specific construction of masculinity articulated in sales is based on the discourses of, on one side, autonomy and independence, and on the other, the careful development of the concept of the 'breadwinner'. Through the selection, training and day-to-day reinforcement of supervisors and colleagues, life assurance sales representatives are encouraged to construct a subjectivity reliant on their ability to act as 'breadwinner' through the heroic, individual pursuit of 'business' in the 'wide world'. By this means, a self-disciplinary form of control is potentially inculcated in the sales representative, which can operate without the direct supervision of sales management to ensure the representative maintains a high level of activity and makes every effort to maximise sales.

This self-discipline is reinforced by a structure of individualising mechanisms in the organisations, from complex systems of financial incentive schemes to the engineering of inter-personal competitions for social recognition and affirmation through sales contests and league tables. All of these to some extent depend on the individualised salesperson's reliance on relative sales performance and conspicuous recognition to reaffirm his/her identity as a capable and independent 'breadwinner'. I then examine the use of surveillance within Lifelong as an attempt to intensify control of the salesforce in a more direct form than the self-disciplinary action of subjectivity affords. This operates through a number of techniques, including the quantification of the conduct of a subject in a form which enables the direct comparison of behaviour and the construction of norms against which subjects may then be *judged*. The surveillance not only isolates the individual salesperson by such judgements, but the technologies are then integrated with the sales competitions for scarce rewards to further individualise the salesforce.

The potential of IT-based surveillance is restricted, however, by technical limitations and more fundamentally by the resistance of the salesforce to what they perceive as a dehumanised form of control which undermines their autonomy. Thus misrepresentation and fabrication of information are used to further undermine the already slender reliability of the 'knowledge' produced by the system. This form of resistance, despite its effectiveness in marginalising systems of bureaucratic surveillance, reflects a preference for a more *personalised* form of sales management. Without other forms of reassurance and support, the individual salesperson is reliant upon their Sales Manager for 'knowledge' on their performance, to secure their construction of their identity. This dependence opens up the salesforce to a return to an intensified form of self-discipline; a more insidious and pervasive form of control through relationship, operating through their subjective reliance on their Sales Manager. I have therefore examined this relationship and in particular the regular 'one-to-one's conducted in terms of Foucault's analysis of *the confession* as a mechanism of power operating on and through the subjectivity of the sales staff.

The Intensification of the Sales Ethos in Life Assurance

The financial institutions' responses to deregulation, as noted in Chapter 4, have led to increasing levels of competition in all sectors of the 'Financial Services' industry. In life assurance in particular, the entrance of the bancassurers and direct providers began to be felt throughout the industry in the late 1980s. Among the existing life assurers, this led to greater pressure on the direct salesforces and IFAs to maximise sales, and a number of wider initiatives took place to respond to the rapid increase in competition. The overall aim of most institutions within life assurance in the late 1980s was to gain an increased share of what promised to be a substantially larger cake, thanks to deregulation and polarisation and the supportive policy of the Conservative government of the time. As the traditional basis of the industry was the selling efforts of the salesforce, the route taken by many organisations involved establishing a more aggressive selling culture in the fieldstaff. The rapid recruitment and training of large numbers of direct salespeople also took place throughout the industry in an attempt to take advantage of this ongoing and predicted expansion.

However, this expansion and intensification has been interpreted by many as directly contributing to the pensions mis-selling scandal which was to come to light in 1993. An SIB investigation found that thousands of people had lost out when transferring from an occupational to a personal pension scheme. In many of these cases, it was found that the advice given by life assurance salespeople had significantly disadvantaged clients, while substantially increasing the sales of private pensions (and boosting the commissions earned by the salespeople themselves). It has been persuasively argued that the provision of advice 'in the best interest of the client' by tied salesforces motivated by the payment of *commissions* is a contradiction at the heart of life assurance sales practices. Thus financial advice remains motivated to a large degree by the commissions that the salesperson will earn as a result. As Grey suggests;

> "salespeople are supposed to recommend the best product for a customer regardless of commission incentives, whilst all of the life offices subject their salespeople to intense pressure to sell high volumes of business and to maximise commission earnings" (Grey, 1992: 226).

Nonetheless, the majority of the blame for the mis-selling of personal pensions appears to have been attributed to 'cowboy' salesmen and small firms, operating outside of the control of the large and presumed 'responsible' organisations (Grey and Knights, 1990). Where the larger firms were implicated, there has often been the suggestion that such mis-selling was accidental, down to the poor and often hurried training of new sales-staff to cope with steep increases in demand in the late 1980s (Mintel, 1995a). Equally, salespeople within the industry have defended their conduct by pointing to the role of the government of the time in promoting the opting-out of state pension provision through campaigns in the media, and thus creating a demand which they then "had to deal with".

The stereotype of the 'cowboy' as individual operator, usually in the smaller life assurers, who takes advantage of public gullibility to maximise his/her own earnings is frequently reproduced in such accounts to explain the mis-selling of personal pensions. Interestingly, the 'cowboy' stereotype has continued despite the findings of several SIB-sponsored reports which indicate that the widespread contravention of regulations by the major life assurers as well as smaller firms was roughly proportional. Thus the Prudential, for instance, as the largest institution had the largest number of 'priority cases' to review, more than 50 000 (TG 14/5/97). The 'cowboy' stereotype therefore exculpates the salesforces of the major institutions in life assurance, allowing them to see regulation as "something forced upon them by the activities of these marginal elements" and "reinforc(ing) the solidity of the established firms" (Grey, 1997b: 56). In doing so, it has the complementary effect of legitimising, even vindicating the continuing operation of the same selling practices in life assurance in general. The day-to-day regulation of the conduct of the salesperson remains therefore the responsibility of organisations whose main concern is with maximising sales and profitability.

Nonetheless, the legacy of the pensions mis-selling scandal continued to reverberate through the 1990s, with persistent front-page headlines naming those institutions which failed to meet investigation and compensation deadlines set by the regulators. Such publicity ensured that the image of the direct selling of personal pensions was still tainted through the mid-to-late 1990s, affecting the sales of personal pensions and other investment products after the uncertainties of the recession had abated. This had two particularly significant effects. Firstly, after the boom of the late 1980s, recession and increased competition led to significant redundancies and restructuring among life assurance salesforces in the early 1990s. Lifelong was no exception to this process, and the need for an aggressively sales-oriented culture among the remaining employees was emphasised by senior management in the restructuring known ominously as 'Scenario Three' among the salesforce. Secondly, it became harder for the remaining direct sales-forces of the major institutions to achieve their sales in the face of public distrust. It has been argued that this was exacerbated when the requirements for commission disclosure began to reveal the greater margins earned by direct salesforces compared to their independent counterparts (Mintel, 1996b). The combined effect of all of these occurrences in Lifelong was to further intensify the pressure to maximise sales among the remaining salespersons, in the face of a suspicious public and in the shadow of recent and ongoing redundancies.

Although rarely referred to directly, I had a very clear impression that the scandals and the poor image of the life assurance sales in general

214 Discourse, Discipline and the Subject

constituted an unspoken undercurrent to most of the interviews conducted. Brief, euphemistic allusions to 'recent times' or 'difficulties' were frequent, as well as some more explicit references. A particularly striking example occurred while I was starting an interview with one Financial Consultant, Arthur, in the presence of two other Financial Consultants;

> Q. *"Is it alright to tape this?"*
> Arthur: "Er..... er no, I'd rather you didn't."
> Other FC: "You'll get your name on World In Action!" (laughs)
> Q. *"Oh, right, that's fine, right... So can I have your name please?"*
> Another FC: "Daniel O'Hare!" (the name of an FC not present)
> Other FC: "Har har har!!!"

When interpreting the responses of the interviewees, this widespread anxiety should be borne in mind, which among the salesforce led to interviewees being careful to guard against being 'stitched up', and to a general concern to portray the industry and their own conduct in a positive light. At the same time, as will be seen below, a number of interviewees eventually proved to be quite keen to put forward their own perspective on the mis-selling scandal and regulation in general, which often involved a very different interpretation of recent events in the industry to the official position.

Identity and Control

Within this context, significant changes were in progress in Lifelong and other life institutions with regards to the forms of control exercised over the salesforce. These traditionally ranged from the traditionally explicit forms of control, such as the setting of sales targets and the engineering of a form of competition between sales representatives, to less coherent but nonetheless powerful efforts to encourage and reinforce a particular form of subjectivity within the sales function. While these are often seen as distinct techniques, what I intend to illustrate in this chapter is the extent to which the operation of explicit control techniques is dependent upon the formation of a mode of subjectivity in the salesforce which is amenable to such manipulation. The construction of this subjectivity specific to the sales function relies on a number of interrelated contemporary discourses, regarding masculinity, autonomy and individualism. In this section I examine the means by which the salesperson in Lifelong is tied to a specific construction of identity which may then be manipulated through a range of mechanisms in the pursuit of certain company objectives. In the following section, I will look in more detail at the precise mechanisms which operate in Lifelong, through surveillance, normalisation and competition, leading to an examination of the effects of these upon the individual Financial Consultant.

Selling and the Construction of a Valued Identity

A constant theme, reiterated in almost every interview with the branch staff in Lifelong, was the company's complete economic dependency on the success of its salesforce. While this may well be an accurate depiction of Lifelong's major sources of revenue, the constant repetition of this theme indicated its centrality to the salesforce's understanding of its own *identity*. Throughout all of the interviews with the branch staff (with the exception of the Sales Support Analysts), this notion of sales as productive and therefore worthwhile seemed to assume great importance to the subjectivities of not only the Financial Consultants but of the Sales Managers and Branch Managers also, most of whom had been promoted from direct selling roles themselves. In contrast, the accounts of Lifelong Head Office staff did not reflect this reverence for sales, and indeed many of those interviewed at Head Office made no reference to the sales function in Lifelong whatsoever. Numerous interviewees in the salesforce, on the other hand, insistently asserted that they were the most vital part of Lifelong, as the continued existence and success of the company depended on their selling of life assurance and other policies.

The importance of the sales process was frequently stressed by contrasting its usefulness with the secondary function of clerical staff in the branches, associated with the bureaucratic operations upon which they perceived Head Office to be fixated. Thus Ken, a Branch Manager, complained about the time and energy he was forced to devote to such bureaucracy and argued;

"At the end of the day, we're a *sales* organisation, and it's the *bottom line* that counts, and that's what everybody's looking at" (Ken: 39-40).

This complaint about the bureaucratic requirements of Lifelong was a constant theme in the interviews with the salesforce, and the contrast was frequently drawn between paperwork and form-filling and the heroic pursuit of sales, which they saw as their principle concern and responsibility. Thus Denise stressed that;

"What *we* do, with the clients, *that*'s what LL's all about - obviously you need good admin but it's all *done* face-to-face..." (Denise: 432-3).

This unprompted contrast of the sales and the administrative functions in Lifelong reflects the theme explored in Chapter 5 regarding the construction of oppositions to locate and fix identity. Although not cast in terms of a 'culture', there was a widespread consensus among the Financial Consultants, Sales Managers and to a lesser extent Branch Managers over the definition of the salesperson, focusing on notions of heroism, autonomy and rugged individualism. Ken's objections to the monitoring of the Financial Consultants reflected such a conception of his salesforce;

> "I mean, the guys don't like being monitored, I mean, they're in sales to be *salesmen*, they don't *want* to be in some clerical job! (...) They want to be in charge of their own destiny, their future!" (Ken: 261-3)[15]

In describing their own positions, Denise and Ken both clearly reject what they perceive as embodied in the terms 'admin' and the 'clerical job'. This reflects the way 'sales' was normally expressed, constructing a fundamental opposition between the active, 'productive' work done by themselves as salespeople and the clerical, 'pen-pushing' mentality attributed to Head Office staff, and some sales staff included the Sales Support Analysts within the branches in this criticism. This clerical function was portrayed not only as a hindrance to their performance but as a challenge to their identity as proactive and productive salespeople in Lifelong. Some were more charitable in their characterisation of the administrative staff, Denise admitting that the Head Office staff were just doing their job, and that, as far as they were concerned, "they've got a box to fill in and if it's blank, something's got to be done" (Denise: 416-17). However, the most common position was reflected in the angry comments of Arthur within the first few minutes of our interview when I asked for his opinion on recent changes in the organisation of sales in Lifelong;

> "If we didn't do all this (selling), what's the *point* of all the rest? All this Head Office, all this BASIS, it's all *bullshit*! It's what we do *face-to-face*, *that's* what it is!". (Arthur: 32)

---

[15] This image of the enterprising, quick-witted and resolutely independent salesman is one which is identifiable not only within sales departments, but as represented in popular culture. Thus there are a number of similarities between Ken's complaints and the self-pitying monologue of Roma in David Mamet's play about real estate salesmen, *Glengarry Glen Ross* (drawn from his own experiences as a salesman); "I swear... it's not a world of men... it's not a world of men, Machine... it's a world of clock watchers, bureaucrats, office holders... What it is, it's a fucked-up world... there's no adventure to it..." (Mamet, 1984: 62).

Throughout my interviews with the Financial Consultants, the most powerful impression I received was of a significant amount of pride in their construction of their identity as salespeople. Indeed, the salesforce's deep-rooted resistance to what are perceived as attempts to 'bureaucratise' their role reflects this very construction. The maintenance of a 'pride' in the role depends on the distancing of their 'heroic' role of direct selling from the associated administrative tasks, represented as secondary, unskilled and demeaning. In particular, the image of *'face-to-face'* work was used more than once by the salespersons themselves to emphasise the heroic, intrepid nature of sales, with the salesperson 'out there', which might be juxtaposed with the notion of the 'faceless' bureaucrat working 'behind the lines'. This heroic depiction was reinforced by the aggressively *masculine* 'mystique' (Collinson, 1988) surrounding sales, which was a constant theme in the interviews, anecdotes and those interactions I observed within the branches of Lifelong.

*The Construction of the Sales*man*: Masculinity in Sales*

This gendered nature of the sales function in general has been substantially documented elsewhere, not only in academic research (Willis, 1977; Collinson et al, 1990) but also in the representations of 'sales' in popular culture. The selling of financial services is no exception to this, sharing to some extent the macho mystique formerly the preserve of heavy industry in Western societies, such that;

> "the task of selling is described ideologically in terms of a heroic drama in which 'intrepid' and autonomous males stride out into the financial world and against all odds return with new business" (Collinson et al, 1990: 137).

The involvement of female employees in this process tends to be limited to clerical duties, with the inferior status accorded to support functions, regardless of the practical significance of this role. This tradition of sex-based segregation is clearly evident in Lifelong and is immediately noticeable in everyday language used throughout the organisation; the salesforce was generally referred to as 'the guys', 'this guy', 'this bloke', distinctly masculine terminology, even when there were female Financial Consultants present. This representation of sales was borne out by the composition of those branches I visited; in each, the Branch Manager and Sales Managers were all male, as were the overwhelming majority of the Financial Consultants, while all the clerical staff (Sales Support Assistants and Secretaries) were invariably female.

Beyond this, as is discussed at length in Collinson et al (1990), the gendered nature of sales departments also tends to be reinforced in selection procedures, through the promotion of 'masculine' characteristics such as aggression and competitiveness as essential criteria. This was reflected in the constructions of the Sales Managers and the other Financial Consultants at Lifelong, who frequently referred to what they perceived as an ingrained drive, defined as 'the desire' or 'the hunger', when attempting to differentiate between the 'good' and the 'bad' sales representative. A typical example was Dave who, describing one of his 'problem cases', complained;

> "don't get me wrong, he's not a bad FC, in fact he's probably a good FC, but then again, he hasn't really got *the desire*, and if he hasn't got *the desire* to go out there and earn a lot of money, if he's happy earning twenty-odd thousand and... that's very difficult to turn around, especially when he's not doing a bad job" (Dave: 436-9, emphasis added).

Brian, another of Dave's Financial Consultants, was more dismissive of those who (unlike himself, he was at pains to make clear) were content with average levels of commission, or else were not fulfilling what was thought by others to be their potential. However, Dave and Brian were both adamant that the main cause of under-performance was the home circumstances of the representative. This appeared to reflect the situation reported elsewhere, where Collinson et al's detailed analysis of recruitment and selection procedures indicates that;

> "selectors invariably believed that only family bread-winners who would have the added 'motivations' of dependants and mortgage responsibilities ... retain the necessary calculating orientation towards social relations" (1990: 152).

Generally, Collinson et al describe this assumption as leading to a clear preference among selectors for the young, married male, although they do indicate exceptional cases where women are recruited with family responsibilities which enable them to be taken as "honorary male breadwinners" (1990: 160).

In the understanding of Dave and Brian, the 'hunger' or otherwise of a salesperson was thus explicitly linked to the weight of their domestic responsibilities. Brian's immediate explanation for poor sales on the part of a Financial Consultant was significant;

> "If you know somebody's under-performing, and as Dave probably knows, he probably knows what their wife does for a living, there might be very good reasons for that! They're just... they're just not hungry enough!" (Brian: 569-71).

The heroic and emphatically masculinist representation of the sales ethos, where only 'real breadwinners' have 'the hunger', is reflected in several other accounts of the sales process in Lifelong. The recruitment of representatives, usually assumed to be men, with the responsibility of the sole breadwinner in a household is thus instrumental to the control of the salesforce at Lifelong. In the accounts of the employees, this is represented as operating in a direct fashion, such that the unavoidable financial commitments of such an employee *ensures* that he/she maintains a high level of activity and can be relied on to maximise sales as far as possible.

The relationship between identity and this construction of masculinity, however, means that this form of control operates more fundamentally upon the subjectivity of the individual salesperson, through the *constructed image* of the 'breadwinner'. Sales performance and the consequent level of remuneration are framed as confirmation of the salesperson's capability as 'breadwinner'. Managers, therefore, attempt to inculcate a reliance upon the masculine role of breadwinner in both the selection of and in their everyday communication with their Financial Consultants. A link is therefore forged between sales performance and masculinity in the subjectivity of the Financial Consultant. Brian proved to exemplify perfectly the internalisation of this discourse, as he stated proudly;

"I am a bringer-home of income, I am! I am a Susan's husband, Jamie, Gareth and Nicolas's father, and they *need* me to earn money" (Brian: 455).

The emphatic manner in which Brian identified himself as a 'breadwinner' is clearly bound up with his construction of himself as capable patriarch, and his reliance on his identity as wage-providing husband and father. As a consequence, 'earning money' can be seen to be the main way in which Brian attempts to affirm a stable identity in line with his construction of masculinity.

Brian went on to identify himself more explicitly by differentiating his successful discharge of his responsibilities from the conduct of certain other, less 'successful' Financial Consultants in the branch. In keeping with the masculine discourse of the 'breadwinner', the all-important 'hunger' needed by the real sales*man* is represented as being undermined by the existence of a professional *wife*.

"I am the method through which my family enjoys the lifestyle it enjoys, as long as *I* bring the business home - you may have another FC, we've got other FCs, who're married to professional women - teachers, doctors, nurses - *their* need for income in their family through the husband isn't as acute as in my family, because I've got to provide everything on one wage, when somebody else has got two." (Brian: 560-65)

The clear implication here is that unlike them, Brian was also carrying out his responsibility to Lifelong as well as to his family;

> "So the fact that somebody else might not be doing as well as I am - because they probably don't have to! They don't need to! And the company's not getting their slice of the action from that particular person - the fact that they're comfortable with what they are bringing in has got nothing to do with it!" (Brian: 565-68)

Thus the notion of a mutually beneficial relationship is constructed; Lifelong depends on representatives who control themselves because of their perceived commitments as 'breadwinner'. At the same time, the transient and insecure 'pride' derived by Financial Consultants relies on participation and success in the direct sales process which bolsters a specifically masculine and heroic construction of their identity as breadwinner and salesman. The conception of the autonomous, enterprising and specifically *masculine* salesman is fundamentally dependent on its differentiation from clerical positions, defined as secondary, bureaucratic and essentially *feminine*. As we will see below, this leads to a significant level of resistance to the bureaucratic forms of surveillance and control which operate in the sales environment. Nonetheless, the specific way in which this resistance is articulated means that this enforced antipathy and resistance to the more bureaucratic aspects of control is balanced by the self-disciplinary operation of masculine constructions of the salesman. Indeed, the overall effect of surveillance is to intensify this internalised form of control.

The Growth of Surveillance in Life Assurance Sales

The issue of *surveillance*, effected through the application of recent developments in information technology, has risen to new prominence in the strategies of financial services institutions over the last decade. The demands of compliance with the regulators play a significant role here; the life assurance institutions are required by the regulator to keep records of transactions and to monitor the enforcement of compliance regulations within their own operations (SIB 1996a). In gathering and centralising this information, however, the financial institutions have recognised the considerable potential of such a network to provide what is known as 'Management Information'(MI), for purposes other than compliance. Thus in Lifelong, gradual developments in technology led to the introduction of what was known as BASIS, an IT system implemented to monitor the activities of the direct salesforce. The information gathered from this system covers a vast range of areas; the number of appointments made by each representative, the number of regulated/non-regulated policies written by an individual in each category, the ratio of unacceptable fact-finds each representative submits, the number of complaints each receives, the number of policies sold which are not cancelled within two years (known as 'persistency'), how punctually representatives pay out maturities, the percentage of sales each representative makes to new customers, and so on.

This information centralised in BASIS is gathered from a number of sources, being mainly drawn from either the reports of the Financial Consultants and their Sales Managers or else from the data produced by the Lifelong clerical staff at Oxford and Head Office in processing policy documentation. This information is entered either directly in the branches by the Sales Support Analysts or is downloaded weekly from other databases at Head Office. The information captured and represented through BASIS is necessarily selective, focusing on certain aspects of the Financial Consultant's behaviour. While a number of these measures are required by the regulator, known within Lifelong as Key Performance Indicators (KPIs), the other aspects of behaviour made visible by this process are chosen by senior management and tend to focus on the most profitable areas of business (thus brokering mortgages, for instance, is seen as 'low revenue business' and is included but often ignored). Other aspects which appear less directly related to profit margins, such as activity (i.e. the number of appointments made by Financial Consultants) are also monitored for purposes of appraisal and control. The reports created from BASIS information are also put to a number of uses, ranging from regulatory compliance and revenue forecasting to providing a basis for appraisal meetings. As far as the Financial Consultants themselves were concerned, however, the main role of BASIS was the production of the monthly league tables of Financial Consultants according to the amount of business written by each.

Before continuing, it is important to clarify my interpretation of these developments. I do not mean to imply that such information was not available before the introduction of IT systems into life assurers; extensive bureaucratic and accounting systems had long been established in the large institutions to monitor and co-ordinate the operations of the salesforce, and these systems were gradually transferred onto mainframes and PCs in the course of the 1980s and early 1990s. Nonetheless, the enormous reported cost of complying with the demands of the regulators can be taken to mean that at least *some* of this information was not already gathered by the life assurance companies (Grey and Knights, 1990). This does not therefore represent the sudden and unprecedented introduction of a system of surveillance into Lifelong. It does, however, represent a more *systematic* and *strategic* attempt to centralise and analyse information on the operation of the salesforce with the aid of recent developments in data transfer and storage. Finally, although IT facilitated this intensification and extension of surveillance mechanisms, I do not mean to attribute this change to the inspired application of recent advances in IT in a technologically-determinist fashion. What I mean to highlight here is the use by senior management of the recent scandals and the introduction of *compliance* regulation to legitimise an extension of surveillance in terms of the types and level of detail of the information gathered.

The rationale for the introduction of BASIS put forward by Lifelong management regularly highlighted these very scandals and the reputation for malpractice with which the life assurance industry had became associated. Simon, in Lifelong's National Sales Operations, had played a large part in deciding upon the features of the latest version of BASIS. He explained the emergence of BASIS by referring to a number of sales practices such as 'churning' that were;

> "all things that perhaps the life assurance industry was renowned for 10-15 years ago - we now monitor and jump on *very* hard if we find anybody doing it - almost all that information comes down on one computer sheet or another" (Simon: 198-200).

The principal benefit of the system of monitoring represented by BASIS was explained both by managers at Head Office and by Branch Managers as the prevention of misbehaviour on the part of individual salespeople. At Head Office, therefore, Simon presented BASIS as an instrument to ensure Lifelong sales representatives met the required standards, and more importantly to provide sufficient information to the regulators to prove this. In doing so, BASIS can be seen as serving to exonerate and justify the practices of all Financial Consultants and branches monitored and *not* caught out and punished for malpractice.

However, the more general information gathered in BASIS related to wider aims than simply compliance. Simon later emphasised that extensions and improvements to BASIS had been made to accomplish a particular strategic aim; namely, to monitor the effectiveness and profitability of the operation of the salesforce. For example, he explained with some pride;

> "we *now* say to the FC's, '*A* - We want to pay out the money on time - that's a service standard we're committed to, but *secondly*, we want to know how much of it is reinvested *with LL*, and how often you replace that insurance policy with a new one'!" (Simon: 395-398).

At the branch level, Jonathan, a Branch Manager, also explained the introduction of BASIS by reference to the monitoring of compliance in his opening words to me on the subject;

"The BASIS system ... the principles of it is twofold in branch level; it's obviously capture of information for compliance, if you know what I mean by that, I mean the regulation side, in other words managing the competency of people..." (Jonathan 1: 5-7).

Jonathan, however, immediately went on to link the system in to the wider potential offered by BASIS in terms of the *maximising of sales* through tighter surveillance and control of the salesforce;

"... while the *other* side of it is the actual sales skills, sales direction, sales opportunities, that side of the business" (Jonathan 1: 7-9).

Thus complying with the requirements of the regulators in terms of monitoring the salesforce also enabled a more strategic use of this information to monitor the effectiveness of selling procedures and of individual employees. This reprises the contradiction in life assurance sales indicated above, between the commitment to 'best advice' and techniques for ensuring maximisation of revenue. The BASIS technology can itself be seen to embody this contradiction: the same surveillance technology is used in Lifelong to monitor and control the salesperson's behaviour in terms of both compliance with regulations *and* the maximising of sales. Both of these objectives, however, rely on the potential for individualisation and normalisation that such technology offers.

The Panopticon and the Operation of Surveillance

The idea of the BASIS system, monitoring the operation of geographically distant sales representatives, might be seen to bear some resemblance to the "panoptic device" referred to by Foucault (1977). Such a device derives from the 'Panopticon', an architectonic design by Jeremy Bentham in 1791 originally envisaged as the design for a prison. In the Panopticon, concentric rings of cells surround a central observation tower, such that from the tower perfect visibility of the inside of every cell is afforded, while each cell is sealed and may only see the tower itself. The principal effect is succinctly summed up by Foucault himself; to "...induce in the inmate a state of conscious and permanent visibility that assures the automatic functioning of a power, as to arrange things so that surveillance is permanent in its effects even if it is discontinuous in its action; that the perfection of power should tend to make its actual exercise unnecessary..."

(Foucault, 1977; 201). This import of this final point is made explicit by Rule; "the risk of instantaneous detection resulting in immediate action makes the member less likely to transgress" (in Sewell and Wilkinson, 1992b; 108). As the Panopticon operates through inducing this state of complete visibility, the optimal situation would be where there is in fact no supervisor in Bentham's tower, merely the potential. The effects of power would therefore have been effectively 'internalised' by the subjects, and surveillance would have become entirely invisible.

As Clegg (1998) notes, the potential of the Panopticon as an architectural design is limited, due to construction costs and the inflexibility of its reliance on unitary, custom-built premises of a fixed capacity. Instead, the importance lies in the principles of permanent visibility and asymmetrical surveillance embodied in the Panopticon (Lyon, 1994), and in particular the individualising effect of the device. By sequestering subjects, each is tied to his/her own conduct and made individually responsible for his/her own behaviour. In the case of direct sales, hierarchical surveillance from a central point is clearly not feasible without substantial restructuring of the customer relationship (as is the case with telesales, for instance). As Grey notes, however, the importance of the panopticon lies in its use as a 'metaphor' for hierarchical social relations which "themselves can act as instruments of hierarchical observation without any particular architecture" (1992: 204). Thus, in Lifelong, certain elements of the individual salesperson's behaviour are selected and monitored through a bureaucratic system of reporting. However, for such a system to function, it is essential that once isolated in this way, the conduct of subjects is then translated into a form amenable to measurement and assessment.

This is done in Lifelong by reducing 'conduct' to the quantification of a set of given elements of behaviour, and translating these into statistics which may then be centralised in BASIS. This *quantification* of behaviour in a work-setting has been directly related to the rise of accounting in the twentieth century, through its "ability to render human performance visible and calculable as a rational economic action" (Ezzamel, 1994: 219). It has been powerfully argued by Miller and O'Leary (1987) that this 'rendering visible' of performance also acted as a contributory factor in the growth of the Scientific Management movement. They contend that Taylorism can be seen as dependent upon to the emergence of standard accounting practices, involving a more direct application of visibility so as to contribute towards the construction of what they term the 'governable self'. Equally, the systems of surveillance in Lifelong contribute to the constitution of the subject as 'calculable man' (Foucault, 1977), i.e. a "human subject (...)

calculable to the extent of being subject to comparative, scalar measures and related forms of training and correction" (Minson, 1986: 113).

A key aspect of this individualisation and quantification of conduct is that it enables what Foucault terms the *normalising judgement* of certain aspects of the behaviour of subjects, in this case the Financial Consultants (and to a lesser extent the Sales Managers and Branch Managers) within Lifelong. The key point in these practices, as noted by Foucault, is not only that it ensures that "all behaviour falls in the field between good and bad marks" but that "it is possible to *quantify* this field and work out an arithmetical economy based on it" (1977: 180). Thus in the case of Taylorism, "money would become the common currency by which to integrate and aggregate the activities of individuals as components" (Miller and O'Leary, 1988: 254). Not only is conduct reduced to numerical data thereby measurable, but it may then be compared positively or negatively with given *norms*.

In Lifelong, the *reductive* nature of this quantification was recognised in the interviews with the Branch Managers. Both Branch Managers nonetheless emphasised the importance of quantification so that information on their Financial Consultants should be manageable and therefore productive. Ken stated;

Q. So do you not find it difficult keeping track of all thirty six (FCs)?
"Well it's impossible - I'd end up with [indicates waist high] that much paper every month if I wanted to look at everybody's, I'd have a two-foot pile of paper you can't relate to, so what do I do, I look at the league table, that sheet up on the top left there, and I get an idea of where people are going." (Ken: 244-9).

Similarly, Jonathan described the reduction of complexity to a useable form, explaining BASIS as;

"a way of capturing all that picture, and feeding it a system which then produces a measurable document, *a bit like an appraisal*" (Jonathan 1: 16-17, emphasis added).

Both comments may be interpreted as reflecting a modernist response to complexity and uncertainty. Ken's difficulty in 'relating to' a relatively limited set of performance indicators for his staff lead him to focus on something manageable and comprehensible; the league table. Jonathan, referring to the 'picture' of what his Financial Consultants do in their jobs, makes it explicit that the representation of this should be 'measurable'. Interestingly, in interviews Ken and Jonathan displayed contrasting perspectives on this process; Jonathan was keen to extol the present and potential virtues of the BASIS system, while Ken became fiercely scathing throughout the interview whenever BASIS was so much as mentioned. Nonetheless, both Ken and Jonathan claimed that the requirements of their position forced them to take part in this process, reducing of complex behaviour to a string of integers which are then made meaningful by comparison with other figures.

The importance of *comparison* must be stressed here, as it is the implicit objective of reducing behaviour to a common, therefore quantitative basis. John's reference to 'appraisal' above is significant here in that it highlights a similar situation, the appraisal procedure, whereby the quantification and comparison of performance is used to productive effect in disciplining an individual (see Townley, 1994). In both situations, where individual effectiveness or productivity is the focus, it should be noted that "the efficiency of the person in the firm ... is not something which can be observed with the naked eye. Indeed, one might say it cannot exist until what is to be regarded as normal or standard has first to be constructed" (Miller and O'Leary, 1987: 262). Thus making such data meaningful involves the construction of *norms* against which the data may be assessed and judged. Such is the importance of the norm that even before it is constructed, "the criterion of the norm (is) implicit in surveillance systems" (Poster, 1984: 114). As noted by Foucault, the norm plays a dual role, "indicating membership of homogeneous social body but also playing a part in classification, hierarchisation and the distribution of rank" (1977: 184). So while BASIS's representation of the Financial Consultant's performance marks him/her out as a salesperson, it simultaneously judges and rates him/her with regard to the given norms.

Norms and Engineered Competition

In Lifelong, these norms are drawn from three sources; the performance of the Financial Consultant's peers, the prior performance of the individual Financial Consultant his/herself and abstract standards set by the company (including KPIs set by the regulators). Comparison against the performance of one's peers is a long-standing form of establishing difference in the form of a hierarchy, particularly in the field of sales. The traditions of sales management involve the construction and dissemination of league tables, displaying the relative performance of Financial Consultants within teams, within offices and within regions. The ubiquity of these league tables, on walls by desks, on general notice-boards, in newsletters, etc. is an essential part of the project of engineering a form of competition between salespeople. The effectiveness of competition is dependent in part on the use of these evaluations as the basis for reward (or punishment), by allocating limited rewards according to the relative performance of each salesperson. Not only does this provide a moving norm which can become self-perpetuating, but the scarcity of the rewards is a powerful means of setting the Financial Consultants off against each other in a particularly individualising way.

This individualised form of manipulation is also enhanced by the routine comparison of the Financial Consultant's present performance with his/her own prior performance. By recording and tracking changes in each indicator, the individual is tied to his/her own (albeit selective) history in the company. Simon in National Sales Operations at Lifelong was involved in implementing a number of changes to BASIS to emphasise this self-comparative aspect, including the reproduction of prior reports at the start of each new one;

> "...to remind themselves of areas they considered important, that they highlighted as needs to be improved, to force them to rediscuss each of the last periods" (Simon: 278-280).

Simon explained this innovation to BASIS with some enthusiasm, stressing that in the latest version, not only is any reading which has decreased since the previous month automatically highlighted in bold, but "a little *grey* box will appear if it's below standard *and* it's gone down compared to the last period" (Simon: 306). Each of these mechanisms is intended to increase the direct pressure on the Financial Consultant, not only by the simple provision of data "so the branch staff can look down and say "Yeah, I know I've got to keep at it". (Simon: 356-359), but by directing the attention of the Sales Managers to any decreasing areas, to encourage the application of personal and individualised pressure. Thus Jonathan, the Branch Manager, underlined the instrumental role he saw BASIS playing in his branch;

> "What the BASIS report does is it highlights areas - again strengths and weaknesses - and it tells you to take action" (Jonathan 1: 234-235).

The interminable, circular nature of this process was also made clear in an off-the-cuff remark made by Jonathan while describing an example of the successful operation of BASIS;

> "if it's an improving trend, and it looks like you've cured the situation, then that's what you've done, so that area then of his overall profile, you can sort of basically sign it off, 'I'm quite happy now with what you're doing, we've cured that issue - *let's move on to one of your other weaknesses!*'" (laughs) (Jonathan 1: 133-135, emphasis added).

The important point here is that while norms constructed on the basis of the performance of other Financial Consultants can stabilise over time, comparing an Financial Consultant's performance with his/her own results in previous months means that *continuous improvement* can be demanded from individual salespeople and reinforced by the direct action of the Sales Manager. In this way, "self-referential targets can work at any level of achievement and not just for those who are already performing at the top of the range" (Knights and Morgan, 1991: 226). As John's semi-humorous remark indicates, this can easily become a perpetual process of identifying weaknesses and demanding improvements (via 'action plans').

Nonetheless, the construction of these norms is not entirely relative, and there is a standard fixed by the company which underpins such comparisons. Over and above these intra-branch processes, the individual and team targets in terms of revenue are essentially dependent on the national target for Lifelong and the breakdown of this target to a regional and branch level. The negotiations which occur between Sales Manager and Financial Consultant to establish and gain each Financial Consultant's agreement to their 'plan' is a key element which *ties* the identity of the Financial Consultant to the targets which they feel they have set themselves. The first step in this process is described by Simon, an ex-branch manager;

"... we ask them right at the start of the year 'What do you think you're gonna be able to sell in the whole year?', because the manager's got to reach a target, the branch has got to reach a target - let's break it down to an *individual* level!" (Simon: 340-3, emphasis added)

Breaking the national target down to this 'individual level' is an essential step in the individualisation of the salesforce, which maximises the visibility of the subjects, allows for highly individualised judgement and through this isolation, reinforces the subjective importance of the material and symbolic rewards. A number of specific techniques are applied to reinforce this individualisation and forge links between targets and the identity of the salesperson, which will be examined in detail in the next section.

'The Levers': Material and Symbolic Rewards

As noted by Knights and Morgan (1990), the potential for sacking under-performing sales representatives is rather restricted in life assurance companies unless they consistently sell less than the minimum company standard, and Lifelong is no exception. More frustrating for the Sales Manager is the Financial Consultant who aims to make the minimum necessary sales and no further. Most forms of control within sales, however, rely on positive incentives, in the form of 'rewards'. Traditionally, in the sales environment, the most obvious manifestation of such rewards are the material bonuses offered to sales staff as a financial incentive. These bonuses range from the basic commission on policies sold to more complex forms of incentive; in Lifelong, for example, earning a certain level of business, or even achieving certain levels of persistency, can mean the multiplication of commissions by a certain figure, the offer of discounted share options, or the possibility of a more expensive and prestigious company car. The staging of these incentives is carefully planned so that there is always a 'carrot' in front of the salesperson, no matter what level of performance they have achieved so far. Thus Jonathan explained eagerly;

> "We really are desperately trying to make sure they really are motivated, from the FC to the Sales Manager, (...) 'Look what you could be doing if you just did a little bit more...'. The payment plan's been designed so that within about £500 to £1000 of earnings, there's always another lever which you can go for, so by being clever about focusing on the yearly position very closely, we can keep pushing our salesmen up to being *more* effective, sell *more*, earn *more*" (Jonathan 1: 467-472).

While the material rewards offered to those who exceed sales norms are substantial, however, equally important to the Financial Consultants are the relatively scarce social and symbolic rewards on offer. In Lifelong, symbolic rewards can range from the sight of one's name at the top of a league table, even the mere mention in a newsletter, up to the public attainment of 'Star Performer' status and a place on the 'Salute the Stars' cruise. As in Foucault's example of the honorary classification of pupils at the *École Militaire* (1977: 181-2), it is the symbolic value of the rank itself which serves as the reward or punishment.

The types of reward used as incentives in Lifelong were represented by Financial Consultants and management as conforming to two basic alternatives, either the *symbolic* or the *material*. Thus one Branch Manager defined his motivation techniques as largely based on these two elements;

> "Well I mean everybody's got different motivators, but the key ones are as I've mentioned league tables and your salary" (Ken: 161-2).

When faced with an Financial Consultant reaching the company minimum requirements but prepared to sacrifice additional bonuses for an lower level of activity, Dave was even more specific about his means of influence, claiming;

"It's just money and pride - that's all you've got. Those two things." (Dave: 766).

In these terms, Sales Management can be seen as a fairly straightforward process. Where the salesperson was thought to value the substantial salary and bonuses offered by Lifelong, then the Sales Manager's task of ensuring maximum productivity from the team was seen as quite simple. Where this didn't work, the Sales Manager was forced to use the possibility of symbolic forms of reward. Brian was highlighted as a perfect example of the self-disciplining, money-oriented salesperson and Dave mentioned with approval his relationship with Brian, who was very clear about the importance of the money to him;

> "I do (keep track of) my own appointments, the prop(osals), the premium, the income and what I've earned... those first four, as far as I'm concerned, are a load of bollocks - if at the end of the day I haven't earned money, I'm not a happy teddy at all. I couldn't give a toss whether LL think I'm brilliant because I've done loads of appointments. loads of PFRs and loads of props, 'cos I personally haven't earned money from that" (Brian : 449-453).

Nonetheless, the financial incentive, while important, is only part of the attraction for Brian; returning later to the 'reasons for his success', he went on to emphasise the importance of his position on the league table, in a particularly masculine assertion of his mastery of the sales process;

> "Some people don't like being at the top, because if you're at the top, or near the top, you're there to be shot down, and some people can't handle that pressure or don't want that pressure. To me it's... you know, bread and milk, I *love* being at the top - I've always been there... well, there or thereabouts... and that's the way it is" (Brian: 588-92).

The relationship between the material rewards and symbolic significantly complicates the simple choice of incentive presented above. Material rewards entail substantial symbolic importance, and the converse is also frequently true, so that rather than the choice of symbolic *or* material reward, what should be stressed is the symbolic *within* the material reward. For example, while the 'star-performers' cruise is seen as a 'financial' motivation, it is intricately linked with the social affirmation provided by the league table and therefore serves as a source of support in the Financial Consultant's attempts to assert a worthwhile, masculine identity.

When working on the symbolic rewards of the league table, for instance, Dave described himself as switching from 'plan A' to 'plan B', from 'money' to 'pride';

> "You sometimes try and get to his pride, don't you? Because, you know, that's the only thing you've got left after that - if you've got a league table, and your name's fourth from bottom on that league table, you know... whether you're not bothered or not about earning money, you wouldn't want to be there, would you?" (Dave: 618).

However, where the rewards appear to be wholly or largely symbolic, it can be difficult to see why they embody such a powerful form of control over the salesforce. In the light of the discussion above, then, it is more accurate to see this as not so much as a *'switch'* from material to symbolic rewards as *making a connection*, so that the Financial Consultant comes to see his/her 'pride', as Dave describes it, as founded on his/her sales performance and thus income. As will be seen below, a range of techniques are used in Lifelong (and other sales organisations) to engineer the reliance of the individual subjects on their position in such hierarchies to secure (relatively) stable and valued identities.

The Individualised Salesforce

The general discussions I had with Lifelong employees suggested that the specific subjectivity reinforced in sales constitutes a subject susceptible to such forms of manipulation. As noted above, the discursive construction of the subjectivity of the salesperson relies on the valuation of an autonomous and independent form of masculinity. This form of masculinity is then particularly susceptible to the individualising effects of surveillance and engineered inter-personal competition; what Knights and Morgan have described as "the individualising effects of competitive struggles for the scarce material and symbolic rewards of success" (1991: 223). The carefully constructed reward systems in Lifelong bear many features of traditional incentive-based sales management practices. The overall effect of this is to create an insecure and individualised sales-force by applying the visibility afforded by surveillance mechanisms, engineering inter-personal rivalry for limited resources and maximising the subjective dependence of the sales representatives on these financial and symbolic resources. This in turn reinforces the construction of a masculine identity and the dependence of the Financial Consultant on material and symbolic rewards for the affirmation of his/her subjectivity. In doing so, the Financial Consultant is subject to a self-disciplinary form of control which, ironically, operates through the value the subject attaches to autonomy and independence from control.

A brief interchange I witnessed between a (male) Financial Consultant and two (female) Systems Support Analysts while waiting for an interview highlighted the normal operation of a number of these themes. Reflecting later, the conversation could be read to typify in an everyday fashion both the operation of mechanisms of control through the internalisation of these values, and equally the opportunistic and individualist pursuit of these values. The mundane and inconsequential nature of the exchange emphasised the unquestioned centrality of these values to the identity of the salespersons.

> (Phone rings and SSA1 answers it)
> SSA1: "It's a Mr Jones... will you...?" (holds out phone)
> FC: (Busying about the office) "Who? Not Mr James?" (Takes the call and after some questions, arranges a meeting)
> SSA1: (When FC has replaced the phone) "Was it Mr Jones?"
> FC: "Yeah, I didn't know him, he was Ted Smith's" (Ted Smith has just left the office).
> SSA1: "Oh, I'm sorry..."
> FC: "No, no, that's fine - absolutely *fine*!" (flashes a satisfied grin at SSAs, inviting comment)
> SSA2: "Was it a good one then?"
> FC: "Yeah, it's another mortgage - another step closer the cruise in the Bahamas!"
> (Unimpressed pause on the part of the SSAs)
> SSA2: "So where are you on the table?"
> FC: "Second, I think - yeah, second, definitely. I'm just five thousand behind the first, and I've got a mortgage this afternoon for £50,000, another tonight for £45,000, another on Monday... yeah!"

Interpreting the exchange, the FC appears to opportunistically poach a potential sale of another FC in his absence, using the occasion to engage the SSAs present in a discussion of his success. The reference to the 'cruise in the Bahamas' highlights the individualising effects of the interpersonal competition for places, where Ted Smith's loss is his gain. It is also interesting to note the way this leads 'naturally' into an enquiry about 'the table' which protocol seemed to demand from one of the SSAs. However, equally important is the way in which the FC draws the SSAs (slightly unwillingly) into a discussion of his good fortune and prowess. This seems to indicate both a typical role of the SSA to affirm the FCs representation of himself, here as the crafty and enterprising hero, and to act as audience to his burgeoning success on 'the table'. The weariness of the SSAs playing this role seemed to indicate that this was a frequent and not entirely welcome duty of theirs. Nonetheless, the FC seemed satisfied, both with the fortuitous commission, his position on 'the table' and with the reassuring responses from the SSAs. At the root of this mundane exchange in Lifelong is the role of surveillance and the reward system in establishing an individualised form of identity among sales staff, which may then be exploited for purposes of motivation. What I intend to examine in the next section are the dynamic processes within the Lifelong salesforce by which the sales identity is reproduced and manipulated.

Beyond Surveillance: Subjectivity and Control in Sales

As competition and incentives operate *through*, rather then *alongside*, the manipulation of an identity specific to sales; I intend to return now to the mechanisms by which this form of subjectivity is reinforced and reproduced on a day-to-day basis in Lifelong. To do so, I will start by examining the salesforce's perception of BASIS and the systems of surveillance they were subject to. The precise focus of the discontent articulated indicates once again the way in which the subjectivity of the salesperson enables the operation of a more subtle and effective form of manipulation through the routine mechanisms which 'tie' of the subject to such a construction of their identity.

The Construction of Knowledge

In line with the anti-bureaucratic and 'autonomous' discourses prevalent in sales, a significant amount of discontent was voiced in my interviews with Lifelong Financial Consultants, Sales Managers and Branch Managers regarding the operation of BASIS within the organisation. At first sight, this appeared to point to the existence of a level of resistance in the face of monitoring. However, further discussion revealed a more complex picture. What employees took issue with was the quantification of their job performance, as they highlighted the ineffectiveness of the system of surveillance and more fundamentally the problems in reducing complex social behaviour to a technicist, numerical formula. Several expressed a preference for a more 'personalised' form of management control, operating directly through their relationship with their Sales Manager. In this section, then, I will attempt to represent the complex position adopted by the salesforce with regard to the more conspicuous structures of surveillance and control.

At first, in the light of my interviews with senior management at Head Office, the comments of the direct salesforce appeared to support notions of perfect panoptical vision throughout Lifelong. A number of interviewees made similar remarks, regarding the visibility they felt subject to as a result of centralisation of information on the performance of individual employees;

> "every man and his dog in the company, from the senior executives who I absolutely love to bits, I think they're wonderful people, can go and tap my computer information and get it up on a computer screen no matter where they are in the country. So there's no hiding now..." (Brian: 395-398)

Brian appeared to dilute his implicit criticism of this total visibility in a typically macho way, by sarcastically feigning an exaggerated love and trust of those utilising the surveillance system which shields him from taking responsibility for his comments. However, he immediately went on to stress that this IT-based system was not a complete innovation, emphasising the continuities between BASIS and its more bureaucratic predecessors;

> "...But those systems have always been there, if somebody had the gumption or the gall to ask that person the question...." (Brian: 398-400)

While the existence of the information in a centralised form is not generally questioned by the Financial Consultants, for it to provide a means of manipulating the subjectivity of employees it is essential that it should attain the status of 'knowledge'. Simply *informing* an employee that his/her performance is substandard by using centralised, quantitative information is a relatively straightforward process once the system of surveillance and norms have been established.[16] However, attempts to construct watertight systems of surveillance aim to construct a form of 'knowledge' such that an employee *internalises* the norms and disciplines his/herself to maintain a valued work identity. Thus Brian himself, explaining the role of BASIS, stated;

> "You've got to have (the Financial Consultant's) perception agreeing that there definitely is something wrong, something's got to be put into place. If they don't agree that, with the best will in the world it's... it's time to hit the highway." (Brian: 701-3)

---

[16] Although, as much Marxist and Labour Process literature on the conflicts over time-and-motion studies indicates, this task in itself is difficult and endlessly contestable; see, for example, Beynon, 1975; Littler, 1982.

In the case of BASIS, elements of technical rationality were invoked in an attempt to persuade the salespersons that the information produced by data is an accurate, objective and therefore 'truthful' representation of their performance. The use of IT and statistics might be expected to represent particularly powerful means of constructing this 'truth'. It is here, however, that the intentions of senior Lifelong management and the perceptions of the salesforce in general appear to diverge.

Dissent and Resistance to Surveillance

The immediate problem with the use of BASIS to construct knowledge regarding the conduct of employees was that not only the Financial Consultants but also the Sales Managers and some Branch Managers deeply resented the inaccuracy of the information held in BASIS. Thus one Branch Manager, Ken, when he finally opened up on his opinion of BASIS, complained bitterly;

"What gets me are the inaccuracies ... you've got inaccurate information in there in the first place, but when you've got all these different individuals, you can't just get an average figure and then make assumptions on that basis, and what they do is they pull together all the information from the regions at a national level... (*Sort of get an aggregate?*) Yeah, and then they make assumptions on the basis of that!" (Ken: 265-9)

Ken's deep scepticism was rooted in what seemed to be a general lack of confidence amongst fieldstaff in the competence of Lifelong's IT function and their systems, as noted in Chapter 6;

[Ken]. "The key issue, which BASIS doesn't give you any credible information on, is customer coverage, in terms of appointments, how many customers is a guy seeing, and most of the information in BASIS on that is inaccurate... I mean, Lifelong systems generally are... (lowers voice) ...pretty crap. You're not reporting this to the company, are you?" (laughing)
[Q]. "No, no chance of that"
[Ken]. (laughs) "So people sort of... there's a lot of mistrust of the..."
[Q]. "You've got to take it with a pinch of salt?"
[Ken]. "Yeah" (Ken: 71-76)

While this specific criticism was restricted to the capacity of Lifelong in particular to operate an effective system of surveillance, there did exist a more fundamental opposition to the functioning of BASIS, and one which seemed common among staff at all levels of the branches. This opposition took issue with the quantification of behaviour, the assumption that the performance of the salespersons could be reduced to a numerical base. Almost all the branch staff I interviewed were fiercely insistent that BASIS ignores and obscures what they perceived as the social and specifically *human* element of selling. Thus Ken, in the middle of a long and passionate attack on the system he saw imposed on himself as Branch Manager, protested;

> "They think of it as a process, and it's *not* a process - I mean, there are processes in there that we try and train people in, but it's a *human* thing, isn't it? It's not just figures and statistics, it's not like manufacturing, you can't just treat it like a manufacturing process..." (Ken: 271-3).

Similarly, Dave, the Sales Manager and Brian, Financial Consultant in his team, agreed on the intrinsic limitations of quantifying the performance of individual salespersons. Dave first emphasised the reductionism implicit in the process;

> "what I'm trying to say is you can't just take those facts and figures, you *can't*, because you've got to know what that individual's about and how he works and how he don't work, and what areas (...) that (BASIS) just helps you put into black and white what probably the strengths and weaknesses are, but you've got to be very careful 'cos you can't just take that as the whole picture..." (Dave: 120-2).

Brian eagerly took up this point, arguing against the impersonal nature of this individualised assessment and linking it to the notion of 'hunger' as the essential requirement of a good salesperson.

> "BASIS is not going to show how hungry somebody is or isn't. It's not going to do that, it can't - it's not complete.... If you ever replaced that system for a manager, you'd be doomed. You'd be doomed". (Brian: 732-4)

Once again, the complaint against BASIS and bureaucratic forms of control centres on its lack of 'humanity', as well as its limited capacity for monitoring. Thus Brian's basic argument was fairly representative of the rest of the Financial Consultants and Sales Managers interviewed, that;

> "when the information's put into the system, it's just asking you for a fact, and that fact's fed in, whatever that fact is. But behind that fact there's a face, and the system, while it's being impersonal - Dave's quite right in my opinion - that system has got to be *personalised* by somebody" (Brian: 131-4).

It is important to note here that what Brian in effectively arguing in favour of is a return to an earlier system where responsibility for managing sales staff is decentralised to their immediate superior, the Sales Manager, as long as the team's revenue meets the target. This, however, is already an essential component of the existing system of control, as Brian admits later, stating;

> "if you liken it to the computer system, it's like a black and white outline and Dave puts the colours in, you know, *he personalises it*" (Brian: 142-3, emphasis added).

The Role of Sales Managers and the 'Personalised System'

As noted above, a system of surveillance supported by established and highly visible norms, even when linked to material and social rewards (and sanctions), does not in itself bring about the internalisation of these norms on the part of the salesforce. Specific mechanisms are needed to tie in the subjectivity of the salespersons with the achievement of these norms; the ultimate intention is that, for the Financial Consultant, attaining a (relatively) secure identity depends on regularly surpassing the norms established. A key element in forging this link is the day-to-day role of the Sales Manager in supplementing the system of surveillance by wider monitoring; for instance, if a Sales Manager is concerned that one of his Financial Consultants is over-reporting their number of appointments,

> "You won't give him notice, you'd say 'I'm coming working with you tonight', and if he says 'A few of my calls have blobbed', you'd probably say 'Well that's alright', and you'd do it again, and... you've got a trend there haven't you!?" (Dave: 300-2).

Apart from such techniques, the relationship built up between the Sales Manager and his/her Financial Consultant allows a supplementary form of discreet yet constant monitoring which is not restricted to quantifiable conduct. As Dave indicated, his sales management role encompassed more than BASIS and on-the-job performance;

> "when you go to their houses, you can *see* why they don't need a lot of money or why they might not be motivated in some things" (Dave: 600-1).

The wider aspects of supervision are used to increase the perceived reliability of the Sales Manager's 'knowledge' in the eyes of the Financial Consultant (particularly when compared to the restricted, quantitative data gathered by BASIS).

In addition to extending the reach of surveillance, however, the fundamental function of the Sales Managers is to gain individual consent to these norms. Through a careful manipulation of their relationship, Sales Managers embed the norms in the subjectivities of their sales representatives. Thus individual salespeople are bound by their constructions of themselves in relation to the knowledge deployed by their superiors. This aspect of the Sales Manager's role, while related to the operation of BASIS, fulfils the complementary requirement of 'personalising the system'.

The personal relationship built up between the Financial Consultant and his/her Sales Manager is the fundamental way in which the form of subjectivity mentioned at the start of this chapter is reinforced and reproduced, and the Financial Consultant comes to construct his/her identity based on company norms and targets. A major part of this is the 'one-to-one', the weekly or monthly meeting between Sales Manager and Financial Consultant where BASIS paperwork is completed and submitted. The 'one-to-one' itself bears a number of similarities to Foucault's description of the modern use of the *confessional* (Foucault, 1978), whereby the individual is constituted as a subject and tied to an identity.

The technology of the confessional is a fundamental technology of power through which 'truth' is produced in Western societies, and Foucault traces its history from the Catholicism of the Middle Ages to the rituals of psychoanalysis of the modern day. As noted by Townley, "the first role of the confessional is to access individuals' deeply held knowledge of themselves" (1994: 119), thus supplementing the limited potential for surveillance offered by BASIS. Dave highlighted the importance of the *personal* nature of these meetings, enabling the Sales Manager to potentially access knowledge inaccessible through other forms of surveillance, as he explained;

> "if you're having a one-to-one and you're in a confined space, they'll tell you things that they might not tell you in a whole group, you know, so it's things like that really, so you've got to have a meeting once a week where they know they can air their views" (Dave: 226-8).

The 'urge to confess' in such situations is reinforced by a number of related features of the position of Financial Consultants. The ephemeral nature of success in sales, measured against steadily increasing standards which are renewed yearly, monthly and even weekly, increases the Financial Consultant's need for social affirmation in the face of this insecurity. As noted above, however, the effect of the reward systems is to engineer an individualising form of competition which serves to isolate each individual from their 'team-members' in the pursuit of scarce rewards.

This leaves the Sales Manager as the main source of support and reassurance for employees in what is an insecure and frequently demoralising job. This dependence should not be seen as simply cynically engineered by Sales Managers, as many managers stressed in interviews the importance they placed on the responsibility they had to provide support to their team; what one described as "the arm round the shoulder, a bit of company" (Dave: 642). However, the isolation of the individualised salesperson and the transient nature of his/her subjective security furnish his/her manager, through the mechanism of the one-to-one, with access to hidden information which may then be used instrumentally to enhance the profitability of the salesperson (and hence the Sales Manager). Dave illustrates this, comparing the one-to-ones with the limitations of BASIS monitoring;

> "Yeah... I mean, it's like I say, we do a one-to-one every week, and sometimes it's like... well, Brian's quite a successful person so we'll be always talking about business, but... there's certain things that can affect what Phil does, next week or the week after, and it might not be pure business things, it might be his family at home, it might be personal things, that doesn't tell you - so if you're not having a one-to-one every week, well you have to go through that (information in BASIS) probably 'cause you haven't got your finger on (the pulse)..." (Dave: 220-5).

The most important aspect of the one-to-one as a mechanism of control is not, however, this extension of surveillance to further *reveal* the subject, but the use of power to actually *construct* the subject through the fixing of his/her identity. There are distinct parallels here with the concept of 'interpellation' (Althusser, 1971) here. The one-to-one is a mechanism by which the subject comes to recognise him/herself in the constructions of the organisation, which thus "become part of the individual's self-understanding" (Townley, 1994: 118). By establishing 'knowledge' regarding the subject of the one-to-one and, more importantly, gaining the subjects acceptance over what this 'knowledge' is, the identity of the subject may be fixed. The role of the 'confessor' is critical here; Foucault notes that the 'master' who listens to the confession "was the master of truth... his power was not only to demand it before it was made, or to decide what was to follow after it, but also to constitute a discourse of truth on the basis of its decipherment" (Foucault, 1981: 67). This form of power relies on a belief in the existence of a 'truth' of an individual, which may be discovered - the presence of the master is necessitated, importantly, by the need to verify that this fundamental 'truth' has indeed been discovered (see Townley, 1995 for a discussion). Thus Townley describes how an appraisee;

"may be ... encouraged to reflect on performance and in collaboration with the head of department (the confessor) to discover areas of individual potential. The views of the confessor are then shared with the individual who, it is hoped, will come to share these perceptions and see themselves in this way" (1994: 118).

A number of tactics are used in the one-to-one to convert the constructions of the organisation into the self-understanding of the individual. One such technique involves the careful blurring of the distinction between the constructions of the subject and the appraiser, as can be seen in the subtle shifting between persons in the following descriptions of one-to-ones;

"*You*, as my Financial Adviser, as one of my staff, *we*'ve identified that *you*'ve got a weakness, an area of development in this area, and *you*'re not quite sure what to do when *you* get to that type of client - *we*'ve found that out through looking at various statistics, so what *we* now need to do is put a development plan in place, so that *the two of us* can work on that over the next month, two months, whatever it takes, so that *I* can give *you* the knowledge *you* need, so that that can be corrected" (Jonathan 1: 116-124, emphasis added).

"if a person isn't very active, and the sales figures say that the sales are declining, if *we* discuss it at a one-to-one and say 'Okay, what *we* need to do is be more active, and *we*'ve agreed that what *you* want to do is make some more telephone calls'" (Simon: 282-4, emphasis added).

In both examples, the Sales Manager, through the careful use of the first person plural, attempts to generate a collaborative atmosphere in the one-to-one, such that the Financial Consultant is encouraged to recognise in him/herself those 'weaknesses' identified by BASIS or the Sales Manager.

BASIS, Knowledge and Self-Discipline

The use of BASIS in the appraisal process serves two purposes. Firstly, it attempts to restrict 'knowledge' to the relatively limited categories of information that are provided by the BASIS paperwork i.e. those deemed to be pertinent by senior management. Secondly, BASIS supplies a foundation of 'objective' information on the subject him/herself to serve as a structure for discussion in the one-to-one. A clear attempt has been made to use BASIS to impose this structure on the Sales Managers conducting the interviews, so that it is no longer 'a case of the big picture', as Ken complains, but instead the statistics provided by BASIS and the forms to be completed for BASIS shape the content and thus the effect of these meetings. In this way, BASIS attempts to define which aspects of the subject are highlighted as 'true'; that their level of activity is below the norm, for instance, or that their projected commission is less than agreed at the prior one-to-one.

However, the practicalities of securing consent to this 'truth' is made considerably more difficult, as seen above, by the unreliability of BASIS data. Forms of resistance to the operation of BASIS include the deliberate fabrication of data for BASIS by the Financial Consultants, either to mislead the Sales Manager or to invalidate certain sets of information. Indeed, there was a clear implication in the accounts of some Sales Managers and even Ken, the Branch Manager, that Sales Managers collude in marginalising the structure imposed by the BASIS system. Thus certain sets of information are ignored or jointly fabricated if seen as less relevant to the 'real' objectives of the salesforce i.e. the maximisation of sales and thereby commissions. What is then *agreed* to be true may be related to the BASIS data, but is more likely to be established by the Sales Manager's knowledge of his/her Financial Consultant through their direct relationship.

Despite the failure of BASIS to construct a reliable and compete body of knowledge on the subjects, some aspects of BASIS data are frequently used in the one-to-ones, such as the 'Total Business Written', although how these are interpreted is often at the discretion of the Sales Manager and Financial Consultant. The day-to-day surveillance conducted through the Sales Manager/Financial Consultant relationship is a supplementary source of what is thought to be more 'reliable' knowledge. This latter knowledge is then deployed by the Sales Manager through this crucial relationship in an attempt to produce and 'fix' the subjectivity of the Financial Consultant, particularly in the appraisal interview. While the one-to-one is an important site of this production and 'fixing' of identity, the process is not restricted to appraisal procedures; from recruitment procedures to the day-to-day interactions of Sales Managers and Financial Consultants, a specifically *masculine* and *individualised* form of identity dependent on commitments to norms in the form of activity and sales targets is constructed and reinforced.

The role of the Sales Manager is to get the Financial Consultant to accept this construction of identity as 'true' about him/herself and to *commit* to altering his/her behaviour in agreed ways to correct this deviation. Thus Jonathan explained the highly-individualised operation of this form of power, stating;

"I think it's important that anyone who works for you has to have a personal goal, and a personal commitment to achieving something. I think what you should do then is break that down into day-by-day, month-by-month tasks, which enables them to achieve that." (Jonathan 1: 285-287)

The *internalisation* of goals and norms is essential here; as Knights and Morgan note, "this mechanism of power depends for its own success on individual managers and sales personnel defining their own sense of themselves (that is *identities*) in terms of achieving or exceeding the targets" (1991: 225). By reconstituting the individual's understanding of him/herself in line with the requirements (or norms) of the organisation e.g. as productive, proactive and reflective, the aim is to instil a form of *self-discipline* in the subject. The importance of identity here is thus the potential it affords for the continuous operation of these techniques of control, as the individual is encouraged to monitor his/herself with regard to norms which are now central to their notion of self. Once these understandings are integral to the notion of self held by the Financial Consultant, "they can function as part of the 'self-steering' mechanisms of individuals" (Miller and Rose, 1990: 19).

By inculcating self-discipline in subjects, the responsibility for monitoring and correcting behaviour is shifted to the subject him/herself. Brian, for instance, was fiercely proud of what he perceived as his independence from BASIS, and emphasising his 'self-motivation', asserted;

> "If the computer's turned off now, or the BASIS system crashes, it's not going to stop me working until somebody tells me to stop working, 'cos I've got... there's four reasons why I go out to work, that's my wife and my three kids, not what BASIS tells me to do" (Brian: 250-3).

What is ironic here is that the very operation of this internalised form of control is constructed by the subject as proof of his/her autonomy and freedom from control. There is no recognition of the control exerted *through* the self-discipline of the Financial Consultant, such is the level of internalisation of this construction of identity. This belief was clear in Brian's proud assertion of his freedom from manipulation by BASIS, where he emphasised that he makes his own calculations, so that;

> "(my personal system) tells me as far as I'm concerned that Dave's not on my back, that John's not on my back, and it doesn't matter what those (BASIS) figures say, 'cos *I've done everything that I as an individual feel I need to do*... which is activity management - I've been active" (Brian: 470-3, emphasis added).

This self-disciplinary form of control is thus enabled by the construction of identity specific to the salesperson, founded on a masculinist discourse of autonomy and independence. The information from BASIS is perceived as the imposition of a direct form of control which 'offends the pride' of the Financial Consultants insofar as it questions the fundamental autonomy and independence of the self-motivated, masculine 'breadwinner'. Through the very rejection of this form of control, the Financial Consultant reaffirms his/her ability to motivate (i.e. discipline) his/her self as a display of 'independence'. Moreover, the need to secure this subjectivity ensures the Financial Consultant's continued dependence on their Sales Manager to confirm their identity and to provide such knowledge on aspects of their conduct which is critical to this subjectivity.

Conclusion

The intention in this chapter has been to outline the complex forms of control by which the sales process is managed within Lifelong Assurance. I started, therefore, by depicting the changes in the life assurance industry which form the context in which these forms of control have been intensified in recent years. The increased demand for pensions in the late 1980s was swiftly followed by widespread publicity over the mis-selling of private pensions, which cut back the burgeoning demand in the industry. The scandal itself can be seen as reflecting a particular contradiction at the heart of life assurance selling, where pressures to maximise sales clash with the requirement of 'best advice' from the sales representative. Nonetheless, such mis-selling has widely been presented as the action of 'cowboy' operators, and thus as an aberration from usual industry practice (contrary to several reports by the regulatory agency which identify major firms as the main offenders). In this way, the pressure to maximise sales has been intensified, not only *despite* such scandals but largely *as a consequence of* the effects on demand of the widespread malpractice in the industry. I read my interviews with employees involved with sales as reflecting a general anxiety in the salesforce as a result of this recent history of intensified pressure to sell combined with increased regulatory sanctions.

The forms which this intensification of control has taken centre on two interrelated elements; the use of monitoring and incentives linked to sales performance, and the construction of a self-disciplinary and predominantly masculine subjectivity specific to the salesforce. Through a discussion of these control mechanisms, I have tried to break down the traditional dichotomy between, on the one hand, forms of control which rely on financial incentives and, on the other, those which operate through manipulating the subjectivity of the salesperson.[17] Instead, I have

---

[17] A dichotomy represented by the Theory X and Theory Y approaches (McGregor, 1987) in the Human Relations School and reproduced in much mainstream managerial work since.

attempted to show the way in which the effectiveness of financial incentives relies, in part, on the social affirmation implicit in such rewards, and in part, on the construction of a restricted and individualised form of subjectivity dependent on this affirmation. More generally, I mean to emphasise the piecemeal, disconnected and often contradictory way in which forms of control are attempted, without imputing any inevitable coherence or common direction to the range of initiatives implemented. Nonetheless, the combined effect is a form of discipline which operates through the interrelated techniques of enhanced surveillance and the instrumental manipulation of subjectivity.

I opened the discussion, therefore, with an examination of the forms of identity encouraged and reproduced through the field of sales, focusing on the constant depiction of sales as productive and heroic by the salespersons interviewed in Lifelong. This image of sales was set against the representation of bureaucracy at Head Office, understood as a faceless and largely parasitic function serving to constrain their own productivity. In contrast, what was emphasised was the fiercely masculine nature of sales, as dependent upon 'the hunger' inside. The connection was frequently made between this understanding of sales and the discourse of the male breadwinner: as a consequence, masculinity and identity were represented as dependent on the salesperson's ability to 'bring home the bacon' i.e. their sales performance. This impression was reinforced by the intense pride evident in several interviewees accounts of his/her sales prowess and 'hunger' being down to (generally his) 'duty' to their families. Moreover, this highly gendered notion of the 'breadwinner' was not only implicit in the recruitment criteria of Lifelong but was actively reproduced both formally, through training and sales management, and informally, in interactions between the sales staff themselves.

In the next section I have developed this theme by examining the use of surveillance to reinforce control of the salesforce. The requirement for certain information to satisfy the regulators compliance criteria serves to justify the use of IT to intensify the levels of monitoring to which the salesperson in Lifelong is subject. Indeed, this dual role of the surveillance systems reflects the contradiction noted above between compliance and sales maximisation. I have adopted Foucault's notion of the panopticon to interpret the surveillance mechanism, BASIS, insofar as it automatically monitors the key aspects of the salesforce's behaviour and, through isolating and quantifying the conduct of each salesperson, reinforces the individualising effect of the organisation of work. The counterpart of this *hierarchical observation* is the exercise of a *normalising judgement* over the salesforce. Such norms are constructed through comparison against the performance of the subject's peers (again isolating individuals), against the subject's own prior performance (as a perpetual form of incentive) and against the bottom line of the company's designated sales plan. A range of material and symbolic forms of reward are then tied to comparative performance, whose importance is magnified by the isolation of the salesperson and their reliance on such rewards to reaffirm their masculine identity.

The somewhat circular structure to the chapter has been chosen to represent the circular way in which such forms of control are reproduced. The management of the salesforce through the construction of a particular subjectivity is a long-standing form of control and pre-dates all of the legislative changes and structural changes to the resultant 'Financial Services' industry in the UK, although there is evidence that a more focused 'sales-orientation' has been encouraged in many institutions. However, it is the specific construction of identity around the masculine notion of the 'breadwinner' which leaves the salesforce vulnerable to manipulation through financial and symbolic incentives and the constant and public comparison of performance. What was interesting in Lifelong was the rejection of the information provided on performance by BASIS as inaccurate and incomplete. Such information was frequently fabricated by sales representatives, in collusion with their managers, and a preference for a 'personalised', more 'human' form of management was expressed. The representative's reliance on his/her manager for affirmation reflects the competition engineered between representatives and the general isolation that surveillance reinforces. The key form of interaction between manager and sales representative, the 'one-to-one' interview, thus forms a kind of 'confessional' in the Foucauldian sense, where the manager can complement the incomplete surveillance system of BASIS. At the same time, the manager does not simply *access* hidden knowledge; he/she actively *constructs* knowledge about the subject, based on the criteria represented in BASIS, and fixes the subject's identity by gaining his/her consent to this representation of him/her*self*, in line with the masculine notions of identity examined above. Thus the inadequacies of surveillance and control through simple incentives are overcome by the self-monitoring and self-control mechanisms provided by the specific construction of the subjectivity of the salesperson. Indeed, salesforce's resistance to simple surveillance, linked to their general pursuit of a masculine notion of autonomy, can be seen to render the individual salesperson even more vulnerable to direct manipulation through their dependence on their sales manager.

8 *Ethos*, Ethics and Financial Services

Discussion and Conclusions

My intentions in this book, as noted in Chapter 1, lie on two levels. My first aim has been to illuminate the ongoing changes in the 'Financial Services' industry in the UK, in relation to the intensification of competition, the action of the regulators and the strategic responses of the senior management of financial institutions such as Buzzbank and Lifelong Assurance. In tracing such changes, I have focused in my empirical work on the experiences of employees of these organisations, specifically in terms of management's attempts at culture management, general forms of surveillance and direct control, the articulation of the associated discourses of professionalism and 'Project Management', and modes of control dependent in part on the construction of a specifically masculine form of subjectivity. Throughout this analysis, I have also paid particular attention to what may be read as 'resistance' of one form or another, usually centring on the rearticulation of discourses, the use of satire and deflationary humour, and occasionally the open articulation of dissent and resistance. At the same time, my wider concern has been to outline the form a critical mode of social research might take, without falling back on an essentialist epistemology nor a universal moral position. In the book, I have structured this critical position around the expansion of my analysis beyond dialectics of control and resistance to encompass power in its broadest sense. As a consequence, I have examined the operation of power in a diverse range of forms in my empirical work, and paid particular attention to the operation of power through the constitution of its subjects. Much of this discussion therefore focused on the construction, reinforcement and manipulation of particular forms of subjectivity in work organisations. Without essentialising any particular form of resistance, or indeed romanticising the notion of resistance itself, I have tried to outline a contingent ethical position which may be taken in relation to each instance of the operation of power, and I have analysed forms of resistance in accordance with such a perspective. I now intend to reiterate in more detail the key elements of the argument, before engaging in a discussion where I will relate these elements to the objectives set out at the opening of the book.

This concluding chapter will therefore consist of three main sections. Firstly, I will provide a brief overview of the preceding chapters, emphasising the key points made in each chapter and highlighting the fundamental connections which are frequently obscured by the division of the book into chapters. I have used *the construction of the individual as object and as subject* as a schema for this discussion, taken from Foucault's retrospective understanding of his earlier work (1982; 1985) and particularly as adopted by Townley (1994). In the light of this overview, I will then draw out the main themes of the book, clarifying the key arguments and revisiting the issues and founding concerns raised in the Introduction.

Review of the Themes

In the book, I have analysed the forms of control exercised over the employees in certain pivotal functions in two organisations within the rapidly-developing 'Financial Services' industry in the UK. I have therefore focused on the IT and Direct Sales divisions of two significant financial institutions; Buzzbank, a telephone-based banking operation, and Lifelong Assurance, one of the largest life assurance companies in the UK. My original theoretical perspective rested on an understanding of, and sympathy for, certain broadly neo-Marxist positions held within the Labour Process field on issues of power, control and resistance in capitalist work relations. Through the period of my doctoral research, I have constantly reviewed my position through an engagement with other literatures which may be understood as 'critical' in a broader sense than neo-Marxist. In particular, my perspective has been informed by a critical interpretation of the work of Michel Foucault, whose work on power and, later, on subjectivity and the self, I feel has provided a number of significant insights into fundamental difficulties which hamper Labour Process analyses of power relations at work.

Developing a Critical Perspective

As I have noted, particular caution needs to be taken in adopting the work of Foucault, given his insistence that his work should not be seen as a coherent *oeuvre*; "what I say ought to be taken as 'propositions', 'game openings'... they are not meant as dogmatic assertions that have to be taken or left en bloc" (Foucault, in Burchell, Gordon and Miller, 1991: 73). It is therefore important that I stress my reading to be a *critical* interpretation of Foucault, assessing works on the merits of the insights they provide. In particular, I have found Foucault's analyses to be useful insofar as they offer a more sophisticated conception of power than the dialectical control-resistance model of traditional Labour Process work, thus also avoiding the implicit dependence on class-based analysis and economistic models of neo-Marxist work in general. The notion of discourse, developed more fully in Chapter 3, also promises a possible way out of the structure-agency dilemma by reformulating understandings of power. Crucially, I feel the adoption of a Foucauldian perspective has afforded the argument a broader and more inclusive appreciation of the operation of power, focusing attention on the capillary 'micro-'operation of power in everyday interactions. As Foucault notes on the subject of prisons and psychiatric internment, for instance, "so long as the posing of the question of power was kept subordinate to the economic instance and the system of interests which this served, there was a tendency to regard these problems as of small importance" (Foucault, 1980: 116). At the same time, a particular advantage of Foucault's position is that it emphasises links between such operations and wider discourses, while avoiding the implication that this may be traced to an originating source or strategist. In addition, Foucault's insistence on the importance of *individual* forms of resistance has focused attention on the domination and repression frequently effected through what superficially appear to be emancipatory discourses.

In developing such a position, I have paid attention to a number of additional and associated concerns. A key element of the argument is the understanding I have adopted of power operating through *discourse*, a notion jointly derived from the (socio-)linguistic conception of discourse and the more material conception adopted by Foucault. For purposes of clarity, I have defined discourse as 'a socially and historically specific system of assumptions, values and beliefs which materially affects social conduct and social structure'. The *materiality* implicit in this formulation of 'discourse' highlights the continuities between Foucauldian discourse and the Althusserian notion of 'ideology'; nonetheless, I have taken some time to delineate the fundamental differences between the theoretical perspectives underlying each. In particular, ideology's reliance on an essential 'Truth' against which it is typically juxtaposed and which it stands to obscure is rejected explicitly by Foucault. Instead, he highlights the operation of power in the very *construction* of knowledge, or 'truths', as outlined in his earlier work on power/knowledge configurations in the fields of psychiatry, medicine, etc. (Foucault, 1975). I have then critically examined the changing understanding of discourse in Foucault's work in the light of the latent determinism which several authors have attacked in his earlier work. I have argued that this implicit determinism can be traced to Foucault's anti-humanism and his early tendency to treat the individual as an 'empty vessel' which is simply *acted upon* by discourse. In his later work, the attention he pays to the notion of 'the self' allows a more active conceptualisation of identity. I have suggested that the concept of *difference* as developed in linguistics and critical psychology provides an insight into the everyday operation of discourses, particularly through the construction of specific forms of *subjectivity*. A final but highly significant point to emphasise is that the reflexive and active role of the individual in this process, unlike the more deterministic notion in Foucault's earlier work, allows space for the introduction of *ethics* into the understanding and the assessment of forms of individual conduct.

The issue of ethics is also central to my broader project; the development of a non-essentialist form of critical social research which can avoid positing and imposing fundamental moral certainties. While providing a body of work which enables the understanding the operation of power in a wider sense, Foucault also undermines the moral imperative which is intrinsic to critical work founded on a Marxist analysis. Foucault's attack is broadly aimed at those 'critical' discourses which claim to speak in the place of the oppressed and to act in their name, justified by their privileged access to the 'real interests' of others. Crucially, as noted by Sawicki, Foucault suggests that such emancipatory theories do not recognise their "dominatory tendencies" and are "historically linked to disciplinary practices that have been more oppressive than liberating" (1991: 97). However, in undermining this universal legitimation, he risks slipping into a dangerous moral relativism, whereby critique of oppression or domination cannot be essentially grounded; indeed, he has been interpreted by several writers of promoting a 'postmodern' celebration of difference and discontinuity. Through a reading of Foucault and associated work, I have attempted to retrieve for myself a position from which I may make judgements and formulate criticisms, while stressing their tentative and contingent nature and openness to dispute. As noted in the opening chapter, this is not for me an abstract and depersonalised synthesis of abstract theoretical literatures; this book forms part of my own (ongoing) construction of myself as socially-aware and theoretically-informed critical academic. What I have tried to develop in the book, therefore, is a mode of analysis which I may use to achieve a form of understanding of the social world, and through which I can pursue my moral concerns. By drawing on both Foucauldian and other critical bodies of work, I intend that this analysis should be adaptable enough to recognise and interpret the wide variety of forms of power relations and modes of discretion/resistance, and should not preclude their evaluation on ethical grounds, yet without imposing a universal and dominatory code of morality.

Interpreting Practice in the 'Financial Services' Industry

My empirical work in the subject organisations has then served as both a focus for this mode of analysis and as a means of developing and assessing the usefulness of the approach. In Chapter 5, then, I have attempted to situate the subject organisations in their social, political and historical context, and draw out the specific relevance of the choice of Buzzbank and Lifelong Assurance. Both organisations operate in financial markets which have been brought into direct contact as a consequence of the restructuring implemented under the Conservative administration of the 1980s and early 1990s in the UK. In particular, the expansion of the 'Financial Services' industry was encouraged by what has been termed the 'deregulation' of financial markets through the 1980s, as well as the dissolution of barriers to competition between European Union member states and the UK government's gradual retreat from various welfare commitments. Two significant and related effects of this have been the tendency of financial institutions to diversify and enter a number of financial markets, as the emergence of the 'bancassurers' exemplifies, and the sudden intensification of competition in a number of these markets, which has had direct implications for the workforce in such institutions.

In Chapter 5, what I have attempted to do, therefore, is to outline these recent developments leading to the construction of a 'financial services industry', and trace the specific implications of these changes on Buzzbank and Lifelong. Both companies can be seen as partly involved in the field of 'bancassurance', although this was not a direct focus of my research. However, this connection does reflect the similarities in the social and institutional environment faced by both, marked by the recent deregulation, the intensification of competition, widespread attempts to diversify and, crucially, the effects of 're-regulation' in the form of regulatory bodies. The action of the regulators has held particular significance for Lifelong in recent years; along with most other life assurers, they have been repeatedly reprimanded for malpractice in the selling of personal pensions in the 'boom years' immediately after 1986 when the Financial Services Act and in particular the Social Security Act was passed. Buzzbank, by contrast, gives the impression of having enjoyed a period of untroubled success and expansion since its inception in the late 1980s, in which it has came to represent a significant proportion of the total turnover of TN Banking. More recently, however, this success has led to changes which have exacerbated difficulties which had until then been carefully managed. Both Buzzbank and Lifelong have recently undertaken a formalisation and bureaucratisation of their business procedures, involving the use of IT to reinforce mechanisms of surveillance, although for apparently different reasons. Thus formalisation at Buzzbank was carried out at the instigation of its 'parent company', TN Banking to ensure that their contribution to the profitability of the company as a whole could be guaranteed, while in Lifelong it was presented as conforming with compliance information demanded by the regulators. However, the senior management interviewed in both companies stressed the importance of this process in providing 'accurate' management information so as to enhance managerial control over certain central functions.

In each organisation, the departments which I chose to research were thus determined partly by their centrality to the operation of each company, and equally by pragmatic concerns regarding access. In focusing on the Information Technology and Direct Sales divisions, there were nonetheless significant contrasts in the positions of each function; IT was moving towards greater strategic and symbolic importance, while Direct Sales had suffered a number of 'difficulties' in recent times, both with the action of the regulators and in terms of significant levels of redundancies since 1990. Thus the way in which this formalisation was attempted was significantly different in each organisation, and the complementary forms of control implemented in each also appeared to be specific to each. Consequently, the responses of the employees of Buzzbank and Lifelong to such initiatives proved to be equally heterogeneous, and were therefore assessed on their own merits, as discussed above.

Power Relations and the Individual

I must now, however, depart from the structure of the book to clarify my key arguments. Within the book, the empirical material has been divided up into three chapters according to empirical focus. Thus in Chapter 5, I focused on issues of culture management and identity in each organisation; professionalism and Project Management in the IT function was discussed in Chapter 6 and control and self-discipline in Direct Sales in Chapter 7. My intention in this section is to emphasise the connections that link these chapters, by paying particular attention to the central arguments that traverse these sections.

In regard to the argument as a whole, what I would emphasise is my understanding of the *complementary* operation of *regimes of power/knowledge* and of *discourse* in the *objectification* and *subjectification* of the modern individual, respectively. In particular, this perspective seems to me to offer the possibility of a *critical* social science which allows sympathy for the position of the individualised subject fundamentally implicated in the reproduction of unequal power relations, without eliminating notions of ethical responsibility for one's own conduct central to critique. As Townley explains, "For Foucault, power operates on individuals in two ways. It *objectivises* them through making them objects of knowledge - that is, they become known objectively and thereby able to be managed in a particular way - or they become *subjectified*. They are presented with an image of themselves, an identity, which then becomes the basis of their self-knowledge" (1998: 199, emphasis added). I should stress that this notion of the individual constituted as object and subject (Townley, 1994) is by no means self-evident throughout Foucault's work; it is a specific reading of certain themes developed in his later work. However, these modes of the operation of power are implicit in Foucault's reference to the "two meanings" of the word *subject*; that is, "*subject to someone else* by control and dependence, and *tied to his own identity* and conscience or self-knowledge" (Foucault, 1983: 212, emphasis added). Thus in the first case, power/knowledge may be read as operating through as the 'human sciences', such as orthodox psychology, economics, and sociology, to construct a concept of the unitary individual as an *object* with an identifiable and consistent nature. Related to this are the forms of control exercised over individuals based on knowledge obtained through the use of examinatory mechanisms in specific settings - in the hospital, prison, workplace, school, etc. In the second case, Foucault can be seen as admitting the importance of a reflexive mode of subjectivity, the "relation of self to self", in the reproduction of power relations. In this work, he thus highlights the application of mechanisms such as the *confession* to construct a 'truth' and inscribe this truth as 'self-knowledge' onto the subjectivity of the individual. In addition, I would emphasise that the objectification and subjectification of the individual must be seen as complementary and interdependent processes, rather than alternatives, and I will focus on this 'dual operation' of power in my discussion of the empirical material below.

I will therefore draw together a number of arguments central to the argument in this chapter by focusing on the twin themes of the *objectification* and *subjection* of the individual. I will then return to the empirical material, outlining how I understand this objectification and subjection to have been attempted in the fields of IT and of Direct Sales through what are superficially quite distinct techniques. Throughout, I will clarify the relationship between my analysis of the empirical material on Buzzbank and Lifelong and the theoretical debates which underpin the analysis of the empirical material throughout. I will also take care to delineate the fundamental interdependency between the construction of the individual as object and as subject. Finally, I will return to the ethical theme in the book, by drawing together and assessing the effects (and effectiveness) of attempts made by employees within Lifelong and Buzzbank to subvert and/or resist such techniques.

The Constitution of the Employee as Object

In tracing the objectification of the individual, Foucault stresses throughout his work that this should be interpreted as the operation of power through *specific* technologies and mechanisms, reflecting his focus on the question 'how is power exercised?' rather than 'what is power?'. His early work emphasises the importance of the notion of *power/knowledge*, undermining the purported objectivity of the human sciences by revealing their reliance on power to produce 'truth' as well as the power effects of such 'truths'. In keeping with this focus on the *operation* of power, Foucault emphasises the importance of new technologies and mechanisms for the emergence of these human sciences "all the sciences, analyses or practices employing the root 'psycho'" (1977: 193). Foucault therefore highlights the central role of the human sciences in effecting the individualisation and objectification of the human subject, by "substituting for the individuality of the memorable man that of the calculable man" (Foucault, 1977: 193). The diverse forms of normalisation and control exercised in the workplace can be seen to draw on these power/knowledge regimes so as to discipline the employee and ensure his/her productive conduct (Townley, 1993a). Thus psychology, sociology, economics and related human sciences have been drawn upon throughout this century in the construction of systems of management, applying models of the worker as object to support the development of techniques of selection, motivation, performance appraisal, and so on (Rose, 1990).

In retrospect, Foucault then describes a 'theoretical shift' in his work, as his focus moved away from studies of power operating through "the discursive practices that articulated the human sciences" (1985: 6). Instead, he describes a turn to the "objectivising of the subject" (1982: 208), through 'dividing practices' which rely on the operation of forms of power which serve to *discipline* the individual. In *Discipline and Punish* (1977), he conducts an analysis of 'power' in what he terms its "manifold relations, open strategies and the rational techniques that articulate the exercise of powers" (1985: 6), without losing sight of the relations with power/knowledge configurations. Although his empirical focus in *Discipline and Punish* is the prison system, his main focus is the practical instances of the *application* of these techniques of power, specifically as they have been articulated in the context of the prison. As he explains, strikingly similar forms of disciplinary technologies have been implemented in a range of locales, such that "prisons resemble factories, schools, barracks, hospitals, which all resemble prisons" (1977: 228). In particular, he sees enclosure of spaces, the partitioning of space into a grid and the ranking of bodies to fill positions within this network as characteristic of such disciplinary regimes. Foucault sets out two cardinal elements in such disciplinary technologies; firstly, the institution of a system of *hierarchical observation*, and secondly, the application of a mode of *normalising judgement* (Foucault, 1977). In particular, Foucault stresses the importance of *the examination*, wherein the individual is simultaneously subjected to both hierarchical observation and this normalising form of judgement. The implications of such a system are described by Foucault as "two correlative possibilities: firstly the constitution of the individual as a describable, analyzable object (...) and secondly, the constitution of a comparative system that made possible the measurement of overall phenomena, the description of groups..." (1977: 190). These elements of a disciplinary technology are reflected in a number of themes of Labour Process Theory, particularly regarding workplace surveillance and direct control, leading a number of commentators to suggest the compatibility of Marxist and Foucauldian analyses of the capitalist workplace. Despite the superficial similarities, I have indicated in Chapter 2 what I feel are insurmountable difficulties implicit in such a synthesis, arising from fundamental epistemological and philosophical differences.

Through my empirical work in the IT functions of each organisation, I have attempted to highlight the correspondence between this mode of *disciplinary power*, particularly as interpreted in the field of management theory, and the application of techniques associated with Project Management. The immediate objective of Project Management is defined as achieving tighter control through monitoring the conduct of the employees and assessing this conduct in line with certain norms. The key effect of Project Management is therefore to enhance the visibility and calculability of those employees engaged in project work, through a variety of mechanisms and techniques. Thus the work that the project involves is fragmented according to the Work Breakdown Structure and set out in a clearly visible format through the construction of a Gantt chart or Critical Path diagram. The immediate effect of these techniques is to break up a complex project into a form amenable to calculation and prediction, so that tasks may be apportioned to individual employees. The individualising effect of such technologies is critical here, through the division of work and through the routine surveillance of employees who are then held accountable for the completion of tasks to a quantifiable standard within a defined duration. Monitoring may be carried out directly, by the project manager him/herself, or through the use of IT applications which automatically request and log status reports and which then notify the project manager of any deviation from plan. A graphic example of this form of control in operation was provided by Doug in Lifelong, who, indicating his 'team' all around who were clearly working under some pressure, explained;

> "Last week we had a bit of slack, but the development environment went down so we used up all the leeway we had ... so now I've broken the WBS down to hours, and I'm going round checking every few hours to make sure they're up to speed ... checking hourly gives me tighter control, basically" (Doug 1: 5).

This 'control' is dependent on the prior structuring of work through Project Management, such that employees may be individualised and their conduct quantified and compared to a fixed norm. Although this comparative performance was not directly related to any explicit financial incentives, reports on the project worker's performance were taken into account in appraisals and/or informal disciplinary meetings when required. The implications were yet more direct in the case of contract staff, with regular renewals of their contracts dependent on performance.

In a different context, my empirical work on the management of the salesforce of Lifelong Assurance centred on similar themes although articulated in different ways. Here, the main forms of direct control were seen by staff and management as being based on an increasingly computerised form of bureaucratic surveillance, linked to a complex system of material and symbolic incentives. Traditionally, this had depended on an enormous bureaucratic operation, based on the completion of an array of documentary forms to inform Head Office of each individual Financial Consultant's performance in terms of activity and sales. The recent need to fulfil compliance requirements of financial services regulators legitimated and in part instigated the application of IT to reinforce this monitoring function in such institutions. The recent development of 'BASIS' in Lifelong was intended to fulfil and partially automate this function, by instituting a system of monitoring not dissimilar to the notion of the panopticon; thus Sales Support Administrators at each branch were to gather and input information on all relevant aspects of an individual's conduct. These could then be centralised within BASIS, which would present these in a quantitative, therefore calculable form. The emphasis on quantification is highly significant, as it not only enhances the visibility of the behaviour of the salesforce but moreover enables the direct comparison with the performance of others. This comparison is instrumental in the construction of 'norms', which in this case are derived from the prior performance of the individual, as well as the performance of others and arbitrary company standards. Unlike the situation with Project Management staff in IT, the normative element here is reinforced by the *formal* linking of performance relative to these norms to a complex system of material and/or symbolic bonuses and incentives.

Both forms of management closely resemble Foucault's description of discipline as dependent on *hierarchical surveillance* and *normalising judgement*, applying IT in both cases to routinise the process of *the examination* (Foucault, 1979). As Townley notes, "Constructing the individual as an object of knowledge ... involves the delineation of components of individuality identified through (examinatory) technologies, enabling the individual to be located on a matrix. Literally, the individual becomes an object of knowledge, and an object to be commanded" (1994: 107). This objectification of the individual is not therefore an abstract, classificatory operation; it is fundamental in the creation of the individual as an object which may be manipulated in the instrumental pursuit of certain goals. The genealogical studies of Foucault and of Foucauldian writers thus focus on the historical application of such techniques of objectification through the human sciences in constructing 'docile' yet 'productive' individuals in Western societies (Foucault, 1975, 1977; Rose, 1990; Townley, 1994). In doing so, such regimes of power/knowledge act to monopolise constructions of reality and thus marginalise and disqualify subjective, embodied and ethically-conscious accounts of lived experience in favour of functional models which open up the subject to instrumental forms of control. Both Project Management and the systems of surveillance centralised through BASIS rely on similar techniques to facilitate this mode of domination and manipulation in Buzzbank and Lifelong.

However, the forms of resistance discernible in each organisation served to highlight the limitations and flaws in such disciplinary forms of control. In general terms, the discontent expressed by those subject to these forms of control in Buzzbank and Lifelong tended to be based on their inaccuracy and 'impersonality'. Although the forms of resistance varied between and within each organisation, there did appear to be general continuities insofar as all types exploited the gaps and inadequacies of the systems of surveillance, occasionally in ways which might be seen as congruent with the objectives of each company. Thus the limitations in the bureaucratic forms of surveillance in Lifelong were exacerbated and made evident by the evasion, misrepresentation and other forms of resistance practised by the sales representatives on a day-to-day basis. The effectiveness of such tactics are evident in the account of Nicky, the Sales Support Administrator, who testified to the unreliability of the data entered into the system, due to the Financial Consultants' tendency to exaggerate the level of their activity, store up policies written to cover themselves in quiet periods, etc.[18] As a consequence, information held in BASIS on the activity of the Financial Consultants was generally considered suspect and frequently ignored by Sales Managers and Branch Managers in their dealings with staff, whose complicity served to reinforce the marginalisation of the system of monitoring. Although actions were being instigated at Head Office and within IT to 'tighten up' the system, I would suggest any efforts made in this direction might be subordinate to the reliance on other forms of institutionalised control in the branches, a point I will return to in the next section.

Equally, the everyday, widespread use of discretion in Buzzbank highlights the limitations of the forms of surveillance in operation through the technologies of Project Management. The importance of discretion within the strictures of Project Management was emphasised by a number of staff, generally through stressing that such models were overly bureaucratic and that compliance with all the requirements was therefore hugely inefficient. In addition, the fact that such systems of monitoring and control were only partially implemented by management and the use of discretion was informally encouraged in a very open way reflects the general recognition that such panoptic technologies were inadequate for the task of retaining direct control over tasks of such complexity and unpredictability. Indeed, the infrequency with which surveillance was mentioned by IT staff in both companies reflects the laxity of the implementation of such mechanisms. These insights in themselves are by no means novel; the inadequacies of such forms of control in Buzzbank and Lifelong reflect the limitations of such techniques in workplaces more generally, as has been reiterated to exhaustion in the post-Braverman industrial relations and Labour Process literature on direct control (e.g. Friedman, 1977; Edwards, 1979; see Thompson and McHugh, 1995, for an overview). However, from the specifically Foucauldian approach I have adopted, I would interpret this not as a failure, leading to the eventual rejection of such forms of control; instead, I would underline the connections between such disciplinary forms of control and the constitution of the employee as a subject and thus subject to reflexive and *self-disciplinary* modes of control.

---

[18] Not dissimilar to accounts of 'making out', the informal regulation of output on the shopfloor, in traditional industrial sociology and Labour Process work on assembly lines (e.g. Roy, 1969; Burawoy, 1979).

The Constitution of the Employee as Subject

In my earlier discussion of Foucauldian theory, in Chapter 3, I have noted that Foucault's analysis of the objectification of the individual, particularly as presented in *Discipline and Punish* (1977), risks marginalising the potential for resistance to such practices, and thus implying a deterministic notion of power. In turning to the notion of 'the subject' and the *subjection* of the individual in his later work, Foucault attempts to remedy this implication by focusing on the *active* role played by the individual in the reproduction of power relations through the construction of his/her own subjectivity; what he describes as "the way a human being turns him or herself into a subject" (1982: 208). The use of the technology of *the confessional*, deriving from the rituals of Catholicism and present in modern psychoanalytic techniques, is a specific mechanism described by Foucault by which the 'truth' of the individual is not merely 'discovered' but is *constructed* in a specific form. Fundamental to this power relationship through which truth is produced is the role of the confessor, "who requires the confession, prescribes and appreciates it, and intervenes in order to judge, punish, forgive, console, and reconcile; a ritual in which the truth is corroborated" (Foucault, 1978: 62). Thus Miller and Rose explain that "the authoritative norms, calculative technologies and forms of evaluation can be translated into the values, decisions and judgements of citizens in their professional and personal capacities ... (to) function as part of the 'self-steering' mechanisms of individuals" (1990: 19). In particular, what must be stressed here is the emphasis on a form of *reflexivity*, of the self-discipline of a continuous subjective assessment and reassessment of one's conduct and feelings to conform to the truth of one's 'self' as revealed through these mechanisms.

Objectification and Subjection in Practice

A Discursive Analysis of Culture Management

My discussion of culture management in Chapter 5, while introducing notions of identity in organisations, serves in many ways to frame the core arguments in the rest of the book, by outlining the role of culture management in supporting a reflexive and self-disciplinary form of control within each organisation. I have used the notion of *discourse* here to examine the construction of *culture* in organisations and the relatively recent emergence of a discourse of 'culture management' in Western work organisations. More broadly, I have supplemented this analysis with work in the field of critical psychology and its use of structuralism, which focuses on the relational construction of identity based on notions of *difference*. I have approached this notion of constructed differences as embodied in discourses which may be internalised by the individual to secure a robust subjective notion of his/her own identity. These discourses can therefore be seen operating on a day-to-day basis, drawing on the objectified notion of the individual but relying on the *active* internalisation of such constructions by their subjects. To set this in context, I have discussed the key elements in the debate over organisational culture, particularly insofar as they has been interpreted in the literature by critical theorists. While recognising the dangers of an uncritical acceptance of the claims of culture management gurus, I would maintain that the ubiquity and the 'taken-for-granted' nature of notions of organisational culture reflects the importance of the concept to an understanding of forms of control in the contemporary workplace. In particular, I have interpreted 'culture management' as a technique which, despite the unsophisticated and transparent manner in which it is frequently applied, draws on significant themes in the construction of an identity and reflexive attention to 'self' within the workplace. In doing so, culture management initiatives may be read as attempts to control this process in a systematic and strategic manner in order to manipulate meaning and identity in organisations, and instigate a reflexive form of identity management amongst employees in line with organisational objectives.

The key aspect of 'culture management' initiatives therefore lies in the way they seek to advance a reflexive form of self-monitoring among employees. This reflexivity was typified within Buzzbank by the company signs displayed prominently on monitors and walls throughout the site which asked simply "*Why are you doing this!!??*". More generally, management in Buzzbank particularly attempt to disseminate a set of 'core values' through induction and training, and to reinforce these through day-to-day interactions with employees, internal bulletins, PR communications in the media, etc. Senior management's depiction of a coherent and universal 'Buzzbank culture' was not, however, reflected in the accounts of most non-managerial employees. In general, it appeared that the articulation of such values was infrequent, being invoked opportunistically in support of particular courses of action; thus Lee, for instance, defended his decision to prioritise his own e-mail project over certain others by making a sudden and uncharacteristic reference to culture, stating "one of (Buzzbank)'s key values is communication, without that we're up the Swannee, basically" (Lee 1: 222). This selectivity reflects the reliance of 'culture' on the situationally-contingent construction of oppositions to derive meaning and identity through differentiating not only Buzzbank but also specific departments within Buzzbank from 'what they are not'. Thus the notion of a culture specific to Buzzbank was riven with further subdivisions and internal oppositions, such as those between permanent staff and contractors, for example, or between project workers and fire-fighters. In Lifelong, despite the lack of explicit attention to constructing a unitary 'Lifelong culture', such oppositions were also widely evident, between IT and 'the Business', for example, or between the Salesforce and Head Office bureaucracy. The construction of such oppositions is not a neutral process; all of these oppositions are related to issues of status and identity, and involve the construction of a hierarchy which promotes one side of the opposition at the expense of 'the Other'. This hierarchical difference allows the subject to maintain a symbolic distance between themselves and those constructed as 'other', which facilitates their disregard of feelings of empathy when dealing with, or 'managing their relationship' with, these 'others', as in Dan's description of the 'lowlifes' in the Customer Services department. The importance of this is evident where the subject's own action (or inaction) is either instrumental in, or dependent upon, the domination and exploitation of those they deal with as individuals on a day-to-day basis.

To highlight *strategic* attempts to manage the construction of meaning, I have made a very broad distinction between those discourses which are promoted as part of an 'organisational ideology' (Kunda, 1992) and those emergent discourses which are 'embedded' within the subjectivities of the employees (and frequently the management as employees). Culture management can therefore be seen as setting up certain 'reference points' (Garsten, 1994) for the construction of identity; by encouraging the perception of TN Banking as staid and bureaucratic, for example. Discourses embedded within the subjectivies of Buzzbank staff include the valuation of innovation, creativity and autonomy, which were repeated drawn on in conversation. I have carefully tried to avoid a simplistic representation of both of these concept in terms of control and resistance, however, not least by stressing the constant dynamic interaction between the promotion of organisation ideology and embedded discourses. As a key example, I described in some detail the attempts made to institute bureaucratic control of IT staff in Buzzbank, to "bring a level of discipline" (Angus 1: 130). Significant problems were encountered regarding the centrality of notions of innovation and autonomy to the employees' sense of a worthwhile identity. Senior management response was to rearticulate the values of innovation and creativity as *dependent* on such formalisation initiatives; thus it was claimed that management were "not actually slowing down the ability of certain areas to change, (but) actually enabling change to take place, fast but in a controlled manner" (Jack 2: 228). This transformation of embedded discourses which were not consistent with the formalisation project was repeatedly described by management as an 'education', a term which reflects Buzzbank management's recognition of the link between culture and identity, and the intended manipulation of employees through a reconstruction of their subjectivity in ways conducive to control techniques.

Implicit within this process of transformation is the potential for employees in turn to transform discourses through their rearticulation, albeit more restricted than the ability of senior management. Taking the example of the notices demanding "WHY ARE YOU DOING THIS!!??", although clearly meant to reinforce the reflexive operation of culture by encouraging employees to evaluate their actions against company values and objectives, a more radical reading on the part of an employee might encourage a deeper reflexive questioning of their role and conduct in Buzzbank. Management's depiction of the organisational ideology as effectively internalised was challenged by the employees' widespread use of deflationary humour, and on occasion open dissent, particularly regarding the bureaucracy perceived in the formalisation initiatives. The effect of both forms of conduct may be read as not only distancing the employee from such values but also as generating a form of social support for further articulations of dissent and even actively resistant conduct.

Project Management: The Professionalisation of IT

Culture management was not the only technique by which control was attempted through the manipulation of subjectivity in each organisation. In interviews and discussions in the IT function in both companies, it became apparent to me that the notions of *Project Management* and *Professionalism* were fundamental to the systems of control and the notions of a valued identity asserted by the IT staff. Above, I have stressed the disciplinary effects of Project Management. More broadly, I have also examined Project Management in two related senses; firstly in the *abstract* construction of Project Management as an academic and vocational discipline, and more directly in the specific articulation of Project Management in day-to-day practices in Lifelong and Buzzbank. In the first sense, I have outlined the ongoing attempts to construct Project Management as a profession are based on the construction of an nationally and internationally accepted terminology and 'Body of Knowledge' upon which can be founded accreditation procedures for the membership of professional bodies. This 'Body of Knowledge' and the dedicated terminology which accompanies it is instrumental in the construction of a specific mode of subjectivity among employees; what is described within

Lifelong as "changing their mindsets", a point I will return to below. Although Project Management tends to be concentrated in the construction and engineering sectors, it has been adopted in a specific form in the field of Information Technology. The promotion of Project Management in this area has relied on the activities of a network of public and private institutions, from academia and governmental bodies to consultancies and professional organisations.

In the specific articulation of Project Management in Buzzbank and Lifelong, I have interpreted the implementation of Project Management methodologies and systems as instrumental to the growth in importance of the IT function; indeed, its introduction can be seen as a central element in the widespread attempts of the IT function to professionalise and hence achieve a higher status and greater strategic influence in the organisations examined. The hierarchical privileging of Project Management in the field of IT is evident in the accounts of Buzzbank employees, such as the assertion of Buzzbank's Head of IT Applications that "we're luckier than most in that we don't have operational responsibilities in here at all, it's all project work" (Angus 2: 282). However, alongside the benefits in terms of status and rewards, the attainment of (or at least the aspiration to) professionalism entails a number of key changes in terms of the form of control exercised over and through such employees. Related to this is the double-edged nature of the professionalisation of Project Management, entailing the increase in material and symbolic rewards tied to the intensification of both the monitoring of staff and their self-disciplinary control.

Beyond the Project Management's technologies of surveillance and direct control, as discussed above, a critical element of its articulation in Lifelong and Buzzbank is the responsibility for self-discipline implied by the promotion of a 'professional' ethos among IT staff. In a brief review of studies of professionalism and professionalisation, I have drawn on a wide range of literature from the trait and functionalist schools reference to 'professional spirit', through the critical work of Marxist writers' focus on the operation of power through the professions. In the light of this work, I have attempted in particular to integrate two key elements of the debate with my broader Foucauldian perspective; the importance of 'professional conduct' highlighted by the symbolic interactionists, and the social construction of professional knowledge, not dissimilar to Foucault's notion of power/knowledge and the production of 'truth'. This understanding of professionalism highlights the productive operation of power through the importance of professionalisation to the identity projects of the employees concerned. As a consequence, 'professional' Project Management staff in each organisation displayed a concern to act in keeping with constructed professional norms, in terms of both knowledge and conduct. Thus IT routinely engaged in competition to display a knowledge of the terminology and the ontology of Project Management to secure their conception of themselves as competent, 'professional' IT staff. Indeed, such behaviour reproduced a monopoly over the representation of organisational reality as structured by Project Management models; constructions of events not in keeping with such models, including my own, were delegitimised as 'unprofessional' and hence marginalised. Again, the double-edged nature of professionalism is evident here; the reflexive construction of an identity which conformed to the ideal of the 'professional project manager' served as an effective form of self-discipline, while providing a (relatively) secure subjectivity for such employees. Thus, as Fournier notes, "Professionals are both the instrument and the subject of government, the governor and the governed" (Fournier, 1997: 5).

Evidence of resistance to this self-disciplinary mode of control among the Buzzbank Project Management staff was complex and often ambiguous. In interviews and particularly through my observations in the division, humour was frequently used to dismiss the importance of 'professionalism' and distance the speaker from the values and norms implied by the notion. The communication of this humour may well have supported the development of a discourse based on the rejection of professionalism, by legitimating action not in keeping with the 'professional ethos', including short-cuts and a disregard for elements of Project Management deemed to be over-bureaucratic and in conflict with the autonomy of Buzzbank IT staff. At the same time, this use of humour also reflected the insecurity of employees in their attempts to live up to the demands of professionalism, as may be seen in the recurrence of the notion of the 'cowboy'. Thus the reluctance to accept the description of 'professional', as in Kevin's ironic "Well what do you expect from consummate professionals such as ourselves?", may be more indicative of a defensive reluctance to claim the status of 'professionalism' rather than a refusal of its values. However, I will return to the complex notion of resistance after discussing my analysis of subjection in the Sales Division in Lifelong.

Subjectivity and Control in Sales

In the field of life assurance sales, professionalism itself did not appear to be a critical issue, although some managers predicted that trends towards professionalisation in the US would soon have an impact in the UK. Nonetheless, interviews with both management and sales representatives highlighted the ongoing importance of similar issues to those in IT; in particular, the management of staff within the Sales division through the encouragement of a reflexive attention to identity and self-disciplinary forms of control. Importantly, such forms of control should be seen as complementary to and dependent upon, rather than superseding, the attempts to establish a panoptical system of monitoring, through BASIS, linked to material and symbolic rewards. Thus the salesperson's individualisation as the object of mechanisms of hierarchical surveillance and normalising judgement, as well as his/her isolation through engineered interpersonal competition for scarce rewards, served to increase his/her vulnerability to such forms of subjection. In addition, I would argue that the very types of resistance to surveillance and bureaucratic monitoring practised by the salesforce in Lifelong were instrumental in enabling and supporting the inculcation of a self-disciplinary mode of control within these employees. Not only did the attempts to undermine surveillance lead to efforts of management to establish supplementary mechanisms of control, but the salesforce's demand for a 'personalised' system of management to replace such objectification provided the means for control through the *subjection* of the sales staff.

Crucially, this mode of subjection drew on the historically-specific discursive construction of masculinity characteristic of the field of sales. The forms of subjectivity created and reproduced by practices in Lifelong were linked to the construction of a masculine and heroic identity to represent 'the salesman'. Through recruitment and selection policies, training and induction and the day-to-day management of staff, a certain understanding of 'the competent salesman' was constructed and reproduced as a valued form of identity for sales representatives within Lifelong. This discursive resource embodied a specific understanding of masculinity as predicated on assertiveness, self-reliance, productivity, and self-motivation, driven by what was repeatedly referred to as 'the desire' or 'the hunger inside'. There were signs that this construction of masculinity was dependent on the discursive construction of hierarchical difference vis-à-vis the 'non-productive' and 'secondary' functions of bureaucracy and administration in the organisations. This masculine subjectivity was also coupled to the discourse of 'the breadwinner' which held particular significance to the salesforce; the image of the wage-earning patriarch with the responsibility to 'bring home the bacon', vividly depicted in Brian's assertion; "I am a bringer-home of income, I am! I am a Susan's husband, Jamie, Gareth and Nicolas's father, and they *need* me to earn money!" (Brian: 455). The salesperson's need for the affirmation of their identity was therefore dependent on their conduct as a 'salesman', and this was seen to be directly represented by their sales performance as defined by BASIS.

As seen above, however, the salesforce and branch management tended to put very little faith in the information gathered and presented by BASIS, in part due to the evasive tactics of the sales representatives themselves in collusion with the Sales Managers and some Branch Managers. It is here that the role of the Sales Manager becomes critical. Through personal contact and direct monitoring, involving the breaking down of the boundary between 'work' and 'home', the Sales Manager acts to overcome the inadequacies of other systems of surveillance; thus one Sales Manager explains;

"when you go to their houses, you can *see* why they don't need a lot of money or why they might not be motivated in some things" (Dave: 600-1).

Moreover, by drawing on information held in BASIS on the performance of the individual sales representative in the context of this supplementary knowledge, the Sales Manager can 'personalise the system' and thus may validate such judgements in the understandings of the salesforce themselves. The 'one-to-one' in Lifelong is a particularly significant site for the construction and fixing of an identity for the subjects structured by the norms of the organisation as specified in BASIS. To analyse this process, I have used Foucault's understanding of *the confession* as a mechanism whereby the truth of an individual is not 'extracted' but is *produced* and embedded in the subjectivity of the confessor as 'self-knowledge' (Townley, 1995). The 'urge to confess' is reinforced here by the individualisation and isolation of the individual Financial Consultant, which leaves the Sales Manager as principal source of support and reassurance, particularly in the salesperson's attempts to maintain a sense of a stable and worthwhile identity. Thus, in the one-to-one, the Financial Consultant is called to 'confess' their weaknesses, difficulties, and self-doubts to account for the 'data' on their performance as revealed by BASIS. The Sales Manager, however, is the final arbiter of truth in this process, and judges the confession of the subject "to constitute a discourse of truth on the basis of its decipherment" (Foucault, 1981: 67). This 'truth' is partly structured by the bureaucratic requirements imposed by BASIS in terms of forms to be filled, but, as noted above, this structure is frequently marginalised by the joint efforts of Sales Manager and Financial Consultant, such that information regarding compliance, admin and activity is devalued in favour of a focus on directly sales- and commission-related information. The most importance effect of this process, however, is the *internalisation* of these norms, as the salesperson comes to understand his/her identity in terms of this 'truth' and therefore as dependent on the achievement of the targets as 'agreed'. Where successful, this 'truth' serves as a form of self-discipline, where the Financial Consultant can be relied upon to reflexively monitor his/her own behaviour in line with these norms and this construction of subjectivity. The irony here is that this self-disciplinary form of control is frequently understood and presented by Financial Consultants as proof of their masculine autonomy, 'drive' and freedom from manipulation; thus Brian proudly asserts;

> "If the computer's turned off now, or the BASIS system crashes, it's not going to stop me working until somebody tells me to stop working, 'cos I've got... there's four reasons why I go out to work, that's my wife and my three kids, not what BASIS tells me to do." (Brian: 250-3)

In contrast to Buzzbank, I had difficulty in identifying any explicit behaviour in my research in Lifelong which might be construed as resistance to this process, although this may be partly due to the restricted access I gained to the organisation, which did not stretch to the observation of routine practices. However, the operation of an individual form of resistance is at least implicit in the remarks of Sales Managers on the problems they encounter in their position; in particular, Dave's reference to a Financial Consultant who was "happy earning twenty-odd thousand and... that's very difficult to turn around, especially when he's not doing a bad job" (Dave: 436-9). Without resorting to what Knights and Morgan (1991) term "physical distancing" (i.e. leaving the job), it seemed clear that the conscious decision on the part of representatives to 'satisfice', to restrict their effort to the achievement of minimum sales and little else, entailed the rejection of both 'money and pride'. Nonetheless, in a general sense the isolated position of the sales staff and the masculinist discourse of 'the breadwinner' appeared to have enabled the operation of a particularly insidious form of manipulation whose strength lay in the production of identity through the use of technologies of subjection.

Ethics and Resistance

Overall, then, what I have attempted to outline above is the operation of complementary yet distinct modes of power in the control of employees in IT and Sales in Financial Services. I have firstly analysed the *objectification* of employees in these areas through the application of a number of fields of power/knowledge, based in the human sciences and operationalised through their embodiment in the practices and techniques of Human Resource Management, personnel, accounting, etc. In particular, I have focused on the operation of disciplinary power through mechanisms of hierarchical surveillance and normalising judgement, in the construction of the employee as an object to be understood and instrumentally manipulated. However, through my empirical work I have highlighted the potential for a number of resistant practices to frustrate and undermine the operation of disciplinary power, ranging from widespread forms of evasion and misrepresentation to the deliberate use of discretion and deviant conduct. The difficulty in defining all of these actions as 'resistance' serves to underline the problems inherent in the term; frequently such practices were applied to further the pursuit of organisational objectives, with the collusion of middle and occasionally senior management. In addition, the ethical complexities of resistance also bear out Foucault's assertion that there is "no single locus of great Refusal, no soul of revolt, source of all rebellions or pure law of the revolutionary" (1979: 95); the evasion and misrepresentation practised by life assurance salespersons, for instance, was historically linked to the exploitation of the ignorance of consumers for personal (and organisational) profit. While I would maintain that such conduct was frequently effective in disabling disciplinary mechanisms, the ethically-dubious nature of many practices serves to reinforce Sawicki's caution regarding the importance of "social and historical investigation" of forms of resistance rather than "a priori theoretical pronouncement" (1991: 26).

The mechanisms for the *subjection* of the individual, however, operate in many ways to overcome the limitations of surveillance and disciplinary power by working *on* and *through* the subjectivity of individuals, their reflexively-maintained conception of self. This subjection of employees, crucially, relies on their vulnerability to such forms of control as a consequence of their individualisation and isolation through mechanisms of surveillance and judgement. I have examined the confessional as a mechanism which is representative (but not exhaustive) of technologies of subjection, whereby the 'truth' of an individual is produced and inscribed upon his/her notion of self. As Townley notes, the idea that a 'truth' of the individual does exist is precisely that which enables the manipulation of an individual and the self-disciplinary control; "it is a mechanistic and functional view of the self, an object to be worked on and changed. Rational mastery proffer's the possibility of instrumental control" (1995: 279). What should therefore be stressed here is the role of the 'confessor' as final arbiter of 'truth', and the intention that such 'truth', internalised as 'self-knowledge', should operate continuously through the efforts of the individual to maintain a secure and valued sense of identity. Thus Townley notes the dominatory and manipulative effect of such technologies, as "the individual becomes tied, through the desire to secure the acknowledgement, recognition and confirmation of self, to practices confirmed by others as desirable" (1994: 142).

I have analysed the construction of the subject by focusing on three general instances in Buzzbank and Lifelong; culture management, professionalism in IT through Project Management, and the confessional function of the one-to-one in Sales. In each, my interest has been in the inculcation of a reflexive attention to the construction and defence of certain forms of subjectivity, leading to a self-disciplinary form of control, and in particular, the means by which this has on occasion been resisted or subverted. The subjective operation of power indicates the importance of resistance through a politicisation of the personal and the everyday, a 'politics of the self' implicit in Foucault's *The Care of the Self* (1986); thus practices of resistance must be grounded in the everyday conduct of the individual in their dealings with others. I have paid particular attention to the frequent use of humour to lampoon and to symbolically distance the speaker from aspects of professionalism or certain company values. In contrast to the solitary and introspective impression often presented of such forms of resistance, I would underline the potential for such humour to encourage the interpersonal, collective construction of a discourse which validates and supports the rejection of imposed values or ideals. However, I would also suggest that the use of humour is often deeply ambiguous, and its defensive and insecure nature frequently reflects the employee's simultaneous *attraction* to such discourses which appear to offer, albeit fleetingly, the security of an organisationally-affirmed sense of 'self'. I would also draw attention to the possibility of deleterious effect of such distancing techniques on the employees themselves, in terms of insecurity and alienation. This is not to deny the potential effectiveness of humour as a form of resistance to subjection, only to inject a note of caution; just as subjection has its beneficial, productive aspects, so resistance to subjection carries its own price.

Conclusions

As with any academic piece of work, there are concerns, problems and anxieties imperfectly buried throughout this book. To set the final comments in perspective, I feel bound to disinter some of these issues so as to undermine any lingering impressions of objectivity, neutrality and 'scientific' precision in this text.

In particular, it is important to note the sometimes uncomfortable personal changes which have accompanied these four years of work. The experience of conducting empirical work has entailed often awkward and disconcerting recognitions of the preconceptions and prejudices with which I entered each organisation and in the light of which I have analysed much of the material. In terms of research technique, I can identify a number of difficulties which I encountered in both my approach and manner in both organisations. To give one example, my concern over securing continuing access within the companies, linked to a fear of offending the subjects of interviews, meant that I have at times avoided questions which explicitly focused on contentious issues, including, significantly, the theme of resistance. At the same time, this fear of appearing as an *agent provocateur* may have increased the risk of my perception by employees as the agent of management, and again led to a reticence over the more delicate themes central to the research. Although the experience of conducting empirical research may have led to improvements in my technique, the general concerns remain in reassessing and analysing the material. With this recognition, I do not mean to imply that these have been eliminated and in the final draft of the book you find an objective and 'professional' piece of research, only that the gradual recognition of such limitations has influenced my interpretation and analysis of the empirical material.

Possibly the most central objection which may be levelled at the conclusions I have drawn regards the extent to which I have developed an identifiable ethical and political position through my engagement with the individuals and changes in Buzzbank and Lifelong. In view of my citation of Parker's statement, "I do not claim access to a transcendental Truth to speak for others, only to state my own truth because I wish to condemn" (1996: 576), I feel I could be accused of a Foucauldian 'crypto-normativism', of failing to articulate the condemnations I suggest in my analysis. In my defence, I would like to make clear that my direct engagement over a period of months with employees in both companies has led me to anger, despondency and a level of sympathy in equal measure. Nonetheless, my understanding and sympathies inevitably lie more with certain individuals as I encountered them in specific contexts and attempted to understand them within the confines of the unfamiliar and artificial 'researcher-subject' relation. This tension is evident in the style in which I have written this book; despite my best efforts, there are no doubt times where the reflexive and embodied stance I have tried to adopt will give way to the security of a depersonalised and objective academic account. In the light of my ethical position, however, I have tried to walk a very thin line, to assess modes of conduct in terms of their ethical worth and emancipatory potential without adopting the position of 'armchair moralist', and without losing sympathy where appropriate for those 'subjects' caught up in reproducing systems of power relations at the expense of themselves and their colleagues.

Given the shortcomings, limitations and missed opportunities I have identified in the book and detailed above, it would be worthwhile now to conclude by establishing those areas in which I feel the book *may* make a contribution. Returning to the very first chapter, I would present my contribution as falling in two areas; work towards the development of an ethically and politically grounded critical theory, and relatedly, insights into specific forms of power relations and forms of resistance within certain areas of the Financial Services industry. In my discussion of Foucauldian theory, therefore, I have tried to integrate work in the related fields of critical social psychology and socio-linguistics to bolster the approach and specify a way to utilise the theory through empirical research. Through this research, I have attempted to derive a form of research which, without falling back on epistemological or moral essentialism, enables a politically engaged mode of critical social research. I have therefore underlined a particular reading of the notion of *ethics* as a basis for critique which does not impose a universal moral code and allows for the contingent interpretation of forms of conduct in the light of the specific situation.

In line with this emphasis on specific instances of power relations, I have focused on a number of areas within the general field of Financial Services and attempted to apply a specific and contextualised critique. Thus I have examined culture management in this light, underlining the forms of resistance to managerial efforts to strategically manipulate meaning and values in each organisation. I have examined in some detail the field of Project Management within IT, one which to my knowledge has not been subject to any sustained form of critical analysis, to draw out the both the disciplinary forms of power and the reflexive operation of self-discipline through the discourse of professionalism. Finally, I have examined the predominant forms of control in the field of Sales, again focusing on forms of disciplinary power allied to a subjectifying mode of control drawing on constructions of masculinity. Across these areas, I have tried to outline the operation of power through the interdependent mechanisms serving to construct the employee as both the object and the subject of power. My hope is that the form of analysis I have employed helps not only to interpret and assess forms of power and of resistance on a *contingent* basis, but that in stressing this contingency, it aids in the development of "the ethics, the *ethos*, the practice of self which would allow these games of power to be played with a minimum of domination" (Foucault, 1988: 18).

Appendix

This appendix explains the system by which the empirical material in the book is referenced. This empirical material includes interview transcripts and notes, notes taken during observation, official documentation from each organisation and relevant articles in the media. The sources include those employees formally interviewed in each organisation, as well as those with whom I spent significant periods of time while engaged in non-participant observation. It is important to note here that the distinction between formal interview material and observation notes is largely arbitrary. Thus observation periods provided the opportunity to interview staff 'informally' that I would not otherwise have been able to contact, and equally, the observations made by myself in the course of conducting interviews were often as useful as the interview content itself.

To preserve the anonymity of the interviewees, I have given each a pseudonym when drawing on the empirical material. For material taken from interviews, the interview is indicated by the pseudonym of the subject, followed by a number if the subject was interviewed on more than one occasion e.g. (Ian), (Doug2). If the material is a direct quote from a recorded interview, this is followed by the line number or line numbers of the quote e.g. (Simon2: 325), (Sue1: 618-624). Where the interviewee did not consent to the interview being recorded, it is followed by the page number of the notes taken during the interview e.g. (Doug1: 2). Material taken from a period of observation is referenced by the pseudonym of the interlocutor followed by OBS1, indicating it is drawn from the first period and OBS2 for the second period e.g. (Martin: OBS1), (Dan: OBS2). Again, where this is a direct quote the page number of the notes is added to this e.g. (Martin: OBS1: 3).

Additional material is drawn from an analysis of official documentation provided by each company. Within Buzzbank, this mainly encompasses the Buzzbank Information Sheets, a set of notes distributed to new members of staff and also used on occasion for PR purposes. As each sheet covers a different area, such as "People", "IT", and so on, these are referenced as BBIS followed by the sheet number and where necessary the page number e.g. (BBIS1: 1). Although there was no equivalent in Lifelong, sources

271

used include the Annual Reports followed by the year and page number e.g. (LLAR86: 2). Other documentary sources include the media, which is noted as the name or initials of the newspaper/magazine followed by the date e.g. FT: 12/8/96. Any other sources used are explained in the text.

Bibliography

Abbott, A. (1988) *The System of Professions: An Essay on the Division of Expert Labour* London: University of Chicago Press

Abercrombie, N. and Urry, J. (1983) *Capital, Labour and the Middle Classes* London: Allen and Unwin

Althusser, L. (1971) 'Ideology and Ideological Apparatuses (Notes towards an Investigation)', reprinted in *Subjectivity and Social Relations* (1985) Beechey, V. and Donald, J. (eds.) Milton Keynes: Open University Press

Alvesson, M. (1987) *Organization Theory and Technocratic Consciousness: Rationality, Ideology and Quality of Work* Berlin: De Gruyter

Anderson, R.J. Hughes, J.A. and Sharrock, W.W. (1986) *Philosophy and the Human Sciences* London: Croom Helm

Anthony, P. (1994) *Managing Culture* Milton Keynes: Open University Press

Armstrong, P. (1989) 'Management, Labour Process and Agency' in *Work, Employment and Society* Vol. 3 (3) pp. 307-322

Bahktin, M. (1986) *Speech Genres and Other Late Essays* (eds.) Emerson, C. and Holquist, M. Austin: University of Texas Press

Baran, P.M. and Sweezy, P.A. (1968) *Monopoly Capital* Harmondsworth: Penguin

Barber, B. (1963) 'Some Problems in the Sociology of the Professions' in *Daedalus* (Fall)

Bauman, Z. (1993) *Postmodern Ethics* Oxford: Blackwell

Bauman, Z. (1996) 'From Pilgrim to Tourist - or a Short History of Identity' in *Questions of Cultural Identity* Hall, S. and DuGay, P. (eds.) London: Sage

Beaumont, P.B. (1992) 'The US Human Resource Management Literature: A Review' in *Human Resource Strategies* Salaman, G. *et al* (eds.) London: Sage

Becker, H. and Geer, B. (1960) *Latent Culture* in *Administrative Science Quarterly* Vol. 5 pp. 304-13

Becker, H.S. (1970) 'The Nature of a Profession' in *Sociological Work: Method and Substance* Harmondsworth: Allen Lane

Becker, H.S. and Carper, J. (1970a) 'The Development of Identification with an Occupation' in *Sociological Work: Method and Substance* Harmondsworth: Allen Lane

Becker, H.S. and Carper, J. (1970b) 'The Elements of Identification with an Occupation' in *Sociological Work: Method and Substance* Harmondsworth: Allen Lane

Beecham, B.J. (1994) *The Monetary and Financial System* London: Pitman

274 *Discourse, Discipline and the Subject*

Beechey, V. and Donald, J. (1985) (eds.), *Subjectivity and Social Relations*, Milton Keynes: Open University Press

Beer, M. Spector, B. Lawrence, P. Mills, Q. and Walton, R. (1984) *Managing Human Assets* New York: Free Press

Bennatan, E.M. (1992) *Software Project Management: A Practitioner's Approach* London: McGraw-Hill

Benson, J.K. (1973) 'The Analysis of Bureaucratic-Professional Conflict: Functional versus Dialectical Approaches' in *The Sociological Quarterly* Vol. 14 pp. 376-394

Berger, P.L. and Luckmann, T. (1966) *The Social Construction of Reality* Harmondsworth: Penguin

Bernauer, J.W. and Rasmussen, D. (eds.) (1994) *The Final Foucault* Cambridge, MA: MIT Press

Beynon, H. (1975) *Working for Ford* Wakefield: E.P. Publishing

Blau, P.M. (1970) 'A Formal Theory of Differentiation in Organizations' in *American Sociological Review* Vol. 35 pp. 201-218

Blyton, P. and Turnbull, P. (1992) (eds.) *Reassessing Human Resource Management* London: Sage

Braverman, H. (1974) *Labor and Monopoly Capital* New York: Monthly Review

Brewis, J. (1996) 'The Making of the Competent Manager: Competence Development, Personal; Effectiveness and Foucault' in *Management Learning* Vol. 27 (1) pp. 65-86

Brubaker, R. (1984) *The Limits of Rationality: An Essay on the Social and Moral Thought of Max Weber* London: Allen and Unwin

Burawoy, M. (1979) *Manufacturing Consent* London: University of Chicago Press

Burawoy, M.(1985) *The Politics of Production* London: Verso

Burchell, G. Gordon, C. and Miller, P. (eds.) (1991) *The Foucault Effect: Studies in Governmentality* London: Harvester Wheatsheaf

Burns, T. and Stalker, G.M. (1961) *The Management of Innovation* London: Tavistock

Burrell, G. (1988) 'Modernism, Post Modernism and Organizational Analysis 2: The Contribution of Michel Foucault' in *Organisation Studies* Vol. 9 (2) pp. 221-235

Burrell, G. and Morgan, G. (1979) *Sociological Paradigms and Organizational Analysis* London: Heinemann

Butler, J. (1993) *Bodies That Matter* London: Routledge

Callinicos, D. (1990) *Against Postmodernism: A Marxist Critique* Cambridge: Polity Press

Casey, C. (1995) *Work, Self and Society: After Industrialism* London: Routledge

Cash, J.I., McFarlan, F.W. and McKenney, J.L. (1992) *Corporate Information Systems Management: The Issues Facing Senior Executives* Homewood: Irwin

Child, J. (1972) 'Organization Structure, Environment and Performance: The Role of Strategic Choice' in *Sociology* Vol. 6 (1) pp. 1-22

Child, J. (1985) 'Managerial Strategies, New Technology and the Labour Process' in *Job Redesign: Critical Perspectives on the Labour Process* Knights, D. *et al* (eds.) London: Gower

Clark, J. (1993) (ed.) *Human Resource Management and Technical Change* London: Sage

Clegg, S.R. (1988) 'Radical Revisions: Power, Discipline and Organisations' in *Organization Studies* 10 (1) pp. 97-115

Clegg, S.R. (1994) 'Weber and Foucault: Social Theory for the Study of Organizations' in *Organization* Vol. 1 (1) pp. 149-178

Clegg, S.R. (1998) 'Foucault, Power and Organizations' in *Foucault, Management and Organization Theory* McKinlay, A. and Starkey, K. (eds.) London: Sage

Cleland, D.I. and King, W.R. (1968) *Systems Analysis and Project Management* New York: McGraw-Hill

Cleland, D.I. and King, W.R. (1975) *Systems Analysis and Project Management (Second Edition)* New York: McGraw-Hill

Cleland, D.I. and King, W.R. (1988) *Project Management Handbook* New York: Van Nostrand Reinhold

Clifford, J. and Marcus, G.E. (1986) *Writing Culture: The Poetics and Politics of Ethnography* Berkeley: University of California Press

Clough, P.T. (1992) *The End(s) of Ethnography: From Realism to Social Criticism* London: Sage

Collins, R. (1986) *Max Weber: A Skeleton Key* London: Sage

Collinson, D. (1988) *Engineering Humour: Masculinity, Conflict and Joking in Shop-floor Relations* in *Organization Studies* Vol. 9 (2) pp. 181-99

Collinson, D. and Knights, D. (1986) *"Men Only": Theories and Practices of Job Segregation in Insurance.* in *Gender and the Labour Process* Knights, D. & Willmott, H. (eds.) Aldershot: Gower

Collinson, D., Knights, D. and Collinson, M. (1990) *Managing to Discriminate* London: Routledge

Cooper, R. and Burrell, G. (1988) 'Modernism, Post-Modernism and Organisational Analysis: An Introduction' in *Organization Studies* Vol. 9 (1) pp. 91-112

Cotterell, M. and Hughes, B. (1995) *Software Project Management* London: International Thompson

Cousins, M. and Hussein, A. (1984) *Michel Foucault* London: Macmillan

Cressey, P and MacInnes, J. (1980) 'Voting for Ford: Industrial Democracy and the Control of Labour' in *Capital and Class* 11 pp. 5-33

Crosby, P. (1984) *Quality Without Tears: The Art of Hassle-Free Management* New York: McGraw-Hill

Davis, S.M. and Lawrence, P.R. (1977) *Matrix* London: Addison-Wesley

Day, D.W.J. (1994) *Project Management and Control* Basingstoke: Macmillan

Deal, T. and Kennedy, A. (1988) *Corporate Cultures* Harmondsworth: Penguin

Dean, M. (1994) *Critical and Effective Histories: Foucault's Methods and Historical Sociology* London: Routledge

Deetz, S. (1992) 'Disciplinary Power in the Modern Corporation' in *Critical Management Studies* Alvesson, M. and Willmott, H. (eds.) London: Sage

Derrida, J. (1981) *Positions* Chicago: University of Chicago Press

Dews, P. (1987) *Logics of Disintegration: Post-Structuralist Thought and the Claims of Critical Theory* London: Verso

Dews, P. (1989) 'The Return of the Subject in Late Foucault' in *Radical Philosophy* Vol. 51 pp. 37-41

Douglas, M. (1975) *Implicit Meanings* London: Routledge and Kegan Paul

Dreyfus, H.L. and Rabinow, P. (1982) *Michel Foucault: Beyond Structuralism and Hermeneutics* Brighton: Harvester Press

du Gay, P. (1993) 'Numbers and Souls; Retailing and the De-differentiation of Economy and Culture' in *British Journal of Sociology* 44 (4) December pp. 563-588

du Gay, P. (1994) 'Making Up Managers: Bureaucracy, Enterprise and the Liberal Art of Separation' in *British Journal of Sociology* Vol. 45 (4) pp. 655-674

du Gay, P. and Salaman, G. (1992) 'The Cult(ure) of the Consumer' in *Journal of Management Studies* 29 (5) pp. 615-633

Durkheim, E. (1992) *Professional Ethics and Civic Morals* London: Routledge

Edwards, P.K. (1990) 'Understanding Conflict in the Labour Process' in *Labour Process Theory* Knights, D. and Willmott, H. (eds.) London: Macmillan

Edwards, P.K. (1991) 'Comparative Industrial Relations: The Contribution of the Ethnographic Tradition' Paper delivered at Colloque International, August 1991

Edwards, P.K. and Scullion, H. (1982) *The Social Organisation of Industrial Conflict: Control and Resistance in the Workplace* Oxford: Basil Blackwell

Ezzamel, M. (1994) 'Organizational Change and Accounting: Understanding the Budgeting System in its Organizational Context' in *Organization Studies* Vol. 15 (2) pp. 213-40

Fairclough, L. (1989) *Language and Power* London: Longman

Fairclough, L. (1992) *Discourse and Social Change* Cambridge: Polity Press

Fernie, S. (1998) 'Hanging on the Telephone' in *Centrepiece: The Magazine of Economic Performance* Vol. 3 (1) February pp. 6-11

Fitzgerald, B. (1996) 'Formalized Systems Development Methodologies: A Critical Perspective' in *Information Systems Journal* 6 (1) pp. 3-23

Fitzgerald, T. H. (1989) 'Can Change in Organizational Culture Really Be Managed?' in *Organizational Dynamics* Vol. 17 (2) pp. 5-15

Fombrun, C.J. Tichy, N.M. and Devanna, M.A. (1984) *Strategic Human Resource Management* Chichester: John Wiley

Foucault, M. (1972) *The Archaeology of Knowledge* London: Tavistock

Foucault, M. (1975) *The Birth of the Clinic: An Archaeology of Medical Perception* London: Tavistock

Foucault, M. (1977) *Discipline and Punish: The Birth of the Prison* Harmondsworth: Penguin

Foucault, M. (1979) *The History of Sexuality Volume I: An Introduction* London: Allen Lane

Foucault, M. (1980) *Power/Knowledge - selected interviews and other writings 1972-1977* Gordon, C. (ed.) Brighton: Harvester Press

Foucault, M. (1982) 'The Subject and Power' in *Michel Foucault: Beyond Structuralism and Hermeneutics* Dreyfus, H.L. and Rabinow, P. (eds.) Chicago: University of Chicago Press

Foucault, M. (1984) 'What is Enlightenment?' in *The Foucault Reader* Rabinow, P. (ed.) Harmondsworth: Penguin

Foucault, M. (1985) *The History of Sexuality Volume II: The Use of Pleasure* Harmondsworth: Penguin

Foucault, M. (1986) *The History of Sexuality Volume III: The Care of the Self* Harmondsworth: Penguin

Foucault, M. (1988) *Politics, Philosophy, Culture: Interviews and Other Writings 1977-1984* Kritzman, L.D. (ed.) London: Routledge

Fournier, V. (1991) 'The Concept of the Profession and its Inscription in the Discourse of Enterprise', paper presented at ISA Working Group 02 *Occupations and Professions*, September 1991

Fournier, V. (1997) 'The Appeal to "Professionalism" as a Discursive Device of Control', paper delivered to 15th Annual International Labour Process Conference, March 1997.

Fraser, N. (1989) *Unruly Practices* Cambridge: Polity Press

Freidson, E. (1970) *Professional Dominance: The Social Structure of Medical Care* Chicago: Atherton Press

Freidson, E. (1977) 'The Futures of Professionalization', reprinted in *Professionalism Reborn: Theory, Prophecy and Policy* (1994) London: Polity Press

French, J.R.P. and Raven, B. (1959) 'The Bases of Social Power' in Cartwright, D. (ed.) *Studies in Social Power* Ann Arbor: University of Michigan Press

Friedman, A. (1977) *Industry and Labour: Class Struggle at Work and Monopoly Capitalism* London: Macmillan

Friedman, A. (1990) 'Managerial Strategies, Activities, Techniques and Technology' in *Labour Process Theory* Knights, D. & Willmott, H. (eds.) London: Macmillan

Game, A. (1991) *Undoing the Social: Towards a Deconstructive Sociology* Milton Keynes: Open University Press

Geertz, C. (1973) *The Interpretation of Cultures* New York: Basic Books

Gergen, K.J. (1985) 'The Social Constructionist Movement in Modern Psychology' in *American Psychologist* Vol. 40 (3) pp. 266-73

Gherardi, S. (1995) *Gender, Symbolism and Organizational Cultures* London: Sage

Giddens, A. (1979) *Central Problems in Social Theory* London: Macmillan

Giddens, A. (1991) *Modernity and Self Identity: Self and Society in the Late Modern Age* Cambridge: Polity

Giddens, A. (1993) *New Rules of Sociological Method*: Second Edition Cambridge: Polity Press

Gill, J. and Johnson, P. (1991) *Research Methods for Managers* London: Paul Chapman

Goffman, E. (1959) *The Presentation of the Self in Everyday Life* Harmondsworth: Penguin

Gordon, C. (1980) 'Afterword' to *Power/ Knowledge- selected interviews and other writings 1972-1977* Foucault, M. Brighton: Harvester Press

Gordon, D. M. (1976) 'Capitalist Efficiency and Socialist Efficiency' in *Monthly Review* 28 (3) pp. 19-39

Grey, C. (1992) *Governing Life Assurance, Governing Lives* Unpublished PhD Thesis, submitted to UMIST

Grey, C. (1994a) 'Career as a Project of the Self and Labour Process Discipline' in *Sociology* Vol. 28 (2) pp. 479-497

Grey, C. (1994b) 'Debating Foucault: A Critical Reply to Neimark' in *Critical Perspectives on Accounting* Vol. 5 pp. 5-24

Grey, C. (1997a) 'Management as a Technical Practice: Professionalization or Responsibilization?' in *Systems Practice* 10 (6) pp. 703-725

Grey, C. (1997b) 'Suburban Subjects: Financial Services and the New Right' in *Financial Institutions and Social Transformations* Knights, D. and Tinker, T. (eds.) Basingstoke: Macmillan

Grey, C. (1998) 'On Being A Professional In A 'Big Six' Firm' in *Accounting, Organizations and Society* (in press)

Grey, C. and Knights, D. (1990) 'Investor Protection and the "Cowboy" Stereotype: A Critical View' in *Managerial Finance* Vol. 16 (5) pp. 29-30

Guest, D. (1987) 'Human Resource Management and Industrial Relations', in *Journal of Management Studies* 24 (5) pp. 503-21

Habermas, J. (1971a) *Knowledge and Human Interests* Boston: Beacon Press

Habermas, J. (1971b) *Toward a Rational Society* London: Heinemann

Habermas, J. (1987) *The Philosophical Discourse of Modernity* Cambridge, Mass.: MIT Press

Hales, C.P. (1986) 'What Do Managers Do? A Critical Review of the Evidence' in *Journal of Management Studies* 23 (1) pp. 88-115

Hall, S. (1996) 'Introduction: Who Needs 'Identity'?' in *Questions of Cultural Identity* Hall, S. and Du Gay, P. (eds.) London: Sage

Hammersley, M. (1990) *Reading Ethnographic Research: A Critical Guide* London: Longmans

Harré, R. (1984) *Personal Being* Cambridge, MA: Harvard University Press

Harrison, F.L. (1981) *Advanced Project Management* Aldershot: Gower

Hatch, M.J. (1996) 'The Role of the Researcher: An Analysis of Narrative Position in Organization Theory' in *Journal of Management Inquiry* Vol. 5 (4) pp. 359-74

Hatch, M.J. and Ehrlich, S.B. (1993) 'Spontaneous Humour as an Indicator of Paradox and Ambiguity in Organizations' in *Organization Studies* Vol. 14 (4) pp. 505-26

Henriques, J., Hollway, W., Unwin, C., Venn, C. and Walkerdine, V. (1984) *Changing the Subject: Psychology, Social Regulation and Subjectivity* London: Methuen

Holliday, R. (1995) *Investigating Small Firms: Nice Work?* London: Routledge

Hollway, W. (1984) 'Gender Difference and the Production of Subjectivity' in Henriques, J., Hollway, W., Unwin, C., Venn, C. and Walkerdine, V. (eds.) *Changing the Subject: Psychology, Social Regulation and Subjectivity* London: Methuen

Hoskin, K.W. and Macve, R.H. (1986) 'Accounting and the Examination: A Genealogy of Disciplinary Power' in *Accounting, Organizations and Society* Vol. 11 (2) pp. 105-36

IEEE (1987) *Standard for Software Management Plans* The Institute for Electrical and Electronic Engineers Inc.: New York

Jacques, R. (1996) *Manufacturing the Employee* London: Sage

Jermier, J. M. Knights, D. and Willmott, H. (1994) (eds.) *Resistance and Power in Organizations* London: Routledge

Johnson, T.J. (1972) *Professions and Power* London: Macmillan

Jones, B. and Rose, M. (1985) 'Managerial Strategy and Trade Union Responses at Establishment Level' in *Job Redesign: Critical Perspectives on the Labour Process* Knights, D. *et al* (eds.) London: Gower

Jordan, E. (1996) 'The Lady Clerks at the Prudential: The Beginning of Vertical Segregation by Sex in Clerical Work in Nineteenth-Century Britain' in *Gender and History* Vol. 8 (1) April pp. 64-81

Kelly, J.E. (1985) 'Management's Redesign of Work: Labour Process, Labour Markets and Product Markets' in *Job Redesign: Critical Perspectives on the Labour Process* Knights, D. *et al* (eds.) London: Gower

Kerfoot, D. (1993) *Clerical Work in Banking*, Unpublished PhD Thesis, submitted to UMIST

Kerfoot, D. and Knights, D. (1996) 'The Best is Yet to Come?: The Quest for Embodiment in Managerial Work' in *Men as Managers, Managers as Men* (eds.) Hearn, J. and Collinson, D.L. London Sage

Kerzner, H. (1995) *Project Management: A Systems Approach to Planning, Scheduling and Controlling* New York: Van Nostrand Reinhold

Knights, D. (1990) 'Subjectivity, Power and the Labour Process' in *Labour Process Theory* Knights, D. and Willmott, H.(eds.) London: Macmillan

Knights, D. (1995) ' "Hanging Out the Dirty Washing": Labour Process Theory in the Age of Deconstruction' Paper presented at 13th Annual International Labour Process Conference, March 1995

Knights, D. (1997a) 'An Industry in Transition: Regulation, Restructuring and Renewal' in *Financial Institutions and Social Transformations* (eds.) Knights, D. and Tinker, T. Basingstoke: Macmillan

Knights, D. (1997b) 'Organization Theory in the Age of Deconstruction: Dualism, Gender and Postmodernism Revisited' in *Organization Studies* Vol. 18 (1) pp. 1-19

Knights, D. and Collinson, D. (1985) 'Redesigning Work on the Shopfloor: A Question of Control or Consent?' in *Job Redesign: Critical Perspectives on the Labour Process* Knights, D., Willmott, H. & Collinson, D. (eds.) Aldershot: Gower

Knights, D. and McCabe, D. (1995) 'Managing Quality Strategically: Change Initiatives and HRM in Financial Services' Financial Research Report Ref. No. 000234403 submitted to the Economic and Social Research Council

Knights, D. and Morgan, G. (1991) 'Selling Oneself: Subjectivity and the Labour Process in Selling Life Insurance' in *White-Collar Work: The Non-Manual*

Labour Process Smith, C., Knights, D. and Willmott, H. (eds.) London: Macmillan

Knights, D. and Morgan, G. (1994) 'Organization Theory, Consumption and the Service Sector' in *Towards a new Theory of Organizations* (eds.) Hassard, J. and Parker, M. London: Routledge

Knights, D. and Murray, F. (1994) *Managers Divided: Organisation Politics and Information Technology Management* Chichester: John Wiley

Knights, D. and Sturdy, A. (1997) 'Marketing the Soul: from the Ideology of Consumption to Consumer Subjectivity' in *Financial Institutions and Social Transformations* (eds.) Knights, D. and Tinker, T. Basingstoke: Macmillan

Knights, D. and Tinker, T. (eds.) (1997) *Financial Services and Social Relations: An International Perspective* Oxford: Blackwell

Knights, D. and Vurdubakis, T. (1994) 'Foucault, Power, Resistance and All That' in *Resistance and Power in Organisations* Jermier, J., Knights, D. and Nord, W. London: Macmillan

Knights, D. and Willmott, H. (1985) 'Power and Identity in Theory and Practice' in *Sociological Review* Vol. 33 (1) pp. 22-46

Knights, D. and Willmott, H. (1987) 'Organizational Culture as Management Strategy: A Critique and Illustration from the Financial Services Industry' in *International Studies of Management and Organization* Vol. 18 (3) pp. 40-63

Knights, D. and Willmott, H. (eds.) (1988) *New Technology and the Labour Process* London: Macmillan

Knights, D. and Willmott, H. (1989) 'Power and Subjectivity at Work: From Degradation to Subjugation in Social Relations' in *Sociology* Vol. 23 (4) pp. 535-558

Knights, D and Willmott, H. (1990) (eds.) *Labour Process Theory* London: Macmillan

Knights, D., Willmott, H. and Collinson, D. (1985) (eds.) *Job Redesign: Critical Perspectives on the Labour Process* London: Gower

Kristeva, J. (1966) 'The System and the Speaking Subject' in *The Kristeva Reader* (1986) Moi, T. (ed.) Oxford: Basil Blackwell

Kunda, G. (1992) *Engineering Culture* Philadelphia: Temple University Press

Landes, D.S. (1986) 'What Do Bosses Really Do?' in *Journal of Economic History* XLVI (3) September pp. 585-623

Larkin, G. (1983) *Occupational Monopoly and Modern Medicine* London: Tavistock

Larson, M. (1977) *The Rise of Professionalism: A Sociological Analysis* London: University of California Press

Law, J. (1994) 'Organization, Narrative and Strategy' in *Towards a New Theory of Organizations* Hassard, J. and Parker, M.(eds.) London: Routledge

Lawrence, P.R. and Lorsch, J.W. (1967) *Organization and Environment* Cambridge, MA: Harvard University Press

Lifelong Assurance Company (1948) *A Century of Service: The Story of Lifelong 1848-1948 (Centenary Volume)* London: Lifelong Assurance Company

Littler, C.R. (1978) 'Understanding Taylorism' in *British Journal of Sociology* Vol. 29 (2) pp. 185-202

Littler, C.R. (1982) *The Development of the Labour Process in Capitalist Societies* London Heinemann

Littler, C.R. (1990) 'The Labour Process Debate' in *Labour Process Theory* Knights, D. & Willmott, H. (eds.) London: Macmillan

Littler, C. and Salaman, G. (1982) 'Bravermania and Beyond: Recent Theories of the Labour Process' in *Sociology* 16 (2) pp. 251-269

Lock, D.L. (1968) *Project Management* Gower: London

Longworth, G. (1992) *A User's Guide to SSADM: Version 4* Oxford: Blackwell

Lukes, S. (1974) *Power: A Radical View*. London: Macmillan

Lykes, M.B. (1985) 'Gender and Individualistic vs. Collectivist Bases for Notions about the Self' in *Journal of Personality* Vol. 53 (2) pp. 356-83

Lyon, D. (1993) 'An Electronic Panopticon? A Sociological Critique of Surveillance Theory' in *The Sociological Review* Vol. 41 (4) pp. 653-678

Lyon, D. (1994) *The Electronic Eye: The Rise of Surveillance Society* Cambridge: Polity Press

Macey, D. (1993) *The Lives of Michel Foucault* London: Hutchinson

Mamet, D. (1984) *Glengarry Glen Ross* London: Methuen

Manwaring, T. and Wood, S.J. (1985) 'The Ghost in the Labour Process' in *Job Redesign: Critical Perspectives on the Labour Process* Knights, D.; Willmott, H. & Collinson, D. (eds.) Aldershot: Gower

Marchington, M. (1992) 'Managing Labour Relations in a Competitive Environment' in *Skill and Consent* Sturdy, A., Knights, D. and Willmott, H. (eds.) London: Macmillan

Marglin, S. (1976) 'What Do Bosses Do?' in *The Division of Labour: The Labour Process and Class Struggle in Modern Capitalism* Gorz, A. (ed.) Atlantic Islands, NJ: Humanities Press

Martin, L.H. Gutman, H. and Hutton, P.H. (eds.) (1988) *Technologies of the Self: A Seminar with Michel Foucault* London: Tavistock

Marx, K. (1951) *Theories of Surplus Value* London: Lawrence and Wishart (originally published between 1905 and 1910)

Marx, K. (1976) *Capital; Volume I* Harmondsworth: Penguin (originally published 1867)

Marx, K. (1978) 'The German Ideology' in *The Marx-Engels Reader* Tucker, R. (ed.) New York: Norton

Mayo, E. (1946) *Human Problems of an Industrial Civilization* New York: Macmillan

McGregor, D. (1960) *The Human Side of Enterprise* New York: McGraw-Hill

McKinlay, A. and Starkey, A. (1998) (eds.) *Foucault, Management and Organization Theory* London: Sage

McNay, L. (1992) *Foucault and Feminism: Power, Gender and the Self* Cambridge: Polity Press

McNay, L. (1994) *Foucault: A Critical Introduction* New York: Continuum

Mead, G.H. (1934) *Mind, Self and Society* Chicago: University of Chicago Press

Merton, R.K., Reader, G.G. and Kendall, P.L. (1957) *The Student Physician: Introductory Studies in the Sociology of Medical Education* Cambridge: Harvard University Press

282 *Discourse, Discipline and the Subject*

Miller, P. and O'Leary, T. (1987) 'Accounting and the Constru.tion of the Governable Person' in *Accounting, Organizations and Society* Vol. 12 (3) pp. 235-65

Miller, P. and Rose, N. (1990) 'Governing Economic Life' in *Economy and Society* Vol. 19 (1) pp. 1-31

Minson, J. (1986) 'Strategies for Socialists? Foucault's Conception of Power' in *Towards a Critique of Foucault* Gane, M. (ed.) London: Routledge

Mintel Marketing Intelligence Report (1995a) *Financial Direct Salesforces* (February)

Mintel Marketing Intelligence Report (1995b) *Life Assurance* (November)

Mintel Marketing Intelligence Report (1996a) *21st Century Consumer Financial Services Providers* (February)

Mintel Marketing Intelligence Report (1996b) *Direct Salesforces* (June)

Mintel Marketing Intelligence Report (1996c) *Information Technology in Financial Services* (July)

Mintel Marketing Intelligence Report (1997) *Personal Pensions* (January)

Mintzberg, H. (1973) *The Nature of Managerial Work* New York: Harper and Row

Mintzberg, H. (1975) 'The Manager's Job: Folklore and Fact' in *Harvard Business Review* July-August pp. 49-61

Mintzberg, H. (1978) 'Patterns in Strategy Formation' in *Management Science* Vol. 24 (9) pp. 934-48

Morgan, G. (1986) *Images of Organisation* London: Sage

Morris, P.W.G. (1994) *The Management of Projects* London: Thomas Telford

Mulkay, M. (1988) *On Humour* Oxford: Basil Blackwell

Murphy, R. (1988) *Social Closure: The Theory of Monopolization and Exclusion* Oxford: Clarendon Press

Nichols, T. and Armstrong, P. (1976) *Workers Divided* Glasgow: Fontana

Nichols, T. and Beynon, H. (1977) *Living With Capital: Class Relations in the Modern Factory* London: Routledge

Noble, D. (1979) 'Social Choice in Machine Design: The Case of Automatically Controlled Machine Tools' in *Case Studies on the Labor Process* Zimbalist, A. (ed.) London: Monthly Review Press

O'Neill, J. (1986) 'The Disciplinary Society: From Weber to Foucault' in *British Journal of Sociology* 37 (1) pp. 42-60

Ogbonna, E. (1992) 'Organization Culture and Human Resource Management: Dilemmas and Contradictions' in *Reassessing Human Resource Management* Blyton, P. and Turnbull, P. (eds.) London: Sage

Ogbonna, E. and Wilkinson, B. (1990) 'Corporate Strategy and Corporate Culture: The View from the Checkout' in *Personnel Review* Vol. 19 (4) pp. 9-15

Ouchi, W.G. (1981) *Theory Z: How American Business Can Meet the Japanese Challenge* New York: Addison-Wesley

Pahl, R.E. (1984) *Divisions of Labour* Oxford: Basil Blackwell

Pahl, R.E. (ed.) (1988) *On Work: Historical, Comparative and Theoretical Approaches* Oxford: Basil Blackwell

Parker, I. (1989) 'Discourse and Power' in *Texts of Identity* Shotter, J. and Gergen, K. J. (eds.) London: Sage

Parker, M. (1995a) 'Working Together, Working Apart: Management Culture in a Manufacturing Firm' in *The Sociological Review* Vol. 43 (3) pp. 518-547

Parker, M. (1995b) 'Critique in the Name of What? Postmodernism and Critical Approaches to Organization' in *Organization Studies* Vol. 16 (4) pp. 553-564

Parker, M. (1995c) 'Angry Young Man Has Egoistic Tantrum' in *Organization Studies* Vol. 16 (4) pp. 575-577

Parker, M. (1997) 'Dividing Organizations and Multiplying Identities' in *Ideas of Difference* Hetherington, K and Munro, R. (eds.) Oxford: Blackwell

Parkin, F. (1979) *Marxism and Class Theory* New York: Columbia University Press

Pawley, M. Winstone, D. and Bentley, P. (1991) *UK Financial Institutions and Markets* London: Macmillan

Peters, T. and Waterman, R. (1982) *In Search of Excellence* New York: Harper

Pettigrew, A. (1979) 'On Studying Organisational Cultures' in *Administrative Science Quarterly* Vol. 28 pp. 570-581

Poster, M. (1984) *Foucault, Marxism and History: Mode of Production versus Mode of Information* Cambridge: Polity Press

Pratten, S. (1993) 'Structure, Agency and Marx's Analysis of the Labour Process' in *Review of Political Economy* Vol. 5 (4) pp. 403-426

Pugh, D.S. and Hickson, D.J. (1976) *Organization Structure in its Context: the Aston Programme 1* London: Saxon House

Ray, C.A. (1986) 'Corporate Culture: The Last Frontier of Control' in *Journal of Management Studies* Vol. 23 (3) pp. 287-297

Reed, M.I. (1992) *The Sociology of Organizations* Hemel Hempstead: Harvester Wheatsheaf

Roberts, J. (1984) 'The Moral Character of Management Practice' in *Journal of Management Studies* 21 (3) pp. 287-302

Rodrigues, S.B. and Collinson, D.L. (1995) 'Having Fun?: Humour as Resistance in Brazil' in *Organization Studies* Vol. 16 (5) pp. 739-768

Rorty, R. (1989) *Contingency, Irony and Solidarity* Cambridge: Cambridge University Press

Rose, N. (1990) *Governing the Soul: The Shaping of the Private Self* London: Routledge

Rose, N. (1996) 'Identity, Genealogy, History' in *Questions of Cultural Identity* Hall, S. and Du Gay, P. (eds.) London: Sage

Roy, D. (1969) 'Making Out: A Worker's Counter-System of Control of Work Situation and Relationships' in *Industrial Man* Burns, T. (ed.) Harmondsworth: Penguin

Sakolsky, R. (1992) ' "Disciplinary Power" and the Labour Process' in *Skill and Consent* Sturdy, A., Knights, D. and Willmott, H. (eds.) London: Macmillan

Salaman, G. (1992) 'Work Design and Corporate Strategies' in *Understanding Modern Societies: An Introduction* Allen, J., Braham, P. and Salaman, G. (eds.) Milton Keynes: Open University Press

Sampson, E.E. (1989) 'The Deconstruction of the Self' in *Texts of Identity* Shotter, J. and Gergen, K. J. (eds.) London: Sage

Saussure, F. de (1974) *Course in General Linguistics* London: Fontana

284 *Discourse, Discipline and the Subject*

Sawicki, J. (1991) *Disciplining Foucault: Feminism, Power and the Body* London: Routledge

Sayer, A (1992) *Method in Social Science* London: Hutchinson

Schein, E. (1985) *Organizational Culture and Leadership* San Francisco: Jossey-Bass

Schroeder, R. (1992) *Max Weber and the Sociology of Culture* London: Sage

Scott, A. (1994) *Willing Slaves? British Workers Under Human Resource Management* Cambridge: Cambridge University Press

Sewell, G. and Wilkinson, B. (1992a) '"Someone to Watch Over Me": Surveillance, Discipline and the Just-In-Time Labour Process' in *Sociology* 20 (2) pp. 271-91

Sewell, G. and Wilkinson, B. (1992b) 'Empowerment or Emasculation: Shopfloor Surveillance in the Total Quality Organisation' in *Reassessing Human Resource Management* Blyton, P. and Turnbull, P. (eds.) London: Sage

Sheridan, A. (1980) *Michel Foucault: The Will to Truth* London: Tavistock

Shotter, J. (1989) 'Social Accountability and the Social Construction of 'You' ' in *Texts of Identity* Shotter, J. and Gergen, K. J. (eds.) London: Sage

SIB (1996a) *An Introduction to the Securities and Investments Board* London: SIB

SIB (1996b) *The Background to Investor Protection* London: SIB

Silverman, D. (1970) *The Theory of Organizations* London: Heinemann

Silverman, D. (1985) *Qualitative Methodology and Sociology* Aldershot: Gower

Silverman, D. (1993) *Interpreting Qualitative Data: Methods for Analysing Talk, Text and Interaction* London: Sage

Smircich, L. (1983) 'Concepts of Culture and Organizational Analysis' in *Administrative Science Quarterly* Vol. 28 (3) pp. 339-358

Stubbs, M. (1983) *Discourse Analysis: The Sociolinguistic Analysis of Natural Language* Oxford: Blackwell

Sturdy, A., Knights, D. and Willmott, H. (eds.) (1992) *Skill and Consent: Contemporary Studies in the Labour Process* London: Macmillan

Sturdy, A.J. (1992) 'Clerical Consent: Shifting Work in the Insurance Office' in *Skill and Consent* Sturdy, A.J., Knights, D. & Willmott, H. (eds.) London; Routledge

Thomas, P. (1995) 'Age Old Problems in the Factory of the Future: Power and Resistance Amongst the Managers of Technological Change' Paper presented at 13th Annual International Labour Process Conference, March 1995

Thompson, P. (1989) *The Nature of Work* London: Macmillan

Thompson, P. and Ackroyd, S. (1995) 'All Quiet on the Workplace Front? A Critique of Recent Trends in British Industrial Sociology' in *Sociology* Vol. 29 (4) pp. 615-633

Thompson, P. and McHugh, D.(1995) *Work Organisations: A Critical Introduction* London: Macmillan

Toffler, A. (1980) *The Third Wave* London: Pan Books

Tolliday, S. and Zeitlin, P. (1991) 'Introduction' in *The Power to Manage? Employers and Industrial Relations in a Comparative Historical Perspective* Oxford: Basil Blackwell

Torrington, D and Hall, L. (1995) *Personnel Management: HRM in Practice* London: Prentice Hall

Townley, B. (1993a) 'Foucault, Power/Knowledge and its Relevance for Human Resource Management' in *Academy of Management Review* Vol. 18 (3) pp. 518-45

Townley, B. (1993b) 'Performance Appraisal and the Emergence of Management' in *Journal of Management Studies* Vol. 30 (2) pp. 221-38

Townley, B. (1994) *Reframing Human Resource Management: Power, Ethics and the Subject at Work* London: Sage

Townley, B. (1995) 'Know Thyself: Self-Awareness, Self-Formation and Managing' in *Organization* Vol. 2 (2) pp. 271-89

Townley, B. (1998) 'Beyond Good and Evil: Depth and Division in the Management of Human Resources' in *Foucault, Management and Organization Theory* McKinlay, A. and Starkey, K. (eds.) London: Sage

Van Maanen, J.(1988) *Tales of the Field* London: University of Chicago Press

Wastell, D.G. (1996) 'The Fetish of Technique: Methodology as a Social Defence' in *Information Systems Journal* 6 (1) pp. 25-40

Watson, T.J. (1994) *In Search of Management: Culture, Chaos and Control in Managerial Work* London: Routledge

Watson, T.J. (1995) 'People, Processes and the Labour Process' Paper presented at 13th Annual International Labour Process Conference, March 1995

Weber, M. (1967a) 'Bureaucracy' in *From Max Weber: Essays in Sociology* (eds.) Gerth, H.H. and Mills, C.W. London: Routledge

Weber, M. (1967b) 'The Meaning of Discipline' in *From Max Weber: Essays in Sociology* (eds.) Gerth, H.H. and Mills, C.W. London: Routledge

Weedon, C. (1991) *Feminist Practice and Poststructuralist Theory* Oxford: Basil Blackwell

Whittington, R. (1992) '*Putting Giddens Into Action: Social Systems and Managerial Agency*' in *Journal of Management Studies* 29 (6) pp. 693-712 November

Wilensky, H.L. (1964) '*The Professionalization of Everyone?*' in *American Journal of Sociology* 70 pp. 137-58

Wilkinson, B. (1983) *The Shopfloor Politics of New Technology* London: Heinemann

Willis, P. (1977) *Learning to Labour* London: Saxon House

Willmott, H. (1986) 'Unconscious Sources of Motivation in the Theory of the Subject; An Exploration and Critique of Giddens' Dualistic Models of Action and Personality' in *Journal for the Theory of Social Behaviour* 16 (1) pp. 105-121

Willmott, H. (1987) 'Studying Managerial Work: A Critique and a Proposal' in *Journal of Management Studies* Vol. 24 (3) pp. 249-70

Willmott, H. (1990) 'Subjectivity and the Dialectics of Praxis: Opening Up the Core of Labour Process Analysis' in *Labour Process Theory* Knights, D. and Willmott, H. (eds.) London: Macmillan

Willmott, H. (1993) 'Strength is Ignorance; Slavery is Freedom: Managing Culture in Modern Organizations' in *Journal of Management Studies* Vol. 30 (4) pp. 515-552

Willmott, H. (1994) 'Bringing Agency (back) into Organizational Analysis: Responding to the Crisis of (Post) Modernity' in *Towards a New Theory of Organizations* Hassard, J. and Parker, M. (eds.) London: Routledge

Willmott, H. (1995) 'From Bravermania to Schizophrenia: the Diseased Condition of Subjectivity in Labour Process Theory' Paper presented at 13th Annual Labour Process Conference, March 1995

Willmott, H. (1997) ' 'Outing' Organizational Analysts: Some Reflections Upon Parker's Tantrum' in *Organization* Vol. 4 (2) pp. 255-268

Wilson, F. (1994) 'Introducing New Computer-Based Systems into Zenbank' in *New Technology, Work and Employment* Vol. 9(2) pp. 115-126

Winch, P (1958) *The Idea of a Social Science* London: Routledge

Wittgenstein, L. (1953) *Philosophical Investigations* Oxford: Blackwell

Witz, A. (1992) *Professions and Patriarchy* London: Routledge

Wood, S.J. (1982) *The Degradation of Work?* London: Hutchinson

Wood, S.J. (1989) *The Transformation of Work?* London: Hutchinson

Wood, S.J. and Kelly, J. (1982) 'Taylorism, Responsible Autonomy and Management Strategy' in *The Degradation of Work* Wood, S.J. London: Hutchinson

Woodward, J. (1970) *Industrial Organisation: Theory and Practice* London: Oxford University Press

Zimbalist, A. (ed.) (1979) *Case Studies on the Labour Process* London: Monthly Review Press

Index